THE REAL BLAKE

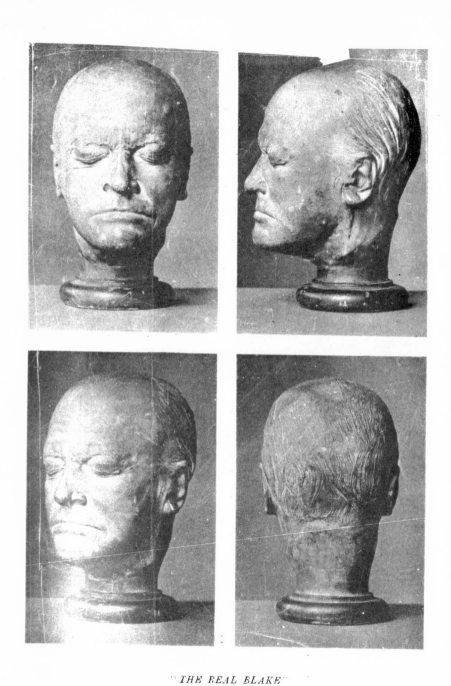

"THE REAL BLAKE"

From the life-mask by Deville, the phrenologist.
Reproduced by special permission of Sir W. B. Richmond, R.A.

THE

REAL BLAKE

A PORTRAIT BIOGRAPHY

BY

EDWIN J. ELLIS

WITH 13 ILLUSTRATIONS

HASKELL HOUSE PUBLISHERS Ltd.

Publishers of Scarce Scholarly Books

NEW YORK. N.Y 10012

First Published 1966

HASKELL HOUSE PUBLISHERS Ltd.
Publishers of Scarce Scholarly Books
280 LAFAYETTE STREET
NEW YORK, N. Y. 10012

Library of Congress Catalog Card Number: 75-117994

Standard Book Number 8383-1049-4

Printed in the United States of America

TO

MY FRIEND

MARK PERUGINI

PREFACE

THIS biography was written as a companion volume to the edition of the complete *Poetical Works of William Blake* which Messrs. Chatto and Windus have recently issued. Both works were prepared and put in type at the same time, in 1904 ; but there has been an unavoidable delay in their production.

For two years they lay dormant. But as they were already in type the present writer, though author of the one work and editor of the other, could not use this time by making any substantial improvements either in the notes or the narrative. Other works have come out since, but none that attempts to take the place either of the edition of the poems or of the biography, and none that adds anything important to our knowledge of Blake's life or mind. A portrait-biography of Blake is as much needed now as it was in 1904, and by a larger group of readers, as a wider knowledge of his importance has begun to grow up.

The present writer regrets not to have seen the edition of the shorter poems published by Mr. Frowde of the Clarendon Press, Oxford, under the editorship of Mr. Sampson, in time to make any use of it in the complete *Works*. Mr. Frowde's edition notices some few slight errors in the first full edition of Blake, that prepared by the present writer aided by Mr. W. B. Yeats for Mr. Quaritch. These slips of the pen have sometimes found their way into the present edition.

Mr. Sampson had much good and careful assistance in preparing his work. He is a professional teacher of bibliography, and gave his whole attention to verbal accuracy. He took plenty of time, and has produced a work which is

a monumental record of every error that the hasty pen of
Blake himself or any of his previous editors had ever committed. The work shows every ailment from which every
text of Blake has suffered, and its long pages of notes are
like the wards of a hospital.

But Mr. Sampson, so skilled in extracting motes from the
eyes of his predecessors, has come before us with a beam or
two in his own eye, which may be mentioned here; for it is
to be hoped that no serious student of Blake will omit to
get his volume, which is well printed and full of biblio-
graphical information, though empty of interpretation or
intelligent poetic study.

Mr. Sampson says of some pieces in the early collection
called Blake's *Poetical Sketches*: "Mr. W. M. Rossetti (in the
Aldine edition) places the pieces in an order of his own,
omitting the prose, with the exception of the *Prologue to
King John* and *Samson*, which he prints as blank verse.
Ellis and Yeats follow the Aldine edition, omitting *Samson*."

This is all absurdly wrong. The pieces "printed as blank
verse" *are* blank verse with a few irregularities, not more
frequent than those in many of Blake's other poems. They
were first printed *as prose* merely because Mrs. Barbauld,
author of the once celebrated *Hymns in Prose*, was one of
the literary people among whom Blake lived at the time of
writing. Ellis and Yeats did not "follow the Aldine edition,"
as they had the advantage of using the exact facsimile of
the original issue which was executed for Mr. Quaritch by
the lithographer, Mr. Griggs, of Peckham Rye. Mr. Sampson's
wildest error is, however, the statement that Ellis and Yeats
omit the poem (which he miscalls prose) called *Samson*. It
almost covers pages 179 to 182 of their second volume. It
was, therefore, not invisible. *The Couch of Death*, omitted
in the Aldine edition, is also to be found on page 183. After
this we are not surprised when Mr. Sampson, rashly ven-
turing beyond the bounds of bibliography a very little way
into criticism, is equally unfortunate. He accuses Ellis and
Yeats of error in saying that Blake's poem called *The Everlasting Gospel* "terminates, for us, with a loose end," simply

because he overlooks the words "for us," and considers that
Ellis and Yeats "failed to see" that the last part on the
MS. as we have it, which leaves off in the middle of a line
with an "&c.," was not meant by Blake for the close of the
poem, but implies that there was more, written on another
piece of paper, which is lost to us. He considers, in spite of
the words "for us" in Ellis and Yeats, that in observing, for
himself, that some of the poem must be lost, he is making
a critical discovery that had not been made by others before
him. He is similarly elate over having noticed one of the
many repetitions from *Vala* to be found in *Jerusalem*. He
should not call *Vala*, *The Four Zoas*. This was an early
title rejected by Blake.

Mr. Sampson's most unpardonable error is in calling his
collection *Blake's Poetical Works*, without any mention of the
fact that it contains less than half of these. He excludes all
those known as "Prophetic Books," as though that title (not
used by Blake in all cases) ranked them as prose : neglecting
to recognise the magnificent verse in which most are written.
or the fact that the god of whom Blake himself claimed to
be a prophet is explained to be the Poetic Genius.

By the kindness of Mr. Russell, Mr. Sampson is enabled to
give (in a note) these few lines by Blake, which were unknown
to the present writer, or they would have been included in the
biography, being his own account in brief of the story of his
life.

To MY DEAREST FRIEND, JOHN FLAXMAN—THESE LINES

I bless Thee, O Father of Heaven and Earth, that ever I saw John Flaxman's
    face.
Angels stand round my spirit in Heaven, the blessed of Heaven are my
    friends upon Earth.
When Flaxman was taken to Italy, Fuseli was given to me for a season.
And now Flaxman has given me Hayley, his friend, to be mine—such my
    lot upon Earth.
Now my lot in Heaven is this : Milton loved me in childhood and show'd
    me his face :
Ezrah came with Isaiah the Prophet, but Shakespeare in riper years gave
    me his hand.
Paracelsus and Behmen appeared to me : terrors appeared in the Heavens
    above.
The American war began : All its dark horrors passed before my face

Across the Atlantic to France.   Then the French Revolution commenc'd in
  · thick clouds.

And my Angels have told me that in seeing such visions I could not
    subsist on the Earth

But by conjunction with Flaxman, who knows how to forgive nervous fear.

12 Sep. 1800.

The date at the end is almost unnecessary.   Readers of this
volume will see that it was most certainly written in 1800.
Its authenticity is obvious.   The last lines are the most
valuable, pointing as they do to telepathic experiences and
horrors at this perturbed period of which we have no other
hint.   " Nervous fear " is not to be mistaken for either what is
usually called nervousness or for what is usually called fear.

The most surprising thing about these lines is the omission
of Swedenborg's name from them, showing that Blake was
at this time much more conscious of the distance beyond
Swedenborg's tether that he had travelled than of the help
which he owed to Swedenborg at an earlier stage of the
journey.   Shortly after writing these lines to Flaxman, when he
had overhauled his old papers and "re-collected his scattered
thoughts on art," he wrote the few and generous words about
Swedenborg in the poem called *Milton*, produced at that period.

I owe thanks to Mr. Fairfax Murray for permitting me to
print the whole of the *Island in the Moon* here, in 1904,
before he presented the original manuscript to the Fitzwilliam
Museum, Cambridge; and for placing his collection of Flaxman's letters at my service for this volume, and showing me
some valuable letters of Blake, one of which, that to Mr.
Cumberland, is given in full here.   The kindness of the Linnell
brothers has enabled me to see others in the original that have
been published elsewhere, and to re-examine the poem of *Vala*,
too hastily transcribed in the early excited pioneering days
when the Quaritch edition was under preparation.

The edition of Blake that is wanted in the future would
be one in which a capable and careful editor corrected for
Blake *every* line that his hasty hand mis-wrote, relegating to
foot-notes the record of the original slips of the pen.   Then
the reader who loved poetry, and loved Blake for poetry's sake,
would be able to read him with uninterrupted pleasure, and

the mere pedant would have a means of making himself uncomfortable that would satisfy even Mr. Sampson. When there is enough general understanding of Blake to enable a *full* edition to dispense with all interpretation, then the space given to notes would always find room for this, their natural use. But the creation of such a text is an invidious task, and no editor will undertake it who is not prepared to be stoned publicly by every pedant, as Mr. Sampson stones all editors indiscriminately. But one day, perhaps, poetry, calling for volunteers as an officer does before a breach is stormed, may find men ready for the work.

Meantime, a valuable sidelight on the real Blake comes from an unexpected quarter since the printing of this biography, and must be noticed here. In the number for July 1905 of the *Occult Review*—a well-printed sixpenny magazine—Miss M. Bramston, the novelist, has written, under the title *Automatic Romance*, a cold, lucid, prosaic account of her own experiences in involuntary production of fiction, in which she relates how non-existent individuals, acting apparently with wills and personalities of their own, literally guide the pen when she is in a purely passive state, and create dialogue for her which seems quite new to herself when she reads it, and not due to any action of her own brain. She explains how she acquired, cultivated, lost, and found again the faculty of yielding her pen to such guidance, and why she selected generally the names of personages whom she knew to have only an imaginative existence, lest the complete splitting up of her own personality into several should seem too like the reception of " messages " from " spirits," as it does to most " mediums," until it deceived herself, as it often deceives them. The question whether real spirits give real messages *also*, and whether there are real mediums, is not touched by Miss Bramston's experiences : but her case, and the way she used, acquired, and lost her power so closely resembled Blake's, and her account of this is so exactly like that to be collected from isolated expressions in Blake's poems and " prophetic " writings, that her self-analysis is invaluable to any one who would understand Blake's mind. There are two differences between Miss Bramston and Blake. Blake wrote poetry, Miss Bramston prose. Blake had metaphysical opinions about "imagination" and "eternity," due to considerations about his experiences which do not seem to recommend themselves to Miss Bramston's mind. Blake was stimulated to the "creation" of his personages by thoughts of a myth-making, impersonating kind, such as the ancients had when meditating on the moods of human character. Then he mounted the tripod and surrendered himself to oracular impulse. Miss Bramston, when preparing herself for the exercise of similar faculties, only yields to the novelist's artistic pleasure in conjuring up personalities. Therefore Miss Bramston has produced picturesque and impressive dialogue and romance, and Blake a great, if fragmentary, philosophic myth.

At this moment, while the Preface is still in proof, a volume of *Blake's Letters* appears, containing also his *Life* by F. Tatham, published by Methuen under the editorship of Mr. G. B. Russell. Tatham's *Life* does not quite fill fifty pages, though printed in large type with widely separated lines. It is the contemporary memoir bound up in MS. with Blake's one coloured copy of *Jerusalem*, formerly owned by Mr. Quaritch, and lent to me when the Memoir for the facsimile edition of Blake's works was prepared for him. Afterwards Mr. Quaritch sold this *Jerusalem* with Tatham's MS., and made a trade secret of the purchaser's name. I am glad that it has at last come to light and is published in full.

Not having my old notes by me here, I now look through Mr. Russell's volume to see if any essential matter from Tatham's *Life* has passed unnoticed. I find pleasant personal descriptions of Blake's good looks, good manners, good temper, and patience under pain during his last illness, his knowledge of languages, and the fact that Mrs. Blake always kept for him a guinea in the house more than he knew of, and kept him well fed and "comfortable," though not "portly"; also that in his later years he always dressed neatly in black (Gilchrist says, in knee-breeches), and wore his hair falling down on his shoulders—facts not indicated in the life-mask.

Tatham defends, by a curious sentence telling how Blake "enjoyed in the early part of his life not only comforts but necessaries," the story that Blake was really robbed of £60 worth of plate at Hercules Buildings. Whether £60 worth of plate was a comfort or a necessary to a quiet man whose entertainments consisted, so far as we know, of sometimes giving Fuseli a chop or Flaxman a cup of tea, does not appear. Perhaps Blake, who had fashionable pupils at this time, received presents of plate from them which his enthusiastic gratitude valued at £60, along with what he himself bought.

Tatham gives no hint that he disapproved of any of Blake's views, only saying that much of his poetry was "unintelligible," that he "wrote a good deal," and that he published those of his works that were "most mysterious." Perhaps the tale that Tatham committed wholesale destruction after Blake's death may prove to be an exaggerated report, and some "prophetic works" may yet be found.

Passing to the letters collected by Mr. Russell, I find, besides the one containing the few lines to Flaxman quoted above, two or three that were unknown to me. They are about a Dr. Trusler who was nearly persuaded by Mr. Cumberland to employ Blake, but found his designs too symbolic.

They contain passages about art of interest to artists, and show Blake's views at the period before the eighteenth century was quite over, when, as his own designs to *America* show, he was not yet out of sympathy with Greek art—a state at which he seems to have arrived later through rebellion against the frigidities of Flaxman and Hayley.

This collection also includes part of a letter from Flaxman in which there is indicated an unfulfilled project at one time existing among Blake's friends to get him taken to Rome to study art there; and Mr. Russell in some of his brief and useful notes adds to the sparse allusions made by Blake to a Work on Art (much of whose intended material is given in the present volume from the MS. book, and collected under the title "Public Address") which went no farther towards production than Blake's announcement that he had "found a publisher" for it.

The biographical contributions, therefore, for which I am indebted to Mr. Russell's volume consist of information about how a journey was not taken, a book was not published, and a patron did not employ.

Mr. Russell's book, however, contains some good reproductions, notably of Blake's engraving of a horse from his own design, perhaps the most unreal horse ever drawn; and the picture of the Last Judgment, whose first pencil sketch is given here. This reproduction, which might have been larger, is very valuable, as it is enough to prove that this is the most beautiful, poetic, and decorative picture the world contains, and also perhaps the most populated. Its figures are literally innumerable. It is a sufficient answer to all doubts that Blake's feebler drawings suggest as to the overwhelming value of his genius. He was always drawing, almost always " out of his own head "; and living as he did under depressing and distracting artistic influences, he not only sometimes did badly, but when he did so was too enfeebled by the eighteenth-century influence to know it. In this picture and in the *Job* he takes a supreme place among the world's artists.

Mr. Russell does ill to express a fear that Rome would have done Blake harm. It is true that the " school " of Michael Angelo, a school of mannerism and little else, influenced him for a moment when, as a boy, he engraved his "Joseph of Arimathea among the Rocks of Albion." But the roof of the Sistine Chapel was painted many years before Michael Angelo acquired the mannerism that his imitators exaggerated, and would have been like new wine to Blake.

Some apology is perhaps due to the reader for the very slender account given in the present work of what was real and essential in Blake that may be found in the artistic story of his life. But only poetic artists who have vision themselves would understand it. These are few, and their experiences will explain to them better than words can even the most paradoxical of the doctrines, and most puzzling of the changes, in Blake the Artist.

EDWIN J. ELLIS.

Paris, *December* 1906.

CONTENTS

xv

ILLUSTRATIONS

THE REAL BLAKE

CHAPTER I

In the year 1804, a century ago, William Blake sat in his London rooms on the first floor of No. 17 South Molton Street, dating the engraved title-pages of his two final poems, each a volume in itself, feeling sure that at last he had turned the corner in the pathway of his daily life, and believing that he saw how he had come to that corner through the past, and that he could see how to go forward from it into the future.

Of ordinary daylight he had enough, but by no means too much to work by. At the present day, as we walk down the shady side of the street, going perhaps by the convenient slanting short cut that it offers from the Bond Street Station of the Central or "Tube" railway to the heart of Bond Street itself, we can still look up and see several such windows as he sat near. They have six small panes in the lower, and six small panes in the upper half. But the front of No. 17, where he laboured for seventeen years, is now re-glazed with modern plate. Here, feeling at peace with all men, and glowing with the warmth of affection and gratitude to some, he began confidently to prepare for printing and illustrating with his own hands the most picturesque and profound symbolic poems that have ever been produced in our language. The main subject of them was the imaginative and affectionate moods of life, of how art leads to brother-hood, and the two together to visionary power, and so to immortality—to "eternal salvation"; for, as he held, "in eternity all is vision." He began his last poetic task with confidence, for he had reason to trust his friends, and to trust his employments, and to trust his visions. He was

B

practically certain that he could make his living by means within his power, without laying aside his poetic art.

And yet it was here that he was to feel the bitterest disappointments of his life, and the deepest resentments. It was here that he, who had harmed no man and helped more than one, who had been consistently courageous and incessantly industrious, was soon to be reduced to writing in his private MS. book this entry: "Between two and seven in the evening: despair." His difficulty in the ordinary intercourse of life partly sprang from the fact that he always claimed to be a man of genius. His claim is now allowed so fully that when the merest tinted sketch, or book of poetry illuminated by his hand, is put up publicly for sale, about fifty times the price that he obtained is frequently given without hesitation, as the account-books of the Carfax Gallery, late of Ryder Street, or of Sotheby in Wellington Street, undoubtedly show.

Records of pounds, shillings, and pence, if they are not the history of art itself, go a long way towards telling us its history, as a heap of dead shells go far towards revealing to us the story of the sea. This amazing increase in the recognised value of Blake's original work has not come suddenly, nor can it be put aside as a whim of fashion. It has grown up slowly as the man himself has become more widely known, and has reached its towering height this year, when gossip whispers that there are many new books of different kinds in preparation that are intended to show him to us more fully— possibly more truly—than he has ever yet been shown.

We all know something about him. Whoever has heard the name of William Blake knows that he was a poet of great sweetness, but great difficulty, and a painter of great spirituality and power, but of visionary extravagance and more than dream-like unreality; but behind the poet and the painter is the man, and it is only beginning to be known that this man was as well worth understanding for his character as for his work.

When, after his first and last attempt to live and labour in the country, he returned to the London battlefield of art, pitching his tent in South Molton Street in 1804, he was forty-seven years of age, and in the very prime of his vigorous development. He had seen visions for forty years, and had kept his head. He had been married for twenty-two years, and his heart was fresh. He had been all his life confident of his genius, but was still the hardest of plodding workers. He had been poor and obscure from the beginning of his career, and had lived in the company of well-known men, eminent men, and men of property: and he had not become tainted with subserviency, but had remained independent in heart and mind, and had paid his own debts from his own earnings. He had more imagination than any man of his age, but had never allowed it to betray him into deceiving any one. He had the temperament of a Turk and the fidelity of a knight. His hopes of position as an artist, as a poet, and as a husband were disappointed, for his pictures were undervalued, his poetry was very little read, and his wife was childless; and yet he remained as cheerful and pleasant in all companies as the luckiest of the lucky, and in his gloomiest moments kept his sorrow strictly at home.

The first event of poetic importance in Blake's life happened when he was four years old. He saw God in a vision put His forehead to the window. This set the child screaming. We only know of the incident through Mr. Crabb Robinson, in whose diary is an allusion to it made many years later. There had been some conversation about visions, and Mrs. Blake reminding her husband of this one, Mr. Robinson jotted it down. Nothing more is told us beyond the bare fact. The probability is that when the little boy's screaming was over he told no one near him at the time about what he had seen. It was too awful and confidential an experience. Possibly the vision was only of a huge forehead and eyes appearing at the window of an upper story, and seeming to imply a figure of supernatural dimensions in the street. It proves at least that William Blake had heard much of God when he was only four years old, and had thought much of what he had heard. His thoughts even then were pictorial. What he thought, he *saw*.

He was a child who had plenty of time to think. His life and mind in early years were not turned into mere foolishness by constant endearments and amusement. He had the advantage of not being a favourite. He was the third son, though some of his contemporaries, who had never heard of the eldest, afterwards thought that he was the second. John, the first son, turned out a scapegrace, and the family did not speak about him after his death. The next brother, James, took his place, passed for the eldest, and became the favourite. Although John turned out ill, yet, while the boys were still all at home together, their parents used to hold him up as an example to William, who, for being so foolish and unpractical as to wish to be an artist, was told that he would one day beg his bread

at John's door. The contrary of this is what happened. John
died young—it is hinted, from the effects of dissipation—after
being a soldier. In some of Blake's verses written at Felpham
he is recalled :

> My brother John, the evil one,
> In a black cloud making his moan.

No more is known about him. But in the early days the
fact that he was the favourite, and James the next in esteem
as in age, gave William a certain freedom from the frequent
notice of his parents, an isolation that must have been of use
to him, enabling him to dream unmolested.

That he said nothing about his first vision is not only to
be inferred from the awfulness of it, but from the fact that
Mrs. Blake, to whom he probably told of it during the summer
days of his courtship, had no further details to relate to Mr.
Crabb Robinson—or rather, none to remind her husband to
relate. There is not a word about how his family took it.
He would certainly have told her something about this if
the family had ever heard of it at all. He probably had
never spoken of the vision to any one until he mentioned it
to her that once, just as she recalled it to him afterwards.
Then through the hurry and rush of business and struggle,
and the crowding-in of other visions upon his mind, he
seems to have forgotten it altogether.

The next experience of the same kind of which we know
anything was three years later, when Blake was seven. One
pleasant day at Peckham Rye, where every house has a pretty
garden, he saw a tree full of angels, "their bright wings be-
spangling the boughs like stars," as he said in describing it,
for in his natural delight he related this to his family, and
his father decided to give him a thrashing for telling a lie.
He probably began to do so with some severity. His mother
begged him off. His friend Frederick Tatham, who gathered
facts about him in his old age, whether from himself or his
wife, says that his mother herself beat him afterwards for
having a vision of Ezekiel. Tatham's memoir is bound up
with the handsomest coloured copy known of the poem called
"Jerusalem." It was in the possession of Mr. Quaritch ten
or eleven years ago, when the present writer was privileged
to consult it.

We also learn that Blake's fit of fury at being struck was so
violent and appalling that it resulted in the decision that he was
not to go to school. In later life he wrote of himself :

Thank heaven I never was sent to school
To be flogged into following the style of a fool.

It is more probable that if he had been flogged at school at all, the style into which this would have driven him would have been that of a madman or a murderer. His feeling of personal dignity was, next to the love of art and vision, the ruling passion of his life. He long disliked the very word *father*. It is often a term of reproach in his poems. He was intensely affectionate, but held as a fixed rule that he must be neither controlled nor criticised. His pride, like his genius, was beyond all ordinary measure, and grew with his growth. He could not be made to understand for many years that people could disagree with him even in the mildest way, unless they were actually wicked. He had from childhood a gift of words as much above that of all other boys as his gift of love and his gift of pride, and we may exercise our more limited imaginations till they are tired without any danger of going beyond what he is likely, in his indignation, to have said to his parents about the flogging. He obtained the mastery over them. They must have been of unusually kind dispositions if their consequent dislike of him did not rise to absolute hatred.

Among the other children that were born to these parents was a daughter, of whom little is known but that she lived longer than all the rest of the family, died unmarried, and had to the last some distinction of bearing which seems to have always been remarked in this family. Besides John and James, William had a third brother, Robert, the best beloved and youngest.

They grew up in the house behind their father's shop. He was a draper,—a hosier as it was called then,—and attended seriously to his business, saved a little money, and left a respectable goodwill to James, the son who took his place at his death. But he was not an ordinary shopman. His name was not really Blake, but O'Neil. No one can study the cast of William Blake's head made for Deville the phrenologist without seeing that he was an Irishman. His grandfather was an O'Neil in Ireland when his father was born,—the family does not know from what mother. This O'Neil married a woman named Ellen Blake, who had some money that came through whisky, and she gave him not only her dowry but her name, for he was in trouble that tradition says was political, and no one in Ireland was ever anxious to know more about a gentleman's misfortunes when so satisfactory an explanation could be offered. There were many honourable men of good blood and good standing who were in political trouble in those days, and not all of them found a kind Ellen Blake into whose family their identity could vanish, while debt and all other troubles were also left outside. John O'Neil's motherless boy, William Blake's father, probably had no very legal name of his own. At any rate, he accepted the name of Blake when his father adopted it, and there would have been an end of the story had not Ellen Blake borne to John O'Neil children of her own, and if Dr. Carter Blake, who was descended from one of these, had not told the whole story to Mr. W. B. Yeats, on whose authority it is given here.

William Blake's mortal and perishable existence is like a sentence in a parenthesis. With a father across whose shield is a bar sinister, he not merely left no children of his own, but he had no nephews or nieces. The family begins and ends in one generation from the date of its pseudonymous founder, and no kin or next of kin to William Blake survives. Even his grave is difficult to identify now, though its number and place in the cemetery of Bunhill Fields is recorded.

Should those hidden bones ever be disturbed, the cast of the head that answers for William's nationality will answer for his identity. A copy of it is in the possession of Sir William Richmond, who was named after him; and it is reproduced in this volume by his kind permission.

CHAPTER II

HOW HE GREW UP

AT first an attempt was made to teach Blake to be a hosier. Unfortunately, he had a constitutional aversion to anything like commerce. He hated money transactions, and even hated money. In later days a patron who was buying a copy of his *Songs of Innocence and Experience* as a sort of "veiled charity," because Blake was dependent on such sales for his bread, was rather taken aback when he tried to make him a present of the work.

By adding to this spirit of anti-commercialism the wild ways of his brother John, we can form a guess of how their grandfather, the John O'Neil who married Ellen Blake, came to be in both financial and political trouble at once. Fortunately, there was a strain of severe conscientiousness in the blood, and William had his share of this, and his long life of struggle was an honest one.

When his parents gave up the idea of teaching him to be shopman, they did not altogether deprive him of pocket-money, and they allowed him to spend it as he chose. For this a white stone must mark their memory. It is true, of course, that they did not, because they could not, foresee what lasting and wise use the character of the boy would enable him to make of his opportunity. They were probably glad enough that he seemed quiet, and was not heard of as being in any mischief.

But, going back to his childish years with the knowledge his writings give us, we can see into the silent places of his mind now, better than his father and mother could see then. They noticed that the once bragging boy seldom spoke, though he looked as vivacious as ever, going quickly about with his flame-like golden-red hair on end, curling up all over his head, his lips sometimes moving as though he talked to himself, but his large, dark, flashing eyes very seldom

seeking theirs either with anger or in confidence. He was a
complete mystery. He did what they told him in the small
matters of daily life. We even suspect that he went so far
as to allow his upright flames of waving hair to be combed
down for him sometimes. The drawing that he afterwards
made to the "Nurse's Song," among the *Songs of Experience*,
shows a boy quite big enough to comb his own hair, who
stands folding his hands resolutely with the deliberate meekness of a martyr, while golden locks, the colour of Blake's
own, are flattened on his head and reduced to respectability
by a young woman, perhaps his elder sister. There is no
allusion to combing in the verse. If this drawing is not a
fragment of autobiography it is incomprehensible. It is
certainly not introduced to serve a purpose either decorative
or pathetic, nor is it symbolic as are the drawings to some of
the songs.

Now, at between eight and ten years of age, he was growing into a more and more complete estrangement from his
parents, partly caused by resentful remembrance making
permanent the results of the appalling fits of fury that he
had shown when they had struck him, to teach him not to
pretend to have visions; for Vision became more and more
sacred to him. But a deeper cause was at work. He had
made a discovery. The figure is formed *for beauty*. From
that moment he was an artist. It is usually thought, even
by the educated classes, that an artist is different from other
people merely because he has a talent for drawing or painting,
and likes pictures and the making of pictures, but that the
difference goes no deeper.

A boy who has discovered that the figure is formed for
beauty has in his mind an idea that alters the whole nature
of his thought and character from those of another boy
who does not know yet that it is formed for anything else
but use and strength, measuring and boasting, dressing or
washing, playing or whipping. As he grows up it even gives
him a delight in a quality of the flesh—*form*—which is
independent of the attractions of sex.

The delight in form, and the belief that beautiful form is
one of the things chiefly worth considering in life, give the
mind food that it cannot obtain from gossip, philosophy,
religion, or commerce. History knows nothing of this delight.
It merely knows that, somehow or other, there were statues
well done by a few people at a particular time, and ill done
before and afterwards by everybody else.

If we are to have an idea of Blake as he grew up we must first get to know what it is to discover the delight in form and the belief in form, and we must at every moment remind ourselves how much, and of what sort, is the difference between the mind of any one to whom this is a leading thought, and the mind of those who divide man into flesh and spirit and forget form—that is neither the one nor the other. Form can be loved in those whom we absolutely dislike, both for their flesh and their spirit. Were this not so, the majority of artists' models would starve.

We cannot go so far as to suppose that our doctrine, *the figure is formed for beauty*, came into Blake's head in dogmatic style when he was a little boy. We should not say of Sir John Franklin that the notion that the North Pole was formed for exploration was in his mind, as a set phrase, in childhood, when his mother found him on the floor instead of in his bed one night, and he gravely assured her that he was hardening himself for his coming privations when he should be a great traveller. Yet the emotional perception of *purpose* in this world of ours, and of duties arising from this purpose, is perhaps among the youngest of thoughts, even if it is obliged to wait till years bring maturity before it can be given out as statement or shown in action.

Much in the same way as that in which a lad whose pet idea is the sea will devour heavy books about Nelson or Captain Cook, while the sporting boy reads about Mr. Selous, and the mechanical boy about Watt, Stephenson, or Edison, Blake worshipped and studied Raphael, Michael Angelo, and Albert Dürer. Religion awoke in him. As he said later, "The worship of God is honouring His gifts in individual men." So he used to go to the sales of prints where threepenny bids were taken in those days, and where Langford, the auctioneer, took a fancy to him because he showed knowledge enough to pick out the best masters, called him his "little connoisseur," and often knocked down lots to him "with friendly precipitation." His father even bought casts for him to copy at home—the Gladiator, Hercules, and Venus de' Medici—and at ten years old sent him to draw at Parr's Life School in the Strand.

The styles of prettiness and ugliness which in our own day, like blue and brown streams, unite their currents, but not their waters, to form the great river of modern art, have so swept most of us along with them that it is difficult now to realise that the old masters and the classics are not necessarily severe, distasteful, or at least disciplinarian to a young mind. To those who take their first and best artistic delights from these, they are as exciting as the story called *Treasure Island* or as the best orchestral music. Our first admirations are always exciting. The Old Testament was a novel to the Puritans, and even now the grimmest and sternest works of art in all the history of the world—the Pyramids themselves —rouse to quick beating of the heart, and the deep breath of excitement, ardent artistic youth, as they did in the days of the Pharaohs.

From prints of Raphael's and Michael Angelo's works, as from the Gladiator, the Hercules, and the Venus, Blake now began to learn the artistic joys of the mind, the seed-sowing delights of which he afterwards told in one of his proverbs that says—

Joys impregnate : sorrows bring forth.

When it was considered time to apprentice the boy to a master that he might learn a trade or craft of some sort, it was undoubtedly his wish to be made a painter. Gilchrist has recorded for us that it was only because indentures to an engraver cost less that he was bound to Basire, after he had refused to be articled to the fashionable and fascinating Ryland, because, as he said after being taken to see him, " the man's face looked as though he would come to be hanged."

This was a really surprising bit of second-sight, because not only was Ryland prosperous and well liked universally at the time, but he must have had an essentially honourable expression as he had an essentially honourable nature, for about ten years later, when he was in prison before execution for the forgery on a chartered company, made under temptation and to the hurt of no visible and lovable individual, for which he ultimately suffered the death penalty, he was trusted on parole by his jailer, and allowed to walk out with him, after giving his word that he would not use this indulgence to make his escape.

It was not in order to rise in the social scale that young Blake wished to be an artist instead of a draper. Nor did he merely come to the conclusion that he must be one because he liked art. A voice that others could not hear laid this command upon him in plain words; it said, " Blake, be an artist." As for the social position of an artist then, he recalled many years later, in writing to Mr. Cumberland, who was trying to found what has become our National Gallery, how they could both "remember when a print-shop was a rare bird in London," and adds in the same letter: "I myself remember when I thought my pursuits of art a kind of criminal dissipation and neglect of the main chance, which I hid my face for not being able to abandon as a passion which is forbidden by law and religion."

The fact that Blake's father bought casts for him of antique statues (reduced copies, we must conclude), seems to indicate that he was a very superior man, and to suggest that the only source of estrangement between himself and his son—the vexed question of art—had turned into a source of union. Other discord arose, however. One account of Mr. Blake the hosier tells us that he was a dissenter. This is a softening of the truth, and leaves it open to us to imagine that he was a Wesleyan. In actual fact he was one of a much smaller minority than any group of Evangelists or Methodists: he was a Swedenborgian. Swedenborg, of course, was a visionary, a man to whom angels appeared, and to whom they taught a special and, it must be confessed, a profoundly interesting and fascinating as well as an almost credible and not at all improbable interpretation of the Bible. We feel as we read his works that there is nothing like them in all literature, and those of us who believe anything at all do not find it easy to resist his teaching unless we close our ears entirely. Hardly any one ever read him without admitting his fascination, and even a Comtist will turn regretfully rather than contemptuously from accepting all that he puts forth, while marvelling at the mind that invented the system, and admiring the character that moulded this mind.

A father may accept Swedenborgianism, however, without being in the least inclined to admit that, because Swedenborg's angels told him divine truth from vision, a little boy may start up in his own family and claim to do the same thing.

Mr. Blake seems to have considered that too close an acquaintance with Swedenborg's doctrines would not be particularly good for such a boy, and it can hardly have been less than an equal cause of estrangement to put beside the general want of acceptance of William's divine call that his father should have discouraged him (to say the least) in learning about the elder visionary. It had required evidently no more than the meagre outlines of family instruction to show Blake as a boy what he announced later—that it would be part of his duty in life to outdo Swedenborg, correct him,

and leave him high and dry as a mere writer of footnotes to
elder prophets, though he might have been of their company
himself.

We require no friend of the household to tell us, on the
authority of personal memory, how irritating it was to Mr.
Blake, perpetually conscious of his position as an exile and
shopman, when he had made a pedestal for himself out of the
courage with which he had embraced the rarest, latest, and
at the same time the most deeply-thought religious opinion
of his day, to find his little boy growing up in a state of
indignant repudiation of the claim to prophetic sufficiency of
the teacher of this new and beautiful reading of the Bible.
What was good enough for the lad's father, what was a great
deal too good for the capacities of most of his father's contemporaries, was not to be treated with contempt and called
merely good enough, *as far as it went*, by the fiery-haired
stripling.

When the apprenticeship to Basire the engraver was a
settled thing Mr. Blake must have gone home with rather
a grim smile, reflecting that this rebellious boy would have
seven years of bending over copper plates, with a strong glass
fixed in his eye and his nose nearly touching the square of
metal, while he laboriously cut lines and dots to represent
the shading of drawings that some artist, whom he probably
thought inferior to himself, had swept in with a free brush
at his ease.   There would not be much room for preposterous
visions in the three inches between that arrogant young face
and the pitiless sheet of cold copper.   Let the boy learn what
work was; it would do him good.

If such thoughts as these did not pass through the mind
of Blake's father he would have been more than human, but
it is right to record that he did not arrange the apprenticeship with any purpose of inflicting on William a period of
discipline.   William chose the life of an engraver for himself.
Mr. Blake had gone so far on the road of concession as to
approve of the scheme that he should be a painter.   Art
instruction was not to be had for nothing then, and the
painter to whom he applied—(Blake never seems to have
told Tatham, or any one else, who it was)—asked such a
heavy sum that the boy refused to have it spent upon him,
because "it would be unfair to his brother and sister."   This
must have been final, as showing to the father how unfit
William was for the career of a shopman.

From the point of view of professional success Basire was

not the best master to have chosen. His style of engraving soon went out of favour, and the soft manner of Bartolozzi replaced it. Blake was always indignant about this, and always fiercely loyal to Basire, while his favourite aversions were Bartolozzi, Woollett, and Strange. He began his apprenticeship to Basire (at 31 Great Queen Street) in 1771, and as long after as 1810 was still his faithful and enthusiastic upholder against all rivals, as we see by these few lines in his MS. book :

Woollett I knew very intimately by his intimacy with Basire, and I knew him to be one of the most ignorant fellows I ever knew. . . . Woollett I knew did not know how to grind his graver : I know this. He has often proved his ignorance before me at Basire's by laughing at Basire's knife tools and ridiculing the form of Basire's graver, till Basire was quite dashed and out of conceit with what he himself knew. But his ignorance had a contrary effect upon me.

A partisan like this would have made a son worth having if his father could have understood him in time.

CHAPTER III

BLAKE only worked for two years continuously at Basire's,—the years 1771 and 1772. It was during this time that he saw Goldsmith, who, as will be remembered, did not live beyond 1774. Goldsmith was then over forty, and his large, round Irish forehead was bare to the crown of the head. Blake, looking out from under his thick crop of hair that started its flaring upright life two inches above his eyebrows, immediately said that he wished he could have a head like that when he became a man. The short Irish nose and large Irish eyes of Goldsmith he had already. As time went on, his hair receded till it came no further forward than the exact middle of the top of the head, although he was never bald. The portraits and the cast from life show that his wish was fulfilled. The upper part of Blake's brow attained Goldsmith's full roundness. The lower part grew more protuberant than Goldsmith's, and the back of the head with the chin that balanced it became much longer and stronger. It is noteworthy that both men were very envious and were exceedingly desirous to shine in company, though Blake felt this craving aggressively and confidently, and boldly satisfied it, except during his occasional fits of doubt and depression when he was too gloomy to desire anything. Goldsmith felt the hunger for appreciation with a nervous helplessness, which placed him even further from gaining it than he would have been if he had not felt the desire at all. We still see Goldsmith unable to keep away from Dr. Johnson's set of competitive talkers, though he only talked "like poor Poll," and we pity him as he stayed for long hours, watching, watching, watching, in the hope of getting in a brilliant remark, and so making his exit with a decent round of applause to comfort his craving ears, but finally creeping off defeated and angry, with the memory of a stammering blunder at which every one had laughed.

14

In the serious things of character the two men were curiously contrasted. Blake hated money, and died poor but solvent. Goldsmith actually worried himself to death in his last illness over a debt of two thousand pounds, and when he died earned Dr. Johnson's caustic funeral oration,—" Was ever poet so trusted?" But the thing that both Blake and he had in common was conscience. It restrained the strong man who hated restraint, and killed the weak one who could not restrain himself.

But Blake was only as yet arriving at the possession of a knowledge of his own character. He tried to feed his emulousness now with the consolation that he knew how to grind his tools better than Woollett, who became a more popular engraver.

After the first two years, however, his position with his master changed. Two new pupils came. They seem to have been idle apprentices. Basire desired to exercise his authority, and expected Blake, who he had discovered was the strongest character in his studio, to help him to do so. He had got quite a wrong idea of Blake. To shine, to be accounted a leader and a hero, was one thing, but to play chief constable to a master as magistrate was quite another. Blake was, in blood and spirit, an Irish chieftain. He was not a Dogberry. Malkin says that the new pupils were too cunning for him, and that he was too simple for them. Nothing is more probable. Here he began to feel the first disadvantage of having had no school experience. Blake had not only escaped being " flogged into following the style of a fool," but he had also escaped seeing little fools growing up and revealing their little meannesses as they did so. He was always ready to suspect authority, but was not shrewd enough to suspect rebellion. Veneration or regard was a feeling that during his whole life he only felt towards two qualities, genius and forgiveness.

Basire needed careful drawings made in Westminster Abbey for some engravings that he was commissioned to execute. He could not leave Blake in charge of his other apprentices. He had only one thing to do. He sent him to the Abbey to make the drawings. That he worked well and faithfully now—1772-1773—is seen by the fact that he was allowed to continue copying the tombs month after month, and that a scaffolding was erected for him to study details that could not be seen from the ground. He not only worked with fidelity but with delight, and exultation, which had both an immediate and a lasting result.

The lasting result was that he ceased to admire Greek form exclusively and adopted Gothic form as his favourite. " Greek form is permanent in the mathematical memory," he afterwards wrote, " Gothic is living form." He even so far abused the word Gothic as to apply it to all art that was not directly derived from the antique without fresh reference to imagination through nature. Raphael and Michael Angelo became Gothic in his mind, and certainly there have been terms applied to them less illuminating and descriptive than this.

The immediate result was that, in the state of imaginative rapture in which he brooded while working, he was visited by a vision of Christ and His apostles. They appeared, as all his visions did, to have life of their own, just as the personages do who appear to us in dreams. That they shared his views on Gothic form is certain, for long afterwards he puzzled good Christians by writing that our Saviour and His chosen twelve were artists.

The effect of this visit did not wear off. We must not suppose that it consisted merely of an insane delusion, an affection of the optic nerve or the centres immediately behind, such as persons in a state of alcoholic poisoning suffer from when they begin to see black dogs. It shows the beginning of Blake's symbolic system of thought, although it came some years before that system took literary shape as a myth and became the great message of his life. None the less, that it was a hallucination in the ordinary sense we need not doubt; only, it did not hallucinate. He believed it to be real only in a particular sense. It was not real as nature is, for the best of all reasons. Nature is not real. Blake never forgot that. Nature is a mental conception as much as vision is a corporeal appearance. He may have been frightened childishly or delighted childishly with his visions at an earlier time. They were beginning to be viewed now by his mind from a very high philosophic standpoint. He had, as it were, a private scaffolding built in the region of his intellect, and when he climbed this he was above the level of insane delusions. Of this mental scaffolding some account will be given when speaking of the period, not many years later, when he lived on it altogether, like St. Simeon Stylites on his column.

It has been recalled that at the time when Blake was

copying in the Abbey for Basire, a company of learned persons belonging to the Society of Antiquaries, for which Basire was making the engravings, obtained Royal permission to open the tomb of Edward I, and saw for a moment the King's face as it was at the time of his death. It fell to dust under the outer air immediately. Blake probably saw it. He represented Basire, and would not be likely to have refrained from using his position.

In our own time a similar visit was paid to the body of Charles I. The head was found replaced on the neck, neatly sewn round, the stitches being in the skin of the throat. The face looked calm and handsome. No excuse, such as was valid in Blake's day, can be offered for the fact that a flash-light photograph was not taken at the very first moment of exposure. While the selfish and unprovident persons for whom the tomb was opened were gloating over the sight, the nose of the King's face fell in, and the mask became a horror. Such must have been what the desecrators of King Edward's rest saw. It is hoped that they all went home feeling like regicides, and dreaming of it for a month after. Perhaps the next time such disgraceful permissions are granted, proper precautions will be taken to save for history a sight that no group of antiquarians has any right to possess exclusively and to destroy for posterity.

There was another result of Blake's Westminster Abbey studies. He altogether ceased to be even in the remotest degree tied and bound with the consciousness of his social position. At school and college he would have been constantly reminded of it. The Kings, whether on—or in—the tombs at Westminster, knew nothing about it, and in their company he ceased to know more. He became their equal. In the *Poetical Sketches* that were written at about this time, the drama of *Edward III* is not composed by a plebeian. The author is as much on a level with the King and his nobles as Shakespeare himself was, although it was by seeing the great ones of the earth reposing in eternal sleep that he acquired his equality, and not by observing them at their revels.

Both poets had, for their medium of expression, a certain literary convention to start with. But the greater miracle remains to us in Blake's one unfinished historical play. He was a boy in his teens when he wrote it. He had an overwhelming amount of suggestion in Shakespeare's plays and yet was not overwhelmed by it. He had the most meagre

C

fragment of document outside the pages of books to reveal majesty to him as it lived—merely its carven effigy made after death, and perhaps one spice-bound corpse. Yet the vitality of his work is as easy and as complete as that of Shakespeare's, who must have been behind the scenes with the British royalty and nobility in more senses than one.

Did visions of Edwards or Dagworths come to Blake and perform before him? Were they real? Were they lost echoes of now silent truth, from the far-off lives of the men themselves? We are not yet advanced enough on the road that begins in a rash guess and ends in a truism, to attempt to chronicle our conjecture of the answer to this riddle. One result, certainly, is left by Blake's historic poetry. The argument against Shakespeare's authorship of his own plays, which gentlemanly but unilluminated minds occasionally feel the weight of oppressively, and that consists chiefly in the suspicion that a man of the middle classes could not have written as Shakespeare wrote of the highest in the land, is laid to rest for ever, and becomes as unfit for public gaze as the face of a dead monarch when the cold air has destroyed its form and dignity.

But the *drawing-room fallacy*, as this absurd contention may be called, is not an enemy to be despised. It seems to have been against Shakespeare's reputation, even in his own lifetime. It continually revives. Men of the highest literary position are known to have allowed it lately to use their superciliousness to obscure their judgments. Their raised eyebrows (to translate the long word) really seem to have taken something away from the strength as well as from the height of their foreheads. They are not to be too severely blamed. All second-class literature is full of amusing failures in the tempting task of describing classes of society to which the writer had no entrance. The modern Baconian's error lies in judging the best by the second best.

One reason may be offered for supposing that Blake had visions among the tombs. He considered the heads as portraits. He can hardly have given this opinion merely from the fact that they were not of academic or classic type. He is not at all likely to have thought that institutions like Parr's life school existed then, or could have obtained casts of antique statues whose originals were still hidden, to make the taste of the sculptors of our early Westminster tombs so classical that only portraits from life could escape the academic influence or exhibit natural types different from those that are to be learned from Greeks and Romans. This was true in the times of the Kings George, but in Blake's most fanciful moment he did not suspect the days of the Kings Edward of any such misfortune. He probably took the short cut of consulting vision, and formed his opinion of the portraits from this, though we have often to remind ourselves that he sometimes criticised and distrusted vision itself. He did not on that account omit to make what use he could of it, or cease to believe that it arose in some way out of a vanished actuality. It was part of God's mind, like everything else, and, coming to him through his own imperfect mind, was liable to perversion or, as he called it, "infection." Still, in some cases, it is all that a man can have to go by, and Blake made what he could of it, as a historian will make what use he can of the gossip in some scrap of an ancient private letter, while admitting that gossip is not gospel.

But Blake had visitors in the Abbey of a less august and dignified character than learned committees in the flesh, or historical or sacred visions. The boys of Westminster School had, in those days, the privilege of considering the Abbey as "within bounds," and went there as often as they liked. It is possible that Blake, innocently supposing that some of them took a real interest in the monuments, allowed them to climb up on his scaffolding. He once more had reason to feel the disadvantage of not having learned at school what mischievous young savages the youths of our civilised nation often are. One of the rascals climbed a cornice, especially to get above Blake and annoy him,—probably by scattering dirt on his drawing. This would quite account for the fury which seized on Blake then and there. He did not recall afterwards that he said a word to that boy. He simply grasped him like a sack and flung him down on to the floor of the Abbey below, and then, leaving him lying there, walked off without waiting to see whether he was dead or alive, and laid a complaint before the Dean. He was only sixteen, but he made the Dean listen to him. It may be supposed that the boy recovered, as the only result of the affair recorded is that Westminster boys lost their privilege of making the Abbey a part of their playground.

All his life Blake claimed to recognise a sharp distinction between friends and enemies. Nothing was too good for a friend. Magnanimity to an enemy was not only absurd, but

was a sort of treachery to friends in itself. "I am no
Homeric hero," he says. He was a born partisan, and never
outgrew his inherited character. These words, which are to
be found on the margin of a divided part of a proof of his
engraving (1779), *King Edward and Queen Eleanor*, reveal
him as he was through life: "The Christian religion shows
that no man is indifferent to you, but that every one is either
your friend or your enemy—he must necessarily be either
the one or the other—and that he will be equally profitable
both ways if you treat him as he deserves."

Occasional outbursts of fury remained always noticeable
in Blake, but as time went on he became wary, and his
violence had a limit even during the very moment of its
explosion. When he admitted once having flung a copper-
plate across the room when out of patience with his own
engraving upon it, and was asked, "Did you not injure it?"
"I took good care of that," he answered. This very frank
reply at once recalls the mingled caution and frenzy of his
great ancestor of Elizabethan days, Shawn O'Neil, who, when
he felt an uncontrollable fit of rage coming on, would order
his followers to bury him up to the neck in sand, so that he
might not do something to one of them which he would be
sorry for afterwards.

The digging-up of Shawn when his meekness returned to
him would offer the subject for a very pleasing historical
picture which seems to have escaped the attention of the
humorists of our day.

Blake, whose respectable father never seems to have mentioned to him his Irish origin, was always true to his ideal
of wrath as a righteous and justifiable emotion. "The tigers
of wrath are wiser than the horses of instruction" is well
known as one of his aphorisms. It is among the *Proverbs of
Hell*, but this exhortation, written about fifteen years later in
Milton, page 25, lines 57, 58, may be read with it—

———— pity the weak as your infant care.   Break not
Forth in your wrath.

One terrific outbreak of wrath in others—this time wrath
of the multitude, of the weak grown strong for a moment
—was seen by Blake in 1780. The lower orders, who had
a very small amount of consideration in those days, suddenly
burst into tumult, and the Lord George Gordon No Popery
Riots gave all Europe a hint of what a mob could do that,
imitated and exaggerated at the other side of the Channel,

was to produce the French Revolution. Gilchrist has a paragraph about this:—

Half London was sacked, and its citizens for six days laid under forced contributions by a mob, some forty thousand strong, of boys, pickpockets, and "roughs." In this outburst of anarchy Blake long remembered an involuntary participation of his own. On the third day, Tuesday, 6th of June, "the Mass houses" having been demolished —one in Blake's near neighbourhood, Warwick Street, Golden Square, and various private houses also,—the rioters, flushed with gin and victory, were turning their attention to grander schemes of devastation. That evening the artist happened to be walking in a route chosen by one of the mobs at large, whose course lay from Justice Hyde's house, near Leicester Fields—for the destruction of which less than an hour had sufficed—through Long Acre, past the quiet house of Blake's old master engraver Basire in Great Queen Street, Lincoln's Inn Fields, and down Holborn, bound for Newgate. Suddenly he encountered the advancing wave of triumphant blackguardism, and was forced (for from such a great surging mob there is no disentanglement) to go along in the very front rank and witness the storm and burning of the fortress-like prison and release of its three hundred inmates.

Gilchrist remarks also that Blake was lucky to have escaped hanging *for being there*. He seems to believe that Blake only looked on. This is incredible. He must have rioted with the rest, for he was "in the very front rank," and could not shirk. He probably liked it, but it does not follow that he boasted of it afterwards. His friendly hustling of Tom Paine, a little later on, showed that he knew the value of a quiet tongue.

CHAPTER IV

BUT besides poetical *Sketches* that were soon to be published by his friends, and bursts of wrath that, but for Tatham's careful though brief record, would never have been published at all, Blake seems to have begun to form his philosophy while working alone in the great Abbey.

It is not certain how far he did so, because it is not clear how much of the inscription that he placed on a plate that he engraved for himself—that called *Joseph of Arimathea among the Rocks of Albion*—is as early as the rest of the engraving. That some of it is so is probable, but the inscription is long, and there was nothing to prevent his adding to it after the date was put down. Its appearance suggests that he did so. The interval may have been only of minutes, but it may have been of years.

His poetry of this time was still entirely free from any trace of philosophy, but the vast idea may have come to him now, to be afterwards put into verse under other influence. The engraving itself shows a massive, antique hero, in a helmet, walking slowly down a barren path between rocks, with folded arms, and an expression of tranquil meditation. The attitude of the legs suggests that this design may possibly have been made from a sketch prepared by Michael Angelo for a figure on Christ's left hand in the *Last Judgment*. The arms and head are different. Perhaps there exists, painted by Michael Angelo, some figure in a position exactly like that in Blake's engraving, but which is now hidden in a private collection.

Blake put "Michelangelo *pinxit*" on his plate, yet says that it was made from a drawing. The plate bears the date 1773, and was therefore done when he was still sixteen, in the year of the casting down of the Westminster boy, after not more than two years of study with Basire. It is a fine work of its kind, and shows a quality that teaching did not improve afterwards. The engraving measures 10 inches by 5½, and may be seen in the Print Room of the British Museum. It is in the title that he gave to this that, if we can believe it to be all belonging to 1773, we find how early in life Blake began to form his philosophic system. The full title of the print, a representation of which is here given, is :

Joseph of Arimathea among the Rocks of Albion, engraved by W. Blake, 1773, from an old Italian drawing.   Michelangelo pinxit. This is one of the Gothic Artists who built the cathedrals in what we call the Dark Ages, wandering about in sheepskins and goatskins, of whom the world was not worthy.   Such were the Christians in all Ages.

"Rocks of Albion" are symbolic. By them Blake here, and throughout his life, meant the "hard, cold, restrictive" portions of mind that forbid imagination and say that the five senses are the only gates by which truth can reach man. In religion they mean the literal sense of Scripture that is symbolised as a tomb in which the inspired Word, or Christ, is laid. Joseph of Arimathea is the "Just Man" of whom we shall hear soon in the "Argument" of *Heaven and Hell*. He takes the form of a mythic personage later in Blake's poetic life, and is called "Los," the "friend of Albion," the spirit of poetry and probity. "Albion" is the ideal man, not a human being, but the abstract of manhood who, when inspired, becomes Christendom, and finally Christ, that ideal Christ whose essence is inspired imagination, whose limbs and members are ideas, when ideas are incarnate in living persons, and who died and was laid in the rocks when inspiration, entering fact, turned it to symbol, became dead in it for a time, while only the literal meaning of that symbol was apparent,—and arose when it was revealed. In these few words on Blake's early engraving is told somethirg of the central tenets of a religion that he gave his life to developing through art, myth, and poetry.

That he should have gone so far into symbolic Christianity already will seem even more amazing than it is unless we remember that he had been accustomed at home to hear Swedenborgian talk, in which the Scriptures were treated always as having a symbolic meaning. Unless we go to Swedenborg's own works and see what he has to say, we cannot form any picture to ourselves of either the character or the power of Blake's mind, and we shall at one moment over-estimate him, while at another we shall do him very much less than justice.

Swedenborg, whom Blake may have met in the streets as
an old man, had only died in 1772, a year before the date of
this design of *Joseph of Arimathea.* He had lived to a great
age, having been born as long ago as 1688, and his great
Symbolic Dictionary of the Bible was published in Latin
during the years 1749 to 1756, being completed the year
before Blake's birth. It is called *Heavenly Secrets,* if that be
a sufficient rendering of *Arcana Cœlestia,* its original title, by
which it is still known, even in translations. This, and the
Apocalypse Revealed, and the treatise *On Divine Love and
Wisdom,* seem all to have been owned by Blake's father,
though they were not studied by Blake himself till later.
The Symbolic Dictionary is the work of which it may be said
that Swedenborg stands or falls by it. A good English
translation nicely bound in slate-coloured boards may be
bought now in Bloomsbury Street, near the British Museum,
at the offices of the Swedenborg Society. There are twelve
volumes, none of them much more than an inch in thickness,
and the cost of each (at the office) is 2s. 3d. The last,
containing an index which is a dictionary in itself, is the
most necessary to readers of Blake, but all are full of suggestions by which, partly through direct analogy, partly through
mere acceptance, and partly through positive opposition,
interpretations of Blake's myth are to be sought. Here again,
to most of us, the general morality and the sweet religious
tone of Swedenborg are the most attractive qualities, while
we admire his amazing lucidity, and the perfect if prolix
manner in which he has set forth his views, even if we with-
hold our assent from his claim that he could interpret the
arbitrary symbols in which, as Scripture itself informs us, all
who were not in the secret must expect to find the Word
hopelessly and purposely hidden, that seeing we might
see and not perceive, and hearing we might hear and not
understand, lest we should see with our eyes, and hear with
our ears, and understand with our hearts, and be converted
and healed. We are at first inclined to deny that Swedenborg had any special means of knowing more about the
matter than we could conjecture without his help. There
are so many religious maniacs, that we are tempted to set
him down as one of them when we learn that he claimed to
have been directly and plainly taught by angels, and to have
been specially permitted to give that teaching to the world.
On the other hand, even if every tenth man had delirium
tremens, we should not doubt the reality of the retriever that

goes out shooting with us or with our friends and comes to the whistle.

Blake accepted at once the angels and a very large portion of the doctrine of Swedenborg. But when he came to look into it a little later, as he tells us, he found it fatally incomplete. He accounted for this by saying, not as a profane jest, but in sober seriousness, that Swedenborg had received his teaching from angels only, while he ought to have consulted devils also. This was in 1790. After 1804 he wrote *Devils are False Religions*. One Swedenborgian idea Blake had accepted on the mere hearsay of home teaching, and adopted without any hesitation already, and he never abandoned it. As time passed it was more and more approved by his imagination, and its importance to us, now that we are all trying to understand him, consists in the fact that it changed every idea that he would otherwise have found in religion, and affected his standard of poetry and directed the flight of his poetic imagination.

This idea was that the Bible is a secret writing that inspiration contrived and that inspiration only can read. As men of business, when describing certain stocks and shares that they wish to buy or sell, conceal these under the names of animals, countries, and articles of furniture or food, and yet, when they read the documents in which these things are written, see only the financial meaning of the words through their knowledge of the "code," and not for one instant picture to themselves the actual articles of commerce, of utility, of landscape, or geography which, to an outsider, would seem to be the subject of their correspondence, so Swedenborg assures us the angels read the Old Testament (through our eyes), seeing in its apparently matter-of-fact histories a prolonged gospel relating only the sacred things of the story of Christ's birth, growth, and character.

Blake adopted the code idea as not merely true of the Bible, but as containing the essence of the highest poetry wherever found. Inspiration he took to be truly one of the intellectual powers of man, high above that lower faculty called *reason*, which is a mere "ratio of the five senses," and not properly intellectual at all. "Allegory," as he wrote after he had used it for thirty years, "which is addressed to the intellectual powers, while it is altogether hidden from the corporeal understanding, is my definition of the most sublime poetry." This passage occurs in a letter to his friend and patron Mr. Butts, dated July 1803.

Not from any single sentence, but from all the many allusions he makes to such matters, we can gather what he meant by "intellectual powers," and why he demanded of all those of us who had any that we should understand his allegories and visions. It is evident enough that in his final poems, where all these names occur, the symbolic relationship of Albion, Joseph of Arimathea, and Los—that is to say, of an impersonation, a person, and a myth—must be altogether hidden from the "corporeal understanding" or every-day common sense.

His theory seems to have been that there was not, as science teaches, matter from all eternity, but that there was mind. Our own minds were portions of this before the disadvantage of birth caused the five senses to claim too much of our attention through that corporeal understanding which is composed from a mixture of their teachings from moment to moment with a mingled memory of what they have recorded since they began to inform us. It follows, of course, that inspiration is a perception of that eternal mind to which we have a perfect right, whether we are good or wicked men, and to attain such inspiration is the duty of all who can do so, while to strive towards it is the universal duty.

The exact time when Blake formed this opinion is not certain. It relieved him of the necessity which Swedenborg felt of hearing imaginative interpretations of Biblical symbols from angels who were invariably, Swedenborg says, the souls of the dead. It did not require of others that they should go to such source for similar interpretation. At the same time, it did not invalidate such authority, for into this world of imagination, this region of eternal mind, we shall all enter after death, and it is not surprising if some are allowed partly to return so as to communicate to us mentally what neither we now, nor they when in life, could fully know. During our period of "sleep" — our mortal seventy years — the clamorousness of bodily sensations and thoughts interferes with our hearing of the divine voice, and there is no reason why we should not attend to what the dead have to say if they are allowed to speak to us.

We all know that memory is bodily as well as mental. The scrapings upon hills in Scotland, made in ancient times by glaciers that crept downhill past their upright rocky portions, are their memory of the ice-fields of the past. When our brains are in such a state that the motion of substance caused by the disturbance aroused by any mental act of perception leaves no scraping signature on the impressionable wall past which the disturbance moves, we have no memory. Memory may be called a scar's consciousness, as perception is that of a blow. But when we look for as accurate and convenient a figure in which to describe an intention, the difficulty is greater; and when we wish to describe a tendency to form an intention, it is still further increased. Even the last of these three stages is, however, readily conceived as the *virtual velocity* of the glacier before it began to move.

Blake, who had never been to school, had probably never heard so technical an expression as "virtual velocity," coined a term for it himself. It was mind in a state of patience. He accounted for motion by the idea that mind is eternal, but patience is not. Patience removed, mind moves; the circle of Destiny begins, and all that our consciousness perceives is generated. As a result, *Man* (as he called primæval mind, afterwards altering the name to *Albion* on reconsidering the engraving now before us when writing a quarter of a century later) — Man the eternal went through changes, became the creator, produced matter by a contraction of intellect, produced error, entered into it himself, became one of us (who are *naturally* a mass of error), and on leaving the state of error and returning to that of mind, now become imaginative instead of patient, he taught us all how to do the same; and, in fact, *did* it *in* us, and does it in us only, and when we ourselves do it. This is Christendom. We are the Saviour and the saved.

In an article on Magic published in a volume of meditations, called by the Blakean title *Ideas of Good and Evil*, by the former collaborator of the present writer, Mr. W. B. Yeats, all who are interested in it may find an account of certain experiences that caused Mr. Yeats to form a belief in the objective existence of a *general memory*, which is not that of any individual, which exists as it were in the air, and on which, by means of magical invocations or symbols, we can draw at will. Events are recorded in the air, not the respirable air, the astral, and magic gives us ingress to that reservoir of unspoken history.

Blake's theory went further. He held that all imaginations are accompanied by a movement of an unknown something that never forgets its own movements, and unites us to one another. He held that those of us who cultivate this faculty of imagination enrich that vast store, and ultimately go to dwell in the part of it usually called "heaven," but that he preferred to call "the Mind." Into this Flaxman went when he died, Blake wrote, and he himself expected to follow Flaxman there. Into this the fool cannot go, and to plead personal holiness is not to be admitted, for "holiness is not the price of entrance into heaven" (Preface to *Jerusalem*). In heaven all is brotherhood. "In eternity all is vision." There is a socialism of the soul there, and communism of property. Those of us who would understand Blake's designs when still alive are invited by him to go to this heaven and study them there.

CHAPTER V

WHEN ART PUT ASIDE LETTERS

In 1778 Blake's apprenticeship came to an end, and he did some artistic study in the life-schools of the Royal Academy, then a new institution. It is said that at Parr's when he was ten he only studied from casts, though Parr's was called a life-school. It is probable that he was now so deeply interested in the human form that he left off writing poetry altogether. It is a crucial moment in life when a boy begins to draw from life, to see what the men and women among whom he is to live are like without their clothing. From casts and from the glass Blake had already learned that form exists. This seems a most unnecessary thing to say, yet those of us who are not artists do not so much as suspect what it means, any more than children suspect what a lover sees in the offered lips that he loves besides what they see in the lips of their playmates.

Let us turn from words to *form itself* for a moment, and consider how much new mental action goes to seeing even a portion. If we look at the shoulder of a woman, and follow the line down its slope to the fullest part that already belongs to the arm, and is one-third of the way to the elbow ; if now we go down to the elbow and see the curve's fresh entrance, like a fresh paragraph of the page, revealing the poetry of the upper part with new meaning, as in architecture the column gives new meaning to the arch ; if we begin again to read what the form has written where the flesh widens for the smooth face of the lower arm, and then learn the outer slope that goes to where the centre line of the wrist, a little more curved than the back of the hand, dies down into it as a wave sinking dies into the flat shining surface of sea-water upon sand ; if we compare the two sides of the arm, and listen to the form as to the metre of a verse, perceiving how its curves are not opposite to one another, but spring at different points.

fading off with different spaces; and if we do the same to the body, rooted into the thighs as the throat into the back and chest, and to the thighs, tapering with such slight difference from straightness on the inner side, and so bold a swing on the outer, we have fifty new and amazing rhymes and melodies to learn, more beautiful than those of shells or of fruits or flowers, and more dignified and less coquettish than pretty schemes of clothing, and therefore more modest.

An ardent boy hungering for the touch and breath, for the mere nearness and voice of womankind, goes to a studio, and passing in to see for the first time the female form entirely undraped, probably catches his breath and wonders whether he will be able to sustain his self-control. He is amazed at the serenity of nerve and the new fascination of mind with which he finds the world's white flower offered without its leaves. Here is something that he had not foreseen. Here is a scheme, a harmony, in beauty. Here generally is also some lapse from beauty, hitherto hidden by costume, a lapse that is positive and aggressive, that repels and startles him, for the fairest of the fair are not always to be obtained in art schools. But at the worst he has a great experience. He expected only to find in woman what man desires. He finds what man admires, and above all what man, especially if pretending to be an artist, should thoroughly learn. For a while the passion of this learning absorbs him, and in the delight of the mental understanding of form he forgets that bodily attraction from one sex to another exists. The novelty of silent cadences will also completely take from him the wish to express himself in poetic words. Here is a poetry without words, yet of more universal meaning.

If experience derived from studying the male form in the same way gives a youth less surprise, it is chiefly because passion is absent, and he knows something of male beauty already. But here also he soon finds—like those who read a great poem complete after only knowing of it from quotations —that there is a bewildering beauty in the harmony, ex- hilarating to learn, and in itself equally able to put all things out of the mind until it is learned.

Above all, it puts out literature and landscape; and music itself, like love, is for a time forgotten. Later on, it produces preference, taste, and distaste. The young artist, in learning what form is, learns what it might be and generally is not. If he is too quick and enthusiastic he comes to this stage, as Blake did, too soon, and turns from the terribly imperfect and sometimes even grotesque types that are offered to him as "*nature.*" He thinks he dislikes "nature." In happy ancient Greece nature was generally sunny, well balanced, easily beautiful, neither knotty nor scraggy. Men were more often like the stems of beech-trees. Now we are too frequently like wind-blown oaks. Their best of art was the produce of their best of luck.

Blake got far enough into the knowledge of modern figure to falsely suspect the types in Greek statues of being mechanically composed; and then he turned away from the actual men offered to him for nude study because of their lack of architectural harmony and of open-air colouring. His drawing from himself naked, done in 1780, and called *Morning* or *Glad Day* by Gilchrist, is his triumphant announcement that he had found at home the solution of the artistic problem of form.

We are not told by Gilchrist (who reproduced the print at the head of his fifth chapter) that the limbs are Blake's own, but that they are so is undoubted. To be certain of this, it is only necessary to compare the way in which the arms grow from small, smooth, and oval shoulder muscles, and from very large chest muscles, with either the Greek or the English types of strength. If we alter them in outline just enough to make them feminine instead of masculine we shall see that they belong to the well-known type of Irish beauty, which is admired, year after year, in evening dress at the Castle balls in Dublin, and still more in London drawing-rooms, where it is more rare.

The whole form is also exactly the same as that of the figure called "William" in *Milton*, page 29, and even of the "Robert" which on page 33 repeats it in reverse. We cannot but see that whatever model sat was Blake's source of reference for anatomy during many years. It could only be himself. The *Los* on page 21 is of the same type. The way in which the full and rounded thighs grow from the body further identifies it. This is not the figure of a tall man, but certainly of a very strong one. Blake was not tall but remarkably strong. He defines the type of greatest strength as that which shows its power concentrated in the trunk and tapering to the extremities, and that of greatest beauty as the one that varies least from infancy to old age. If he had trained from childhood he could have become a "Strong Man" at a fair, and earned his living much more easily by lifting big brass balls than by scraping little copper plates. It would have been much less of a tax on his vitality and endurance. In *Job*, 1827, his last work, the same figure is repeated, undistorted by time,—varied little " from infancy to old age."

With the pedantry of an enthusiast, Blake became at once intolerant of all art that was weak in the places where his own artistic tastes were strong, and with his usual uncalculating and simple truthfulness he entirely forgot that he might seem to be a " hater of dignitaries " if he uttered aloud what was in his heart. His interview with Moser, Keeper of the Academy, is quite natural, like his interview with the Dean of Westminster, when one remembers that he had never been taught the fear of the schoolmaster as a little boy. He recalls it in a note, pencilled on the margin of Reynolds' *Discourses*. The date of the incident cannot be later than 1782, as Moser died and was buried in the month of January 1783. Blake was probably a student at the time,—if so, the incident related belongs to 1778, when he was twenty-one.

I was once looking over the prints from Raffaele and Michelangelo in the library of the Royal Academy. Moser came to me and said, " You should not study those old dry and stiff unfinished works of art. Stay a little and *I* will show you what you should study." He then went and took down Le Brun and Ruten's *galleries.* How did I secretly rage! I also spoke my mind. I said to Moser, "These things which you call finished are not even begun ; how then can they be finished ? "

The fact that even genius can be mingled with a quality so much the contrary of itself as mental vulgarity has been proved to us lately by Gustave Doré, and in literature by other gods of a day. But Blake reverenced the word genius, and would not hear of such a thing—a picture was only *begun* to him when it had begun to have that *line* which is the apostolic succession of the elect among artists. " True art and science," he has laid down, " cannot exist but by naked beauty displayed." To him it was unfortunately never really displayed enough.

In his faculty of " vision " he had a substitute for nature which enabled him to work with less return to study, and less loss by the lack of such return, than any other artist known. He also had more advantage than most from the habitual inspection of his own and his wife's figures undraped. His imagination suffered less from this home-study than from any other kind, though he says, " Nature does and always did weaken, deaden, and destroy imagination in me." It always does this to all of us, as a hearty meal reduces (at the moment) muscular strength. He did not always remember that at the same time nature, when studied, strengthens talent, nor across the blinding vision did he see, when drawing from imagination, the piece of paper on which he was wrongly tracing the shape of his idea. He said, " I draw perfectly from vision," and added, that others drew imperfectly from nature.

But the study of nature improves the faculty of comparison between art and the idea, even if it weakens the idea, and the study of vision weakens this, even if it strengthens the idea. A *purely* visionary artist would *never* know when he drew correctly from vision. His correctness would depend entirely on a harmony between the nerves of the hand and the nerves that produced the vision, an inborn harmony, unaided and uncriticised, and his work would therefore be wonderful when he was at peace with himself and in solitude, but easily spoiled by distraction, irritation, or fatigue, and diverted or weakened even by poetry.

Therefore when Mr. Mathews, in the preface to the *Poetical Sketches*, explains the fact that these verses were not corrected, by saying that since 1777 Blake was too busy with " his profession " to attend to poetry, he must have been repeating an expression of Blake's own, a recollection of the absorbed fascination of original art study that had suddenly taken him away from the pen so soon after the time when he wrote these early poems. None of them bears a later date than the last year of his apprenticeship.

His writing, whose recommencement was put aside by art study, had probably stopped when the composition of the drama of *Edward III* came to an end, in that year before he began his new course of life-study.

He does not tell what broke it off. It was probably some chilling lack of sympathy in some friend ; but once checked, all poetry was forgotten for the human form, and lines that can be drawn must have filled his mind, not lines that could be written.

He could to a certain extent draw whenever he chose, but he could no more command himself to be poetic when distracted by the irritations of daily life than we can command ourselves to go to sleep when we are worried or cross. In later years he wrote a good deal of verse when angry, and it is so remarkably poor that it makes his real poetry even more of a miracle.

His great secret was, that when he was able to devote himself to imagination entirely he had genius. When distracted by the miserable self-consciousness that either doubts itself or rages at the doubts of some one else, his mind was unable to free itself from self-consciousness and enter into the absorbed trance of poetic creation.

He therefore was wise in resenting, as he always did, the disparagement which those who cannot criticise believe to be criticism. " Doubts are always injurious, especially when we doubt our friends," he says; and also, " Doubt is self-contradiction"; and again, " If the sun and moon should doubt they'd immediately go out." Later he says, in one of his letters, " I must be shut up in myself or reduced to nothing." He talks of the mythic persons of his imagination, when they became destroyed by arguments or other distractions of the mind, as being " dissipated and drawn out into nonentity."

Some one once told him that Raphael died of dissipation. He appears to have understood by dissipation distraction, especially distraction from artistic contemplation—the tearing to pieces of a mind continually trying to concentrate itself and continually disturbed. He therefore answered that he thought what was related was quite possible, and added that " some people had nothing to dissipate," which was probably true of the imagination of those to whom he was speaking. This *dissipation* caused by any interruption and disturbance is always painful. It is like being awakened from a sweet, warm sleep to encounter some disagreeable task on a winter's morning. It is, in fact, so very like this, that Blake always called unimaginativeness " winter." The loss to us all from the foolish disturbance of imaginative peace that checked the growth of the play *Edward III* must always remain irreparable.

As the blood of martyrs, however, is the seed of the Church, some good may yet come of that broken poem if even one of those who read it achieves a perception how much easier it is to injure an artist than to produce a work of art. Those who are not artists are constantly injuring those who are, beyond all power of reparation. The result is that the art, even of the most gifted periods, only grows by fits and starts when the destroyer is otherwise occupied. The destroyer is sometimes an individual, sometimes a vast chorus, and not infrequently acts as the perverter, believing himself to be the helper of art. He renders only such kinds possible as can be done with his foolish approval. Most art students are such perverters, and they injure each other. We have the decadence of art in art-schools, and the perpetuation of mediocrity and imitation as a consequence. A true dream is never mediocre. We all paint the darkness in our sleep with a force above that of an Academician. Our minds are then at liberty. We have no self-consciousness, and therefore no self-contradiction. We are not what Blake, in *The Keys of the Gates*, calls " a dark Hermaphrodite."

CHAPTER VI

IN what poetry Blake wrote during the years of his apprenticeship there is no trace at all either of Swedenborgianism or of the myth of Los, Albion, and the four Zoas which was the subject of his chief works later on. He was an enthusiastic reader of Shakespeare at this time, and it was remarked with surprise that he took a great pleasure in the poems, the *Venus and Adonis*, and the *Lucrece*. They were not fashionable. The taste that admired Pope could hardly be expected to enjoy them.

His own first poems were written between the years 1768 and 1777, or, as the preface to the volume of *Poetical Sketches* says, were " commenced in his twelfth and occasionally resumed till his twentieth year." Chatterton produced his poems, attributed to " Thomas Rowley, a monk of the fifteenth century," in the year 1768. He was born in 1752, five years before Blake, and is credited with being the first of the moderns to break away from the poetic standard of the misguided eighteenth century. It is just possible that he influenced Blake, who afterwards upheld his pretended " Thomas Rowley " poems as being really written (he meant inspired) by Thomas Rowley, or an influence or spirit so called. Blake had a way of attributing the good in art to influences or spirits as the " authors " rather than to the man that held the pen or pencil. He disclaimed the authorship of his own poems more than once.

He would have considered it as quite probable that even an actual Thomas Rowley, having died three hundred years before, might have influenced Chatterton's mind from his eternal station in the Universal Mind to which he had entered. If so, what Chatterton wrote he rightly attributed to dictation. Blake would even speak of a mental influence that produced work of any sort as having " dictated " it, as we shall see in the letter to Hayley about his brother Robert, after Robert's death. It is in this sense that he continued to attribute the *Ossian* of Macpherson to a real Ossian, after Macpherson had admitted having written the poems himself.

But the early verses in the *Poetical Sketches* are stamped with a quality that shows them as essentially and intimately Blake's own, and if he began them in 1768, as Mr. Mathews tells us, he is undoubtedly a pioneer.

None the less, he was continually roused to complete artistic acts by hints, just as people unable to originate are roused to imitation and distortion by completed artistic work. We could wish to know, though we must always despair of knowing, the order in which these poems were written. The most surprising thing about them is that they are so easy in style and so few in number. They are all he has to show during seven years, and yet each probably only occupied a few minutes. The reason must have been that his solitude was still used more for reading than for writing, and more for walking than for either. He always delighted in long country walks, and the engraving for his apprenticeship filled up most of the hours that found him unfatigued.

How much and how often he loved lightly, in a dreamy and silent way, before he met Polly Woods, we shall also never know. We suspect that the persons spoken of in the poems were not the subjects of any long or intimate affection. They were certainly not Kate his wife, though he addresses "Kitty" in one of them, perhaps by a marginal insertion in the MS. which is lost to us. He was already married when she good-naturedly allowed them to be published.

The unfinished drama *Edward III*, being taken as the last, would leave the years of his real romance, its breaking off, the meeting of his future wife, his twelve months' engagement, and the twelve months after his marriage, without any poetical production at all, which was probably the case.

"Clara Woods," who seems to have been called "Polly" familiarly, since we are told of "Polly" without being told that Clara had a sister, was the name of the girl who was his real first and last love.

After something less than a year the courtship came to a sudden end. Blake was jealous. Polly was flirting. He protested. We know of what kind his protests were. Polly may be glad not to have been treated like the Westminster boy. She kept the upper hand in the quarrel. He probably considered her want of strict fidelity as a crime of *lèse-majesté* against himself, for his view of woman was always Miltonic, and was founded on Old Testament ideas. To himself, as we know, he gave later the very frank if well-deserved title, "a mental prince."

But we can only guess at the terrific thunder of his reproaches, whose poetry was incomprehensible to the girl, by her answer. She listened to his tirade, and at the end, "Are you a fool?" said she. "That cured me of jealousy," said Blake afterwards, doing himself rather more than justice, for more than two years later, in his own handwriting, on the margin of a book of Lavater's aphorisms, we find, where jealousy has been mentioned with rebuke, these words: "Pity the jealous!"

The shock, however, was a severe one. Blake's temperament being ardent, his character confident, and his heart affectionate and trustful, the whole woof and warp of his emotional fabric was torn to scraps at once. Love, self-regard, and hope were wounded. Such a fit of extreme wretchedness came upon him that, strong as he was, or rather precisely because he was strong, he became seriously ill. Like "William Bond" in the ballad, he "came home in a black, black cloud, took to his bed, and there lay down." In fact, he never entirely recovered, for to the end of his life he was liable to suddenly fall into short illnesses that were only fits of extreme and helpless melancholy, for which he himself said he found "no cause." They were echoes of that first thunder-clap of disappointment. His parents, taking serious alarm, arranged with a friend of theirs, a market-gardener named Bouchier, that he should go and live at the garden-house for a while, in the hope that he might recover his health among the flowers.

Mr. and Mrs. Bouchier had a dark-eyed pretty daughter of four-and-twenty, named Catherine, who knew how to love though she did not know how to read and write. She had her own ideal, and was waiting for it. She was not to be deceived by small civilities. She had admirers, and one of them seems to have induced her mother to speak in his favour, for there is no reason to suppose that it was merely to get her out of the house that Mrs. Bouchier had already asked Catherine to make up her mind about marriage. But all the answer Catherine had given was: "I have not yet seen the man." Now on the night of Blake's arrival, as she came into the room where he was sitting with her family, she *saw the man* and grew faint. It was love at first sight, and never changed from that hour, but was still fresh and

whole all through Kate's long married life, and even during her short widowhood, between forty and fifty years later.

In the summer of 1782 she began to love. In 1827 Blake died. In 1831 she followed him.

Of his proposal to her we have a few words only, as of his jilting by his former love, but this is more than history has kept for us of all the other poets of the world. The words have been told over and over again, and it may almost be said that until they are known Blake's symbolic system itself is only half revealed. When the declaration was made Blake had been describing his ill-treatment by Polly Woods, and telling how miserable it had made him.

"I pity you from my heart!" Catherine exclaimed.

"*Do* you pity me?" he said. "Then I love you for that."

"And I love you," she answered.

This is certainly a true account of what was really said. The authority for the words must have been Mrs. Blake herself. Her memory was always good, as is that of most healthy and clever people not taught to read and write, and in this matter there is every reason to trust it, for the words she remembered were evidently the middle of a day's talk, the turning-point of the conversation, the climax that is not easily forgotten.

The response of Blake to her offer of pity tells several things. The "*then*" shows Catherine's love to have been betrayed by a look if not by a word already, so that Blake knew quite well that *she* loved *him*. Probably the true writing of his words would be: "Then *I* love *you* for that." But we are not forced to emphasise the point in order to find it evident. Whichever way the expression is read it means: "I, who have so lately loved, have already seen that you love me; and you are so pretty and dear that I have been sorry to think that I could not love you for such qualities—Polly Woods was pretty and dear—and I have often wished that I could find something different to love you for. I find it now in your pity."

Here indeed was something entirely unlike Polly Woods, and fit to win a new kind of love. It was a problem solved, and Blake never lost a second in pouncing on the solution of a problem while it was still red-hot in his heart.

Then came her formal acknowledgment of what he knew already. We are not told where the words were spoken, but in the long pathway of a nursery-garden is the probable place, for lovers can be seen so clearly, and from so far, that a chaperon was not likely to be any nearer than the window of the house. This, though open to let in the warm air, and convenient for observation, would be well out of hearing.

It was not till he was more than forty years old that Blake had a garden of his own, but all through his works gardens are mentioned as places "of delight"—"a garden of delight" is the usual phrase in *Vala*. "Vala" herself is an allegoric personage, the essence of simplicity and feminine love, and an allegory of masculine love meets her in her garden, where it is said that "impressions of Despair and Hope for ever vegetate" (Night IX, line 375).

From what we know of the way in which Blake would snatch up an experience, treat it as what Swedenborg calls "representative," and use it for a symbol, it is easily to be understood that his place of love-making was Mr. Bouchier's garden. But Mr. Bouchier the gardener was a practical man, and so was Mr. Blake the hosier. Mrs. Bouchier had her own favourite suitor for her daughter, the one whose cause she had meant to plead when she received the discouraging answer, "I have not seen the man." No one but the girl herself wanted the jilted invalid apprentice just out of his articles and his first love.

Finally it was decided that Blake should not see nor even communicate with Kate Bouchier for a year. If he was still in earnest at the end of that time, and if he had shown himself worthy, opposition was to be withdrawn.

Blake, though he loved, was not a lover, and therefore not madly impatient. He himself wished to show what he was made of. The plan suited him. There was never much doubt that he would stand the test. He stood it, and on Sunday, August 18, 1782, he was married in the church at Battersea, then newly rebuilt and decorated with painted windows to imitate real stained glass, which was not in that day so easily procurable as in our own.

Blake's father was only half pleased that his son had behaved steadily and gone through this year of trial that ended in marriage. His disapproval of a mere uneducated country girl was strong. He had looked on himself as patronising the Bouchiers when he sent his son to board with them. It was quite another thing to unite his family to theirs. To our eye the difference in social height between a hosier's son and a market-gardener's daughter may be too subtle for appreciation, but Mr. Blake felt it not merely because of the position, but chiefly for a reason he could not

give. He could not say that it was a derogation because
he was really Mr. O'Neil. In actual fact, of course, he was
Mr. Nobody—he was not even Mr. Blake.

He appears to have kept his counsel, if not his temper, and
said nothing to his son. Of this we may feel certain. It is
wholly incredible that William Blake could have known the
story of his father's birth, and have made no symbolic use of
it. On the contrary, he calls himself "English Blake."

After his marriage there was a period of estrangement
from home affections. He set up house at 23 Green Street,
Leicester Fields, a street in which Hogarth lived then, and
where "junior branches of Royalty had lately abode." This
surely ought to have comforted Mr. O'Neil Blake. Whether
it did so or not, he kept his tent like Achilles. At this time
also Flaxman married and settled down. He had been
introduced to Blake by Stothard, whom Blake knew through
Basire. Flaxman had spent several years in Italy, and had
now returned to work entirely in London. He was one of
Blake's best friends for many years from this time. His
reputation helped Blake's *then*. Blake's memory perpetuates
his *now*. A pitiful misunderstanding separated them at
the last. In the end, which seemed a long way off in those
honeymoon days, they both died in the same year: Flaxman
going first, but only preceding Blake by a few months. Their
names will always be remembered more closely together than
those of most "tigers of wrath" and "horses of instruction"
that are fated to run side by side on life's dusty road.

They did many services to each other. Blake lent
Flaxman so much of his imagination that he began to
recognise it again in Flaxman's designs, tame, sedate, and
well schooled as Flaxman's drawing always was, like his just
character and his formal handwriting.

Flaxman was one of the two artists referred to in the
little couplet in Blake's MS. book, written in the times of
their misunderstanding.

> I found them blind, I taught them how to see,
> And now they know neither themselves nor me :

and in this couplet to Flaxman's wife, written at the same
late period (it is to be hoped that she never saw it)—

> To NANCY F——.

> How can I help thy husband's copying me ?
> Should that make difference between thee and me ?

Blake's politeness to Mrs. Flaxman has led him to overlook the obvious fact that *thee* should be the last word of the second line, and the shallow, unpoetical state of mind in which he wrote all his irate couplets, of which this is a good specimen, concealed from him the fact that if he had placed Mrs. Flaxman's pronoun at the end he would have placed it at the highest point of emphasis, and given his guest, as it were, the head of the table, as a man may in his wife's absence,—and certainly Mrs. Blake is not present in the couplet. The repetition which he gives instead of real rhyme is not, of course, wrong in itself, but is clearly so in this place. Blake's very smallest errors have so much narrative hidden in them,—narrative of the mind, for whose sake only that of the body is worth recollecting,—that this has its claim not to be passed over. Here, as in many other places, what seems merely literary criticism will often be found to help the personal story, as the personal story helps to direct literary criticism by explaining symbolic suggestions.

The first benefit that Blake received from the Flaxman family was an important personal service, one that showed kindness and courage on their part, for Blake was an alarming guest to take into society among quiet folk. They introduced him to Mr. and Mrs. Mathews, of 27 Rathbone Place.

While Blake is remembered Mr. and Mrs. Mathews cannot be forgotten, though he came to them only to be encouraged and patronised, as Michael Angelo went to Lorenzo dei Medici. Mr. Mathews was a clergyman, and not a merchant prince like Lorenzo, but he and his wife encouraged young artists and musicians, and he was not without a touch of that urbane generosity with which some of the best of artistic people who are not artists have, in periods of taste, won to themselves immortality, when they only intended to do an unrewarded kindness.

Flaxman was not, any more than Blake, a distinguished man when Mr. Mathews first took him up. A few years before he brought Blake to the house he was only a quiet boy, son of a plaster-cast seller, and very much in earnest about classical art. Mrs. Mathews read Homer with him in Greek, translating and explaining as she went along. This alone must have meant many long hours of patient kindness.

Since then Mr. and Mrs. Mathews had attained the leading position that they deserved. It was known that something better than gossip was to be heard at their house, and many people of admitted literary distinction were glad to be received there. No. 27 Rathbone Place became known as a *salon*. Gilchrist has preserved some of the names of the regular guests, recalling how Mrs. Montagu and Mrs. Vesey (whose blue stockings made "blue-stocking" a popular term for literary ladies) set the fashion in London of literary "*réunions*":—Mrs. Brooke (novelist and dramatist), Mrs. Carter (learned and awful), Mrs. Montagu (sprightly and fashionable), and Mrs. Barbauld—this is Gilchrist's catalogue of celebrities among the friends of Mrs. Mathews. He adds, that this is the Mrs. Montagu of whose mental powers Dr. Johnson had a high opinion, and that she gave a dinner to chimney-sweeps on May Day. We have here the evident reason for the poems about the chimney-sweeps in Blake's *Songs of Innocence and Experience*, where they seem, without this explanation of their presence, to have been inserted merely as a piece of far-fetched poetic humility.

When we recall, however, how at this time the pathos and picturesqueness of chimney-sweeps were actually thrust on Blake's attention this suspicion vanishes. It was at the house of Mrs. Mathews that he began to write his *Songs of Innocence*, and there is nothing more probable than that the favourite subjects of conversation among the people whom he met there roused him up, not only to the verses about chimney-sweeps, but to more of what is said and sung in these *Songs* than we can now trace. It is certain that he left off this kind of writing soon after he left off being among the habitual guests of Mrs. Mathews, and that he never seriously adopted it again.

Mrs. Barbauld is still faintly remembered by many people now fifty or sixty years old, who were taught her *Hymns in Prose* when they were children. These miserable metreless paragraphs of gently devotional dreariness were composed under the impulse of an idea that was in the air then, and that made people think themselves original and superior for trying to write in prose what is usually written in verse. In America this kind of originality arose again lately, but Walt Whitman was old-fashioned before he began. Blake's desire to "out-do" all writers in his own day accounts for the printing as prose of several pieces of not very irregular verse in the *Poetical Sketches*, and for the composition of the piece called "The Passions," first published in the August number of the *Monthly Review* in 1903, rather more than a century after it was written.

In this poem is Blake's first piece of what would have

been called by readers of Rousseau "confession." This is what he said of himself, writing it as prose. The editor who prepared it for its appearance in the *Monthly Review* cut it up into these lines:

> My cup is filled with envy's rankest draught,
> Desire still pines but for one cooling drop,
>   And 'tis denied.
> While others in contentment's nest do sleep,
> It is the cursed thorn wounding my breast
>   That makes me sing.
> However sweet, envy inspires my song:
> Prict by the fame of others, how I mount!
> And my complaints are sweeter than their joys.

This admission is one for which any admirer of Blake, who wishes to keep himself free from timid insincerity when trying to describe him, must be thankful. The truth of it is evident enough to whoever enters into Blake's character, but to announce it as the result of critical research would seem ill-natured. It would even appear to be insincere,—to be itself a disparagement growing out of envy of a great man who is gone,—perhaps the most detestable of possible qualities in a biographer.

Yet if we are not to descend to a tone of childish and sentimental worship, but to admire Blake as Ben Jonson admired Shakespeare, keeping just a little "on this side idolatry," then this thing had to be said, and it can come from no one with a better grace than from the man himself. About twenty years later he repeated the confession of envy in his MS. book, where he says that the sarcastic verses to be found there in derision of Sir Joshua Reynolds were "written by a very envious man."

CHAPTER VII

THE boast that his "complaints are sweeter than their joys" that Blake makes in speaking of those whom he envied, and his calling what he writes "my song," are, of course, perfectly justified expressions, but they take all justification from the writing of this passage for print—it was certainly written for print—as prose. There are several pages of it. A further sin against his own poem done by the ever-gifted and ever-reckless Blake was purposely wiped out, as the quotation was copied for insertion in the last chapter merely by the omission of three words, that seem to have been inserted by an enemy expressly to injure the music. In fairness, in stern and disapproving fairness, they must be now put back. In the fourth line of the quotation "downy" must be re-inserted before "nest," and in the seventh "'tis" must be restored before the word "envy" and "that" after it. Then the passage stands, ready to trip up the reader as well as to delight him, just as Blake left it. We read:

> While others in contentment's (downy) nest do sleep,

and

> However sweet, ('tis) envy (that) inspires my song.

When Blake came to the drawing-room of Mrs. Mathews he found an interior as picturesque for its appearance as for its guests. There were even statuesque decorations made by Flaxman in a kind of artificial stone composed of sand and putty that could be worked in the hands like clay when it was fresh, and would harden afterwards. There were painted glass windows by Oram, another of the protégées of Mrs. Mathews, and "bookcases, tablets, and chairs ornamented to accord with those of antiquity."

Blake brought with him his early ballads and poems, and

sang some of them to his own tunes, which the musicians of the drawing-room praised and noted down. But either they are lost or have been quietly inserted in the compositions of these people, who perhaps also had drunk of Envy's black liquor. Perhaps every tune contained one or two impossible notes which completely spoiled passages of value. If so, probably Blake was most deeply attached to these, as it is said the mothers of deformities are to their distressing children. In any case, as Fuseli said some years later, " Blake is dam' good to steal from."

The songs were certainly beautiful, however lawless, and they made for Blake a party within a party in the drawing-room of Mrs. Mathews, for " Nollekens " Smith, a fellow-guest who heard the singing, tells us that, though some who came disliked Blake for his " unbending deportment," yet he had " adherents " who praised him for his " manly firmness of opinion."

In the early days, before it was known that he was a devoted lover of his own errors and slips, Blake won so much admiration for his first songs, those that he had written in the time before Polly Woods, that Mr. Mathews wished some of them published, and was even willing to bear half the cost of their printing. Flaxman, young and warm-hearted then, not yet disguising under prim and cold impartiality his natural faculty of admiration, undertook to bear the other half. Between them the little volume still known as *Poetical Sketches* was printed, and the sheets were presented to Blake to sell or distribute to his friends. We are nowhere told that the copies were all bound, and there is reason to suspect that they were not, and that the " sheets " were quietly used by Blake afterwards chiefly to light his fire. Newspapers were rarer and smaller then than now, and fires must be lit with something.

This publication should have been, and with any other man would have been, the cause of real gratitude and lasting friendship. To Blake it was an almost undiluted annoyance, and he found it, after the first moment of hope, an offence very difficult to forgive.

The outrage began when the proofs came home, and Mr. Mathews asked him to correct them. We can see, from our side of the sandbank that more than a century has caused to rise as the grains fell from the never-turned and bottomless hour-glass of Old Time, how this must have revolted Blake. He stood smiling in the sunny glow of his own self-satisfaction, which may be called self-worship, since he believed his

verses to be the voice of God within him, and held that the
only "worship of God is the honouring of His gifts in individual men." Mr. Mathews showed him his first work in print.
Mr. Mathews had admired it (*very naturally*, we hear Blake
say in the silence of his own bosom). Mr. Mathews had
desired to have it printed (*very proper*). He had borne half
the cost (*quite so ; well, even half is something*), and now
just before issuing it he wanted it corrected. (*What ?*)
Behind the good-natured Irish smile, and hidden by the
musical and murmurously caressing Irish voice, Mr. Mathews
probably did not detect the amazed contempt with which
Blake received the suggestion. He accepted from Blake the
commonplace excuse, quite sincere as far as it went, that
since writing these things he had been too busy with art to
correct them ; and this, intended as a mere bit of personal
conversation, he put into a preface as an apology, to
Blake's intense disgust ; further offending him by calling the
compositions "sketches," a word hateful to Blake, as we know
by the indignant tone in which he made long afterwards the
perfectly absurd statement, "Michelangelo never *sketched*."

The one quality of Blake that, like his genius, those around
him could not measure was the enormous capacity for contempt that his pride gave him. In the confidential pages of
his MS. note-book we find him, twenty years later, writing—

> The only man I ever knew
> Who did not almost make me spue
> Was Fuseli. . . .

The reason why Fuseli was an exception was because he had
original powers of imagination. These were very much
inferior to Blake's own, as Blake knew perfectly well, but
yet they were very much superior to those of any other poetic
artist of his day. Fuseli, like Blake, had dignity, impressiveness, massive movement in his art, the poetic style, knowledge of the nude, a power of serious and almost sublime
composition. Who else could claim to possess these things
then ? Blake measured every one by his power to answer
that question.

It did not impress him with any feeling of respect that
Mr. Mathews stood far above the clergy about him in matters
of taste, as his wife did above their wives in knowledge of
Greek. He did not appreciate the beautiful voice in which
we are told Mr. Mathews read the service, nor the church
that was built for him by his admirers. He did not even

discover that Flaxman had dealt generously in arranging
that he should be admitted at all to their house.

The Mathews family, who appeared to themselves to be
kind patrons of a clever boy; and the other guests, who
seemed to themselves to be eminent and important friends of
the kind patrons, willing to tolerate and even encourage the
clever boy,—seemed to Blake rather less than so many monkeys.
They almost "made him spue," because his mind was fixed
with devoted ardour upon passion, poetry, art, and beauty,
and they were tame dabblers in careful little pomposities.
Yet it requires intellect and taste superior to that of nine
people out of ten to be even a tame dabbler in little pomposities. Blake in cool moments did as much justice to his new
friends as any one, only he seldom had cool moments. He
was almost always in a fever of artistic and poetic enthusiasm,
and he despised the amateurs as an ardent soldier in war-
time despises the fat merchants and futile mayors and aldermen of towns that he alone can defend and his equals alone
can endanger. Let those who have felt either the military
or the poetic temptation to contemptuousness treat Blake's
arrogance as it deserves. No one else has the smallest chance
of suspecting what it is or measuring its desert. The poorest
artist on the pavement has sinned the same sin. If he reads
this he will (if regenerate) beat his breast, and say in the
mood of the publican in the parable, "God be merciful to
me, a painter."

Below all emotional difficulty caused by red-hot egotism
that was so disinterested as to seem to its owner to be self-
devotion, there was another reason why Blake did not correct
the pages of the *Poetical Sketches*, and it is final. He did
not because he could not. Any one who has handled or
studied his original manuscripts, and has seen the changes he
made from time to time as he re-read them, is continually kept
in a state of irritated wonder by finding that, though he often
retouched to alter, it was hardly ever to correct. Corrections
can be made when a man, taking up his work once more after
his mind is released from the chain of composition, sees that
what he has written is not, whether for sound or for sense, a
satisfactory embodiment of the idea which is the reason of
its being. If this is still unchanged, and the writer's purpose of giving it a true expression still uncooled, he will
take the pen and strike out the stumbling words, put in
those that lift the meaning on their shoulders, and do *at last*
what he did *at first* in other places, where his energy worked

without hitch or oversight. The corrections are unseen, and all is unity. Blake hardly ever—it would be almost true to say never—had this needful prolongation of his mood lof conception, so that it could run on into a mood of judgment. When he came out of the poetic fit he came like the three Israelites from the furnace—scarcely was the smell of fire left on his garments. If he tried to restore his burning mood by lighting up his mind at his own pages, he generally set up a new productive heat, not exactly the same as before, that urged him to make changes, not corrections. This is true to a certain degree of the best Irish poets now writing in English. It seems to be a national characteristic.

Blake had this defect, as he had all his qualities, in an exaggerated degree. He was so totally without the real talent of criticism, that sees the *should have been* in the *has been*, that he did not know the difference between this and its opposite, the pedantic and mischievous primness that so often causes a merely smooth revision and defaces what it should vitalise. While still smarting under the offence that he had endured in being asked to *correct* the *Poetical Sketches,* he wrote :

Improvement makes straight roads, but crooked roads without improvement are the roads of genius.

Perhaps this will be remembered as the most outrageous and inartistic piece of nonsense this truly great artist has left us. He could not see that crooked roads, when not crooked as genius hastily thought it had crooked them, could be improved so that their beautiful crookedness should really at last become what it had only seemed to be to their designer in his preoccupation, caused by the mental absorption of the act of creation. This deficiency in Blake, this critical blindness, was almost always absolute and unconscious, like colour-blindness or tone-deafness to others. Those that have it suffer, as of course we all know now, from a mild form of a disease that is well understood. But Blake had never even heard of *aphasia,* and his misfortune cost him friend after friend, all through an enthusiastic life in which, nevertheless, *friendship* was the one ideal that he held to be of truly divine origin, and equal to genius.

This is the preface, or, as Mr. Mathews called it, the " Advertisement," written for the *Poetical Sketches*:

The following Sketches were the production of untutored youth, commenced in his twelfth, and occasionally resumed by the author till

E

his twentieth year; since which time, his talents having been wholly directed to the attainment of excellence in his profession, he has been deprived of the leisure requisite to such a revisal of these sheets as might have rendered them less unfit to meet the public eye.

Conscious of the irregularities and defects to be found in almost every page, his friends still believed that they possessed a poetical originality which merited some respite from oblivion. These, their opinions remain, however, to be reproved or confirmed by a less partial public.

The plea that the writer of this "Advertisement" urged against the possible oblivion of the *Poetical Sketches* by the public, need not be urged in favour of the preface itself. It will be sufficiently protected by the charming vagueness of the first sentence, in which we are not told what profession the youth adopted in his untutored state, and by the pleasant distinctness of the second, where we are told that *his friends* believed that *they* (there is no other plural nominative in the paragraph as yet) possessed a poetic originality. What other opinion they had of themselves is not told us. Only one is mentioned, and "these, their opinions" remain but inaccurately counted, however frankly expressed. The style of the "Advertisement," at least, encourages in us a cheerful frame of mind, and offers, unconsciously, a sufficient apology for Blake's contemptuous feeling towards the writer. Yet there is still interest for all who use the pen in looking to see *what it was* that Blake (in six years since writing) had not "leisure" to correct in these *Poetical Sketches*! We must look closely at the weakness of a partly paralysed Hercules if we are to value his strength.

In *Edward III* the play begins with a prayer. It is before the battle of Cressy:

KING.

O thou to whose fury, the nations are
But as dust, maintain thy servant's right—

The first line, by the inevitable if irregular pause after "fury," is splendidly fit for its purpose, of course, but we are caught at the second line and tripped up. What "genius" is there in such a "crooked road without improvement" as this? None, obviously. Let us venture to correct the metre and go on again:

KING.

O thou to whose fury, the nations are
But as the dust, maintain thy servant's right.
Without thine aid the twisted mail and spear,
And forgèd helm and shield of seven times beaten brass,
Are idle trophies of the conqueror.

Two words too many trip us up again in that last line but one. Why "seven times"? Was not "beaten brass" enough? Here is an idle trophy indeed. The speech goes on:

> When confusion rages, when the field is in a flame,
> When cries of blood tear terror from heaven,
> And yelling death runs up and down the ranks—

We are forced to stop again. Let us drop one word from the first of these three lines, and its extra length then has poetic value by forcing a great rapidity into the words "when confusion rages," which become "when c'nfusion rages," with a distinct and startled pause before the rest, which gives a panting reality to the emotion. Then in the second line "from" ought obviously to be read "out of," or we are a syllable short:

> When confusion rages,—when the field's aflame,—
> When cries of blood tear terror out of heaven,
> And yelling death runs up and down the ranks,
> Let Liberty, the chartered right of Englishmen,—
> Won by our fathers in many a glorious field,—
> Enerve my soldiers. Let Liberty
> Blaze in each countenance and fire the battle,
> The enemy fight in chains, invisible chains, but heavy,—

We are once more tripped. The line,

> Enerve my soldiers. Let Liberty,

need not be complained of, because any actor or reader, even one who reads to himself, would have the sense to put a vocative "O" before "Let Liberty," as all is vocative here, for the day when "soldiers" could be pronounced as a word of three syllables has passed; but the line about the chains requires thought. It would be unreasonable to ask Blake to take off the last two words, because, though redundant, they are graphic, and happily add to the terribleness of the idea and to the emphasis of the word "invisible." But as "unseen" means practically the same thing, and the word "chains" need not occur twice, a correction, obvious to every one but the flame-headed author, could have been made. With no further changes than to take off the word "then" from the next line, that Blake made to end

> . . . then how can they be free?

and adding the word "now," curiously missing at the end of the sentence, we may get through this fine passage without more trouble:

> The enemy tight in chains, unseen but heavy.
> Their minds are fettered ; how can they be free ?—
> While like the mounting flame
> We spring to battle o'er the floods of death ?
> And these fair youths, the flower of England,
> Vent'ring their lives in my most righteous cause,—
> O sheathe their hearts in triple steel, that they
> May emulate their fathers' virtues now !

Beside the retouched verses here we find fine irregular lines, unimproved because needing no improvement. The pause after the short one about the mounting flame, which is needful that it may not cause us to step out of time to the march music of the whole passage, is irregular, of course, but eloquent. It gives us a moment in which to *see* " mounting flame " in the figure of speech. During the pause of four syllables' worth of silence that flame leaps up before us, and if our prosody is less full, our minds are fuller. In the word " England " the letter *l*, lovingly prolonged, is a syllable in itself. This now admittedly is correct prosody as well as good poetry, and it is not, as we may remember, a new device. We have in Shakespeare's *Troilus and Cressida*—

> The policy that's in a watchful state
> Knows almost every grain of Pluto's gold,—
> Keeps pace with thought, and almost, like the gods,
> Does thoughts unveil in their dumb crad-l-es ;

which is perhaps authority enough, without a citation from Shelley, who came after Blake, and did not even know of his existence, but who has the same thing in his poem on Leonardo's Head of Medusa.

> It lieth gazing on the midnight sky,
> Upon the misty mountain peak supine,
> Below, far lands are seen tremb-l-ingly,
> Its power and its beauty are divine.

But while accepting without pedantry the irregular as well as the regular beauties of this prayer of King Edward in Blake's play, we cannot suppose that the slips, which are not beauties of any sort, were due to a mental bashfulness in the presence of the royal person whom his imagination had conjured up, for the whole poem shows that he treats the King as a god, or as " the policy that's in a watchful state " treats mere subjects when it dares to " thoughts unveil in their dumb cradles." The poet is the superior throughout. The King's mind is the servant of his.

Another utterly superfluous blunder, the result of over-sight, not of temptation, consisting of the mere intrusion of little unneeded words, is soon to follow. The next line is not the sinner, though it scans only by compression. The King now speaks to the Prince of Wales—

> And thou, my son, be strong. Thou fight'st fr a crown
> That death can never ravish from thy brow—
> A crown of glory ; but from thy very dust
> Shall beam a radiance to fire the breasts
> Of youth unborn. Our names are written equal
> In fame's wide trophied hall. 'Tis ours to gild
> The letters and to make them shine with gold
> That never tarnishes. Whether Third Edward,
> The Prince of Wales, Montacute, Mortimer,
> Or even the least by birth gain brightest fame
> Is in His hands to whom all men are equal.

It seems hardly credible, but in the unrevised sheets that poor Mr. Mathews so regretfully and kindly published the two lines above the last run :—

> The Prince of Wales, or Montacute, or Mortimer,
> Or even the least by birth shall gain the brightest fame.

The editor of Blake's poems in "Gilchrist" quietly skips all this fine opening, and begins the play at the words "Our names are written equal." But to fully appreciate the fatal incapacity to correct which caused Blake to leave his manu-scripts so full of flaws, it is not enough to have noticed cases of oversight where, among whole pages that were flung aside unread, there are lines left with the overgrowths of the first hurry and fever of improvisation unpruned. It is necessary to look at the kind of slips he leaves untouched in lines that he has read over and altered, believing that he had corrected them, and to see in these the halting and incomplete nature even of his alterations. The MS. of *Vala* has many such oversights. The poem is written entirely in a fluent and melodious line of fourteen syllables, on which Blake has so stamped the signature of his genius that he has made it his own for ever, as Spenser made the stanza of the *Faery Queen* and Petrarch the sonnet. It is a line almost as elastic as that of Shakespearian blank verse, and its elasticity enables it to fill itself with every different form of emphasis and significance. Here is an example of its use with an extra but unaccented syllable, a style of ending for which the technical term "weak" is so ridiculous and misleading :

> Terrified, Urizen heard Orc, now certain that he was Luvah ;
> And creeping Orc began to organise a serpent body.
>
> Vala, Night VII, line 153.

The second line is not very sonorous, but it has its just place in the general sound-scheme, as can be seen by even the hastiest reference to the page where it is found. Blake, whose pen was going at its usual headlong pace, did not set down the words so as to hit the true measure at once.

The line was first written thus :

> Creeping, he began to organise a serpent body,

which lacks weight in two of the syllables. If we add to it the words " did Orc " at the end, it would be rhythmical, but, in the mouth of any one but a peasant, impossible.

Blake of course did not add the deficient syllables. He left the line at the moment, but he felt vaguely that something should be done to show that Orc, and not Urizen or Luvah, was the organiser of the serpent body. He changed the line into

> And Orc he began to organise a serpent body,

and left it, again forgetting that he had lost the word "creeping," which is technical in his system and essential to the myth, for it implies that the state "length and breadth" is entered, and the state "height and depth" is abandoned. What remained was still not a line at all. But he was at the end of his patience, and he never took the trouble to make it one. The present writer, as editor, has been obliged here, as in other lines of *Vala*, to come to his aid, and this time actually to compound a line from his fragments. But this has not been done, as similar service was rendered in Rossetti's freer day, without a note (in the Quaritch edition) enabling the reader to see what had happened. Another example—lines 163 and 164 of Night IX, as numbered in the Quaritch edition—stood thus in the MS. :

> Saying, O that I had never drunk the wine nor eat the bread
> Of dark mortality, nor cast my eyes into futurity, nor turned
> My back, darkening the present, clouding with a cloud.

Originally the second of these lines was written—

> Of dark mortality, nor cast my eyes into the west, nor turned,

which would have been a good line if it had ended at " west," a pause being suggested after " cast," thus emphasising " my

eyes." The words "nor turned" would then begin the next
line. That they belong to that line is seen by the fact that
it is too short without them. Blake, going over his MS., did
not make the obvious correction that would at least sort up
the lines into verses, and not leave syllables hanging to the
end of one that were required to begin another. But, on
consideration, he decided that the associations with the
symbolic west and Urizen's journey (it is Urizen who is
speaking here) did not make out his meaning clearly enough.
He substituted the word "futurity" for "west," striking his
pen through it. He even made this incorrect correction
incorrectly, for he omitted to strike his pen through the
word "the." So line 164 now stood thus:

Of dark mortality, nor cast my eyes into the futurity, nor turned,

in which swollen and chaotic state he left it, and it is so left
in the Quaritch edition, the unerased definite article before
"futurity" only being omitted, though the present writer
regrets now that, weary with many emendations, he did not
put the whole passage into metre with a note to tell what
was done. It should obviously read:

Urizen wept in the dark deep, anxious his scaly form
To reassume the human, and he wept in the dark deep,
Saying—"Oh that I had never drunk the wine, nor eat the bread
Of dark mortality, cast eyes into futurity,
Nor turned my back dark'ning the present, clouding with a cloud,
Building arches high and cities, turrets, towers, and domes."

"Saying" at the beginning of the third line has the value
of a single short unaccented syllable only. But this is only
one of many places where editorial duty became too heavy to
bear. So I left Blake, by an oversight, in the tangle of his own
oversights, as he was left under compulsion in the days of the
Poetical Sketches by Mr. Mathews. Yet whole paragraphs
and pages in the finest parts of *Vala*, as in those of all his
long poems, are flawless, musical, dignified, firm, melodious,
and original in a degree, as is now gradually becoming
admitted, above the highest reach of any other writer of
English whatsoever.

Gradually we are forced into seeing that Blake, in his
inspired moods, had the power of hypnotising himself.—
unless indeed other powers of a spiritual nature, as he himself suspected, hypnotised him. However this may have
been, the result was that he became, when the fit was on

him, like Trilby in Du Maurier's novel, singing the divine *bel canto* when under the nervous concentration of Svengali's influence. When this went off she, it will be remembered, could not sing a musical note, and Blake, who did not always correctly record the song he sang, when in the fit, in his everyday state could not correct an erroneous line, even when its own musical form was plainly indicated in its errors.

He fully recognised these two states in himself, but the account he gave of them was by no means always the same. When "exalted in terrific pride," he would claim that his errors were beauties, and that they were proofs of his genius, while every one who wished them changed was a mischievous fool, and his enemy. In saying this he was perfectly sincere, and in many cases perfectly justified. The people of his day would probably have been mischievously willing to see his few really good irregularities also ground down into flatness.

In another mood he simply said that his poems were "dictated to him," and that he "might praise them, since the authors were in eternity."

Whichever account we may accept, one thing follows. There were two Blakes, and they could not edit one another. Yet he absolutely requires editing. Rossetti solved the problem by touching him up secretly. The present writer, for sincerity's sake, and to relieve the reader from being distracted from enjoyment of the poems by a nervous apprehension that he is not really reading the author but the editor, has noted every emendation he has ventured to introduce. But to leave what Rossetti happily called the "pious duty" of correction unperformed would have been the very cowardice of pedantry, unfair to reader and to author.

The few examples of Blake's blunders here given are not intended as literary criticism, but as part of the material without which a narrative of the growth of his mind could not have been written, and Blake without Blake's mind would have been as far from the real Blake as was the Blake of the earlier biographical and critical essays, among all of which is to be found no portrait whatsoever. But however necessary it may be to know truly the paradoxical story of his metrical errors, even when we have dug up the root of this mystery we are still outsiders, and have not entered into his living mind. We must know also the causes and origins of his inspired moments. Many of the experiences in his daily life that suggested symbols to him are not to be recovered now. They were trifles that left no trace before

Apparently illustrating the lines,

" Jocund Day stands tiptoe on the misty mountain tops—"

they foundered in the stream of time. They live in his poetic use of them only. But to know of a few is to know of them all. Some have been already mentioned, but one or two more may be considered.

We have already seen how the country walks of Blake while still apprentice produced his first lyrical utterances, while the cold tombs of the Abbey were the parents of his red-hot scenes of Elizabethan drama. It was Elizabethan, of course, from the pricking of the cruel spur of envy that goaded him to try to "out-do" Shakespeare. Sometimes a mere word let fall by chance would set him off into a productive fever of imagination, and be the cause of a sweet and never-to-be-forgotten poem or ballad.

There is a revelation of how this happened. The word "jocund," which also perhaps inspired his drawing of *Jocund Day*, called *Glad Day* by Gilchrist, was first to inspire a poem, as may be gathered from the notes written in later life that have been already referred to, about Woollett the engraver, who dared to be contemptuous of Basire. From those reminiscences we also learn that among Woollett's prints was one called *Jocund Peasants*. At the moment when this was under Blake's eye, and he saw "Jack Brown" working on it for Woollett, he was not thinking of writing *Anecdotes of Artists*. He was in the poetic exaltation of the years that produced the verses afterwards printed by the kind Mr. Mathews under the title *Poetical Sketches*.

At that time he was Trilby entranced, and the youthful blood in his veins was the Svengali that made the magic passes as he strode about the green fields in his holiday rambles. To him in this easily inspirable state the word "jocund" was enough. It set him off at once, as a match sets off a firework, and we have—

I love the jocund dance,

a poem whose third stanza begins—

I love the peasant cot,

which is evidently directly produced by the imaginative delight with which he gave life and love from his own mental riches to the title of another print claimed at the same date by Woollett, called *The Cottagers*.

Every one will recall an example of an incident almost similar, noted in Keats's letter to John Hamilton Reynolds,

written April 17, 1817, from Carisbrook. Keats is at the
time nervous from want of regular rest, as he says almost
apologetically, as if to explain such weakness as the fact
that the passage in *Lear*—

> Do you not hear the sea ?

has " haunted him intensely."

Then the letter gives the sonnet beginning—

> It keeps eternal whisperings around,

which was the result of that intense haunting.

In the high tide of what may be called Blake's missionary
activity, when the whole purpose of his life was—

> To open the eternal worlds, to open the immortal Eyes,
> Of Man inwards, into the worlds of Thought, into Eternity,
> Ever expanding in the Bosom of God, the Human Imagination,

he was still caught sometimes by a word.

> I give you the end of a golden string,
>   Only wind it into a ball,
> It will lead you in at heaven's gate
> Built in Jerusalem's wall,

he wrote as a little outburst of cheering to encourage those
who were likely to faint by the way in threading the mazes
of his great poem *Jerusalem*. The verse seems to have been
similarly the result of a chance suggestion in one word.
We find on another page of the MS. book, where this little
quatrain is crowded into a margin and written upside down
so as to catch his eye among its confused and crammed-up
leaves—

> " 2nd May 1807. Found the word Golden."

In the *Jerusalem* the lines are printed by Blake on page 77,
which is known to have been engraved long after 1804—the
date of the title-page. There is only one clue to its period.
The page of the MS. on which it occurs shows, by the
manner in which the entries crowd on one another,—the prose
paragraphs written wherever room could be found for them
in and out of spaces left by epigrams, short poems, and
sketches,—that the reminiscence about Woollett and Jack
Brown was written *after*—probably soon after—the quatrain
about the golden string. These reminiscences were to form
part of an advertisement to the *Canterbury Pilgrims*, including

Anecdotes of Artists, which could not have been written before 1808 or 1809. It was therefore in the mood of reminiscence, and not long before he wrote about the days when he had found the word "jocund," that he "found the word golden." This is natural enough. To the prolific mind the void of nature, when *entered into,* "becomes a womb that heaves in enormous circles." It is probable, in fact, that the verse he wrote after finding "the word golden," by recalling to him a similar experience of earlier years, brought back the time when he used to see Woollett, and to boil with suppressed indignation at his prosperity, while Basire was going out of fashion. This would now lead to the production of *Anecdotes of Artists* in the year 1808 or 1809.

The *Passions,* the one more poem so lately come to light that seems to belong to the period of the *Poetical Sketches,* has a value of a special kind. It enables us to see that *moods* underlie all Blake's mythic names, and that real mental relationships are intended by his mythic genealogies.

The one quality of his work which most encourages the reader, when wearied by its wonders, is its continuity of general scheme from the opening of his life to its close. This quality is difficult to find, however, for a very natural reason. It was a matter of course to Blake, and he only took pains to show it now and then under revolt from the incredulous and patronising contempt of those who excused themselves for not understanding him by whispering that he did not understand himself. He was slow to learn how those who could not comprehend him despised him, though it is the lesson that is the beginning of maturity, and there is perhaps hardly any one, with any strength or generosity at all, who has not at times attempted to gather the feeble as Christ would have gathered Jerusalem, "as a hen gathereth her chickens under her wings," only to find that they "would not." Continuity is difficult to trace in Blake, because the thing in his work that interested him was not its continuity, as a rule, but was each separate flash of imaginative creation as it flared up in his mind. He despises the artistic quality called by painters "getting together" in a picture,—a merit first violently thrust upon the attention of connoisseurs by Rembrandt with his single-spot scheme of illumination. Blake, in furious rebellion against the cheap praise that has grown rank about this, exclaims, "Real *effect* is the making out of parts." He loves "minute particulars," and called them the beloved "little ones" of the parent Imagination.

He loves separate emotions,—first one, then the other. He loves almost anything better than *sequence, gradation, continuity*. His pictures, whether light or dark, are patchy. Sustained will expressed with gradated fervour was unknown to him. There would have been, we see, no *plot* in his *Edward III* or his *Island in the Moon*, as there was none in the lighting of his paintings. In each figure each muscle is " made out " with as much foreground emphasis as each other muscle. The toes and fingers are equally insisted on. In sculpture this is right, no doubt, but it makes the difference, of course, between a painting and a picture in an illusionary art like that which uses a flat surface to express depths and distances. Blake never discovered that he was not a painter, but was constitutionally a born sculptor. He was a pioneer in colour as in verse, but though he has the first place as a maker of lyric maxims or poetic proverbs and of philosophic myth, by a similar oversight he thought himself a writer of epic poetry. His only idea of plot in literature may be symbolised by the numbers 1, 2, 1, or a " fall into division and a resurrection into unity " (*Vala*, Night I, l. 17).

In the *Job* series he seemed to have a plot in his drawings. It is the same thing,—a fall from plenty, a return to plenty. There is no plot. The sons, daughters, flocks and herds that, in the Bible, make Job's plenty at the end are not the same that make it at the beginning, but to Job's elastic mind they seem the same. He really thinks of nothing but himself and his God. All else is an occasion to show his faith and his God's power. No one can call this a plot.

Blake's mythic and symbolic *scheme* is therefore not the backbone of his myth or his symbolism. It is an accident, and is due to the significance, of which he never lost sight, being always a reference to the essentially unchanged truths of life, feeling, and mind. It is precisely its union of the firm and the unsought that makes the unity of his work the irrefragable proof, and the only proof, of his sanity. Let no praise, therefore, be stinted to those who, like Gilchrist, D. G. Rossetti, and Mr. Swinburne, believed in this sanity, and announced it, though the proof was hidden from them.

Only habitual readers of Blake possess it even now, for it is not to be found without going over the whole of his work. It is like the treasure buried in the farmer's field, which he told his sons was two feet below the surface, but of whose place he gave no further indication, with the result that they dug up the whole ground, and when the crops of the deep-turned soil were sold they obtained the treasure. A hint of Blake's continuity of meaning, however, may be offered here, as it is to be gathered from his early poem *The Passions*, which, as belonging to the period of *Poetical Sketches*, is printed in the preliminary pages to the Chatto and Windus complete *Poetical Works of William Blake*. This may be traced by comparing the use of the words *Pride* and *Giant, Flood, City*, etc., and names of cities in the poem with the same words and names elsewhere—

> But Pride awoke, nor knew that Joy was born,
> And taking poisonous seed from her own bowels
>   In the monster Shame infused.
> Forth came Ambition, crawling like a toad :
> Pride bears it in her bosom and the gods
> All bow to it. So great its power is
> That Pride inspired by it prophetic saw
> The kingdoms of the world and all their glory.
>
> Giants of mighty arms, before the flood
>   Cain's city built with murder.
> Then Babel mighty reared him to the skies,—
>   Babel with a thousand tongues.
> Confusion it was called and given to Shame.
>
> This Pride observing inly grieved to see,
> But knew not that the rest was given to Shame
>   As well as this.
> Then Nineveh, and Babylon, and Tyre,
> And even Jerusalem, the Holy City
>   Was shown ;
> Then Athens' learning and the pride of Greece,
> And, further from the rising sun was Rome,
>   Seated on Seven Hills,
> The mistress of the world,—emblem of Pride.
> She saw the Arts their generous treasures bring
> And Luxury his bounteous table spread.

These are lines 11 to 35 of the poem's 165.

We shall be told presently in *Jerusalem* that the *moods* are eternal, and that man passes through them as a traveller through cities. Some of these moods Blake called already by the names of cities. His myth began at this point in fact, since all myths are stories about moods made possible by giving them personal names. But Blake's first step being taken, there was a long pause, while his life was filled with artistic rather than literary thought.

The world in a material sense is, Blake always repeats, the result of an intellectual error in our moods,—indeed, no one looks on it as *real*, except because it gives pain and pleasure, which themselves are two mental experiences. Pain could be got rid of if our minds were in the right state, as it is artificially destroyed by merely distracting attention from it, whether by hypnotism or a martyr's ecstasy. Blake tells how Albion's centres become " open to pain " when he is not in the right imaginative state. He is always spoken of as *the* Giant. His sons are giants. In the *Marriage of Heaven and Hell* we hear of " The Giants who formed this world into its several existence and now live it in chains," and it becomes clear that they are energetic moods. They are, in fact, " portions of Being." Everything and every one in Blake's myth are *portions of Being*. These early " giants " live in chains which are the " cunning of weak minds which have power to resist energy." They " condense into nations " (*Jerusalem*, page 53, line 8), are bound by females (*Jerusalem*, page 67, line 45). Albion's " sons " are the moods that believe in the reality of Nature which obliges them, even when good, to be so far evil as to be haters of free love,—a thing only perfect and happy in Nature's opposite, Imagination, the Eternal. Their father's selfhood, or " reasoning power," builds " Vala," or natural love, by the force of his conviction, and she becomes their mother. They are so many natural demonstrations, and they delight in the war of argument. They destroy even natural love, and make the world what it is to nine-tenths of our labouring and respectable classes, a place with weary certainty of evil and destruction, unrelieved by illusion, pleasure, or hope. They think dreaming to be sinful, and prefer Morality and Mystery (Babylon), thus losing all the brotherhood that imaginative Pity (Jerusalem) would bring to them.

Cities are emotional states. From the book of *Urizen* onwards they are constantly referred to. They are always feminine. Cain's *city* is Cain's emotional condition produced by the murder of a holy capacity of dreaming called Abel. The Flood is the rush of general belief in the five senses that overwhelmed all the mental wisdom of life except such arts as were saved and called Noah and his sons.

The other " cities " in this list may be read of in *Jerusalem* in many places.

Babel—in page 7, lines 18, 20 ; page 8, line 20 ; page 60, line 56 ; page 85, line 18.

Babylon, whose references in *Jerusalem* under this one of her names only here follow, is heard of more frequently, and is also called Rahab and Vala, the goddess Nature, Bacon, Newton, Locke, and the tree of Mystery.

Page 18, line 29	Page 42, line 63	Page 82, line 27
„ 20, „ 26	„ 52, in the prose	„ „ „ 31
„ 21, „ 30	„ 60, line 23	„ „ „ 36
„ 24, „ 25	„ „ „ 39	„ 84, „ 3
„ „ „ 26	„ 61, „ 34	„ „ „ 12
„ „ „ 27	„ „ „ 35	„ 85, „ 32
„ „ „ 30	„ 74, „ 16	„ 89, „ 38
„ „ „ 31	„ „ „ 31	„ „ „ 48
„ 27, in ballad	„ 75, „ 19	„ 93, „ 25
„ 34, line 8	„ 82, „ 18	

The multitude of her names helps the reader to understand her in the end, though they at first require from him a keenly imaginative attention if he is to escape confusion.

Nineveh is scarcely remembered; it is mentioned on page 7, line 18, merely as an "admired palace" of the mind reduced to ruins by the argumentative mood.

Tyre appears on page 63, line 43, and page 86, line 32, first as a limit of the Land of Canaan,—a mood that rolls apart from Albion though it is "higher" or more "inward" than the mood that remains, and as one of the "golden sandals" that once clothed the feet or nether parts of the imagination of Albion.

Athens and Greece suggest the pride of accuracy in art rather than of vitality to Blake. He says that Greek art is mathematic. He did not in the least understand it. Rome, emblem of Pride, is the vicar of that part of Christ, as well as of the feeble matter-of-fact and feminine part. The serpent in Him is that sin that he "put on in the Virgin's womb," as related by Blake in The Everlasting Gospel, given in the Chatto and Windus edition with absolute fulness. Pride is very fully treated there. Keeping constantly in mind that Christ is the Human Imagination, the Eternal Thing in Man that unites us all to one another till we become through it One Man on whom death has no power and for whom the flesh has no illusions and "reasoning from the loins" no fallacies, and remembering that Imagination was so closely interwoven with Art in Blake's mind that he said, "Christ and his Apostles were artists," there is no difficulty in following that poem and uniting its ideas to those of the verses on "The Passions."

> I was standing by when Jesus died :
> What they called Humility I called Pride :

is among its rhymes.

That the masculine or intellectual is attracted by imaginative emotion, and the materialistic or experience-convinced part of our lives is attracted by the emotion of comparison, not of direct enjoyment,—by the feeling of superiority, not of delight,—is declared by Blake in another allusion to pride in *Jerusalem*—

> For Men are caught by Love : Woman is caught by Pride
>> (Page 81, line 6)

—a theory, disguised as a sentiment, repeated on page 87, line 16.

That personal comparison is an essential characteristic of our imaginative mind and actually animates its imagination, producing jealousy and envy, he is always repeating. In *Jerusalem*, a little further on, page 88, lines 22 to 33, we have it set forth again. The male pride is a phase equally the enemy of disinterested imagination (the "Lamb of God"), and may be traced in the poems wherever the Spectre or Reasoning Power becomes Self-righteous. The seventeenth stanza of the long ballad in the preface to the second chapter of *Jerusalem* makes this clear. The feminine Jerusalem herself is here or elsewhere without pride or self-interest or comparison, and is the emotional origin of brotherhood in man, therefore the " Bride " of the " Lamb."

> And thou, O Lamb of God, whom I
>   Slew in my dark self-righteous pride,
> Art thou returned to Albion's land,
>   And is Jerusalem thy Bride ?

Of course Blake was always credulous about the theories and names, and violently opposed to the hierarchical arrangement, of the Roman Church. That the two are opposite to one another is obvious enough, and refusing to shut his eyes to either, he was at one moment found talking like a middle-class Protestant, and the next moment like a sentimental person of good birth and feeble capacities of historical meditation who is being drawn into the great whirlpool by the Church's well-known " influence."

In this first allusion to Rome on its seven hills we see it chiefly as the patron of the lower forms of art. The seven hills are the heads of the seven dragons, of course. For opposite kinds of animus regarding the Church, see the childish passages in the latter part of the preface to the third chapter of *Jerusalem*, the taunting suggestion to the "spectre" in page 64, line 12, and the picture of Urizen as Pope with bat's wings in the ninth page of *Europe*.

The words "flood" and "table" are found elsewhere in Blake with symbolic purpose. The "flood" is that of the "five senses" that overwhelmed all but those forms of art referred to under the names of Noah and his sons.

F

CHAPTER VIII

'THE ISLAND IN THE MOON'

BLAKE'S indignation in 1783 was no longer against Woollett of "the word jocund," but against the kind people who had attempted to correct him while daring to patronise him. In this mood, and, as we must suppose at this time, though there is no date on the MS. and none on the watermark of the paper, Blake wrote his one attempt at a funny book. Like his one attempt at an historical play, it was never finished. It is now printed for the first time.

Its place here is not as a specimen of his work. It is part of his life-story. No one can hope at this distance of time to give a better account of the general impression Blake received from his introduction to educated, tasteful, and literary society than is to be gathered from this pasquinade. The incidents in it are perhaps imaginary, and there are no recognisable portraits. Blake is even careful to avoid them. He gives the dialogue about Voltaire to male voices, though the subject must have belonged especially to Mrs. Montagu. The sketch seems to have been written with perfect good-nature as well as in a mood of perfect contempt.

That Blake himself was in the wrong about the correcting of the *Poetical Sketches,* and that he had behaved badly to the friends who had encouraged and helped him, does not seem to have entered his head. In this piece of sarcasm he rolls his patrons about as a big dog might roll half-a-dozen little dogs with his paw, and he thinks himself very good-natured for not breaking their backs with one snap.

As we read *The Island in the Moon* it is necessary to be at some pains in order not to lose all enjoyment of it, through feeling too much disgust at the offensively conceited ingratitude of the young author who could write such mockery of people at whose house he received his first encouragement in poetry, and from whom he had accepted the substantial and solid benefit of the payment shared with Flaxman for their publication. But the fault of his character was never of the kind that we usually call conceit. From the moment that the Mathews family had ceased to admire him *unreservedly* they had actually ceased to be *his friends*. In *Jerusalem*, page 43, lines 56, etc., we read:

It is easy to acknowledge a man to be great and good while we Derogate from him in trifles and small articles of that goodness. Those only are his friends who admire his minutest powers.

And we have already heard (page 30, lines 10, 11) of "Albion's children"—

Being not irritated by insult, bearing insulting benevolences They perceived that corporeal friends are spiritual enemies.

These lines were written more than a quarter of a century after Mr. Mathews wrote the preface to the *Poetical Sketches*, and so caused all his circle to incur the sarcasm of *The Island in the Moon*, and they referred to Hayley, but the Blake who wrote them was the same man, and his feeling about his work and what his friends owed to it was the same.

THE ISLAND IN THE MOON

In the Moon is a certain Island near by a mighty continent, which small Island seems to have some affinity to England, and, what is more extraordinary, the people are so much alike, and their language so much the same, that you would think you were among your friends. In this Island dwell three Philosophers—Suction the Epicurean, Quid the Cynic, and Sipsop the Pythagorean. I call them by the names of their sects, though the sects are never mentioned there, as being quite out of date. However, the things still remain, and the vanities are the same.

The three Philosophers sat together thinking of nothing. In comes Etruscan Column the Antiquarian, and after an abundance of enquiries to no purpose, sat himself down and described something that nobody listened to. So they were employed when Mrs. Gimblet came in. The corners of her mouth seemed—I don't know how, but very odd, as if she hoped you had not an ill opinion of her,—to be sure, we are all poor creatures! Well, she seated (herself) and seemed to listen with great attention while the Antiquarian seemed to be talking of virtuous cats. But it was not so. She was thinking of the shape of her eyes and mouth, and he was thinking of his eternal fame. The three Philosophers were at this time each endeavouring to conceal his laughter (not at them but) at his own imagination.

This was the situation of this improving company when in a great hurry Inflammable Gas the Wind-finder entered. They seemed to rise and salute each other: their tongues went in question and answer, but their thoughts were otherwise employed. "I don't like his eyes," said Etruscan Column. "He's a foolish puppy," said Inflammable Gas, smiling on him.

The three Philosophers—the Cynic smiling, the Epicurean seeming studying the flame of the candle, the Pythagorean playing with the cat—listened with open mouths to the edifying discourse.

"Sir," said the Antiquarian, "I have seen these works, and I do affirm that they are no such thing. They seem to me to be the most wretched, paltry, flimsy stuff that ever——"

"What d'ye say? What d'ye say?" said Inflammable Gas. "Why —why, I wish I could see you write so."

"Sir," said the Antiquarian, "according to my opinion the author is an arrant blockhead."

"Your reason—your reason?" said Inflammable Gas. "Why—why, I think it very abominable to call a man a blockhead that you know nothing of."

"Reason, sir?" said the Antiquarian. "I'll give you an example for your reason. As I was walking along the street I saw a vast number of swallows on the rails of an old Gothic square. They seemed to be going on their passage, as Pliny says. As I was looking up, a little outré fellow, pulling me by the sleeve, said, 'Pray, sir, who do they all belong to?' I turned myself about with great contempt. i Said I, 'Go along with you, fool!' 'Fool!' said he, 'who do you call fool? I only asked you a civil question.' I had a great mind to have thrashed the fellow, only he was bigger than I."

Here Etruscan Column left off.

Inflammable Gas, recollecting himself (said), "Indeed I don't think the man was a fool, for he seems to me to have been desirous of enquiring into the works of nature!"

"Ha! Ha! Ha!" said the Pythagorean.

It was re-echoed by Inflammable Gas to overthrow the argument.

Etruscan Column then, starting up and clenching both his fists, was prepared to give a formal answer to the company. But Obtuse Angle, entering the room, having made a gentle bow, proceeded to empty his pockets of a vast number of papers, turned about and sat down, wiped his face with his pocket-handkerchief, and shutting his eyes, began to scratch his head.

"Well, gentlemen," said he, "what is the cause of strife?"

The Cynic answered, "They are only quarrelling about Voltaire."

"Yes," said the Epicurean, "and having a bit of fun with him."

"And," said the Pythagorean, "endeavouring to incorporate their souls with their bodies."

Obtuse Angle, giving a grin, said, "Voltaire understood nothing of the mathematics, and a man must be a fool i'faith not to understand the mathematics."

Inflammable Gas, turning round hastily in his chair, said, "Mathematics! He found out a number of Queries in Philosophy."

Obtuse Angle, shutting his eyes and saying that he always understood better with his eyes shut (replied), "In the first place, it is of no use for a man to make queries, but to solve them, for a man may be a fool and make queries, but a man must have a good sound sense to solve them. A query and an answer are as different as a straight line and a crooked one. Secondly——"

"I—I—I—aye! Secondly, Voltaire's a fool," says the Epicurean.

"Pooh!" says the Mathematician, scratching his head with double violence. "It is not worth quarrelling about."

The Antiquarian here got up, and, hemming twice to show the strength of his lungs, said, "But, my good sir, Voltaire was immersed in matter, and seems to have understood very little but what he saw before his eyes, like the animal upon the Pythagorean's lap, always playing with its own tail."

"Ha! Ha! Ha!" said Inflammable Gas. "He was the glory of France. I have got a bottle of air that would spread a plague."

Here the Antiquarian shrugged up his shoulders, and was silent while Inflammable Gas talked for half an hour.

When Steelyard the Lawgiver, coming in talking with an Act of Parliament in his hand, said that it was a shameful thing that Acts of Parliament should be in a free state.

It had so engrossed his mind that he did not salute the company. Mrs. Gimblet drew her mouth downwards.

CHAPTER II

Tilly Sally the Siptippedist, Aradobo, the Dean of Morocco, Miss Gittipin, Mrs. Nannicantipot, Mrs. Jistagatint, Gibble Gabble the wife of Inflammable Gas, and little Scopprell entered the room.

(If I have not presented you with every character in the piece, call me Ass.)

CHAPTER III

In the moon, as Phœbus stood over his Oriental Gardening, a "O ay, come, I'll sing you a song," said the Cynic.

"'The trumpeter (spat) in his hat,'" said the Epicurean.

"——and clapt it on his head," said the Pythagorean.

"I'll begin again," said the Cynic.

> Little Phœbus came strutting in
> With his fat belly and his round chin,
> What is it you would please to have?
> Ho! Ho!
> I won't let it go at only so, so.

Mrs. Gimblet looked as if they meant her. Tilly Sally laughed like a cherry clapper. Aradobo asked, "Who was Phœbus, sir?"

Obtuse Angle answered quickly, "He was the God of Physic, Painting, Perspective, Geometry, Astronomy, Cookery, Chemistry, Mechanics, Tactics, Pathology, Ohrascology, Theology, Mythology, Astrology, Osteology, Somatology (sic)—in short, every art and science adorned him as beads round his neck."

Here Aradobo looked astonished and asked if he understood Engraving.

Obtuse Angle answered, "Indeed he did."

"Well," said the other, "he was as great as Chatterton."

Tilly Sally turned round to Obtuse Angle and asked who it was that was as great as Chatterton.

"Hay! How should I know?" answered Obtuse Angle. "Who was it,—Aradobo?"

"Why, sir," said he, "the gentleman that the song was about."

"Ah," said Tilly Sally, "I did not hear it. What was it, Obtuse Angle?"

"Pooh," said he. "Nonsense!"

"Mhm," said Tilly Sally.

"It was Phœbus," said the Epicurean.

"Ah, that was the gentleman," said Aradobo.

"Pray, sir," said Tilly Sally, "who was Phœbus?"

Obtuse Angle answered, "The Heathen in the old ages used to have gods that they worshipped, and they used to sacrifice to them. You have read about that in the Bible."

"Ah," said Aradobo, "I thought I had read of Phœbus in the Bible."

"Aradobo, you should always think before you speak," said Obtuse Angle.

"Ha! Ha! Ha! He means Pharaoh," said Tilly Sally.

"I am ashamed of you,—making use of the names in the Bible," said Mrs. Jistagatint.

"I'll tell you what, Mrs. Imagerine. I don't think there's any harm in it," said Tilly Sally.

"No," said Inflammable Gas. "I have got a camera obscura at home."

"Law! What has that to do with Pharoe?" said Tilly Sally.

"Pho! Nonsense! Hang Pharoe and all his hosts," said the Pythagorean. "Sing away, Quid."

Then the Cynic sang—

> Honour and Genius is all I ask,
> And I ask the gods no more.
> No more, No more, ⎱ The three philosophers
> No more, No more. ⎰   bear chorus.

Here Aradobo sucked his under lip.

Chapter IV

"Hang names!" said the Pythagorean. "What's Pharoh better than Phœbus, or Phœbus than Pharoh?"

"Hang them both," said the Cynic.

"Don't be profane," said Mrs. Intagatist.

"Why?" said Mrs. Nannicantipot.

"I don't think it's profane to say 'Hang Pharoh and son!'" said Mrs. Sinagain. "I'm sure you ought to hold your tongue, for you never say anything about the Scriptures, and you hinder your husband from going to church."

"Ha, ha!" said Inflammable Gas. "Why, don't you like going to church?"

"No," said Mrs. Nannicantipot. "I think a person may be as good at home."

"If I had not a place of profit that forces me to go to church," said Inflammable Gas, "I'd see the parsons all hanged,—a parcel of lying——"

"Oh!" said Mrs. Istagatint. "If it was not for churches and chapels I should not have lived so long. There was I, up in the morning at four, when I was a girl. I would run like the dickens till I was all in a heat. I would stand till I was ready to sink into the earth. Ah, Mr. Huffcap would kick the bottom of the pulpit out with passion,— would tear off the sleeve of his gown and set his wig on fire, and throw it at the people. He 'ld cry and stamp and kick and sweat, and all for the good of their souls."

"I'm sure he must be a wicked villain," said Mrs. Nannicantipot, "a passionate wretch. If I was a man I'd wait at the bottom of the pulpit stairs and knock him down, and run away!"

"You would, you ignorant jade? I wish I could see you hit any of the ministers! You deserve to have your ears boxed, you do."

"I'm sure this is not religion," answers the other.

Then Mr. Inflammable Gas ran and shoved his head into the fire and set his hair all in a flame, and ran about the room—— No, no, he did not; I was only making a fool of you.

Chapter V

Obtuse Angle, Scopprell, Aradobo, and Tilly Sally all met in Obtuse Angle's study.

"Pray," said Aradobo, "is Chatterton a Mathematician?"

"No," said Obtuse Angle. "How could you be so foolish as to think that he was?"

"Oh, I did not think he was,—I only asked," said Aradobo.

"How could you think he was not, and ask if he was?" said Obtuse Angle.

"Oh no, no. I did think he was, before you told me, but afterwards I thought he was not."

Obtuse Angle said, "In the first place you thought he was, and then when I said he was not, you thought he was not. Why, I know that."

"Oh no, sir, I thought that he was not, but I asked to know whether he was."

"How can that be?" said Obtuse Angle. "How could you think that he was not?"

"Why," said he, "it came into my head that he was not."

"Why, then," said Obtuse Angle, "you said that he was."

"Did I say so? Law! I did not think I said that."

"Did not he?" said Obtuse Angle.

"Yes," said Scopprell.

"But I meant——" said Aradobo, "I—I—I can't think. Law, sir, I wish you would tell me how it is."

Then Obtuse Angle put his chin in his hand and said, "Whenever you think, you must always think for yourself."

"How, sir?" said Aradobo. "Whenever I think, I must think myself? I think I do. In the first place——" said he with a grin.

"Poo! Poo!" said Obtuse Angle. "Don't be a fool."

Then Tilly Sally took up a Quadrant, and asked, "Is not this a sun-dial?"

"Yes," said Scopprell, "but it's broke."

At this moment the three Philosophers entered, and lowering darkness hovered over the assembly.

"Come," said the Epicurean, "let's have some rum and water, and hang the mathematics! Come, Aradobo! Say something."

Then Aradobo began, "In the first place I think. I think that Chatterton was clever at Fissie Follogy, Pistinology, Aridology, Arography, Transmography, Phizography, Hogamy, Hatomy, and hall that, but, in the first place, he eat very little, wickly (*sic*). That is, he slept very little, which he brought into a consumption; and what was that that he took? Fissic (*sic*) or something,—and so died!"

So all the people in the book entered the room, and they could not talk any more to the present purpose.

Chapter VI

They all went home and left the Philosophers. Then Suction asked if Pindar was not a better poet than Ghiotto (*sic*) was a painter.

"Plutarch has not the life of Ghiotto," said Sipsop.

"No," said Quid,—"to be sure, he was an Italian."

"Well," said Suction,—"to be sure, that is not any proof."

"Plutarch was a nasty ignorant Puppy," said Quid. "I hate your sneaking rascals. There's Aradobo in ten or twelve years will be a far superior genius."

"Ah!" said the Pythagorean, "Aradobo will make a very clever fellow."

"Why," said Quid, "I think that any natural fool would make a very clever fellow, if he was properly brought up."

"Ah, hang your reasoning!" said the Epicurean. "I hate reasoning. I do everything by feeling."

"Ah!" said Sipsop, "I only wish Jack Tearguts had had the cutting of Plutarch. He understands Anatomy better than any of the ancients. He'll plunge his knife up to the hilt in a single drive, and thrust his fist in, and all in the space of a quarter of an hour. He doesn't mind their crying, though they cry ever so. He'll swear at them and keep them down with his fist, and tell them that he'll scrape their bones if they don't lie still and be quiet. What the devil should these people in the hospital that get it done for nothing make such a piece of work for?"

"Hang that," said Suction; "let's have a song." Then the Cynic sang—

1.

When old corruption first began,
Adorned in yellow vest,
He committed on Flesh a whoredom,
Oh, what a wicked beast!

2.

From thence a callow babe did spring,
And old corruption smiled,
To think his race should never end,
For now he had a child.

3.

He called him surgery, and fed
  The babe with his own milk,
For flesh and he could ne'er agree,
  She would not let him suck.

4.

And this he always kept in mind,
  And found a crooked knife,
And ran about with bloody hands
  To seek his mother's life.

5.

And as he ran to seek his mother,
  He met with a dead woman,
He fell in love and married her ;
  A deed which is not common.

6.

She soon grew pregnant and brought forth
  Scurvy and spotted fever.
The father grinned and skipped about,
  And said, " I'm made for ever !

7.

For now I have procured these imps
  I'll try experiments."
With that he tied poor scurvy down
  And stopped up all his vents.

8.

And when the child began to swell,
  He shouted out aloud,
" I've found the dropsy out, and soon
  Shall do the world more good."

9.

He took up fever by the neck
  And cut out all its spots,
And through the holes that he had made
  He first discovered guts.

" Ah," said Sipsop, " you think we are rascals—you think we are
rascals. I do as I choose. What is it to anybody what I do ? I am
always unhappy too. When I think of surgery,—I don't know. I do
it because I like it. I think, somehow, I'll leave it off. There was a
woman having her cancer cut, and she shrieked so I was quite sick."

Chapter VII

" Good-night," said Sipsop.
" Good-night," said the other two.
Then Quid and Suction were left alone. Then said Quid, " I think
that Homer is bombast, and Shakespeare is too wild, and Milton has

no feelings : they might easily be outdone. Chatterton never writ those poems ! A parcel of fools, going to Bristol ! If I was to go, I'd find it out in a minute."

"If I don't knock them all up next year in the Exhibition, I'll be hanged," said Suction. "Hang philosophy ! I would not give a farthing for it ! Do all by your feelings, and never think at all about it. I'm hanged if I don't get up to-morrow morning by four o'clock and work Sir Joshua."

"Before ten years are at an end," said Quid, "I will work those poor milksop devils,—an ignorant pack of wretches ! "

So they went to bed.

Chapter VIII

Steelyard the lawyer, sitting at his table, taking extracts from Hervey's *Meditations Among the Tombs* and Young's *Night Thoughts*.

"He is not able to hurt me," said he, "more than making me constable or taking away the parish business. That !

> My crop of corn is but a field of tares,

says Jerome. Happiness is not for us, poor crawling reptiles of the earth. Talk of happiness—happiness ! It's no such thing. Every one has a something.

> Hear then the pride and knowledge of a sailor,
> The spritsail, foresail, mainsail, and his mizen.
> A poor frail man ! God wot I know none frailer.
> I know no greater sinner than John Taylor.

If I'd only myself to care for I 'ld soon make Double Elephant look foolish, and Filligree work. I hope I shall live to see

> The wreck of matter and the crush of worlds,

as Young says."

Obtuse Angle entered the room.

" What news, Mr. Steelyard ? "

" I am reading Thison and Aspasis," said he.

Obtuse Angle took up the books one by one.

" I don't find it here," said he.

" Oh no," said the other, " it was the *Meditations* !"

Obtuse Angle took up the book and read till the other was quite tired out.

Then Scopprell and Miss Gittipin coming in, Scopprell took up a book and read the following passage :—

" *An Essay on the Human Understanding*, by John Lookye Gant."

" John Locke," said Obtuse Angle.

" Oh, ay,—Lock," said Scopprell.

" Now here," said Miss Gittipin,—" I never saw such company in my life. You are always talking of your books. I like to be where we talk. You had better take a walk, that we may have some pleasure. There's Double Elephant's girls. They have their own way. And there's Miss Filligreework, she goes out in her coaches, her footman and her maids, and Stormont's and Balloon hats, and a pair of gloves every day, and the Sorrows of Werther, and Robinsons; and the Queen of France's Puss colour, and my cousin Gibble Gabble says that I am like nobody else. I might as well be in a nunnery. Then they go in post-chaises and stages to Vaxhaul and Raneleigh, and I hardly know what a coach is, except when I go to Mr. Jacko's. He knows what riding is, and his wife is the most agreeable woman. You hardly know she has a tongue in her head, and he is the funniest fellow, and I do believe he'll go in Parliament with his master, and they have black servants lodge at their house. I never saw such a place in my life. He says he has six-and-twenty rooms in his house, and I believe it, and he is not such a bear as Quid thinks he is."

"Pooh! Pooh! Hold your tongue. Hold your tongue," said the lawgiver.

This quite provoked Miss Gittipin, to interrupt her in her favourite topic, and she proceeded to use every provoking speech that ever she could, and he bore it more like a saint than a lawgiver, and with great solemnity he addressed the company in these words :—

"They call women the weaker vessel, but I think they are the strongest. A girl has always more tongue than a boy. I have seen a little brat no higher than a nettle, and she had as much tongue as a city clark (*sic*). But a boy would be such a fool not to have anything to say, and if anybody asked him a question he would put his head into a hole and hide it. I am sure I take but little pleasure. You have as much pleasure as I have. There I stand and bear every fool's insult. If I had only myself to care for I would wring off their noses."

To this Scopprell answered, "I think the Ladies' discourses, Mr. Steelyard, are some of them more improving than any book. That is the way I have got some of my knowledge."

"Then," said Miss Gittipin, "Mr. Scopprell, do you know the song of Phœbe and Jellicoe?"

"No, Miss," said Scopprell.

Then she repeated these verses, while Steelyard walked about the room.

> Phœbe, dressed like beauty's queen,
> Jellicoe in faint pea-green,
> Sitting all beneath a grot
> Where the little lambkins trot ;
>
> Maidens dancing, loves a-sporting,
> All the country folk a-courting,
> Susan, Johnny, Bet, and Joe
> Lightly tripping on a row.
>
> Happy people, who can be
> In happiness compared to ye ?
> The pilgrim with his crook and hat
> Sees your happiness compleat.

"A charming song, indeed, Miss," said Scopprell.
Here they received a summons to the Philosopher's house.

CHAPTER IX

"I say, this evening we'll all get drunk,—I say—dash!—an Anthem, an Anthem!" said Suction.

> Lo the bat on leaden wing,
> Winking and blinking,
> Winking and blinking,
> Winking and blinking,
> Like Dr. Johnson.

Quid. "Oho," said Dr. Johnson
To Scipio Africanus,
"If you don't own me a philosopher,
I'll kick your Roman Anus."

Suction. "Aha," to Dr. Johnson
Said Scipio Africanus,
"Lift up my Roman Petticoat
And kiss my Roman Anus."

And the cellar goes down with a step. (*Grand chorus.*)

" Ho, Ho, Ho, Ho, Ho, Ho, Ho, Ho, Hooooo, my poooooor siiides. I, I should die if I was to live here!" said Scopprell. " Ho, Ho, Ho, Ho, Ho!"

1*st Voice.*	Want matches?
2*nd Voice.*	Yes, yes, yes.
1*st Voice.*	Want matches?
2*nd Voice.*	No.

1*st Voice.*	Want matches?
2*nd Voice.*	Yes, yes, yes.
1*st Voice.*	Want matches?
2*nd Voice.*	No.

Here was great confusion and disorder. Aradobo said that the boys in the street sing something very pretty and funny about matches. Then Mrs. Nannicantipot sang :

> I cry my matches as far as Guild Hall ;—
> God bless the Duke and his aldermen all!

Then sang Scopprell :

> I ask the gods no more,—
> No more, no more.

"Then," said Suction, "come, Mr. Lawgiver, your song."
And the Lawgiver sang :

> As I walked abroad on a May morning
> To see the fields so pleasant and gay,
> Oh there did I spy a young maiden sweet
> Among the violets that smell so sweet.
> Smell so sweet,—smell so sweet,
> Among the violets that smell so sweet.

"Hang your violets! Here's your rum and water. O ay," said Tilly Sally, "Joe Bradley and I was going along one day in the sugarhouse. Joe Bradley saw—for he had but one eye—saw a treacle jar. Soke goes of his blind side, and dips his hand up to the shoulder in

treacle. 'Here, lick, lik, like!' said he.   Ha! Ha! Ha! Ha! Ha!
for he had but one eye.   Ha! Ha! Ha! Ho!"
Then sang Scopprell :

> And I ask the gods no more,—
> No more, no more,
> No more, no more.

"Miss Gittipin," said he, "you sing like a harpsichord.   Let your
bounty descend to our fair ears and favour us with a fine song."
Then she sang :

> This cock he would a-wooing ride,
>   Kitty alone,—Kitty alone,—
> This frog he would a-wooing ride,—
>   Kitty alone and I !
> Sing, cock, I carry Kitty alone,
>   Kitty alone,—Kitty alone,—
> Cock, I carry Kitty alone,—
>   Kitty alone and I !

"Charming !   Truly elegant !" said Scopprell.

> And I ask the gods no more !

"Hang your serious songs !" said Sipsop, and he sang as follows :—

> Fa ra ro bo ro
> Fa ra bo ra
> Sa ba ra za ba rare roro
> Sa ra ra ra bo ro zo zo
> Radara
> Sarapodo no flo ro.

"Hang Italian songs !   Let's have English !" said Quid.   "English
genius for ever !   Here I go :

> Hail, Matrimony, made of Love,
> To thy wide gates how great a drove
>   On purpose to be wed do come.
> Widows and maids and youths also,
> That lightly trip on beauty's toe
>   Or sit on Beauty's bum.
>
> Hail, finger-footed lovely creatures,
> The females of our human natures,
>   Formed to suckle all mankind.
> 'Tis you that come in time of need ;
> Without you we should never breed,
>   Or any comfort find.
>
> For if a damsel's blind or lame,
> Or Nature's hand has crooked her frame,
>   Or if she's deaf, or is wall-eyed,
> Yet if her heart is well inclined,
> Some tender lover she will find
>   That fainteth for a bride.

The universal Poultice this,
To ease whatever is amiss
  In damsel or in widow gay.
It makes them smile, it makes them skip :
Like birds just cured of the pip,
  They chirp, and hop away.

Then come ye maidens, come ye swains,
Come to be cured of your pains,
  In Matrimony's golden cage."

"Go and be hanged !" said Scopprell. "How can you have the face to make game of matrimony ? "

Then Quid called upon Obtuse Angle, and he, wiping his face and looking on the corner of the ceiling, sang :

To be, or not to be,
Of great capacity,
  Like Sir Isaac Newton,
  Or Locke, or Doctor South,
  Or Sherlock upon Death ?
  I'd rather be Sutton.

For he did build a house
For aged men and youth,
  With walls of brick and stone.
He furnished it within
With whatever he could win,
  And all his own.

He drew out of the stocks
His money in a box,
  And sent his servant
To Green the bricklayer
And to the carpenter ; —
  He was so fervent.

The chimneys were three score,
The windows many more,
  And for convenience
He sinks and gutters made
And all the way he paved
  To hinder pestilence.

Was not this a good man,
Whose life was but a span,
  Whose name was Sutton,—
As Locke, or Dr. South,
Or Sherlock upon Death,
  Or Sir Isaac Newton ?

The Lawgiver was very attentive, and begged to have it sung over again and again, till the company were tired, and insisted on the Lawgiver singing a song himself, which he readily complied with.

This city and this country has brought forth many Mayors,
To sit in state and give forth laws out of their old oak chairs,
With face as brown as any nut with drinking of strong ale :
Good English hospitality, O then it did not fail.

With scarlet gowns and broad gold lace would make a yeoman sweat,
With stockings rolled above their knees and shoes as black as jet,
With eating beef and drinking beer, O they were stout and hale!
Good English hospitality, O then it did not fail!

Thus sitting at the table wide the Mayor and Aldermen
Were fit to give laws to the city ; each eat as much as ten.
The hungry poor entered the hall, to eat good beef and ale.
Good English hospitality, O then it did not fail!

Here they gave a shout, and the company broke up.

Chapter X

Thus these happy Islanders spent their time. But felicity does not
last long, for, being met at the house of Mr. Inflammable Gas the
Wind-finder, the following affairs happened.

"Come, Flammable," said Gibble Gabble, " and let's enjoy ourselves. Bring the puppets."

"Hay,—hay," said he, "you,—sho!—why—ya! ya. How can you
be so foolish? Ha! Ha! Ha! She calls the experiments puppets!"

Then he went upstairs and loaded the maid with glasses, and brass
tubes, and magic pictures.

"Here, ladies and gentlemen," said he, "I'll show you a louse, or a
flea, or a butterfly, or a cockchafer, the blade bone of a tittle-back (sic).
No, no. Here's a bottle of weed that I took up in the bog, and—dear,
dear, the water's got into the sliders! Look here, Gibble Gabble!
Lend me your handkerchief, Tilly Sally."

Tilly Sally took out his handkerchief, which smeared the glass
worse than ever. Then he screwed it on. Then he took the sliders,
and then he set up the glasses, for the ladies to view the pictures.
Thus he was employed, and quite out of breath, while Tilly Sally and
Scopprell were pumping at the air-pump. Smack went the glass.

"Hang!" said Tilly Sally.

Inflammable Gas turned short round and threw down the table and
glasses, and pictures, and broke the bottles of wind, and let out the
Pestilence.

He saw the Pestilence fly out of the bottle, and cried out, while he
ran out of the room :

"O, come out! Come out! We are putrefied! We are corrupted!
Our lungs are destroyed with the Flogiston (sic). This will spread the
plague all through the Island!"

He was downstairs the very first. On the back of him came all the
others in a heap.

So they need not bidding go.

Chapter XI

Another merry meeting at the house of Steelyard the Lawgiver.
After supper Steelyard and Obtuse Angle had pumped Inflammable
Gas quite dry. They played at forfeits, and tried every method to get
good-humour.

Said Miss Gittipin, "Pray, Mr. Obtuse Angle, sing us a song."
Then he sang:

Upon a Holy Thursday, their innocent faces clean,
The children walking two and two in grey or blue and green.
Grey-headed beadles walked before, with wands as white as snow,
Till into the high dome of Paul's they, like Thames waters, flow.

O what a multitude they seemed, these flowers of London town !
Seated in companies they sit, with radiance all their own.
The hum of multitudes were there, but multitudes of lambs,
Thousands of little girls and boys raising their innocent hands.

Then, like a mighty wind, they raise to heaven the voice of song,
Or like harmonious thundering the seats of heaven among.
Beneath them sit the reverent men, the guardians of the poor,
Then cherish pity, lest you drive an angel from your door.

After this they all sat silent for a quarter of an hour, and Mrs.
Nannicantipot said, "It puts me in mind of my mother's song—

When the voices of children are heard on the green,
And laughing is heard on the hill ;
My heart is at rest within my breast,
And everything else is still.

Then come home, my children, the sun is gone down,
And the dews of night arise ;
Come, come, leave off play, and let us away
Till the morning appears in the skies.

No, no, let us play, for it is yet day,
And we cannot go to sleep—
Besides in the sky the little birds fly,
And the meadows are covered with sheep.

Well, well, go and play while the light fades away,
And then go home to bed.
The little ones leaped, and shouted, and ran,
And all the hills echoed."

Then sung Quid :—

O father, father, where are you going ?
Oh do not walk so fast ;
Oh, speak, father, speak to your little boy,
Or else I shall be lost.

The night was dark and no father was there,
And the child was wet with dew.
The mire was deep, and the child did weep,
And away the vapour flew.

Here nobody could sing any longer, till Tilly Sally plucked up a
spirit, and he sung :

I say, you Joe,
Throw us the ball.
I've a good mind to go,
And leave you all.

quite dry. They playd at forfeits & tryd every method to get
good humour said Miss Gittipin pray Mr Obtuse Angle sing us
a song then he sung

Upon a holy thursday their innocent faces clean
The children walking two & two in grey & blue & green
Grey headed beadles walkd before with wands as white as snow
Till into the high dome of Pauls they like thames waters flow

O what a multitude they seemd these flowers of Londons town
Seated in companies they sit with radiance all their own
The hum of multitudes were there but multitudes of lambs

Then like a mighty wind they raise to heaven the voice of song
Or like harmonious thunderings the seats of heaven among
Beneath them sit the reverend men the guardians of the poor
Then cherish pity lest you drive an angel from your door

After this they all sat silent for a quarter of an hour
said it puts me in mind of my mothers song

When the tongues of children are heard on the green
And laughing is heard on the hill
My heart is at rest within my breast
And every thing else is still

Then come home my children the sun is gone down
And the dews of night arise
Come home leave off play & let us away
Till the morning appears in the skies

No No let us play for it is yet day
And we cannot go to sleep

Besides the sky the little birds fly
And the meadows are coverd with Sheep

Will Will go & play till the light fades away
And then go home to bed
The little ones leaped & shouted & laughd
And all the hills eechoed

Then ~~~~~~~~~~ Sung Quid

O father father where are you going
O do not walk so fast
O speak father speak to your little boy
Or else I shall be lost

The night it was dark & no father was there
And the child was wet with dew
The mire was deep & the child did weep
And away the vapour flew

Here nobody could say any longer. till Tilly Lally pluckd up a
spirit & he sung.

O I say you Joe
Throw us the ball
Ive a good mind to go
And leave you all
I never saw such a bowler
To bowl the ball in a tansey
And to clean it with my handkercher
Without saying a word

That Bill a foolish fellow
~~~~~~~~~~~~~~
He has given me a black eye
He does not know how to handle about

PAGE FROM THE MS. OF "THE ISLAND IN THE MOON,"
Showing where the *Song of Innocence* afterwards numbered 13 was first written.

> I never saw such a bowler,
> To bowl the ball in a t—d (tansey),
> And to clean it with my handkercher
> Without saying a word.

> That Bill's a foolish fellow,
> He has given me a black eye.
> He does not know how to handle a bat
> Any more than a dog or cat.

> He has knocked down the wicket
> And broke the stumps,
> And runs without shoes to save his pumps.

Here a laugh began, and Miss Gittipin sang :

> Leave, O leave me to my sorrow,
> Here I'll sit and fade away ;
> Till I'm nothing but a spirit,
> And I love this form of clay.

> Then if chance along this forest
> Any walk in pathless ways,
> Through the gloom he'll see my shadow,
> Hear my voice upon the breeze.

The Lawgiver, all the while, sat delighted to see them in such a serious humour. "Mr. Scopprell," said he, "you must be acquainted with a great many songs."

"Oh, dear sir! Ho, Ho, Ho, I am no singer. I must beg of one of those tender-hearted ladies to sing for me."

They all declined, and he was forced to sing for himself :

> There's Dr. Clash
> And Signor Falalasole :
> O they sweep in the cash,—
> Into their purse('s) hole.

> Great A ! Little A,
> Bouncing B.
> Play away,—play away,
> You're out of the key.
>   Fa me sol, Fa me sol.

> Musicians should have
> A pair of very good ears,
> And long fingers and thumbs,
> And not like dancing bears.
>   Fa me sol, La me fa sol.

> Gentlemen, gentlemen !
> Rap, rap, rap,—
> Fiddle, fiddle, fiddle,—
> Clap, clap, clap.
>   Fa me la sol, La me fa sol.

G

Then said the Lawgiver, "Funny enough! Let's have Handel's water piece—

> A crowned king,
> On a white horse sitting,
> With his trumpets sounding,
> And banners flying,
> Through the clouds of smoke he made his way.
> And the shout of his thousands fills his heart with rejoicing and victory.
> And the shout of his thousands fills his heart with rejoicing and victory.
> Victory! Victory! 'Twas William, Prince of Orange,—

(Here a page is wanting, if not more.)

—thus illuminating the manuscript."

"Ay," said she, "that would be excellent."

"Then," said he, "I would have all the wording engraved instead of printed, and at every other leaf a high-finished print,—all in three volumes folio,—and sell them (for) a hundred pounds apiece. They would print off two thousand."

"Then," said she, "whoever will not have them will not deserve to live."

"Don't you think I have something of the goat's face?" said he.

"Very like a goat's face," she answered.

"I think your face," said he, "is like that noble beast the tiger. Oh, I was at Mrs. Sicknacher's, and I was speaking of my abilities, but their nasty hearts, poor devils, are eat(en) up with envy. They envy my abilities, and all the women envy your abilities."

"My dear, they hate people who are of higher abilities than their nasty, filthy selves. But do you outface them, and then strangers will see that you have an opinion.'"

"Now I think we should do as much good as we can when we are at Mr. Femality's. Do you snap, and take me up, and I will fall into such a passion. I'll hollow and stamp, and frighten all the people there, and show them what truth is."

At this instant Obtuse Angle came in.

"Oh, I am glad you are come," said Quid.

Having begun with laughter, Blake ends very suddenly with a mixture of feelings. He has drifted by a mere accident into the idea of the *Songs of Innocence*, the book through which he is still best known all the world over. He was too young and good-natured to keep up the mood of bitter derision for long at a time. He has lost his way into the region of beauty when he intended mere mockery. It occurs to him suddenly that he has hit on a new kind of art, and he pauses. The *Songs of Innocence*, with their pages printed on floating tints of sunrise, with their verses nestled up against quaint or pretty designs, and with the touch of the author's own hand upon every page, have always been an invention about which the world has wondered with increasing delight. The price of a copy (including the second part, the *Songs of*

Experience) in Blake's time was five guineas. A hundred guineas would not be considered unusual now, and more has been paid for the best examples.

Those of us who have been dissatisfied with the mere vague, general attribution of their originality and sweetness to Blake's spirituality and genius are no longer to be kept at arm's length from the author by the prestige of these beautiful words. We can come nearer to his mind. We find that the substance or sentiment of the opening poems was due to his amusement at the sentimentality of the ladies who sang similar songs at Rathbone Place, while the form and appearance were invented as a mock at the hare-brained projects of one of the men who wanted to be preposterously original in order to outdo the others. To *outdo* is a phrase in this caricature which went straight to the centre of Blake's character. There is a similar meaning to the word "work" in these pages. "I could *work* him" simply meant "I could excel so as to humiliate him" in the Rathbone Place drawing-room.

But just as vulgar people become especially revolting and unendurable when they try to be witty, so poetic people— those at least in whom the real faculty of poetry is deep down—cannot remain shallow and childish, even when only intending to make fun, if they compose verse upon really beautiful and lovable subjects. The simplicity of lovers in a grot will bring a sweetness to the tune of their words, and the sublimity and pathos of a crowd of innocent children as they sing tunes, feeling the pinch of mutability as sunset puts a term to their wild play, has a magic power on the nerves of poets as they write, and affects the verse itself; so that what comes forth under such influences is not verse merely, but poetry.

This innate tendency to tune the measure in harmony with the thought was Blake's real muse, though he never knew it. This was the "author in eternity" who "dictated to him" his "mild song." When he wrote mere sarcasm about conceit, envy, folly, and fraud, that author went on a journey like Baal and could not be called, or peradventure he slept and would not be awakened.

In the small portion of the MS. of *The Island in the Moon* here reproduced we see the handwriting of the first of the *Songs of Innocence* as it was composed, and we see beyond that of the second a fragment of how the manuscript ran on,—a sarcastic piece of deliberate foolishness, not even free from the reproach of coarseness. Blake was so deficient in the power of seizing the value of his own literary work that it was only a page or two later that he was pulled up by seeing that he was playing with what should be important and beautiful, when his artistic imagination saw the poems of the future printed on rainbows of beauty and making visible on the page the colours of the excitement that their delight owned as an atmosphere.

We are sometimes reminded that the faculty of seeing colour at all in nature around us is very imperfect still in our branch of the Aryan race, and is of very modern development. There was as little colour in art as there was in music harmony a few centuries ago. The harmony of to-day is as new as the seven colours now commonly found in the rainbow. Our fathers only saw three.

An improvement in general perception seldom comes to a whole race, or even to a whole country, at once. A great man here, and a great man there, first sees or hears in his mind what others are taught to see and hear through him.

Blake's own faculty of *vision* in art will soon be within most people's power, though it still causes his sanity to be suspected by many people who know more of medical text-books than of the imagination which they parcel out so glibly into normal and morbid. The idea that "normal" supplies us with a criterion by which to measure sanity is, Max Nordau notwithstanding, as funny as anything in *The Island in the Moon*. Blake himself deliberately advised artistic youth to " cultivate imagination till it reaches vision."

There is an idea now gaining ground that colours have a direct relation to sounds, as these have to emotions. Blake has left an accidental observation which tells his own position here in a way that reveals, as an inherent quality of his emotional organism, the origin of the colouring that covers the pages of the *Songs of Innocence*, and explains why he instantly saw, even though first conceived in fun, the serious-ness of the idea of treating printed verse in this way. In the description of the appalling vision of Leviathan in the *Marriage of Heaven and Hell* we are told, " His forehead was divided into streaks of green and purple, like those on a tiger's forehead."

These colours are those of the emotions of " vegetative " or physical fury that we cannot separate from our imagina-tions when we think of a tiger's forehead.

With the *Songs of Innocence*, not as printed, but as first

written during the time of *The Island in the Moon*, really closes the first or literary period of Blake's poetic life.

Before the *Songs of Experience* were added to them the great change began in his manner of thought which sets him not merely in advance of all other writers, but apart from them.

He was now about to become altogether a myth-maker. He did not for some years know the fact, and it was still longer before he himself perceived the importance of it. But the need had been felt for this change, and the time for the change was at hand.

Before it is considered, however, a change of another kind that belongs to this period of his life calls aloud to be looked at and understood.

CHAPTER IX

'MARY'

HOWEVER glad we may be to glean something from *The Island in the Moon* about the opening of Blake's career, about how his best-known works came to be produced, or about how he bore himself among the literary people of his day, this, we cannot help feeling, is not enough. The Rathbone Place period was the beginning of his married life. "Here is the poet," we say to ourselves as we read, "but where was the husband?"

Only on the last page of the *Island* is there any indication that such a thing as married life existed. It appears here in the caricature of a couple who are conspiring at home to make a sensation at a literary party. Such a scheme, with no intention that it should be realised, may very probably have been hatched between Mr. and Mrs. Blake. One of the two speakers is the intending author of the ideal volume whose real form, when it came to be produced, was that of the *Songs of Innocence*. The wife in this dialogue seems to have formed a very bad opinion of the "nasty, filthy," and "envious" people of the literary coterie. Envy was one thing when it stimulated a poetic nature to make sweet songs; it was quite another thing when it led mean natures to utter abuse or detraction.

Mrs. Blake must have been, in the early months, several times to Rathbone Place. She had learned to read and write since she married, and that was but lately. She had lived a useful life for five-and-twenty years, and had learned qualities of common-sense without the aid of literature, qualities which in old age were to develop into the marked precision, formal and methodical habits, and primness of manner that were noticed in her during her last years. She was certain to have at this time of her early marriage quite as much contempt as her husband had for the literary *preciousness* that was, along with better things, to be found at the evening parties given by Mrs. Mathews. Of what was worth respecting or enjoying there she probably did not understand enough to enable her to annoy her husband by being any more just to the dilettante circle than he was.

For what happened, and how they both felt about it, we have several sources of information, the best of which are Blake's own poems about " Mary." They are not dated, but were composed probably in 1783 or 1784, since, it seems, they were found by Mr. R. Herne Shepherd jotted down on the fly-leaves of Blake's bound copy of the *Poetical Sketches*, if we read his hint on the subject rightly. In the first of these "Mary" poems we learn that a very pretty and very simple girl (Mrs. Blake was both) went for the first time into a drawing-room among artificial people of eighteenth-century habits, and received the usual high-flown compliments which were considered suitable to good breeding at that period. That Blake would ever have thought of writing verses on such a subject had not Mrs. Blake had such an experience, is not probable. He would not even have discovered the possibility or the possibilities of such a situation. We have already seen how rapidly a suggestion would call up in his mind a poetic conception ; a word would sometimes be enough, or the sight of an engraving. Here he had the sight of the drama being acted in real life, with his wife as heroine.

In the poem, " Mary " does not adopt the tone of mock modesty expected from her in an atmosphere of mock gallantry. She is not well-bred. She shows her love for her husband in the drawing-room as coolly as though she were alone in a wide garden. There was only a look of the eye or a touch of the hand, perhaps. The outrageousness was not so much in the sign of love given as in the shameless sincerity of it. Very naturally, all the others felt outraged. The selfishness of such a proceeding is the sin. Catherine did not know that, so when she was scolded she did not take it meekly. She thought that she had as much right to love her husband in her own way as he thought that he had to write his verses in his own way. Both were con-demned. He was pronounced obstinate, and she indecent.

Cut to the heart, and not at all understanding what she had done, Catherine tried to efface herself as ignorantly as she had put herself forward. She became a dowdy. This was not what was wanted at all. It offended the hostess and the gallant young guests at the same time. They all combined against her once more. She left off going into the little corner of society that she had rashly entered, and took with her sad, bitter, and ineffaceable memories, but not the smallest spark of real comprehension of the fact that would have been obvious to almost any one else—that the whole trouble was at least as much her own fault as that of the people who hurt her feelings. There was just one person who understood it all as little as she did. Blake, his perceptions of conduct darkened by the ideal, could no more see truly what had happened than a man who walks about carrying a large and brilliant lamp in his hand that shines in his face can judge the faces of people at the farther side of that lamp.

Blake certainly continued to go to Rathbone Place for literary purposes, but from now began the "unbending demeanour" that Smith noticed a year after the *Poetical Sketches* were printed. It is not because Blake wrote down the story of his wife's *début* in the poem of *Mary*, or because this is found in the leaves of a book that he had in his hands at the time, that we know the story to be true. All this was so because it must have been. We rather understand the poem from the truth than the truth from the poem. Not in any single page, but yet legibly and plainly, the story of what else happened now is written a little later in Blake's works. When Catherine had first entered the Rathbone Place drawing-room, and Blake, who was not yet quite in love with her, though he loved her, saw her beauty, as all who were there saw it, in its fresh country sweetness and charm, a new and natural love awoke in him that was not merely gratitude nor pity, but actual desire. He saw her in full dress. Her smooth neck and long, slender, but firmly rounded arms were, though he knew them at home, revealed to him all over again, as they bore the looks of admiration that pressed on them from every man in the room. He was roused to a new pride and a new craving. Polly Woods was forgotten at last. Catherine learned that she had married a giant. The volcanic energy with which Blake did all that roused his enthusiasm was now shown in the fire of new-married life lived at its highest and fullest.

In marrying Catherine he had come to his wife as innocent as she had come to him. He had lived at home. He had lived poor. He had spent his little pocket-money on art. He had thrown his energy into long walks and his desires into early love-making of the most chaste and ideal kind. Catherine was not a feeble maid. She was well able to respond to his needs. She had been brought up in the open air, and in future years was to show the vigour that was in her by sharing with her husband the thirty- and forty-mile walks in which he delighted to spend the long hours of a summer's day. But at the very outset of this honeymoon-year she received, along with the revelation of love's violence, the blow of blighting censorious contempt just as her heart was opening out to faith in life, and trust in those whose position enabled them to claim to be her superiors.

Till now she had always been the superior. As the only daughter of a substantial tradesman, and as a pretty brunette, tall, graceful, attractive, she had not lived to be five-and-twenty without being courted over and over again, and learning how to hold her own against the elbow-pinching, waist-gripping, lip-snatching gallantries of the robust seeds-men in her father's nursery garden. Their manners must have been a rough caricature of the liberties that frolicsome young bloods in those days were accustomed to take publicly in Covent Garden. Now she had a new experience. Suave and artificial compliments were followed by the most wound-ing contempt. She had never been so praised before. She had never been despised at all.

In bitter misery of heart she lost the power to find her whole world in her husband's arms, in the divine fever of married love. His confident demands of rapture revolted her. She lost sympathy and unity with him. They saw themselves suddenly as two strangers. The modesty that had been so long the stronghold of her self-respect had only been lulled asleep in the *Venusberg* for a moment. And now, just when it ought to have most firmly and sedulously kept its eyes shut, it woke up. She alienated by rebuke the husband whose love she had won by pity first, and by pleasure after.

The shock to him was as unforeseen and deadly as had been the shock of the drawing-room world's contempt to her. In the perfect selfishness of their warm and undisciplined hearts, they neither of them saw what was happening. It was quite hidden from her that she was telling him that the spite of a few strangers who had no claim whatsoever on her considera-tion was of more weight with her than the whole heart's love and whole body's vigour of her pure, true, and fiery husband, and could sadden her more than his love could delight and absorb. Yet this was exactly what her inability to forget their slights and respond to his love as before, when they

still admired her, said to him more plainly than she could
have spoken it in words. She did not see that she herself
was inflicting on him a slight made up of all that she had
received, that she was passing on the wounds, and in her hands
the knife was driven deep into the soul by the addition to its
power of the vigour of a new love and new hope. But that,
of course, is what he felt. *When his love did first begin she
did call that love a sin,* as he reminded her long afterwards
in the verses called *Broken Love.* She was now like Vala in
the net of religion, and not Vala the innocent, who in olden
days " forgave the furious love " of Albion (*Jerusalem*, page 20,
line 37). Blake did not take his disaster easily. He rebelled
with fury against her pretence of claiming in the bridal room
to repeat the high-handed law-giving from the female to the
male that might have been becoming in her as a pure maid
among enterprising and unpolished suitors. Virginity is a
throne ; matrimony is another. But they are not the same
throne, and the dignity and sovereignty of one is so unlike
the dignity and sovereignty of the other as to be almost its
opposite. What is to be done with a wife whose heart does
not teach her this ?

For a while Blake's fury and indignation made him
almost blunder into wickedness. Modesty seemed to him
now to be the only sin. He never quite disentangled it from
prudery all his life long. He began by making a mistake,
as unjustifiable as his wife had made in claiming to map out
the limits of the passionate love that he offered to her. He
told her that if she set up such boundaries he had a right to
give to others what she shut off from herself. Just as a man
becomes half a thief from the moment that he discusses the
stability of the rights of property, and questions how far
these may be forfeited by a neglect of the duties that go
with them, so Blake became half unfaithful to her in his
anger. Half unfaithful only, however,—the theoretic half.
He fumed out to his wife a theory of matrimony as preposterously arrogant and patriarchal as hers was preposterously
vestal. He claimed the right of Abraham to give to Hagar
what Sarah refused. Both these poor children of the heart
must be forgiven. They were very miserable. They were
lost in the labyrinth of love's forest, and were leading one
another astray.

Blake lay down on his bed, choked with the love that was
flung back on him. His wife sat weeping and pale, feeling
not only despised, but deserted. She did not know that if

her husband had really deserted her he would not be ill in this way, but would be only ill in the soul, while his health would have been sparkling, and his cheerfulness hard, brazen, and inaccessibly unscrupulous. His wife now called in his sister, with the instinct that makes woman turn to woman when in despair of man, and Blake, in a delirium of misery, rebellious and estranged, refusing to be tortured by the frigidity of his foolish and sobbing wife any longer, burst out with his announcement that he would take some one else in her place, some merry and attractive girl who should do him justice.

At this a deadly fear and horror came over poor Catherine, whose sore heart could bear no more. That her husband had led her into the false and falsely-educated world, where she had been despised, was bad enough in him, and that he had shown not an atom of sympathy with her in her misery, but had expected her to come home, forget it all, and blend herself entirely in his masterful appetite, was worse. There was desertion of the heart, in this claim to use her like a slave for his pleasure when unhappiness had taken from her the power to answer as a bride should to his love. But now had come the worst of all. She was to be publicly cast off and shamed before his family. She felt her courage give way, and crying out in her desolation, she fell down in a heap by the bed.

Something else as well as her courage gave way then. In that cry and that heavy fall, and in the great trouble Blake and his sister had to bring her to consciousness again when, with a sudden pang of pity, he threw off selfishness from his heart, and once for all gave himself entirely to her, we have the sad knowledge why this vigorous and unstained young couple lived childless all their lives.

Catherine was at that moment on her way to become a mother. But, as is often the case with those who are checked by a sudden shock or accident when in this condition, she could never from that hour go through it to the end of the allotted months of preparation where another life should wait to meet her, giving and receiving welcome.

Fortunately for us poor mortals, there is nothing so robust in all the world as wedded love. If it is not absolutely killed, nothing can prevent it from recovering most of its youth and strength in a very short time.

Within a month or two after this incident Mr. and Mrs. Blake were laughing together over the follies of the Mathews circle, as he read bits of *The Island in the Moon* to her, which we can guess, though we have no certain knowledge, was written to amuse her while she was regaining her bodily strength after the illness that cost her her hopes of maternity.

When the literary joke had done its work, and had given place to the composition of the *Songs of Innocence*, Blake may have also written the long rigmarole about *The Passions*, in which he tells of the emulousness of his own character, very unkindly calling it envy. Now also he must have written the poems *Mary* and *William Bond*. Writing the *Island* had restored to him his poetic faculty, and while the cause of these poems was not much earlier, the time when he ceased to have leisure or taste to attend to that kind of composition was not much later than the winter of 1783-84. Further allusions to the same incidents are to be found in the poem *Vala*, but the style is now altogether changed, and the allusions are much more difficult to recognise, being now woven closely into the myth, and coloured with the artistic meaning of the surrounding symbolism.

The only difficulty which any reader will have in making up his mind to accept *Mary* and *William Bond* as rhymed reminiscence, thinly masked, comes from the fact that " Mary " is, in these poems, not merely Blake's wife, but the lyrical and emotional side of his genius, and he is not *merely* writing about Catherine, but also about this part of his own nature. This is so strikingly evident that the present writer admits having thought—and said—until but lately that " Mary " was *only* Blake's poetic nature and not a human being at all,—his *Emanation*, to use the term he adopted, and made so well known. *Los* is partly the twin brother, and in a sort of way the mythic husband of *Enitharmon*, who is, in the great dream, the *Emanation* of a being called *Urthona*, who was an aspect of *Los*. *Enitharmon* herself is described as " the vegetated mortal life of Los,—his emanation, yet his wife until the sleep of death is past," in *Jerusalem*, page 14, line 13. And *Los* becomes " one " with Blake himself in *Milton*, page 20, line 12.

" Enitharmon " is not " Mary " merely, but belongs to another order of writing and another period, yet what is said of her partly applies to " Mary," who was both a woman and a symbol.

It will be noticed that in the verses about " Mary " there are lines—

Why was I not born with a different face ?
Oh why was I born like this envious race ?

which occur, hardly changed, as part of a short poem written
in a letter about ten years later, in which Blake laments over
the difference between himself and the people about him.
It is given with the title " A Cry " in the Chatto and Windus
Poetical Works of William Blake. " Mary " *might*, therefore,
have been *only* an aspect of his own mind.

But at the period of the incident from which the poem
Mary sprang, Blake was not yet come to the analysing frame
of mind which would have made it at all likely that he should
have so written about his artistic or poetic frame of mind ; and
even if he had, there was absolutely nothing in the world of
dreams, or in that of common fact, which could have caused
him to write in exactly this manner about his poetry or his
emotions, while there was all the material ready to hand for
such reference to what he had just learned of society, of
beauty, of envy, of jealousy, of love, and of pity, through his
married experiences.   It was still part of his poetic habit to
so treat personal recollection, and when he wrote these lines
he was just at the right distance from the experiences,—not
too far and not too near so to treat them.   In *Broken Love*
he returns to them from farther off, and in a different vein.
Nearly twenty years had gone by.

Hardly were these poems written, and probably while *The
Island in the Moon* was in progress—for this would account
for the *suddenness* of its stopping—when a change came in the
current of Blake's life.   His father died, and was buried in
Bunhill Fields, July 4, 1784.   Mr. Blake's opposition to his
son's marriage with Catherine Bouchier, and his absence
from the ceremony itself, had produced a final estrangement
between them that was never healed.   Blake was not at his
father's deathbed.

We cannot even be sure that he did not write the book of
Tiriel shortly after.   In this poem fathers are first held up
before us as the natural enemies of their children until
a more advanced senility reduces them in their turn to a
childish state.   It dates between 1783 and 1788.   That is
all that we can learn with any certainty from its contents,
but its paper, even without a dated watermark, is enough
to place it earlier than 1790.

CHAPTER X

HOW ROBERT CAME AND WENT

THE MS. of *The Island in the Moon* is written on two half-quires of paper, whose watermark has only the letters G. R., but no date. The outside sheet of the first portion of it is lost. This deprives us of the title-page, which may have borne a date, and also of the last page but one of the MS. itself, in whose dialogue a gap will be noticed. The second half-quire, containing at its beginning the broken final page, was otherwise left nearly blank, as the MS. was abruptly dropped. But it seems to have lain beside Blake for a time, while he was being annoyed by a conversation about some list or catalogue of effects, to which he could only give a divided and forced attention, for this second half-quire has been turned over, and on the back are two slight scribbles representing the lion lying down by the lamb, and a number of horses' heads scattered about, almost repeating one another. Blake's own name is repeated twice near the top, and is smudged out while wet, and a number of letters *n* and *u*, written large in a copy-book hand, spread themselves vaguely among the horses' heads, the full word "numeration" being in the middle of the page. This suggests that the MS. was lying on the table the very day on which James came to talk business with William about cataloguing and dividing their father's personal estate.

Mr. Blake the hosier probably died intestate. If he made a will, the provisions of it left something in common between the brothers, for not long afterwards we find Blake agreeing with Lavater that you do not truly know a man till you have divided an inheritance with him. "Numeration" must have preceded such division.

In Gilchrist's *Life of Blake* we are not told of this, but we learn that "the second son James, a year and a half William's senior, continued to live with the widow Catherine, and succeeded in the hosier's business." In the first paragraph of that biography (which begins with the second chapter, the first being preliminary) we are mistakenly told that William was the second son, a statement in which earlier authorities, deceived by the omission of John's name from the family conversations, agree. Most of Blake's friends simply had never heard of his brother John at all. Catherine was the name of Blake's mother as well as of his wife.

That some money was divided among the brothers is evident in another way, for Blake immediately left his house, 23 Green Street, Leicester Fields, and took No. 27 Broad Street, next door to what was now his brother's place of business. He opened a print-shop here in partnership with an elder apprentice of Basire's named Parker, who is said to have been by six or seven years his senior. J. T. Smith ("Nollekens" Smith), one of the "envious" guests of Mrs. Mathews, who did not follow Blake with unqualified admiration, says (in his *Book for a Rainy Day*) that Mrs. Mathews found the money for this partnership. This has a look of gossip and exaggeration on the face of it, though there may have been some portion of truth in the story. Mrs. Mathews may have continued to help and encourage Blake after the trouble over the uncorrected poetical sketches had cooled her husband's affection for him. Parker must have contributed; but if none of the capital came from the home stock it is difficult to understand why the shop was established next door to James in a house not built for a shop at all, and why James used to "pester" William with "bread-and-cheese advice," as we are told by Smith that he did. There was also some sort of business arrangement made by which Robert, the youngest son, was given to William as an apprentice and lodged in his house. This was not done on payment of a sum for articles, perhaps, but that James considered it to be business we need not doubt. There was a *quid pro quo* of some sort.

Blake was morbid about money, and it was very difficult to make him understand that it is, of all subjects, the one where egotism is especially forbidden, even though competition may be admitted. Like many proud, generous, egotistic people, Blake had not the least idea that his egotism was a particularly unpermissible form of selfishness. He, in later life, told Mr. Robinson that the offer of money used to make him turn pale. No doubt it did, but we should rather have had the fact from any lips but his own. That he had an exaggerated fear of being degraded by money transactions, and so grew to hate money, is known and is easy to understand. He was the grandson of one spendthrift, and the brother of another. He was the son of a careful man of business, and the brother of another. He had in his blood the most irritable impatience of seeming to be a bargainer or a grasper, with the strictest ideas of probity. We can never forget that he lived in poverty and did not die in debt. What this meant to a man of his temperament and his powers must always be a thing to be wondered at, and admired at least as much as his art and poetry. He was an exceedingly hard worker. Between the termination of his apprenticeship to Basire in 1778 and his father's death in 1784 he had done a good deal of work. Much of it must have been distributed into books and portfolios, from which it has slowly vanished; but the industrious compilers of Gilchrist's *Life* have recorded enough to vindicate Blake's character as a man of toil as well as a man of genius.

The titles include, first, those designed and engraved by Blake:

King Edward and Queen Eleanor (no date), a composition with more than a score of figures. The size is not given in the catalogue; but putting together the two fragments, on which Blake afterwards wrote part of *Vala*, Night VII, it must have measured about 18 inches by 10. The figures are grouped in an old-fashioned theatrical style, like the last tableau of a Shakespearian act, and all highly shaded as well as the wall and floor. The shading over the wall spaces only of this represented many days of work.

Morning, or Glad Day (1780).—At this the list of works both designed and engraved by Blake ends, till it is resumed in 1791 with the plates to Mary Wollstonecraft's *Tales for Children*. There is such a striking difference of style between the *King Edward* and the *Glad Day*, that many others after Blake's own designs must have come between that are now lost. Those engraved from other people's compositions do not account for the change of manner. Of these there are mentioned—

The *Joseph of Arimathea* (10 × 5½ in.).

Several plates in the *Memoirs* of Hollis.

Several plates in Gough's *Monuments*, etc.

Asia and Africa (after Stothard), a frontispiece to a *System of Geography*, 1779.

Eight plates, after Stothard, for the *Novelist's Magazine*, 1779, 1782.

Clarence's Dream, for Enfield's *Speaker*, after Stothard. Published by Johnson, 1780.

Four plates for *Scott of Amwell's Poems,* after Stothard. Published by Buckland, 1782.

Two plates, after Stothard, for the *Lady's Pocket-Book*, 1782 or 1783.

Nine or ten plates for *Ritson's English Songs*, out of a total of nineteen, after Stothard.   Published by Johnson, 1783.

The *Fall of Rosamond* (circular; 2 inches), after Stothard. Published by Macklin, 1783.

Zephyrus and Flora, Calisto, after Stothard.   Published after the death of Blake's father by Parker and Blake, 1784, though probably engraved before.

This gives hardly more than thirty plates in six years— five plates a year.   If they averaged in price ten pounds a plate, that was as much as we can suppose to have been paid, and means a pound a week of laborious, artistic, skilful, and anxious work.   If a statistician were to calculate how much an hour Blake made, he would find it amounted to a sum resembling that which is paid now to young doctors, writers, and the clergy, but refused by artists' models in the schools and stevedores at the docks.   There is no reason to believe —even if we suppose the prices paid were the best in the market, and that a dozen or more plates have been lost since Blake's time altogether—that Blake made more than thirty or thirty-five shillings a week.

Though his brother James was acting as the head of the family now, Blake seems to have felt that he had suddenly attained a position of ascendency, after having been looked down upon for the whole of his life up to this time.   **He** was the only married brother.   He had a house of his own, where he was master.   Even from the point of view that a business man takes, he believed that his choice of a profession was about to be justified.   As usual, we find him putting down his personal feelings in a work of art without loss of time.   In the year after that at whose close the death of his father and his own change of house to Broad Street happened, we find that he executed several pictures of *Joseph and his Brethren*, in one of which the brethren bow down to Joseph.   They form (Gilchrist's catalogue says) " a fine sheaf-like group."

H

The works that he had executed with the brush, along with the engravings already quoted, before 1785, are all important:

The Penance of Jane Shore.

King Edward and Queen Eleanor (from which he engraved).

War unchained by an Angel. (Marked *Butts* in the list. We have no letters to Butts till many years later. Presumably the picture was not sold when painted.)

A Breach in a City, the Morning after a Battle.

The Bard, from Gray. (This picture was exhibited in London in 1906 at the Carfax Gallery. Its brown tone curiously recalls Giorgione. We should not have ventured to compare Blake to a Venetian artist in his lifetime. He would have gone into a paroxysm of rage.)

The *Bard* and the *Joseph* series went to the Academy Exhibition in 1785, and were therefore done within nine months after Blake's father died. They must have been his first designs in his new home. The *Josephs* are traced by Gilchrist, who says that they were not marked with the star, that meant *for sale,* not *sold,* at the Royal Academy in those days, he explains (when did the change of meaning begin ?); and he relates how they afterwards were bought by a picture-dealer at a furniture sale in their original and unbecoming rosewood frames (so, gold was not necessary at the Royal Academy then !), and were sent to the International Exhibition of 1862.

For two years and a half Robert lived with William as his pupil. He was always the best beloved and most popular of the Blake brothers. William's affection for him was one of the strongest feelings he had ever known, and its memory lasted all his life. The happy days of brotherhood and close union did not last long. One story from those times makes us intimate with that home and lets us into all its secrets. It is well known now, and has been repeated in every biography. Here it is in the words of Gilchrist :—

"One day a dispute arose between Robert and Mrs. Blake. She, in the heat of discussion, used words to him his brother (though her husband too) thought unwarrantable. A silent witness thus far, he could now bear it no longer, but, with characteristic impetuosity — when stirred — rose and said to her : ' Kneel down and beg Robert's pardon directly, or you never see my face again.' A heavy threat, uttered in tones which, from Blake, unmistakably showed that it was *meant.* She, poor thing, ' thought it very hard,' as she would afterwards tell, to beg her brother-in-law's pardon when she was not in fault! But being a duteous, devoted wife, though by nature nowise tame or dull of spirit, she *did* kneel down and meekly murmur, 'Robert, I beg your pardon, I am in the wrong.' 'Young woman, you lie,' abruptly retorted he, '*I* am in the wrong.'"

Two things we see once more from this, though we already knew them—Blake was not in love with his wife, yet lovingly reconciled to being her husband, but his wife was in love with him fully, absolutely. Robert—"Bob," as every one called him—was a moral education to Blake at this time, and kept his heart alive with brotherly love when it might have fallen into the death of self-satisfaction. So great was the danger and so near, that Blake knew ever afterwards through what peril he had then gone, and what death had been at the farther side for him if he had not been guided through by his affection for Robert.

Love in the one complete sense of that word—the real and perfect madness that inhabits, as Shakespeare has told us, "in the finest wits of all"—would never come to Blake again. He had had it. Polly Woods had brought it and taken it away. That was all she had had to do with him. She had done it, and gone. It could never be done again. Every one noticed through all the mature and all the declining years of Blake's life how devotedly attached he was to his wife. She was his "beloved." That was his name for her. It was a true name. He had earned the right to use it by his fidelity from the hour of his great discovery that love does not live only in the hot sunshine, but even more in the moony night. But she was not his love. As for the girl that was, or that had been, he had no more to do with her. He never wished to see her again, and he never saw her. That was a comfort, so far, of a kind.

But he could not get it quite out of his head that there was something very grand and noble *in himself*, or he would not have made this great discovery of his, and returned to the wife that loved him the gift of pity that she had brought to him in his dark hour, restoring it with such high-piled interest. Bob, with his cheery ways and his cleverness and companionability, put all that now out of the region of Blake's daily meditations. There was a contagious healthfulness about Bob. He was in no sort of moral danger himself, and by his mere presence he saved his brother from drifting into something very like the character of a Pharisee. This was

Robert's "message." It had also been in early times his part in life to attract the affection of his play-fellow, J. T. Smith, whose attention became in this way drawn to William, the arrogant and gifted brother. Smith being of a gossiping nature, the result was that when he came to write his *Book for a Rainy Day* he told us several scrappy but illuminating facts about Blake that we could very ill have spared. Had there been no Bob and no Smith, posterity would now have only half a Blake.

And then Robert, having delivered his message and played his part, seemed to have found no other business in life, and though they tried hard to keep him, he would not stay. Blake did all he could for him. He did not leave the nursing to his wife. He threw himself into the desperate struggle with death, as though he could force the enemy out by his own strength. During the last fortnight he watched day and night by his brother's bed without sleeping. He had his reward. He saw the soul spring from the suddenly still, blind body, and ascend upwards, clapping its hands for joy. Then taking this sight with him Blake went to bed, and slept continuously for three days and nights.

CHAPTER XI

AFTER ROBERT HAD GONE

WHEN he woke up and returned to the activities of life Blake felt an absolute need for a fresh set of opinions to console him and a fresh set of aspirations to arouse him to effort. He could not take up his existence where he had laid it down when he fell into that long sleep, probably with a last conscious wish that he might wake from it as his brother had awakened from the sleep of life.

His wife was now his only companion. As they drew closer together she must have told him something of the sense of desolation and hopeless misery with which she had gone about her household duties during those three long days, while he had lain from night to morning, and round again to night, in an unapproachable isolation of slumber that must have seemed almost more terrifying than that of the dead body which lay in the next room.

Then it must have been that he told her of the vision that he had seen—the soul of Robert escaping, not merely in peace, or in an awful joy, but with childish and exuberant glee.

She had not seen it. What sort of reality had these visions that one could see while they were hidden from another? Blake argued. He was always arguing. It must ever be held as one of the innumerable wonders that cling about him that he alone among our greatest poets was so greatly given to this unpoetic habit. He had argued with the keeper of the Royal Academy when he was only a student. He argued with the guests of Mrs. Mathews. He argued with all the books he read, as we see by his notes on their margins. He was not in the least likely to spare his wife. But at last all argument came down to this—" Were it not better to believe vision with all our might and strength, though we are fallen and lost?" In the first of what are now

101

called his "Prophetic Books," written after Robert's death—
The Ghost of Abel—Blake puts these words into the mouth
of Eve. Probably the question in actual fact was put to him
by his wife, after he himself had treated the visionary
experience with such mercilessly abstract and metaphysical
handling that she had found all its consolation squeezed
out of it.

The view, however, was not that of his wife only, but of
his natural and unintellectual secret inner self. His philosophic self did not rise to the height of such inspired
simplicity till it had passed through self-annihilation, and
Reason had consented to that suicide which is its one sole
and sufficient deed of real virtue.

Never in the higher portions of his poems can the reader
disentangle what he tells us as from himself in the feminine
mood and what as from his wife. Her character was so
natural and frank, and so free from mental coquettishness,
epigram, paradox, and sarcasm, that when she speaks he hears
the eternal voice of the blood that is the liquid soul, and
when he answers with opposition and personal pride and
logic, his own blood feels the hardness of the bones, and
knows that these are the dust of death disguised in the
solidity of the imperative mood, that claims to be the
fraternal and righteous affirmative. The words, "his emanation, yet his wife," tell us from now onwards that Blake
and Catherine had entered together into the composite
solitude of their lives, and he had risen up and shut-to
the door.

Now also he turned with fresh activity to the study of
Swedenborg, which thus led him to form during the years
1788, 1789, and 1790 the complete symbolic system of
thought of which, to our lasting misfortune, we shall never
have more than an imperfect record, for poverty prevented
the printing of many of his books during his life, and his
virtuous but very stupid friend Tatham conscientiously
burned invaluable manuscripts after his death because their
theology was not that of the Irvingite church.

When the inheritance was divided that came to the
brothers at Mr. Blake's death, no one can possibly believe
that most of the books did not come to William. He alone
would have really cared for them. He alone had to take his
revenge for the opposition to his visions, and even the per-
secution—so he considered it—with which his parents had
met his divine call. Perhaps he had not enough time to

read during the first days of Robert's apprenticeship.   Afterwards Robert's illness had absorbed every energy.   Now poor
"Bob" was dead, and the tension was over.   Consolation
was what the thirst of Blake's soul desperately demanded.
Consolation meant vision, and in vision he had no companion
upon earth who could pretend to an equality with him.
That he should turn to Swedenborg was a simple necessity.

What Parker, Blake's partner in the shop, had to say to
this can be guessed, and how ill Blake took attempts to make
him do any ordinary workaday duty in its own time, instead of
at his good pleasure, we can understand.   What is recorded
is simply that the partnership came to an end, and that
Blake gave up the house at 27 Broad Street, which he had tried
in vain to make into a shop, and moved to Poland Street,
undoubtedly to find a cheaper shelter.   Perhaps also he was
glad to get away from his brother James, for it was likely to
be during the disputes with his partner that James wasted
good common-sense upon him and received nothing in return
but that reputation for having "pestered" him with "bread-
and-cheese advice," which is all that has come down to our
own day of his conduct at this time.   But James was a good
brother.   He lent his own house later for Blake's exhibition
of pictures, and he deserved better treatment than he
received.   Blake was in no state to question with himself
how he was treating any one.   The new idea of developing
vision was everything to him.   He had a purpose in life
once more.   Art and poetry possessed a new meaning.   He
also had a message for the world.

Of course, the "rank draught" of envy with which he
complains frankly that his cup of life was filled so full was
not all emptied yet.   He still drank of it, and we detect the
bitter savour of its wormwood even in his most generous
words.   But he was not now trying to out-sing the Islanders
in the Moon, or even to out-dramatise the Elizabethans and
Shakespeare himself.   He would out-prophesy Swedenborg.

If any one who possesses his copy of the *Heaven and Hell,*
of the *Heavenly Mysteries,* and the *Apocalypse Revealed*
would come forward and show us the notes in their margins,
he would shed a light on what still remains dark about
Blake's development of mind at this period.

There is a pause between the date of *Tiriel* and that of
The Ghost of Abel, neither of them later than 1788, and the
Marriage of Heaven and Hell, 1790, with its companions,
Thel, the *Visions of the Daughters of Albion,* etc.   The lost

book of *Outhoon* must go with these in date as in subject. The *Songs of Innocence*, though engraved in 1789, do not fill the gap. They had been written years before. The *Songs of Experience* do not fill it. They were accumulated during five years, and engraved in 1794. The lost though published work, the *French Revolution, a Poem in Seven Books*, whose first book was produced at the price of one shilling by Johnson, does not fill it. This was printed in 1791. The whole seven books were probably never written. The entire edition must have been destroyed in 1793 after the September massacres, and even the few copies that were sold were probably burned by their owners. The one scrap called *Lafayette* is the only certain trace we have left of it.

All this leaves the years 1787 or 1788 to 1790 without any adequate record of the action or growth of Blake's mind. It was the period of incubation, when he laid his golden egg, the great Myth. But this was not a goose's egg, but rather a kiwi's. Du Maurier once reminded us playfully what symbolism is in the fact that "the kiwi bird lays such a large egg that it takes two kiwis to hatch it."

The difficulty of dating Blake's first two books is that, even more markedly than his last two, each has two dates. *Tiriel* may have been written and copied out carefully, all but the last few lines, with the purpose of being read, if not printed, by some one in the Mathews' drawing-room, perhaps Mr. Mathews himself. It was written on the very cheap paper used for *The Island in the Moon*, of which Blake bought a quantity in the very poor days of the first year of his marriage. He certainly did not make himself uncomfortable by buying any more of it after his father's inheritance came to him. Something better was to be found in the stock-in-trade of the firm Parker and Blake.

But the last portion of *Tiriel* is a little later than the rest, and perhaps even later than the words " MS. of Mr. Blake " written on the slate-coloured paper cover into which the poem was stitched with the intention of being handed to somebody, though this label was probably added when Mr. Mathews was given up and the manuscript taken to Johnson the bookseller. No man writes " MS. of Mr. —— (anybody) " on the cover of a work when he merely intends to put it into the drawer of his own desk.

There is an allusion to a lady, a child, a sofa, and a dog, whose history we do not know, in the close of the poem. There are lines that even unite it to *America* and to the *Visions of the Daughters of Albion,* which were poems not even thought of when that spongy paper was bought on which *Tiriel* was written.   *The Ghost of Abel,* in the same way, bears two dates, but these, 1788 and 1822, are printed by Blake himself, and they tell their own story.

CHAPTER XII

THE NOTES TO SWEDENBORG

IF we have not the copies of Swedenborg's books which may have come to Blake from his father's bookshelf, we have, in the library of the British Museum, a copy of the volume on *Angelic Wisdom concerning the Divine Love,* which was published in English in 1787—the year of Robert's death. It was heard of, we need have no doubt, among the very small group of Swedenborgians in London as soon as it came out, and Blake is likely to have acquired it at once, being now not without a few spare shillings. There are notes of his on the margin every few pages, almost all through it. Those on the fly-leaf cover the whole of the blank space. Unfortunately, some tidy person—we do not know who—began to rub them out, and most of them are entirely illegible.

One can trace this curious beginning to the long and effaced paragraph—" There is no good *will.* Will is always evil"; which seems, if not universally applicable, especially written of the man who used that india-rubber. Incidentally, it explains Blake's use of the word "hell." "Will," "evil," "hell," "desire," are practically synonyms. Shakespeare, of course, used "will" frequently in a secondary sense as meaning "lust," just as "desire" is used now.

It is not possible to give a true picture of Blake's mind as he read this book of Swedenborg's without reprinting it as well as copying his notes. But as there is no space here for such ideal completeness of record, the sentence in each paragraph that is nearest the pencil note, or that to which it seems to have been intended as an answer or a comment, is given, and then the note.

The portions of text quoted from Swedenborg are not verbally always exactly the same as Blake's edition, but are from an even better and later translation of the same Latin

original. Swedenborg is so prolix that a few passages are
purposely condensed. Where this is done it is mentioned.
As a rule, the condensation is not a re-composition, but only
the omission of the verbose accumulations of Swedenborg's
elaborate diction.

From now Blake divided the different men, or sorts of
man, in each man as distinctly as Swedenborg does, who
calls them *discrete*. The natural man, celestial man, spiritual
man, and rational man are Swedenborg's divisions. Blake
went further, called them "lifes," then "Zoas," had visions
of them, gave them names (Urizen, Luvah, Tharmas, and
Urthona), and claimed that they were the same that Ezekiel
saw. Blake, going beyond Ezekiel, perceived that each had
an evil as well as a good aspect and action, and that each had
a feminine portion, without which he was altogether evil. The
masculine is, taken alone as a group of tendencies, merely
Will, Selfhood, Reason, symbolically called "Head," "Heart,"
"Loins." The feminine alone is *Sensation, Pity, Sorrow*—
again "Head," "Heart," "Loins." Each when alone fights
imagination, the sacred first-born Word of God, the *logos* by
whom all things are made. Swedenborg never saw this,
therefore the divisions of Swedenborg do not even correspond
exactly to the "four Mighty Ones" in Blake, nor are they
equally descriptive of the truth. Blake also perceived the
personality of states and spaces, and gave many of them
names.

The meaning of this will be seen in the early part of the
notes to Swedenborg. The germ of the idea of the *Marriage
of Heaven and Hell* can be seen in his note to par. 68. We
also see the origin of the expression "Albion's reactor" in
Jerusalem.

In No. 82 we find what was running in Blake's head
while he wrote several well-known passages in the *Marriage*
and in *Jerusalem*.

It is pleasing to the self-love of our century to notice how
childishly lacking in the true self-consciousness of thought
are Swedenborg's dicta about vacuum. If all the world
were abolished to-morrow, we ask ourselves, would nothing
subsist? The fact that something had existed would subsist.
When *is* departs, *was* remains. If, after a gap of vacuum,
the universe were restored, we ask ourselves, would that prove
that something else had existed, when *is* had gone besides *was*?
We suspect that the *tendency* to restore itself must have
existed, called *will be*. We begin to discover that verbs and

tenses are as much forms of existence as nouns, and that the more immaterial a thing is, the easier it is to our minds to conceive it as existing, and that vacuum is the habitat of the most obstinate and irrepressible of all our ideas that insist on considering themselves as existences.

Under No. 169 the ideas of death and life are contrasted, as though they were as simple as yes and no, instead of each being a mental region so *difficult for transport* that the Boundary Commission has not yet succeeded in making the tour and mapping out the frontier of either.

In Swedenborg's No. 295 we have a hint about how Blake composed his mythic names, adapting them from any that he could pick up, and so far altering as to bring in significant letters.

In the note to Swedenborg's No. 315 we have the explanation of the phrase in line 2 of the last page of *Jerusalem*, a poem that began to grow from this seed of Swedenborg's philosophy, turning it into art, vision, myth, as it grew, and adding much philosophy to it also.

By comparing all these notes with Blake's works it will be seen that he never ceased to largely accept Swedenborgian thought, *as far as it went,* and to regret that in this as in other books of Swedenborg he could not adopt without addition or change what he read. Yet, whenever he reflected on Swedenborg's limitations he was stirred to anger. The *Marriage of Heaven and Hell* is full of bitter derision against him, though Blake none the less looked on him as the attendant angel of a risen Christianity. Those of us who have read both will generally feel that Swedenborg is beyond nine men out of ten, while Blake is far beyond Swedenborg.

The present writer's experience enables him to bid the reader hope that after twenty-five years of uncounted and uncountable readings of Blake he will find in him new beauties, new revelations, new suggestions of value continually, and that on a return to consideration of Biblical writers after such finding he will discover new symbolic relations to real life in all early Christian doctrine.

In the end, our personal feelings toward revelation must turn upon our attitude of mind towards the great question of what constitutes *personality*, and upon whether we adopt as the answer " Always one thing," or " Sometimes one thing, and sometimes another," $x = y$ or *sometimes z.*

There will be noticed an instructive and interpreting tone in these notes that makes it seem that they were written by

Blake for some one else,—probably for Mrs. Blake, whom he was now educating. The numbers in the references here are those of the paragraphs of Swedenborg's work, and are the same for all editions and translations of it. S. is put before Swedenborg's words, B. before Blake's.

BLAKE'S MARGINAL NOTES TO SWEDENBORG'S
ANGELIC WISDOM CONCERNING THE DIVINE LOVE

S. (1) The wise man perceives this (that thought, speech, and action grow warm in proportion as the affection belonging to love grows warm), not from the knowledge that Love is the Life of Man, but from his experience that these things are so.

B. They also perceive this from knowledge, but not from the natural part.

S. (2) No one knows what the life of man is unless he knows that it is love.

B. This was known to me, and thousands.

S. (7) It (that the Divine is not in Space) cannot be comprehended by a natural idea.

B. What are natural ideas?

S. (7 again) A man nevertheless may comprehend this by natural thought, provided he admits into it something of spiritual light.

B. Mark this.

S. (7 again) A spiritual idea does not derive anything from space, but it derives its all from state.

B. Poetic idea.

S. (8) It may appear from these premises that by a merely natural idea man cannot comprehend that the Divine is everywhere and yet not in space, and that angels and spirits comprehend this clearly, consequently that man also may, provided he admits into his thought something of spiritual light. The reason why a man may comprehend this is that it is not his body which thinks but his spirit,—consequently not his natural but his spiritual part.

B. Observe the difference between natural and spiritual as seen by man. Man may comprehend, but not his natural or external man.

S. (10) In the spiritual world appear spaces . . . distances . . . appearances according to spiritual affinities, which are of love and wisdom, that is of good and truth. . . . The Lord is everywhere . . . appears high above as a sun in the heavens, of which there are three . . . the hells under them according to their (reception or) rejection of love and wisdom.

B. He who loves feels love descend into him, and if he is wise, may perceive it from the Poetic Genius, which is the Lord.

S. (11) God is very man. In all heavens there is no other idea of God than the idea of a man. The reason is that heaven, as a whole, and in every part, is in form as a man, and the Divine which is with the angels constitutes heaven. . . . The Africans who acknowledge one God . . . entertain concerning God the idea of a man. When they hear that a number of persons entertain the idea of God as of a little cloud in mid air they ask where such persons are, and being told that they are among the Christians they declare it to be impossible.

B. Man can have no idea of anything greater than man, as a cup cannot contain more than its capaciousness. But God is a man, not because he is so perceived by man, but because he is the creator of man.

Think of a white cloud as being holy, you cannot love it ; but think of a holy man within the cloud, Love springs up in your thought. For to think of holiness distinct from man is impossible to the affections. Thought alone can make monsters, but the affections cannot.

S. (12) They who are more wise than the common pronounce God to be invisible.

B. Worldly wisdom, or demonstration by the senses, is the cause of this.

S. (13, end) The negation of God constitutes hell.

B. The negation of the Poetic Genius.

S. (14, middle) Soul is not possible apart from its body, nor body apart from its soul.

B. Thought without affection makes a distinction between love and wisdom as it does between body and spirit.

S. (27, 28) If a person . . . should say that a plurality of Infinites, of Uncreates, of Omnipotents, and of Gods is possible, provided they have one and the same essence . . . is not the same essence one identity ? . . .

B. Essence is not Identity, but from Essence proceeds Identity, and from one Essence may proceed many Identities as from one affection may proceed many thoughts. Surely this is an oversight. That there is but one Omnipotent, Uncreate, and God I agree. But that there is but one Infinite I do not. For if all but God is not Infinite they shall come to an end, which God forbid.

If the Essence was the same as the Identity, there could be but one Identity, which is false. Heaven would, on this plan, be but a clod.

(On opposite margin)

But one and the same Essence is therefore Essence and not Identity.

S. (40) Appearances . . . first form understanding, and these appearances the mind cannot shake off . . . if the cause lies deep, unless it keeps the understanding some time in spiritual light.

B. This it can do while in the body.

S. (41) This can be demonstrated only by such things as a man can perceive by virtue of the sense of his own body. Therefore by these things it shall be demonstrated.

B. Demonstration is only by bodily senses.

S. (49, condensed) The love of God in us is a human and not a divine quality, for if divine it would be part of God's infinity in us loving the rest outside us, and it is contrary to the essence of God to love himself.

B. False. Take it so or the contrary it comes to the same, for if a thing loves it is infinite. Perhaps we only differ in the meaning of the words Infinite and Eternal.

S. (68) Man is only a recipient of life . . . from his hereditary evil he reacts against God. In proportion as he believes that all his life is from God . . . reaction becomes the property of action, and acts with God as from himself.

B. God and evil are here both good, and the two contraries married.

S. (69) Two things are proper to nature—space and time. . . . He who knows how to raise his mind above the ideas which flow from space and time passes from thick darkness into light . . . he disperses the thick darkness of the natural light, and relegates its fallacies from the middle to the sides.

B. (after correcting the word *middle* into *centre*, and *sides* into *circumferences*). When the fallacies of darkness are in the circumference they cast a bound about the infinite.

S. (condensed) Spaces and times in spiritual life are not settled 's in natural life, but have relation to states of love and are mutable with these. Angels do not comprehend when we say that the divine fills spaces, for they do not know what spaces are, but they understand when we say that the divine fills all things.

B. Excellent.

(Blake approves without comment, underlines, or uses several expressions, such as the following.)

S. (72) Natural man . . . relapses into his life's love . . . his will, and this love dissipates these (spiritual) things and immerses his thought in space, in which his *lumen*, which he calls rational light, abides.

(73) Time in the spiritual world is only a quality of state.

(76) Who cannot . . . think of God apart from Time is unable to perceive eternity otherwise than as eternity of time, and then in thinking of God as from eternity he must needs fall into confusion. He thinks from a beginning . . . an attribute of time. . . . His delirium lies in the thought that God has existed from himself, from which he falls headlong into the origin of nature from itself. . . . Between which (the infinite and the finite) there is no ratio.

B. How can life create death ?

(79) The Divine in the whole heaven and the Divine in an angel is the same, wherefore the whole heaven can appear as one angel. . . . The church . . . an entire society of Heaven, has appeared as one man . . . as big as a giant . . . as small as an infant. . . . The Divine is the same in greatest things and least things.

(82) I once heard angels conversing with Newton on vacuum. They said they could not bear the idea of a vacuum . . . as nothing. Newton said that he knows that the Divine which Is fills all things. He exhorts all those who converse with him concerning vacuum to beware of the idea of nothing, calling it a swoon, because in nothing no actuality of mind is possible.

(The following are also among Swedenborgian phrases that entered into Blake's mind and never left it again. They will be recognised as showing through in much of his poetry.)

(84) The two worlds are distinct . . . in the spiritual world is heat and light, the good of charity and the truth of faith. Heat and light cannot derive their origin from any other source than that of a sun . . . in the spiritual world there is another sun than in the natural world.

(86) That sun is the Divine Love and Wisdom that are one, and appear as a sun in that world.

(103) By the Most High is signified the inmost.

(129) Angels constantly turn their faces to the Lord as a sun, and thus have the south to the right, the north to the left, and the west at the back.

(151) The Lord created the universe and all things belonging to it by means of the (spiritual) sun, which is the first proceeding of the Divine Love and the Divine Wisdom.

(154) In the spiritual world are the causes of all things, and in the natural world are the effects of all things.

(After a long gap the direct marginal commentary is resumed.)

S. (163) Without two suns, the one living and the other dead, there can be no creation.

B. False philosophy according to the letter, but true according to the spirit.

S. (164) Natural things in their origins are dead . . . suns are origins . . . the dead sun is created through the living sun by the Lord.

B. How could life create death ?

S. (165) A dead sun was created . . . that things may be fixed . . . that existences may come forth which shall be . . . ever enduring. The terraqueous globe is a basis and firmament upon which they exist.

B. They exist literally about the sun, and not about the earth.

S. (166) All things were created by the Lord through the living sun and nothing through the dead sun.

B. The dead sun is only a phantasy of evil men.

S. (181, condensed) Men in their natural heat and light do not know spiritual heat except by a certain delight of love, nor spiritual light except by perception of truth.

B. He speaks of men as mere earthly men, not as receptacles of spirit, or else he contradicts 257.

(257 is quoted and annotated below, in its place.)

S. (182) Degrees of spiritual heat cannot be described from experience, because love, to which spiritual heat corresponds, does not come under ideas of thought, but spiritual light can be described because light, being of light, falls into those ideas.

B. This is certainly not to be understood according to the letter, for it is false by all experience. Who does not and may not know of love and wisdom in himself ?

S. (220) By works (so often mentioned in the Word, where we are told that a man's salvation depends on them) are meant uses which are actually done, for charity and faith is in uses and according to uses.

B. The whole of the New Church is in Active Life and not in Ceremonies at all.

S. (237) Man comes first into the natural degree. This increases . . . until he reaches . . . the rational. The second degree, the spiritual, . . . is opened by the love of uses . . . love towards the neighbour . . . the third degree . . . by love toward the Lord.

B. Study science till you are blind. Study intellectuals till you are cold. Yet science cannot teach intellect. Much less can intellect teach affection. How foolish it is then to assert that Man is born in only one degree, when that one degree is receptive of the three degrees ; two of which he must destroy or close up or they will descend. If he closes up the two superior then he is not truly in the third, but descends out of it into mere Nature or Hell (see No. 239). Is it not also evident that one degree will not open the other, and that science will not open intellect, but that they are discrete, and not continuous so as to explain each other except by correspondence which has nothing to do with demonstration, for you cannot demonstrate one degree by the other, for how can science be brought to demonstrate intellect without making them continuous and not discrete ?

S. (239) There is in every man a natural, spiritual, and celestial impotency by birth, and in act when they are opened.

B. Mark this. It explains 238.

S. (later in 239) Man . . . after death, if he becomes an angel . . . speaks ineffable things incomprehensible to the natural man.

B. Not to a Man, but to the natural Man.

S. (241) Every one who consults his reason whilst it is in the light is able to see that a man's love is the end of all things belonging to him.

B. *Whilst it is in the light* (underlined).

S. (244) The understanding does not lead the will. Wisdom does not produce love.

B. Mark this.

S. (256) A man, so long as he lives in the world, and is therefore in the natural degree, cannot be elevated into very wisdom as it is with the angels.

B. See Sect. 4 of the next number.

S. (257, Sect. 4) Still, the man with whom the spiritual degree has been opened comes into that wisdom when he dies, and he can also come into it by a laying asleep of the sensations of the body, and by an influx into the spiritual things of his mind from above.

(Sect. 5) Thought comes out of the mind's spiritual substances, not out of its natural substances.

B. This is to be understood as unusual in our time but common in ancient. This is while in the body. Many persons understand him (Swedenborg) as if a man in the natural body was only conversant with natural substances, because themselves are mercenary and worldly, and have no idea of any but worldly gain.

S. (257) It may be confirmed, and indeed is confirmed, by the wicked to themselves that there is no God . . . nature created herself . . . religion is to keep simple minds in bonds . . . human prudence does all things.

B. Who shall dare to say after this that elevation is of self, and is Enthusiasm and Madness, and is it not plain that self-derived intelligence is worldly demonstration ?

S. (294) Those things which constitute the spiritual sun are from the Lord, and are not the Lord, therefore they are not life in itself.

B. This assertion that the spiritual sun is not life explains how the natural sun is dead.

(294, later) As things which flow forth from an angel or a man are not the angel or the man, but are from them, devoid of life . . . making one with them no further than that . . . they have been taken out of the forms of their bodies which were the forms of their life. Men with natural ideas cannot express this.

B. How absurd then would it be to say that no man on earth has a spiritual idea after reading No. 257.

S. (295) Angels were told to think spiritually and . . . tell what they thought. . . . They could not. . . . No word of spiritual speech is like natural speech . . . nor of spiritual writing like natural . . . except the letters, each of which has an entire meaning.

I

B. They could not tell him in natural ideas how absurd must men be to understand him, as if he said the angels could not express themselves at all to him.

S. (304, condensed) There is progression of fibres and vessels in man, and their states from their first *principles where they are in the light* (underlined) and heat to ultimates in shade and not in heat.

B. We see here that the cause of an ultimate is the absence from heat and light.

S. (315) Heat, light, and atmospheres of the natural world conduce absolutely nothing to the image of creation.

B. Therefore the Natural Earth and Atmosphere is a Phantasy.

S. (315, continued) They only open seeds, maintain their shoots in expansion, and put upon them matters which fix them, but this not by Powers derived from their own Sun.

B. Mark this.

S. (316) There is a progression in the forms of animals and vegetables from first principles to ultimates, and from ultimates to first principles. Will and understanding are primes: thought and action ultimates.

B. A going forth and returning.

S. (324) There is nothing in the created universe which has not correspondence with something in man, affections, thoughts, or even organs and viscera of the body . . . not with these as substances but as uses.

B. Things and substances are so different as not to correspond.

(A long portion here of the book has no note made, but Blake read and partly used afterwards many remarks in it, such as: (371) "There is a correspondence of the will with the heart, and of the understanding with the lungs." This recalls all that is said in *Jerusalem* and *Milton* about the furnaces and bellows of Los.)

S. (404, condensed) There is thought out of affection for truth, it is wisdom,—but there is a thought out of memory through the sight of the natural mind.

B. Note this.

S. (410) Love or the will joins itself to wisdom or understanding, and wisdom or understanding does not conjoin itself to love or the will.

B. Mark this.

S. (410, later, condensed) Knowledge which love acquires is not of understanding, but of love. It flows in from the spiritual world not to the understanding but to love in the understanding. It appears as if the understanding received it, but this is a fallacy, and as if love conjoined itself to affection, but this is a fallacy.

B. Mark this. Note this.

S. (410, still later) Love acts through truths, deriving nothing from understanding, but acting as though wisdom came from it, from some determination of Love called affection.

B. Mark this.

S. (411) Therefore love conjoins itself to understanding, not the converse.

B. Mark this.

S. (417) Any one who is familiar with the anatomic structure of the lungs, and collates it with the understanding, can see clearly that the understanding does nothing of itself.

B. Mark.

S. (412, later) My knowledge of the fabric of the lungs fully convinced me that love through its affections conjoins itself to the understanding, and that the understanding does not conjoin itself to the *affection of love.*

B. Mark.

S. (413) The wisdom or understanding, out of the potency given to it by love or the will, is able to receive those things which are light from heaven, and to receive them.

B. Mark this.

S. (414) Love cannot be elevated through honour or gain as an end. . . . Love towards the neighbour from the Lord is the love of wisdom. The light in man corresponding to winter is . . . wisdom without love. . . .

B. Is it not false, then, that Love receives its influx through the understanding, as was asserted in the Society?

S. (419) Material love has become impure through the separation from heavenly love in parents.

B. Therefore it was not created impure and is not naturally so.

S. (419, later) In so far as the love puts heaven in the first place and the world in the second . . . it is raised into the heart of heaven and conjoined to the light of heaven.

B. Therefore it may not receive influx through the understanding.

S. (421) The love or will is defiled in the understanding and by it, if they are not elevated together.

B. Mark this. They are elevated together.

S. (422) The understanding is not become spiritual or celestial, but the love does. When the love is so it makes its spouse, the understanding, spiritual and celestial.

B. underlines this.

S. (432, condensed) The initiament or primitive of man as it is in the womb after conception no man can know because it cannot be seen. It is of spiritual substance that does not fall into natural light. . . . The right half of the brain at smallest is of love, the left of understanding. Its form within is in the form of heaven, but its exterior form was seen in it in opposition to that Order and Form.

B. Heaven and Hell are born together.

In Swedenborg's *Angelic Wisdom concerning the Divine Love* it is also taught that—(288) " Inasmuch as God is a Man, therefore the universal Heaven in the complex is as one man, and it is distinguished into regions and provinces according to the members, viscera, and organs of a man. . . . All these provinces are distinct from one another. . . . The angels who constitute heaven are the recipients of love and wisdom from the Lord, and RECIPIENTS ARE IMAGES."

The last three words relate what may be called the first law of mysticism. It contains a conceivable relation between the IMAGINATION in Blake's sense of the word, and the *Logos*.

CHAPTER XIII

ROBERT'S INVENTION

In the year 1788-89 Blake was not only busy with his studies of Swedenborg, he received from a dream or vision of his dead brother Robert the invention of the kind of printing in which he published all his autograph books. Robert directed him to write and draw in a liquid varnish that would protect a copper plate from being eaten away by acid, and then to leave the plate in an acid bath till only the lines were left standing up. He could then roll an ordinary printing roller soaked with printing ink over the surface and print as from an ordinary block.

As this is usually told from Blake's own account of it, we cannot help understanding it as though Blake were a medium, and the spirit of Robert came to him and spoke to him. Whether such a thing be possible or not seems to be still a matter in dispute with most people, but we have an incorrect idea of Blake if we look upon him as here claiming to be a "medium"; though he would seem to speak as though that were his idea of himself. Whatever the "mediumistic" faculty may be, it is one which imagination does not help, but rather hinders and distorts. Blake's imagination being habitually in a state of boiling activity, ready at the smallest suggestion to boil over, we should expect him to be less of a medium than most people, while his Swedenborgian habit of talk, dating back to before he possessed more than a childish smattering of Swedenborg, would naturally cause him to refer to the dead in such a way that mediums, especially those who were not Swedenborgians, would claim him as one of themselves.

In fact, he seems to have possessed a very slight and easily disturbed and deceived faculty of an occult or psychic sort, showing itself in presentiment and intuition, and leading him as often to errors as to revelations. His views of the subsist-

ence of the influence of the dead upon us were almost
identical with those of Auguste Comte, as was most of his
philosophy. The circle of joined hands at a séance, the
"man exists not but by brotherhood" of Blake's formula, and
the mystic "Humanity" of Comte are all phases of the same
thing, as is the French writer's epigram: "ll y a toujours
quelqu'un qui aura plus d'esprit que qui que ce soit,—c'est
tout-le-monde." The thing is *multiple personality*,—a subject
whose psychology is yet in its infancy. The language in
which Blake spoke was picturesque, and disguised the
Positivism of the ideas, as Positivism, on the other hand,
disguises its own truth by the distressingly unpicturesque
nature of the way in which it is presented.

The letter already referred to of Blake to Hayley, with whom
he was not yet acquainted at the time of Robert's death, written
a few years later, when Hayley had just lost a son, gives a
view of the spiritual communications from Robert that might
have been written by Comte himself, if he had been educated
in the Swedenborgian school. Blake is enclosing a drawing
that he has made of Hayley's son. The letter is dated
Lambeth, May 6, 1800 :—

DEAR SIR—I am very sorry for your immense loss, which is a
repetition of what all feel in this valley of misery and happiness mixed.
I send the shadow of the departed angel and hope that the likeness is
improved. The lips I have again lessened, as you advised, and done a
good many other softenings to the whole. I know that our deceased
friends are more really with us than when they were apparent to our
mortal part. Thirteen years ago I lost a brother, and with his spirit I
converse daily and hourly in the spirit, and see him in my remembrance,
in the region of my imagination. I hear his advice, and even now
write from his dictate. Forgive me for expressing to you my enthusiasm,
which I wish all to partake of, since it is a source of immortal joy, even
in this world. By it I am the companion of angels. May you continue
to be so more and more, and to be more and more persuaded that every
mortal loss is an immortal gain. The ruins of Time build mansions in
Eternity.

I have also sent a proof of Pericles for your remarks, thanking you
for the kindness with which you express them, and feeling heartily
your grief with a brother's sympathy.—I remain, etc.

Some small portion of Blake's ideas of life and death may
be sketched as follows :—Just as while the generations run
on there is seen a personal tendency to *take shape* which is a
spiritual influence that survives the disappearance of a man's
features when they are melted down in his own seed, and is
capable of blending with other features in an equally non-
existent state in a woman's seed, and as it depends on and

yet stamps and moulds mental faculties, when these are still non-existent, so there is something personal that survives by joining in brotherhood the non-existence of each of us through death. In fact, it only becomes free to be fully alive when it ceases to be obliged to work at forming and feeding a mortal body at all. The chief qualities of the framework that is called a mortal body are time and space. The mind, free from these, is necessarily immortal, and is even immortal before it gets free from them. Therefore, the immortal part of the mind (for much of the mind is as mortal as the body, and is only used to keep the body alive and teach it to propagate) is able during life to have communication with immortality, which is the whole mind of those who, being dead, no longer waste mentality on corporeal needs.

The *conditions of identity are different after death*. Minds merge themselves in Mind, as when a sheep-pen is removed the particular portion of the meadow where the sheep were confined merges in the acres around. Yet a characteristic living mind turning itself toward the general mind can communicate with a sympathetic mind merged in the mass. Memory is existence in Time; Imagination is existence in Eternity; Contraries vivify; Space without motion is not yet alive; Space with motion is not space only, but is partly Time; *Space* without *place* is barren; Place is an idea, an imagination; Space is Nature.

This is only a free sketch of a small portion of Blake's creed, not quoted from any particular passages of his, but it may be enough to put us on our guard against reading him in a rough and ready sense which should attribute to him either materialistic spiritualism or Positivist metaphysics.

We must, as Swedenborg warns us, *immerse our minds* in contemplative celestial light for some time before they will work in any other than the corporeal manner, whose *space and time* are its essence, for the corporeal is the manner that our own essence habitually needs for its own purposes, and only habit can conquer habit.

By whatever means of communication Blake received his idea from Robert, even if memory of him produced a vision during waking hours exactly like a dream, and this vision spoke as our dreams do, and told him what to do, the result was that he had a new occupation. It was now possible to print the pictorial poems, and tint them, as his Islander in the Moon had suggested.

After the partnership with Parker was broken off and

the removal completed, Blake gave a large amount of his time in Poland Street to this work, writing little at first, but reading Swedenborg and Lavater when not producing his *Songs of Innocence.*

He also proceeded, with the emulation that was so inherent in him, to *outdo* his own *Songs of Innocence* by beginning to add the *Songs of Experience* to them, though these rather bitter rhymes can hardly have belonged to an *early* period of this secluded and almost solitary section of his life,—the years immediately following Robert's death.

That time is divided—so far as we can learn—in this way. Robert's death in 1787 closes a period that is practically given to art exclusively, and that lasted from the breaking off of the *Poetical Sketches* in 1776, with only *The Island in the Moon* and such *Songs of Innocence* as were written in it at the close and thought too good for its pages.

The troubles over the partnership and its dissolution, with the removal to No. 28 Poland Street, shared the year 1788 with readings from Swedenborg and the writing of the *Book of Thel.* The revelation of the method for printing the *Songs of Innocence* is now received, and these and the *Book of Thel* are put on copper, with the "first stereo" of the *Ghost of Abel*—1788-1789. Blake now writes the part of the *Marriage of Heaven and Hell* aimed at Swedenborg, and begins to put it on copper. While doing so he reads Lavater's *Aphorisms, and annotates them.* (These annotations are given in full in the next chapter. As in the case of the notes to Swedenborg, only just the few lines necessary to understand what Blake was referring to in his note are given from the annotated author.) Then the *Proverbs of Hell* are written and added. This brings Blake's personal work up to 1790, and closes a period. Gilchrist notes the *Flight into Egypt, Christ blessing little Children,* and *Death and Hell teem with Life* (afterwards, he says, engraved in the *Marriage of Heaven and Hell,* leaf 10, as painted in 1790). The reference seems incorrect; page 10 has the Devil reading the *Proverbs of Hell* from a scroll for its pictorial portion.

After this year Blake's style began to change because he was less solitary. He did a long series of fifty plates from designs by Chodowiecki for *Elements of Morality* by Mary Wollstonecraft, and this brought him continually to Johnson's shop, where he met the authoress and also Dr. Price, Dr. Priestley, Godwin, and Tom Paine. Here came Fuseli, who met Mary Wollstonecraft for the first time in 1790.

Blake had struggled through his bereavement and his business disappointments alone, and had struggled through them into poetry, into "believing vision" along with his wife, into an increasing love for her, and the beginning of his great myth, of which the first trace is the mention in *Thel* of the "Eternal Gates' Terrific Porter" who opened the "Northern Bar." We are to know this porter as for many years the laborious spirit inhabiting Blake, who is called *Urthona* and *Los* under different aspects, as told in all the later poems.

Blake was now thirsting for a little "jostling in the street," though he admits that "great things" are not done by it. He threw himself with delight into the revolutionary talk that he heard at Johnson's, and, as usual, was not satisfied unless he could outshine every one else. He came amongst them with his *Song of Liberty* in his hand, and walked out from them into the streets of London with a cap of Liberty on his head. It was a very unsafe thing to do. The mob might have lynched him in the name of order. We do not hear that any other of Johnson's guests defied public opinion in this way.

Blake persuaded himself for a while that he was finding friends. Friendship—the half-way house between selfhood (all evil) and eternal brotherhood, the "multiple personality," the ultimate good—was his ideal all through life, yet it was only in his later years that his exuberant character and terrific self-love could be toned down enough to make any friendship safe from resentment and quarrel, dearly as he loved every human being that came near him and said a few kind words to him. He, in fact, was so eager for unity with his fellows that, in spite of his mental contempt for people, he would respond from the heart to the merest civility. He studied Lavater's *Aphorisms* at this time with the serious intention of educating himself in the art of friendship, as his naïve and shrewd marginal notes show on almost every page.

One touch seems to have roused him particularly. He could not have sat still with quiet pulses when learning that these *Aphorisms* were composed (by the hundred) during a single autumn while Lavater was moving about from place to place.

Here was a record to pull down! The *Proverbs of Hell* were probably written as an "out-doing" of this, in some limited tim : perhaps half-an-hour. There is nothing, even in their concentration, that would oblige Blake to pause and meditate. He became stupid when he thought slowly. Consideration was done by him unconsciously, when he did not know that he was thinking at all. Then, in a state of excitement, the result came tearing forth in "human form," —that is, in living utterance of poetic picturesqueness.

CHAPTER XIV

LAVATER

LAVATER'S *Aphorisms* form a wise and pleasant little book. The style is not without a sort of large-eyed childishness in its innocent depth of well-meaning thought. Blake not only read each one of the aphorisms with careful consideration, but wrote marginal comments on them, which he considered made his own private copy of the book a composite work done in a sort of personally separate, but spiritually joined, collaboration. He wrote "Will Blake" beneath the name "Lavater" on the title-page, and surrounded the two with the outline of a heart, in the conventional form used for valentines and playing-cards.

The sentence of Lavater which led to the making of these marginal notes is this:

APHORISM 633.

If you mean to know yourself, interline such of these aphorisms as affect you agreeably in reading, and set a mark to such as left (*sic*) a sense of uneasiness with you, and then show your copy to whom you please.

On the first page Blake refers the reader to this for the reason of his annotations.

Gilchrist has given a selection from them. But as it is the purpose of this book to set forth Blake visibly and accurately, we cannot spare a word of such valuable help as we get here from his own hand. Gilchrist says that Fuseli remarked, when Blake showed him these annotations, that any one could read his character in them. The frontispiece that Blake engraved to the book is from a painting by Fuseli, representing a theatrical sort of eighteenth-century Hamlet sitting in an elaborate attitude of meditation, while a cherub in the sky shows him a tablet with ΓΝΩΘΙ ΣΕΑΥΤΟΝ

("Know thyself") in capital letters upon it. The engraving is good. It is accurately and conscientiously Fuseli, and Fuseli treated with a silky suavity and richness of surface in the hero's clothing, and a pleasant, not too heavy, obscurity in the mysterious clouds that fill his study. Here follow such aphorisms as are annotated with their numbers, and Blake's comments, printed in Italics:

1.

Know, in the first place, that mankind agree in essence as they do in their limbs and senses.

(*This is true Christian philosophy, far above all abstraction.*)

3.

As in looking upward each beholder thinks himself the centre of the sky, so Nature formed her individuals that each must see himself the centre of being.

(*Let me refer to a remark on Aphorism 533, and another on 630.*)

8.

Who pursues means of enjoyment contradictory, irreconcilable, and self-destructive is a fool, or what is called a sinner. Sin and destruction of order are the same.

(*A golden sentence.*)

11.

The less you can enjoy, the poorer and scantier yourself,—the more you can enjoy, the richer, the more vigorous.
(Underlined by Blake.)
You enjoy with wisdom or with folly as the gratification of your appetites capacitates or unnerves your powers.

(*False, for weak is the joy that is never wearied.*)

13.

Joy and grief decide character. What exalts prosperity? What embitters grief? What leaves us indifferent? What interests us? As the interest of man, so his God. As his God, so he.

(*All gold.*)

14.

What is a man's interest? What constitutes his God, the ultimate of his wishes, the end of his existence? Either that which on every occasion he communicates with the most unrestrained cordiality, or hides from every profane eye and ear with mysterious awe,—to which he makes every other thing a mere appendix ;—the vortex, the centre, the comparative point from which he sets out, on which he fixes, to which he irresistibly returns ;—that, at the loss of which you may safely think him inconsolable ; that which he rescues from the grip of danger with equal anxiety and boldness.

(*All gold.*)

The story of the painter and the prince is well known. To get at the best piece in the artist's collection the prince ordered " Fire ! " to be cried in the neighbourhood. At the first noise the artist abruptly left the prince and seized his darling, his Titian. The alarm proved a false one, but the object of purchase was fixed. The application is easy. Of thousands it may be decided what loss, what gain would affect them most. This the Sage of Nazareth meant when He said, " Where thy treasure is, there will thy heart be also." The object of your love is your God.

(*This should be written in gold letters on our temples.*)

16.

The greatest of characters no doubt would be he who, free of all trifling accidental helps, could see objects through one grand immutable medium, always at hand and proof against illusion and time, reflecting every object in its true shape and colour, through all the fluctuations of things.

(*This was Christ.*)

20.

Distinguish with exactness in thyself and others between wishes and will in the strictest sense.

Who has many wishes in general has but little will. Who has energy of will has few diverging wishes. Whose will is bent with energy on *one* must renounce the wishes for *many* things. Who cannot do this is not stamped with the majesty of human nature. The energy of choice, the union of various powers for one, is alone *will*, born under the agonies of self-denial and renounced desires.

(*Admirable. Regeneration.*)

21.

Calmness of will is a sign of grandeur. The vulgar, far from hiding their *will*, blab their wishes. A single spark of occasion discharges the child of passions into a thousand crackers of desire.

(*Uneasy.*)

28.

The glad gladdens. Who gladdens not is not glad. Who is fatal to others is so to himself. To him heaven, earth, wisdom, folly, virtue, and vice are equal. To such an one tell neither good nor bad of thyself.

(Underlined all but the last sentence by Blake.)

32.

Let the degree of egotism be the measure of confidence.

(*Uneasy.*)

36.

Who begins with severity in judging another ends commonly with falsehood.

(*False. Severity of judgment is a great virtue.*)

37.

The smiles that encourage severity of judgment hide malice and insincerity.

(*False. Aphorisms should be universally true.*)

39.

Who without pressing temptation tells a lie will without pressing temptation act ignobly and meanly.

(*Uneasy: false. A man may tell a lie for his own pleasures, but if any one is hurt by his lying he will confess his lie. See No. 124.*)

40.

Who under pressing temptation to lie adheres to truth, nor to the profane betrays aught of a sacred trust, is near the summit of wisdom and virtue.

(*Excellent.*)

44.

You can depend on no man, on no friend but him who can depend on himself. He only who acts consequentially towards himself will act so towards others, and *vice versa.*

Man is for ever the same,—the same under every form, in all situations and relations that admit of free and unrestrained exertion. The same regard which you have for yourself you have for others, for nature, for the invisible Noumen which you call God. Who has witnessed one free and unrestrained act of yours has witnessed all.

(All but the first and third sentences underlined by Blake.)

54.

Frequent laughing has been long called a sign of a little mind, whilst the scarcer smile of harmless quiet has been complimented as the mark of a noble heart. But to abstain laughing and exciting laughter, merely not to offend, or to risk giving offence, or not to debase the inward dignity of character, is a power unknown to many a vigorous mind.

(*I hate scarce smiles: I love laughing.*)

59.

A sneer is often the sign of heartless malignity.

(*Damn sneerers.*)

61.

I know not which of these two I should wish to avoid most, the scoffer at virtue and religion who with heartless villainy butchers innocence and truth, or the pietist, who crawls, groans, blubbers, and secretly says to gold, Thou art my hope! and to his belly, Thou art my god!

(*I hate crawlers.*) (The epithets here underlined by Blake.)

62.

All moral dependence on him who has been guilty of *one* act of positive cool villainy against an acknowledged virtuous and noble character is credulity, imbecility, insanity.

(—— *is being like him, rather.*)

63.

The most stormy ebullitions of passion, from blasphemy to murder, are less terrific than one single act of cool villainy. A still *rabies* is more dangerous than the paroxysms of a fever. Fear the boisterous savage of passion less than the sedately grinning villain.

(*Brave!*) (All underlined by Blake.)

66.

Can he love truth who can take a knave to his bosom?

(*No.*) (Underlined by Blake.)

67.

There are offences against individuals to all appearance trifling which are capital offences against the human race. Fly him who can commit them.

(Underlined by Blake.)

68.

There ought to be a perpetual whisper in the ear of plain honesty— "Take heed not even to pronounce the name of a knave." He will make the very sound of his name a handle of mischief. And do you think a knave begins mischief to leave off? Know this : whether he be overcome or be foiled, he will wrangle on.

(*Therefore pronounce him a knave. Why should honesty fear a knave?*)

69.

Humility and love, whatever obscurities may involve religious tenets, constitute the essence of true religion. The humble is formed to adore, the loving to associate with eternal love.

(*Sweet.*) (The second sentence underlined.)

70.

Have you ever seen a vulgar mind warm or humble or a proud one that could love ? Where pride begins, love ceases. As love, so humility. As both, so the still real power of man.

(*Pride may love.*)

71.

Everything may be mimicked by hypocrisy, but humility and love united. The humblest star twinkles most in the darkest night. The more rare humility and love united, the more radiant when they meet.

(*All this may be mimicked very well. This aphorism certainly was an oversight, for what are all crawlers but mimickers of humility and love?*)

73.

Modesty is silent when it would not be improper to speak. The humble, without being called upon, never recollects to say anything of himself.

(*Uneasy.*)

78.

The wrath that, on conviction, subsides into mildness is the wrath of a generous mind.

80.

Thousands are hated, while none are ever loved, without real cause. The amiable alone can be loved.

81.

He who is loved and commands love when he corrects or is the cause of uneasiness must be loveliness itself ; and

82.

He who can love him in the moment of correction is the most amiable of mortals.

83.

He to whom you may tell anything may see everything and will betray nothing.

(The above five are underlined by Blake.)

86.

The freer you feel yourself in the presence of another, the more free is he : who is free makes free.

(*Rather uneasy.*)

92.

Who instantly does the best that can be done, what no other could have done, and what all must acknowledge to be the best, is a genius and a hero at once.

(*Uneasy.*)

93.

The discovery of truth by slow progressive meditation is wisdom. Intuition of truth not preceded by perceptible meditation is genius.

(Underlined by Blake.)

94.

The degree of genius is determined by its velocity, clearness, depth, simplicity, copiousness, extent of glance (*coup d'œil*), and instantaneous intuition of the whole at once.

(*Copiousness of glance !*)

96.

Dread more the blunderer's friendship than the calumniator's enmity.

(*I doubt this.*)

97.

He only who can give durability to his exertions has genuine power and energy of mind.

(*Uneasy : sterling.*)

98.

Before thou callest a man hero or genius, investigate whether his exertion has features of durability, for all that is celestial, all genius, is the offspring of immortality.

(*Uneasy : sterling.*)

99.

Who despises all that is despicable is made to be impressed with all that is grand.

(Underlined by Blake.)

107.

Who takes from you ought to give in his turn, or he is a thief. I distinguish taking and accepting, robbing and receiving. Many give already by the mere wish to give, their still unequivocal wish of improvement and gratitude, while it draws from us, opens treasures within us that might have remained locked up even to ourselves.

(*Noble and generous.*)

114.

Who writes as he speaks, speaks as he writes, looks as he speaks and writes, is honest.

(Underlined by Blake.)

124.

Who has a daring eye tells downright truths and downright lies.

(*Contrary to No. 39, but most true.*)

141.

Many trifling inattentions, neglects, indiscretions, are so many un-equivocal proofs of dull frigidity, hardness, and extreme egotism.

(*Rather uneasy.*)

150.

As your enemies and your friends so are you.

(*Very uneasy.*)

151.

You may depend upon it that he is a good man whose intimate friends are all good, and whose enemies are characters decidedly bad.

(*Uneasy. I fear I have not many enemies.*)

157.

Say not you know another till you have divided an inheritance with him.

(*!!*) (Underlined by Blake.)

163.

Who at the pressing solicitation of bold and noble confidence hesitates one moment before he consents, proves himself at once inexorable.

(*Uneasy. I don't believe it.*)

164.

Who at the solicitations of cunning, self-interest, or impudence hesitates one moment before he refuses, proves himself at once a silly giver.

(*Uneasy.*)

168.

Whenever a man undergoes a considerable change in consequence of being observed by others, whenever he assumes another gait, another language than what he had before he thought himself observed, be advised to guard yourself against him.

(*Rather uneasy.*)

170.

I am prejudiced in favour of him who can solicit boldly without impudence. He has faith in human nature.

176.

As a man's salutation, so the total of his character. In nothing do we lay ourselves so open as in our manner of meeting and salutation.

K

177.

Be afraid of him who meets you with a friendly aspect and in the midst of a flattering salutation avoids your direct, open look.

(The above three underlined by Blake.)

185.

All flattery is a sign of littleness.

(*Not always.*)

190.

The more honesty a man has, the less he affects the air of a saint. The affectation of sanctity is a blotch on the face of piety.

(*Bravo !*)

191.

There are more heroes than saints (heroes I call rulers over the minds and destinies of men)—more saints than humane characters. Him who humanises all that is within and around himself adore. I know but of one such by tradition.

(*Sweet.*)

193.

Who seeks those that are greater than himself, their greatness enjoys, and forgets his greatest qualities in their greater ones, is already truly great.

(*I hope I do not flatter myself that this is pleasant to me.*)

215.

The friend of order has made half his way to virtue.

(Underlined by Blake.)

216.

There is no mortal truly wise and restless at once. Wisdom is the repose of minds.

(*Rather uneasy.*)

232.

The connoisseur in painting discovers an original by some great line, though covered with dust and disguised by daubing, so he who studies man discovers a valuable character by some original trait, though unnoticed, disguised, or debased. Ravished at the discovery, he feels it his duty to restore it to its own genuine splendour. Him who in spite of contemptuous pretenders has the boldness to do this, choose for your friend.

(The last sentence underlined by Blake.)

234.

Who writes what he should tell, and dares not tell what he writes, is either like a wolf in sheep's clothing, or like a sheep in a wolf's skin.

(*Some cannot tell what they can write, though they dare.*)

238.

Know that the great art to love your enemy consists in never losing sight of the *man* in him. Humanity has power over all that is human. The most in human man still remains man, and never *can* throw off all taste for what becomes a man. But you must learn to wait.

(*None can see the man in the enemy. If he is ignorantly so, he is not truly an enemy,—if maliciously, not a man. I cannot love my enemy, for my enemy is not a man. But I can love him as a beast, and wish to beat him.*)

243.

He who welcomes the look of the good is good himself.

(Underlined by Blake.)

244.

I know deists whose religiousness I venerate, and atheists whose honesty and nobleness of mind I wish for, but I have not yet seen the man who could have tempted me to think him honest who publicly acted the Christian whilst privately he was a positive deist.

(*Bravo!*) (The last two lines underlined by Blake.)

246.

He who laughed at you till he got to your door, flattered you as you opened it, felt the force of your argument while he was with you, applauded when he rose, and after he went away blasts you, has the most indisputable title to an archdukedom in hell.

(*Such a one I could never forgive whilst he continued such a one.*) (All underlined, though irregularly, by Blake.)

251.

Ask not only, "Am I hated?" but, "by whom?"—"Am I loved?" but "why?" As the good love thee, the bad will hate thee.

(*Uneasy.*) The last sentence underlined by Blake.

262.

Who can act or perform as if each work or action were the first, the last, and only one in his life, is great.

(Underlined by Blake.)

266.

We can do all by speech and silence. He who understands the double art of speaking opportunely to the moment and of saying not a syllable more or less than it demanded, and he who can wrap himself up in silence when every word would be vain, will understand to connect energy with patience.

(*Uneasy.*)

268.

Let the unhappiness you feel at another's errors and the happiness you enjoy in their (*sic*) perfections be the measure of your progress in wisdom and virtue.

(*Excellent.*)   (Underlined by Blake.)

269.

Who becomes every day more sagacious in observing his own faults and the perfections of another, without either envying him or despairing of himself, is ready to mount the ladder on which angels ascend and descend.

(*Noble.*)

272.

The more there is of mind in your solitary employments, the more dignity there is in your character.

(Underlined by Blake.)

275.

He who can at all times sacrifice pleasure to duty approaches sublimity.

(Marginal score by Blake.)

279.

Between the best and the worst there are, you say, innumerable degrees—and you are right. But admit that I am right too in saying that the best and the worst differ only in one thing—in the object of their love.

(*Would to God that every one would consider this.*)

280.

What is it you love in him you love? What is it you hate in him you hate? Answer this closely to yourself, pronounce it loudly, and you will know yourself and him.

(*All gold.*)

282.

If you see one cold and vehement at the same time, set him down for a fanatic.

(*i.e. hypocrite.*)

285.

Who can hide magnanimity stands on the supreme degree of human nature, and is admired by the world of spirits.

(Underlined by Blake.)

291.

He has not a little of the devil in him who prays and bites.

(There is no other devil. He who bites without praying is only a beast.)

292.

He who when called upon to tell a disagreeable truth tells it boldly and has one, is both bolder and milder than he who nibbles in a low voice and never ceases nibbling.

(Damn such.) (Underlined from *disagreeable* to *voice.*)

293.

As the shadow follows the body, so restless sullenness the female knave.

(This form of the aphorism is from the second edition, showing the adoption of a correction of the press made by Blake in the first. The word *sullenness* was there printed *subtleness.*

295.

Be not the fourth friend of him who had three before and lost them.

(Excellent rule.)

298.

Want of friends argues either want of humility or courage, or both.

(Uneasy.)

299.

He who at a table of forty covers, thirty-nine of which are exquisite and one indifferent, lays hold of that, and with a "damn your dinner!" dashes it in the landlord's face, should be sent to Bethlem or Bridewell, and whither he who blasphemes a book, a work of art, or perhaps a man of nine-and-thirty good, and but one bad quality, and calls those fools or flatterers who, engrossed by the superior number of good qualities, would fain forget the bad one (?—the missing query at the end here is added by Blake, who answers the question thus).

(To hell till he behaves better! Mark that I do not believe there is such a thing literally, but hell is the being shut up in the possession of corporeal desires which shortly weary the man, FOR ALL LIFE IS HOLY.)

318.

Keep him at least three paces distant who hates bread, music, and the laugh of a child.

(*The best in the book.*)

323.

Between passion and lie there is not a finger's breadth.

(*Lie is the contrary to passion.*)

324.

Avoid like a serpent him who writes impertinently yet speaks politely.

(*A dog! Get a stick to him!*) (Underlined by Blake.)

328.

Search carefully if one patiently finishes what he boldly begun.

(*Uneasy.*)

329.

Who comes from the kitchen has something of its smoke. Who adheres to a sect has something of its cant. The college air pursues the student, and dry inhumanity him who herds with literary pedants.

(The second sentence underlined by Blake.)

331.

Call him truly religious who believes in something higher, more powerful, more living than visible nature ; and who, clear as his own existence, feels his conformity to that superior being.

(Underlined by Blake.)

332.

Superstition always inspires littleness ; religion, grandeur of mind. The superstitious raises beings inferior to himself to deities.

(*No man was ever truly superstitious who was not truly religious as far as he knew.*

The superstitious is ignorant honesty. This is beloved of God and man.

I do not know that there is such a thing as superstition in the strict sense of the word.

A man must deceive himself before he is superstitious, and so he is a hypocrite.

Hypocrisy is as distinct from superstition as the wolf from the lamb.)

(These comments seem to have been written separately in this order on the margins, and when writing the last Blake drew his pen through the word "Superstition" in the aphorism, and substituted *Hypocrisy*. In the same manner he corrected "superstitious" in the aphorism into *hypocrite*.)

333.

Who are the saints of humanity ? Those whom perpetual habits of goodness and grandeur have made nearly unconscious that they are good or grand,—heroes with infantine simplicity.

(*This is heavenly !*) (The last four words underlined by Blake.)

335.

The jealous is possessed by a " fine mad devil " and a dull spirit at once.

(*Pity the jealous.*)

342.

He alone has energy that cannot be deprived of it.
(Underlined by Blake.)

343.

Sneers are the blasts that precede quarrels.
(*Hate the sneerer !*)

344.

Who loves will not be adored.
(*False.*)

349.

No great character cavils.
(Underlined by Blake.)

355.

He can love who can forget all—and nothing.
(Underlined by Blake.)

356

The purest religion is the most refined Epicurism. He who in the smallest given time can enjoy most of what he shall never repent, and what furnishes enjoyments still more unexhausted, still less changeable, is the most religious and the most voluptuous of men.

(*True Christian philosophy.*) (Underlined as far as *enjoyments* by Blake.)

360.

The generous who is always just, and the just who is always generous may, unannounced, approach the throne of God.

(Underlined from *may* by Blake.)

365.

Let me once more in other words repeat it—he is the king of kings who longs for nothing and wills but *one* at once.

(Underlined from *and* by Blake.)

366.

Spare the lover without flattering his passions. To make the pangs of love the butt of ridicule is unwise and harsh. Soothing meekness and wisdom subdue in else unconquerable things.

(*And consider that* LOVE IS LIFE.)

367.

There is none so bad (as) to do the twentieth part of the evil he might, nor any so good as to do the tenth part of the good it is in his power to do. Judge yourself by the good you might do, and neglect; and of others by the evil they might do, and omit; and your judgment will be poised between too much indulgence for yourself and too much severity on others

(*Most excellent.*)

370.

To him who is simple and inexhaustible, like nature, simple and inexhausted nature resigns her sway.

(Underlined from *like* by Blake.)

373.

How can he be pious who loves not the beautiful, whilst piety is nothing but the love of beauty? Beauty we call the *most varied one*, the *most united variety*. Could there be a man who should harmoniously unite each variety of knowledge and of powers, would he not be most beautiful? Would he not be a god?

(*This is our Lord.*) (*God* underlined by Blake.)

375.

The unloved cannot love.
(*Doubtful.*)

376.

Let the object of love be careful to lose none of its loveliness.

(Marked with a side asterisk by Blake, but not with any comment. Probably intended to arrest the attention of Mrs. Blake.)

379.

We cannot be great if we calculate how great we, and how little others are; and calculate not how great others, and how minute, how impotent ourselves.

(*Uneasy.*)

381.

He loves unalterably who keeps within the bounds of love,—who always shows somewhat less than what he is possessed of, nor ever utters a syllable or gives a hint of more than what in fact remains behind (and who) is just and friendly in the same degree.

(*Is possessed, syllable, more than,* and *behind* underlined by Blake.)

390.

There is a manner of forgiving so divine that you are ready to embrace the offender for having called it forth.

(*This I cannot conceive.*)

391.

Expect the secret resentment of him whom your forgiveness has impressed with a sense of his inferiority. Expect the resentment of the woman whose professed love you have repulsed. Yet, surer still, expect the unceasing rancour of envy against the progress of genius.

(*If you expect his resentment you do not forgive him* NOW, *though you did once. Forgiveness of enemies can only come upon their repentance.*)

397.

Whatever is visible is the vessel, or veil, of the invisible past, present, future. As man penetrates to this more or perceives it less he raises or depresses his dignity of being.

(*A vision of the Eternal Now.*)

398.

Let none turn over books or roam the stars in quest of God who sees Him not in man.

(Underlined from *in quest* by Blake.)

399.

He alone is good who, though possessed of energy, prefers virtue with the appearance of weakness to the invitation of acting brilliantly ill.

(Noble. But, mark! Active Evil is better than Passive good. (*With the appearance, to the invitation, brilliantly ill* underlined by Blake.)

400.

Intuition (what the French call *coup d'œil*) is the greatest, simplest, most inexhausted gift a mortal can receive from heaven. Who has that has all, and who has it not has little of what constitutes the good and great.

(*Uneasy. Doubtful.*)

403.

As the presentiment of the possible deemed impossible, so genius, so heroism. The hero, the man of genius, are prophets.

(The last eight words underlined by Blake.)

(*Note.*—In Blake's edition, the first, this ended with the extra words, "every genius, every hero is a prophet." These were struck out in the second edition, whose corrected numberings, different from those of Blake's copy by a sustained error often after 285, are followed here.)

404.

He who goes one step beyond his real faith or presentiment is in danger of deceiving himself and others.

(*Uneasy.*)

406.

He who to obtain much will suffer little or nothing can never be called great, and none (can) ever (be called) little who, to obtain one great object, will suffer much.

(*The man who does this is a sectary ; therefore not great.*)

409.

You beg as you question, you give as you answer.

(*Excellent.*) (Underlined by Blake.)

413.

He knows little of the man who trusts him with much that cares for no one.

(*So he does.*) (The translator has made this rather obscure by his unhappy arrangement of words. The meaning, of course, is, " He who trusts with much the man who cares for no one, knows little of him.")

414.

Love sees what no eye sees, love hears what no ear hears, and what never rose in the heart of man love prepares for its object.

(*Most excellent.*) (*Hears what no ear hears, never rose in the heart of man,* and *love prepares for* underlined by Blake.)

416.

Him who arrays malignity in good nature, and treachery in familiarity, a miracle of omnipotence alone can make an honest man.

(*No omnipotence can act against order.*)

417.

He who sets fire to one part of a town to rob more safely in another is, no doubt, a villain. What will you call him who, to avert suspicion from himself, accuses the innocent of a crime he knows himself guilty of, and means to commit again ?

(*Damn him !*)

422.

The richer you are, the more calmly you bear the reproach of poverty. The more genius you have, the more easily you bear the reproach of mediocrity.

(The second sentence underlined by Blake.)

425.

There is no instance of a miser becoming a prodigal without losing his intellect, but there are thousands of prodigals becoming misers. If, therefore, your turn be profuse, nothing is so much to be avoided as avarice. And if you be a miser, procure a physician who can cure an irremediable disorder.

(*Excellent.*) (*Your turn be profuse, nothing is so much to be avoided as avarice*, underlined by Blake.)

427.

Avarice has sometimes been the flaw of great minds. Great men produce effects that cannot be produced by a thousand of the vulgar, but great minds are stamped by expanded benevolence, unattainable by most.

(*With expanded benevolence* underlined by Blake.)

430.

He is much greater and more authentic who produces one thing entire and perfect than he who does many by halves.

(*Uneasy.*)

434.

Say what you please of your humanity, no wise man will ever believe a syllable while *I* and *mine* are the two only gates at which you sally forth and enter, and through which alone all must pass who seek admittance.

(*Uneasy.*)

437.

Who hides love to bless with unmixed happiness is great, like the King of heaven.

(*I do not understand this, or else I do not agree to it. I know not wha' hiding love means.*)

(Ambiguous in the translation. The word *his* understood before *love* would suggest the meaning, Who hides the fact that he would love to bless, etc.)

439.

Trust not him with your secrets who, when left alone in your room, turns over your papers.

(*Uneasy, but I hope I should not do it.*)

440.

A woman whose ruling passion is not vanity is superior to any man of equal faculties.

(*Such a woman I adore.*)

441.

He who has but one way of seeing everything is as important for him who studies man as fatal to friendship.

(*This I do not understand.*)

442.

He who has written will write again, says the Frenchman. He who has written against you will write against you again. He who has begun certain things is under the curse of leaving off no more.

(Blake crossed out the second sentence, and corrected the word *curse* in the last into *blessing.*)

450.

Nothing is more impartial than the stream-like public—always the same, and never the same,—of whom, sooner or later, each misrepresented character obtains justice, and each calumniated, honour. He who cannot wait for that is either ignorant of human nature, or feels that he was not made for honour.

(*Uneasy.*)

452.

The obstinacy of the indolent and weak is less conquerable than that of the fiery and bold.

(Underlined by Blake.)

453.

Who, with calm wisdom alone, imperceptibly directs the obstinacy of others, will be the most eligible friend or the most dreadful enemy.

(*This must be a grand fellow.*)

455.

He is condemned to depend on no man's modesty and honour who dares not depend on his own.

(*Uneasy.*)

The frigid smiler, crawling, indirect, obtrusive, brazen-faced, is a scorpion whip of destiny. Avoid him.

(*Never forgive him till he mends.*)

476.

Distrust your heart and the durability of your fame if, from the stream of occasion, you snatch at a handful of foam ; deny the stream, and give its name to the frothy, bursting bubble.

(*Uneasy. This I lament that I have done.*)

477.

If you ask me which is the real hereditary sin of human nature, do you imagine I shall answer pride, or luxury, or ambition, or egotism? No, I shall say, Indolence. Who conquers indolence will conquer all the rest.

(*Pride, fulness of bread, and abundance of idleness was the sin of Sodom. See Ezekiel, chap. xvi. 49th verse.*)

479.

An entirely honest man, in the severe sense of the word, exists no more than an entirely dishonest knave. The best and the worst are only approximations of those qualities. Who are those that never contradict themselves? Yet honesty never contradicts itself. Who are those that always contradict themselves? Yet knavery is mere self-contradiction. Thus the knowledge of man determines not the things themselves, but their proportions—the quantum of congruities and incongruities.

(*Man is a twofold being—one part capable of evil and the other capable of good. That which is capable of good is not also capable of evil, but that which is capable of evil is also capable of good. This aphorism assumes to consider man as simple, and yet capable of evil. Now, evil and good cannot exist in a simple being, for thus two contraries would spring from one essence, which is impossible. But if man is considered as only evil, and God only good, how then is regeneration effected which turns the evil to good by casting out the evil by the good? See Matthew, chap. xii. verses 26, 27, 28, 29.*)

486.

Sense seeks and finds the thought; the thought seeks and finds genius.

(*And vice versa. Genius finds thought without sense, and thought thus produced finds sense.*)

493.

No wheedler loves.

(*Better a wheedler than no lover, though.*)

494.

Great minds comprehend more in a word, a look, the squeeze of a hand, than vulgar men in day-long conversation or the most assiduous correspondence.

(*I agree.*)

496.

The poet who composes not before the moment of inspiration, and, as that leaves him, ceases, composes, and he alone, for all men, all classes, and all ages.

(*Most excellent.*) (*The moment of inspiration, leaves him, ceases, and he alone for all, all classes, all ages,* underlined by Blake.)

497.

He who has frequent moments of complete existence is a hero, though not laurelled, is crowned without crowns, a king. He only who has enjoyed immortal moments can reproduce them.

(*O that men would seek immortal moments! O that men would converse with God!*) (*Who has frequent, complete existence, not laurelled, without crowns, a king, who has enjoyed,* and *moments can reproduce them,* underlined by Blake.)

498.

The greater that which you can hide, the greater yourself.

(*Pleasant.*) (The first five words singly underlined, the last four trebly by Blake.)

504.

He who cannot forgive a trespass of malice to his enemy has never yet tasted the most sublime enjoyment of love.

(*Uneasy. This I know not.*)

508.

You may have hot enemies without having a warm friend, but not a fervid friend without a bitter enemy. The qualities of your friends will be those of your enemies : cold friends, cold enemies—half friends, half enemies—fervid enemies, warm friends.

(*Very uneasy, but* truth.)

511.

He who reforms himself has done more towards reforming the public than a crowd of noisy, impotent patriots.

(*Excellent.*) (All underlined by Blake.)

513.

He will do great things who can avert his words and thoughts from past irremediable evils.

(*Not if evils are past sins, for these a man should never avert his thoughts from.*)

516.

He who is ever intent on great ends has an eagle eye for great means, and scorns not the smallest.

(*Great ends never look at means, but produce them* (*sic*) *spontaneously.*)

522.

Take from Luther his roughness and fiery courage, from Calvin his hectic obstinacy, from Erasmus his timid prudence, hypocrisy and fanaticism from Cromwell, from Henry IV. his sanguine character, mysticism from Fénelon, from Hume his all-unhinging subtilty, love of paradox and brooding suspicion from Rousseau, naivety and elegance of knavery from Voltaire, from Milton the extravagance of his all-personifying fancy, from Raphael his dryness and nearly hard precision, from Rubens his supernatural luxury of colour—deduct this oppressive *exuberance* from each, rectify them according to your own taste ; what will be the result ? Your own correct, pretty, flat, useful—for me, to be sure, quite convenient vulgarity. And why this amongst maxims of humanity ? That you may learn to know this exuberance, this leaven, of each great character, and its effects on contemporaries and posterity, that you may know where the d e f is, there must be a b c. He alone has knowledge of man who raises each character and makes it that which it shall be, and something more or less than it shall be.

(*Deduct from a rose its redness, from a lily its whiteness, from a diamond its hardness, from a sponge its softness, from an oak its height, from a daisy its lowness, and rectify everything in nature as thy philosophers do, and then we shall return to chaos, and God will be compelled to be eccentric, if He creates, O happy philosopher! Variety does not necessarily suppose deformity, for a rose and lily are variations, and both beautiful. Beauty is exuberant, but not of ugliness, but of beauty, and if ugliness is adjoined to beauty, it is not the exuberance of beauty. So, if Raphael is hard and dry, it is not his genius, but an accident acquired; for, how can substance and accident be predicated of the same essence? I cannot conceive. But substance gives tincture to the accident, and makes it physiognomic. Aphorism 47 speaks of the heterogeneous, which all extravagance is, but exuberance not.*)

(Aphorism 47. Man has an inward sense of consequence, of all that is pertinent. This sense is the essence of humanity. This, developed and determined, characterises him; this (when) displayed in his education. The more strict you are in observing what is pertinent and (what is) heterogeneous in character, actions, works of art and literature, the wiser, nobler, greater, the more humane, yourself.)

523.

I have been too often tempted at the daily relation of new knaveries to despise human nature in every individual, till on minute anatomy of each trick I found that the knave was only an enthusiast, or momentary fool. This discovery of momentary folly, symptoms of which assail the wisest and the best, has thrown a great consolatory light on my inquiries into man's moral nature. By this the theorist is enabled to assign to each class and each individual their own peculiar fit of vice or folly, and to contrast the ludicrous or dismal catalogue with the pleasing one of sentiment and virtue more properly their own.

(*Man is the ark of God. The Mercy Seat is above upon the Ark. Cherubims guard it on either side. In the midst is the Holy Law. Man is either the ark of God or a phantom of the earth and of the water. If thou seekest by human policy to guide this ark, remember Uzzah, 2 Samuel, chap. vi. Knaveries are not human nature. Knaveries are knaveries. See No. 559. This aphorism seems to me to want discrimination.*)

No. 559. He who feels himself impelled to calumniate the good need not much doubt the existence of dæmoniacs.)

524.

He who is master of the fittest moment to crush his enemy, and magnanimously neglects it, is born to be a conqueror.

(*This was old George the Second.*)

529.

A great woman not imperious, a fair woman not vain, a woman of common talents not jealous, an accomplished woman who scorns to shine, are four wonders just great enough to be divided among the four quarters of the globe.

(*Let the men do their duty and the women will be such wonders. The female life lives from the light of the male. See a man's female dependants; you know the man.*)

533.

Depend not much upon your rectitude if you are uneasy in the presence of the good ; nor trust to your humility if you are mortified when you are not noticed.

(*Easy.*) (This to the first part, underlined by Blake. To the second part—*Uneasy.*)

539.

He who hates the wisest and best of men hates the Father of men, for where is the Father of men to be seen but in the most perfect of his children ?

(*This is pure worship.*) (The last part underlined ; in the first part the word *hates* in each place where it occurs is crossed out and *loves* written over.

542.

He who adores an impersonal God has none, and without guide or rudder launches on an immense abyss that first absorbs his powers and next himself.

(*Most superlatively beautiful, and most affectionately holy and pure. Would to God that all men would consider it.*) (Underlined all through by Blake.)

544.

The enemy of art is the enemy of nature. Art is nothing but the highest sagacity and exertion of human nature ; and what nature will he honour who honours not the human ?

(*Human nature is the image of God.*) (The last part underlined, in this and the two next, by Blake.)

546.

Where is much pretension much has been borrowed. Nature never pretends.

546.

Do you think him a common man who can make what is common exquisite ?

549.

Whose promise may you depend upon ? His who dares refuse what he knows he cannot perform,—who promises calmly, strictly, conditionally, and never excites a hope which he may disappoint.

(*Promise may you, who dares refuse, he cannot perform*, and all from *calmly* underlined by Blake.)

550.

You promise as you speak.
(Underlined by Blake.)

552.

Avoid him who speaks softly and writes sharply.

(*Ah, rogue! I would be thy hangman!*) (All but the first two words underlined by Blake.)

556.

Neither patience nor inspiration can give wings to a snail. You waste your own force, you destroy what remained of energy in the indolent, by urging him to move beyond his rate of power.

(The first sentence underlined by Blake.)

563.

Your humility is equal to your desire of being unobserved in your acts of virtue.

(*True humility.*) (All underlined by Blake.)

564.

There are certain light, characteristic, momentary features of man which, in spite of all masks and all exterior mummery, represent him as he is, and shall be. If once in an individual you have discovered one ennobling feature, let him debase it, let it at times shrink from him, no matter ; he will in the end prove superior to thousands of his critics.

(*The wise man falleth seven times in a day, and riseth again, etc.*)
(Underlined from *let it* by Blake.)

566.

The man who has and uses but one scale for everything, for himself and his enemy, the past and the future, the grand and the trite, for truth and error, virtue and vice, religion, superstition, infidelity ; for nature, art, and works of genius and art—is truly wise, just, and great.

(*This is most true, but how does it accord with* 451 ?)

(No. 451 in the first edition, wrongly numbered, is given here, with Blake's other comment on it, as No. 441.)

L

567.

The infinitely little constitutes the infinite difference in works of art, and in the degrees of morals and religion. The greater the rapidity, precision, acuteness with which this is observed and determined, the more authentic, the greater the observer.

(*Uneasy.*)

570.

Range him highest among your saints who, with all acknowledged powers and his own steadfast scale for everything, can, on the call of judgment or advice, submit to transpose himself into another's situation and adopt his point of view.

(*Himself into another's situation and adopt* underlined by Blake.)

512.

No communications and no gifts can exhaust genius or impoverish charity.

(*Most excellent.*) (Underlined by Blake.)

575.

Distrust yourself if you fear the eye of the sincere, but be afraid of neither God nor man if you have no reason to distrust yourself.

(The last part underlined, and all the next one, by Blake.)

576.

Who comes as he goes, and is present as he came and went, is sincere.

578.

He loves grandly (I speak of friendship) who is not jealous when he has partners of love.

(*Uneasy, but I hope to mend.*)

580.

He knows himself greatly who never opposes his genius.

(*Most excellent.*) (Underlined.)

586.

"Love as you could hate, and might be hated," a maxim of detested prudence in real friendship, the bane of all tenderness, the death of all familiarity. Consider the fool who follows it as nothing inferior (? superior) to him who at every bit of bread trembles at the thought of its being poisoned.

(*Excellent.*) (*Fool who follows, inferior to him, bit of bread trembles, of its being poisoned,* underlined.)

587.

" Hate as if you could love, or should be loved." Him who follows this maxim, though all the world were to declare an idiot and enthusiast, I shall esteem of all men the most eminently formed for friendship.

(*Better than excellent.*)

590.

Distinguish with exactness if you wish to know yourself and others what is so often mistaken—the *singular*, the *original*, the *extraordinary*, the *great* and the *sublime* man. The *sublime* alone unites the singular, original, extraordinary, and great with his own uniformity and simplicity. The *great* with many powers and uniformity of ends is destitute of that superior calmness and inward harmony which soars above the atmosphere of praise. The *extraordinary* is distinguished by copiousness and a wide range of energy. The *original* need not be very rich (if) only that which he produces is unique, and has the exclusive stamp of individuality. The *singular*, as such, is placed between originality and whim, and often makes a trifle the medium of fame.

(From *the extraordinary*, where the word first occurs, to *calmness* underlined, and also *the original need* and *very rich*.)

591.

Forwardness nips affection in the bud.

(*The more the pity.*)

592.

If you mean to be loved, give more than what is asked, but not more than what is wanted, and ask less than what is expected.

(*The whole aphorism an oversight. This is human policy.*) (The last seven words crossed out.)

593.

Whom smiles and tears make equally lovely all hearts may court.

(This aphorism is altered into *Whom smiles and frowns make equally lovely only some hearts may or dare court.*)

594.

Take here the grand secret, if not of pleasing all, yet of displeasing none. Court mediocrity, avoid originality, and sacrifice to fashion.

(*And go to hell.*)

595.

He who pursues the glimmering steps of hope with steadfast, not presumptuous eye, may pass the gloomy rock on either side of which superstition and credulity spread their dark abysses.

(*Superstition has been long a bugbear by reason of its being united with hypocrisy. But let them be firmly separated, and then superstition will be honest feeling, and God, who loves all honest men, will lead the poor enthusiast in the paths of holiness.*)

596.

The public seldom forgive twice.

(*Let us take their example.*)

597.

Him who is hurried on by furies of immature impetuous wishes, stern repentance shall drag, bound and reluctant, back to the place from which he sailed. Where you hear the crackling of wishes expect intolerable vapours or repining grief.

(*Uneasy.*)

598.

He submits to be seen through a microscope who suffers himself to be caught in a fit of passion.

(*And such a one I dare love.*)

599.

Venerate four characters—the sanguine who has checked volatility and the rage for pleasure ; the choleric who has subdued passion and pride ; the phlegmatic emerged from indolence ; and the melancholy who has dismissed avarice, suspicion, and asperity.

(*Four most holy men.*)   (Closely underlined from *and the rage for pleasure* to end.)

600.

All great minds sympathise.

(Underlined.)

602.

Men carry their character not seldom in their pockets. You might decide on more than half of your acquaintance had you the will or the right to turn their pockets inside out.

(*I seldom carry money in my pockets. They are generally full of paper.*)

605.

Not he who forces himself on opportunity, but he who watches its approach and welcomes its arrival by immediate use, is wise.

(Underlined throughout.)

606.

Love and hate are the genius of invention, the parents of virtue and vice. Forbear to decide on yourself till you have had opportunities for warm attachment or deep dislike.

(*True experience.*)   (Second sentence underlined.)

609.

(This is an aphorism a page in length; Blake only annotates the last sentence.) Be assured, then, that to know yourself perfectly you have only to set down a true statement of those that ever loved or hated you.

(*Uneasy, because I cannot do this.*)

613.

Avoid connecting yourself with characters whose good and bad sides are unmixed, and have not been fermented together. They resemble phials of vinegar and oil, or pallets set with colours. They are either excellent at home and intolerable abroad, or insufferable within doors and excellent in public. They are unfit for friendship merely because their stamina, their ingredients of character, are too single, too much apart. Let them be finely ground up with each other, and they will be incomparable.

(*Most excellent.*) (This note is written against the middle part of the aphorism, *insufferable within doors*, etc.).

614.

The fool separates his object from all surrounding ones. All abstraction is temporary folly.

(*Uneasy, because I once thought otherwise, but now I know it is truth.*)

616.

Let me repeat it. He only is great who has habits of greatness: who, after performing what none in ten thousand could accomplish, passes on like Samson and "*tells neither father nor mother of it.*"

(*This is excellent.*) (*Like Samson* to end underlined notwithstanding the italics of the text.)

620.

A god, an animal, a plant are not companions of man, nor is the faultless—then judge with lenity of all. The coolest, wisest, best—all without exception have their points, their moments of enthusiasm, fanaticism, absence of mind, faint-heartedness, stupidity. If you allow not for these, your criticism on man will be a mass of accusations or caricatures.

(*God is in all. That is our companion and friend, for our God Himself says—" You are My brother, and My sister, and mother": and St. John —" Whoso dwelleth in God, and God in him," and such an one cannot judge of any but in love, and his feeling will be attraction or repulsion. See Aphorisms 549, 554. God is in the lowest effects, as well as in the highest causes, for He is become a worm, that He may nourish the weak. For let it be remembered that creation is God descending according to the weakness of man, for our Lord is the Word of God, and everything on earth is the Word of God, and in its essence is God.*)

(No. 549, referred to above, and so numbered in the first edition, is 539 in the fuller edition, whose numbers are used here. It has been printed above. Similarly what Blake cites as 554 is the 544 printed above.)

623.

You think to meet with some additions here to your stock of moral knowledge, and not in vain, I hope. But know (that there are) a great many rules (which) cannot be given by him who means not to offend, and many of mine have perhaps offended already. Believe me, for him who has an open eye and ear every minute teems with observations of precious import, yet scarcely communicable to the most faithful friend, so incredibly weak, so vulnerable in certain points is man. Forbear to meddle with these at your first setting out, and make amusement the minister of reflection. Sacrifice all egotism. Sacrifice ten points to one, if that one have the value of twenty. And if you are happy enough to impress your disciple with respect for himself, with probability of success in his exertions of growing better, and, above all, with the idea of your disinterestedness, you may perhaps succeed in making one proselyte to virtue.

(*Lovely! Those who are offended with anything in this book would be offended with the innocence of a child, and for the same reason, because it reproaches him with the errors of acquired folly.*)

625.

Keep your heart from him who begins his acquaintance with you by indirect flattery of your favourite paradox or foible.

(*Unless you find it to be his also, previous to your acquaintance.*)

626.

Receive no satisfaction for premeditated impertinence. Forget it; forgive it, but keep him inexorably at a distance who offered it.

(*This is a paradox.*)

628.

Let the cold who offers the nauseous mimicry of warm affection meet with what he deserves—a repulse; but (from) that moment depend upon his irreconcilable enmity.

(*Uneasy, because I do not know how to do this, but I will try to do it the first opportunity.*)

630.

The moral enthusiast who in the maze of his refinements loses or despises the plain paths of honesty and duty is on the brink of crimes.

(*Most true.*)

At the end of the volume, on the fly-leaves, we find the following written by Blake at the same time, and printed here in italics also for the sake of not interrupting the mood of the eye:—

(*I hope no one will call what I have written cavilling, because he may think my remarks of small consequence, for I write from the warmth of my heart, and cannot resist the impulse I feel to rectify what I think false in a book I love so much, and approve so generally.*

Man is good or bad as he unites himself with bad or good spirits. Tell me with whom you go, and I will tell you what you do.

As we cannot experience pleasure but by means of others who experience either pleasure or pain through us, and as all of us on earth are united in thought—for it is impossible to think without images of somewhat on earth—so it is impossible to know God or heavenly things without conjunction with those who know God and heavenly things. Therefore all those who converse in the spirit converse with spirits.

For these reasons I say that this book is written by consultation with good spirits, because it is good, and that the name Lavater is the amulet of those who purify the heart of man.

There is a strong objection to Lavater's principles (as I understand them), and that is he makes everything originate in its accident. He makes the vicious propensity not only a leading feature of the man, but the stamina on which all his virtues grow. But as I understand Vice it is a Negation. It does not signify what the laws of kings and priests have called Vice, we who are philosophers ought not to call the Staminal Virtues of Humanity by the same name that we call the omission of intellect springing from poverty.

Every man's leading propensity ought to be called his leading Virtue and his good Angel.

But the Philosophy of Causes and Consequences misled Lavater, as it has all his contemporaries. Each thing is its own cause and its own effect. Accident is the omission of act in self, and the hindering of act in another. This is Vice, but all act is Virtue. To hinder another is not an act. It is the contrary. It is a restraint on action both in ourselves and in the person hindered, for he who hinders another omits his own duty at the time.

> *Murder is hindering another,*
> *Theft is hindering another.*

Backbiting, undermining, circumventing, or whatever is negative is vice.
But the origin of this mistake in Lavater and his contemporaries is—they suppose that Woman's Love is Sin. In consequence, all the loves and graces, with them, are sins.)

So end Blake's notes on Lavater's *Aphorisms.* Have we lost the long day passed in reading them?

CHAPTER XV

MUCH of the origin and the meaning of many otherwise inexplicable passages in the *Marriage of Heaven and Hell,* which has been called "the high-water mark of Blake's intellect" by Mr. Swinburne, will now be sufficiently clear to enable our minds to enter into Blake's with some companionship as we read it. "High-water mark" is perhaps an exaggeration. The book is but prose, after all, and the compliment was paid to it partly because the critic found himself less humiliated than when reading the *Jerusalem* by an excess of unexplained symbolism. Yet the seeming ease with which we understand the *Marriage* in its outbursts of choleric irony is not a sign of any real, intimate, brotherly nearness of our minds to the author's mind unless we have trodden with him at least as much of the same mental road that led him to this point as—without being ourselves such a man—we can tread. Even this much is worth doing. Desdemona, without being Othello, came near enough to him to love him as he told "the dangers he had passed."

While Blake was preparing the plates of the *Marriage* and printing them with his wife's assistance, and she was even learning to colour copies of the *Songs of Innocence,* on which he began to rely for a valuable help to the very dry bread that was all he could earn by engraving, he wrote a good deal of prophetic poetry. He was stimulated to do so partly by the recoil on his own mind from the heavy stones with which he had stoned Swedenborg for not having done the same in his time.

So, when Blake had done deriding him, and making Ezekiel say that the voice of the Lord was the voice of mental enthusiasm, which cares not for consequences, he, still adopting the perverted language which he had borrowed from the over-mild angels of Swedenborg, promised the

152

Bible of Hell to the world. He had already written the sweetest, most musical, and most religious of the books of this terrible Bible—*Thel*—in whose pages the fourteen-syllabled line was first made his own.

That line, in its highest perfection, is one which the ear of our educated classes, perverted by Latin verses in youth, had not yet opened itself to fully accept. A man, as Blake soon discovered, may be grown up in the taste that can detect the savour of Horace, Virgil, and Lucretius, and yet be a conceited and destructive baby, breaking a toy that he has not wit enough to play with, when the metre of *Thel* is offered to his cramped mind, and its music to his prejudiced ear. The bad influence of Latin classics on the ear that would use English is now well known. From Ben Jonson to Landor men were made stiff by it all through the intermediate period remembered as Dr. Johnson's time. Milton alone escaped alive. We shall have to wait until the accumulated prides of the men of a rising generation educated in contempt of Latin create a living taste strong enough to eat up the heavy body of tradition left us by those whose ears were stunted through the language of poets that never knew the music of our tongue. Then Blake's fourteen-syllabled line will be known as an enjoyment classed among the accepted advantages of education. Then, also, it is to be feared, will come a flood of such tepid imitations of it that the true lovers will regret that a Blake Church was never founded in time, so that its worshippers might revere his verse too much to repeat it, while his opponents should think it too wicked and blasphemous to be endured.

In the absence of that church a general suspicion of Blake's sanity, caused by the general miscomprehension of his work, has done literature very good service in keeping him out of the hands of the educator. He is still fresh. The reputation of madness has come down on him like the cinders of Vesuvius on Pompeii. It killed many a happy hour and many a lovely verse in Blake's life, as the cinders killed the Pompeians; but now that the accumulation is being dug away from the buried town, we at least find fruit paintings and portraits of fair dames upon the walls, as fresh as they were on the day when the master's brush left them. In the same way, misunderstanding is being dug away from Blake, and his prophetic books shine out clear and sweet for us now.

How thick is the accumulation of the ashes of super-ciliousness that had fallen both on his symbolism and his music may be seen in a pamphlet published by Dr. Garnett, of the British Museum, *after* the Quaritch edition of Blake's works was already in his hands. *Thel* Dr. Garnett patronises : " Could Blake have schooled himself to have written (*sic*) such blank verse as he had already produced in *Edward the Third* and *Samson*, *Thel* would have been a very fine poem. As it is, its lax, rambling semi-prose is full of delicate modulations."

Thel really is, of course, far more correct than *Samson* in metre. Dr. Garnett adds : " In every succeeding production, however, there is less of metrical beauty, and *thought* and *expression* grow continually more and more amorphous."

Amorphous (would not *formless* have done ?) is the last word which will be applied to Blake's thought by those who know what its form was, and what the form of its two parents —Swedenborg's visions and his own. But it is true that, as Blake grew older, and was more and more worried by the perpetual misunderstanding of every one—*every one*, think what that meant to a man hungry for friendship !—he began more and more to struggle to be explanatory, and it is this that ruined his poetic mood, made his song fall into assertion, and his assertion into interpretation, more and more. He tried in vain to shake this off, and claimed that when he told a truth it was not to convince those who did not know it, but to protect those who did. This was not always enough for his heart. He wanted those whom he was so protecting to know that he had put on his intellectual armour for them, but if he did not explain his symbols they would never know this unless expressly inspired. So he fell into a patchwork style of composition, at one moment giving the best verse, but at another spoiling it with an intrusion of statement and comment. In the books written when Blake still thought to be understood, and had not been pestered by the Dr. Garnetts of his time, most is still unexplained and beautiful.

And yet, after all, he did not explain enough for doctors of literature to even discover that he was trying to do so. On the contrary, Dr. Garnett says that "no man ever wilfully put more obstacles into the way of his success than Blake, whether as artist, thinker, or poet." When will the closed eye and the preoccupied ear of clever men cease to believe that original men put obstacles into the way of their own success ? The closed eye and the preoccupied ear are the obstacles, and not the originality.

" This incarnate enigma among men could manifestly be

as transparent as crystal," Dr. Garnett also says, "when he knew exactly what he wished to say—a remark that may not be useless to the student of his mystical and prophetical writings."

Dr. Garnett admitted once to the present writer that he was never *a student* of these writings. This admission was made after his unfortunate pamphlet was written. In fact, he read Blake as people read novels, not as he himself would have read a work that he approached in the spirit of a student. He therefore never knew what was the position of Blake's mind with regard to his own meaning, or in what his difficulty in expressing it consisted.

How much of thrust-in explanation may have occurred in poetic works now lost to us, written by Blake in 1792, we do not yet know. He probably kept it at arm's length at first, though if it be true, as we suspect, that the *Book of Tiriel* was shown to Johnson, then the passage about parents and education towards the end may have been added at this time.

What more there may be of the same kind in the *French Revolution* (a poem in seven Books), written immediately after *Tiriel*, we cannot tell, since a copy of even the first Book, published now by Johnson as a sort of experiment, cannot be found. Gilchrist says that Blake's name was not on the title-page. We must suppose that when the September massacres in 1792 came with a shock of horror to all Europe, either Johnson or Blake, who then took off the red cap of Liberty with which he had alarmed his friends, burned the whole issue. If there had been any copies sold, they were burned by the buyers in the same mood of horror. The six unpublished books of the poem were perhaps never written out for the press. We may conjecture *Lafayette* to be a trace of the contents of one of them, though it must be of later date in the form we find it in Blake's MS. book. There are many rewritings of it there, verses changed, the order changed, and a reference to "Paul, Constantine, Charlemagne, Luther," as divisions of truth. We can now see that they correspond to Urizen, Luvah, Tharmas, and Urthona, a quaternary which also belongs to a time later than 1792 in Blake's progress, so far as record enables us to conjecture.

So the fragment that survived his lost *French Revolution* was probably only a few lines that belonged to a chance memory developed later, when the main subject had been long forgotten.

That *Tiriel* must have been written at the same time or

earlier is, of course, an assertion based only on inference. The evidence that would date the *Tiriel* earlier or later than 1789 is the following. *Thel's Motto* is the name given to a quatrain at the beginning of the *Book of Thel* :

> Does the eagle know what is in the pit,
> Or wilt thou go ask the mole ?
> Can wisdom be put in a silver rod,
> Or love in a golden bowl ?

The last two lines of this seem to have been written before the first two, and we find them in *Tiriel*, crossed out, as though Blake had decided not to leave them there after the lilt of line (for they are only one long line in *Tiriel's* metre) had shown him that the proper treatment was to take it out, cut it into two natural divisions, and put two lines of similar metre above it.

Then, it is probable, he asked his imagination to refer him to some contrast, some pair of suggestive contraries that would balance those that he had now on the paper before him.

Silver is, in his system, the metal of heart's love ; *Gold*, of mind's enthusiasm. *Brass* is the "spiritual hate, origin of earthly love," and *Iron* is generative magnetic attraction, and the hardness and solidity that this seems to give to Nature.

Without going further into the symbolism we see that the last two lines meant—

"Can wisdom be stored in that which is packed full of heart's love, or love in the part of our minds that is all abstract enthusiasm ?"

The mocking reminder of the first two lines, that we cannot expect expert opinion on any subject from the expert to whom another subject belongs, enforces this, and the whole together brings out a mistake which was first made by the maiden called Thel, and afterwards by the old man Tiriel, each a wanderer. Thel is the tender shyness that wishes the loins to be altogether spiritual, and shrinks from seeing herself—her evanescent and pearly beauty—turned into the exciter of fleshly passion, as actual virgins do actually at times shrink from seeing their beauty arouse passion. "Food of worms" must be read with "Man is a worm renewed with joy," and with "Vala is a worm," and with "Hyle" (also called once a worm) as "arched over the moon" in *Jerusalem*. The moon with its silver light is the region of love. Tiriel, with his senile sterility, at the same time a contrast to and a bitter imitation of virginity, with the jealous

antagonism to all joy that belongs to incapacity, is evidently
a personage designed to show a picture of the error of Thel,
seen under a mask that is its counterpart. The *Book of
Tiriel* means "Resent not"; that of *Thel*, "Censure not."

Therefore these two books, showing how these two sides
of one command may be disobeyed, are two aspects of one
subject, two enemies of "Infant Joy." But the one is kind
and the other malignant. Blake was never on the side of an
enemy of joy, for joy is beauty, beauty is life, and life is
holiness. Only murderers hate joy, though not all who hate
the babe know in what bad company they do so.

In subject, therefore, *Tiriel* and *Thel* are linked, but this
does not make us certain that one grew out of the other.
They both sprang from the same root, the great poetic tree
now pushing its way from the good soil of Blake's mind.
Possibly most of *Tiriel* was written after *Thel* was composed,
and *Thel's Motto* was taken from its pages after *Thel* was
written, and during the preparation of the plates.

Then the copying out of *Tiriel*, perhaps, as has been already
suggested, first offered in vain to Mr. Mathews, was finished
for Johnson, and slight changes were made. There is an
uncouth name or two (such as "Chthyrra" and "Mahnoth")
struck out from Section IV, where Ijun calls Heuxos forth.
They are the names of other members of Tiriel's family, are
never heard of again in any manuscript of Blake's that we
possess, and no line of poetry is attached to them. Their
presence merely shows, as does the conjunction with which
the book begins, that in what we possess of *Tiriel* we have a
copied-out segment of some longer poem. The last pages, in
a hand somewhat more mature and less neat than the rest,
were probably written out in 1801, and the line that had
been taken for part of the motto of the *Book of Thel*, from
the first draft, though now copied with the rest in the
swing of the labour, was duly crossed out. At the same
time the deleted lines about the king—

> Is the king's son warmed without wool, or does he cry with a voice
> Of thunder, or look upon the sun and laugh, or stretch
> His little hands to the depths of the sea to draw up
> The deadly cunning of the flatterer and then read it to the morning?

may have been crossed out because Blake remembered that
he had used them for the *French Revolution* already published by Johnson, and with these went perhaps two or three
of the lines through which the pen was also drawn, whose

style is elaborated later in the *Visions of the Daughters of
Albion*.   They lead up to the reference to the silver rod and
golden bowl.   Different kinds of men are described—the
lion and ox, etc. :

Some nostrils wide, breathing out blood, some close shut
In silent deceit, poisons inhaling from the morning rose,
With danger hid beneath their lips and poison in their tongue,
Or eyed with little sparks of Hell, or with infernal brands,
Flying flames of discontent and plagues of dark despair ;—
Or those whose mouths are shut, whose teeth are gates of eternal death,
Can wisdom be put in a silver rod, or love in a golden bowl ?

Then the whole manuscript was stitched, and " MS. of Mr.
Blake " written on the slate-coloured cover only to identify
it among Johnson's other manuscripts, as it was probably to
have been published anonymously, like the *French Revolution.*

At his private press Blake had enough to do still with the
Marriage of Heaven and Hell.   He had learned from this
and from the *Book of Thel* even more about the laboriousness
of copying out a whole manuscript in reverse, every letter
and word written backwards, with varnish on metal, than
even the *Songs of Innocence* had taught him.   The *Songs of
Experience* were already coming into existence, and he looked
forward to expending the same kind of labour upon them.
If any one would print a book for him and save him this
trouble he would be too glad.

As a matter of fact, that identical fair copy of *Tiriel* made
for Johnson was eventually printed, being unstitched for the
purpose ; but it was for the Aldine edition of Blake's Works,
published in our own time, that the lines were put in type.
The comforting presentiment of coming publication with
which Blake copied them out had not deceived him, though
he must at one time have thought that it had done so.
Later books, all those written after 1795, contain no further
cuttings from *Tiriel*, and those nearest to 1791 only a few
words.   When writing the " generation " of the " Sons and
daughters of Los " in *Vala* (Night VIII, line 350 and
following), in the last years of the century, he seems not to
have had *Tiriel* to refer to, and not even to remember completely the persons there mentioned.   From this we can only
suppose that the " MS. of Mr. Blake " was lost at Johnson's,
being perhaps lent to some one else who never returned it.
But it may only have been put into a box and forgotten—a
fate to which it succumbed during more than the last quarter
of the nineteenth century, for after the Aldine edition was

printed the publisher put it away and no one remembered
what had become of it, though the editor of that edition
tried in vain to do so. The son of the publisher discovered
it while looking over the boxes of his late father, and sold it
at Sotheby's in 1903, when it was bought by Mr. Quaritch.

The difference in the quality of the verse between *Thel*
and *Tiriel* was probably an effect of the change from almost
complete silence to the conversation at Johnson's weekly
parties. To test the effect of conversational habits on Blake's
style at any time of his life, a page of *Thel* may be read
close to almost any page of *Tiriel*, and then between any of
the passages that occur first in *Vala*, and afterwards, whether
or not slightly altered, in *Jerusalem*. Sometimes the *Vala*
lines are transferred unchanged, and then they contrast with
the rest of the page as a bit of *Thel* let into a chapter of
Tiriel would with the rest of the text. There is more
assertiveness, but the fluent beauty and liquidity have gone.

The influence of Felpham arguments with Hayley was
what made *Jerusalem* different from *Vala*, added to the
constant interviews on business with all kinds of people that
worried Blake during his first years in South Molton Street.
Thel was written in the period of little talkativeness before
Blake met Fuseli and Godwin at Johnson's parties; *Vala*
some years after them, and before the annoyances of Felpham
and the return to London.

So far as *Tiriel* had a personal father who really walked
this world, we must look for him in Godwin. He is the
incarnation of the "hypocritical self-righteousness," "the
moral virtues of the heathen"—everything that Blake held
in most horror. In Godwin's time there was a general
belief that all who did not attain to virtue through a respect
for the divine commands and a fear of the divine threats
of punishment were sunk in vice. We know what good
service he did in battling with this prejudice. But Blake was
not able to feel the value and courage of Godwin when he
insisted on teaching an unwilling world that to behave well
was as much a part of the natural character of man as to
behave badly, and would necessarily survive religion even if
religion were to vanish to-morrow. Blake, as he tells us,
held that "man is naturally altogether evil, and requires to
be continually turned into his direct opposite."

Besides, Nature is a "delusive goddess" who, if believed
in, has a disastrous effect, namely, eternal death. To Godwin
this was a matter of course, about which the less said the

better. Blake grew to look on Godwin as summing up all that is most dangerous and abominable, as being the typical weak tyrant who, aided by cunning and pretended mildness, destroys life and love, pretending to preach an absurd thing called morality, that pleases no emotion but the vanity of self-righteousness.

This morality, so far from being good, was deadly. It was the wrong way to do right. Sin might, though evil, at least be an indirect means of good when, meeting with forgiveness, it turned into divine gratitude and love. Righteousness was not only deadly in its influence. It was as much a delusion as nature. One of its strongholds was virginity. The virginity that does not think lustfully is not human at all. The virginity that "thinks but acts not" is anything but righteous, except in that unimportant, exterior, and temporary part of life that is furthest from imagination, and therefore from the true and the eternal. This doctrine can only have appeared to be raving wickedness to Godwin. He probably had heard something that sounded very like it from others than Blake, who had other objects in preaching it. Antinomians were always various. St. Paul was an antinomian; so is the hardest anarchist and the most slippery cynic.

Blake was a good man who insisted on his right to be a wicked one, and avowed his total absence of merit if he was only good in act and not in thought. There are not, as yet, enough of such men in the world for moral volumes written for their use only to be required in sufficiently large editions to be successful. Godwin had written a successful though much-abused book.

Blake always liked to draw his descriptions from what he thought a typical model, one who contained a whole group in himself, and there was no one whom he met in his life, either now or later on, so well fitted to serve him for the figure of Natural Morality as Godwin. But when Natural Morality was to be *named* he did not think Godwin important and influential enough to use his name. Bacon, Newton, and Locke, with their preaching of Nature as a fit object for the intellect to dwell on, might be considered, if rolled into one, as the real enemy. Blake rolled them into one and called it Rahab. He chose a female name because female meant to him *matter-of-fact*. The sweet beauty of nature through which its erroneous convictions got their force, the other aspect of those convictions, he called Vala. He said that this universal enemy was therefore Rahab "in Time," but

Vala "in Eternity," and Rahab could be redeemed by
becoming Vala, and Vala by becoming "Jerusalem," which was
his name for the "emative portion that unites man to his
fellow." By character Vala, the beauty, is a dragon. Natural
beauty tends to devour eternal beauty, but let her get free
from the belief in the five senses, let her become only the
basis for sympathy in love, and she will be an innocent
shepherdess of happy flocks, and we can all delight in her,
and enter into brotherhood with one another while doing so
as much as by pitying the afflicted.

This is the symbol and this the doctrine that next occupied Blake. He took every opportunity to rail at the
"hypocritic selfish righteousness of the heathen," and whenever he did so he inevitably thought of Godwin, the only
man who had taught him about this, and had taught his age
and country about it, though whether it would be more
correct to say that he recognised in him old Tiriel, or drew
Tiriel consciously from him, must remain matter of guess-
work. We have no sufficient certainty about the date of
the long-destroyed first draft of the book to decide.

CHAPTER XVI

LIBERTY AND VISION

WE hear of Blake among the Johnson group as calling himself a true "Liberty boy" and son of the "Revolution" (before "1792" was become a name for massacre), and we hear of him giving naturalistic reasons for this, making it the result of a personal bodily peculiarity, pointing to the protuberance of his own forehead over the eyes, and saying that here one could see the head of a natural republican. Gilchrist tells us how Blake saved Tom Paine, who had now, in 1792, published the second part of the *Rights of Man* :

A few months later county and corporation addresses against "seditious publications" were got up. The Government (Pitt's) answered the agreed signal by issuing a proclamation condemnatory of such publications, and commenced an action for libel against the author of the *Rights of Man*, which was to come off in September, all this helping the book itself into immense circulation. The "Friends of Liberty" (as the society got up among some of those who met Blake at Johnson's was called) held their meetings too, at which strong language was used. In September a French deputation announced to Paine that the Department of Calais had elected him member of the National Convention. Already, as an acknowledged cosmopolitan and friend of man, he had been declared a French citizen by the deceased Assembly. One day in this same month Paine was giving at Johnson's an idea of the inflammatory eloquence he had poured forth at a public meeting of the previous night. Blake, who was present, silently inferred from the tenour of his report that those in power, now eager to lay hold of obnoxious persons, would certainly not let slip such an opportunity. On Paine's rising to leave, Blake laid his hand on the orator's shoulder, saying, " You must not go home or you are a dead man ! " and hurried him off on his way to France, whither he was now in any case bound, to take his seat as a French legislator. By the time Paine was at Dover the officers were in his house, or, as Mr. Cheetham designates it, " his lurking hole in the purlieus of London," and some twenty minutes after the custom house officials at Dover had turned over his slender baggage, with, as he thought, extra malice, and he had set sail for Calais, an order was received from the Home Office to detain him. England never saw Tom Paine again. New perils awaited him : Reign of Terror and near view of the guillotine, an accidentally open door and a chalk mark on the wrong side of it proving his salvation. But a no less serious one had been narrowly escaped from the English Tories. Those were hanging days ! Blake on this occasion showed greater sagacity than Paine, whom, indeed, Fuseli affirmed to be more ignorant of the common affairs of life than himself even. Spite of unworldliness and visionary faculty Blake never wanted prudence and sagacity in ordinary matters.

It is well known as characteristic of the more imaginative men of Irish blood that whether their own lives succeed or fail in a worldly point of view, their practical advice to others is of the best. Blake had the special advantage in coolness that contemptuous courage gives. He could choose the right moment. He knew exactly how much the mob would stand and how much the Government.

Tom Paine was not the only oppressed person whom Blake was now the means of saving from the oppressor, though the other is not known to us by name.

The original edition of the *Song of Liberty* contains two little figures of horses, capitally drawn, minute in size, wedged into a space among the print. They are walking about on their hind legs, pawing the air like circus horses. They are much better drawn than seems explicable at first, better, for example, than the horses' heads scribbled on the blank leaves of the *Island in the Moon.* Symbolically, of course, they are the " horses of instruction," maddened by poetic freedom and excitement, like those described in the story about " Palama-bron " in the first part of the *Book of Milton.*

There is an explanation of how these horses came to be put here. Blake probably had his press, that press for which he paid £40, in a back room at 28 Poland Street. The windows at this side looked out upon the premises of Mr. Astley, the original proprietor of the well-known circus that did not change its name for a century. Here Blake used to amuse himself by watching the grooming and exercising of the animals. One day he saw something else. There was a boy limping up and down, dragging pain-fully at every step a heavy block, to which he was chained by the foot. Blake called his wife to come and look, and asked her what she thought could be the meaning of this. It does not appear to have occurred to either of them that the meaning was that the boy was a mischievous and lying young rascal who deserved a whipping that Mr. Astley was too good-natured to give him, or had already given without doing any good by it. Mrs. Blake suggested that the log was a hobble, used to prevent the circus horses straying too far when they were turned out to graze on a common during the summer trips of the circus, and that the boy was fastened to it now as a degrading punishment.

Blake took fire at once, and in a minute was out of his house and down among the circus people, giving them his ideas on liberty with an outburst of eloquence, and appealing cleverly to their sentiment of patriotism by asking them if this was treatment that an English boy ought to suffer when it would be humiliating to a slave. He carried his point, and the boy was let loose. Mr. Astley was out at the time, and when he returned and learned what had happened he flew into a rage and came round at once to Blake's house to give him eloquence for eloquence, and indignation for indignation. His strong point, of course, was the hatefulness of busybodies who interfered in the affairs of other people.

The interview was rather heated at first, and poor Mrs. Blake, who expected it to come to blows, trembled as she heard the loud voices of the men. But Blake remembered in time that he had a purpose to serve. His object was the protection of a helpless boy, and this could hardly be achieved by putting the boy's master into a towering rage. He set himself to appeal to this master's better feelings, and succeeded so well that before Mr. Astley went back to his circus he was completely won over to Blake's views, and the two men parted civilly, with feelings of cordial respect for one another.

But Blake never forgot the sight of that chain, and we who have seen it so often in the *Book of Urizen* and the designs to Young's *Night Thoughts* can never forget it either. It is enough to make memorable in Blake's life the short period of five years between 1788 and 1793 during which he lived in Poland Street.

These two *deliveries*, that of Tom Paine from the Government and that of the circus boy from his master's chain, are the only two incidents that we know of for certain in which Blake is seen as an active defender of liberty, but they are not likely to have stood alone, and they increase our suspicion that he was, quite willingly, something more than a mere spectator of the fall of Newgate in 1780. When, after the September massacres in Paris of 1792, Blake threw off his revolutionary badge, he had another reason for ceasing to appear in public with a red cap on, which had nothing to do with the crimes

of either rulers or rebels.   In the first week of this month of
September his mother died.   She was buried on the 9th
in Bunhill Fields, a few days after the massacres ceased.

Blake would have respected her death, though she seems
never to have been important to him since early childhood.
The punishment she was induced to inflict on him for seeing
the vision of Ezekiel seems to have been a permanent source of
estrangement.   Blake's friends in later life did not remember
having heard him speak of her, though he often referred to
his favourite brother Robert.   Her funeral oration is found,
however, in the song *To Tirzah* among those *of Experience.*

The *Visions of the Daughters of Albion* were probably
now written, and were the first result of the break-up of the
" Friends of Liberty " and Blake's return to solitude.   " I
must be shut up within myself, or reduced to nothing," he
said when he knew himself better.

There are here some passages so closely akin to two struck-
out lines in the latter pages of *Tiriel*, that it is even
possible that before the copied-out MS. of this book was
prepared and, as we have supposed, handed to Johnson, the
Visions were already begun.   They seem to have absorbed
Blake as soon as *Tiriel* was out of his sight.   It is exceedingly probable that passages from the unprinted books of the
French Revolution are used here, as Blake issued parts of
Vala afterwards in *Jerusalem* and *Milton.*

If we take up this book, remembering the *Thel* and
Tiriel, and read it through quickly, reading *America* next
after it, we shall need no commentator to tell us that here
we have a pair of utterances that are related to each other
very much as *Thel* and *Tiriel* are related.

In the *Visions of the Daughters of Albion* innocent and
sweet exuberance of life that hardly yet knows itself to be
desire, flowing from the spiritual into the corporeal by what
Swedenborg calls " influx," becomes passion, and suffers
reproach from jealousy.   It cries out now for its own life,
denies that its corporeal consequences have permanently
stained it, and says that in spiritual realms it still flows
straight towards brotherhood, as joy *must*, and, like each joy,
is willing to serve unity by changing into another joy.   In
the symbols this is related under poetic form, but readers will
remember that Blake knew of a happy time, known to mystic
tradition, before the three obstructive powers Flesh, Morality,
Reason—the Head, Heart, Loins of that portion of the
Creator that fixed the limit called " Adam "—so influenced or

"darkened" Tharmas, or liquid, overflowing sympathy, as to make him evil. In his luminous condition Tharmas had once vegetated so spiritually that desire developed into friendship, and this into the eternal Unity, without any check from duty, jealousy, or pride (again a Head-Heart-Loins group), but now this once innocent "Angel," or *chief propensity* of the tongue, ceased to be an impulse that leads us all *outwards every way*, and became his own spectre—eternal death. He ceased to propagate eternal sympathy, and became matter-of-fact in language and in feeling, mere fleshly desire, the evil desire that seeks only its own gratification—mortal generation—the worm's family —and not its own development towards brotherhood by progress. The greatness of the evil of this descent is because the form of life called "Tharmas" is incalculably good, and is as necessary to man as roots are to trees. Only, roots must not be "brandished in the heavens, and fruits in the earth beneath."

The symbol of Tharmas is therefore in the West, in Water —the region where the sun darkens—the element by which all vegetation is enabled to grow. Theotormon, the hero of the *Visions of the Daughters of Albion*, represents the sorrow in particular that jealousy brings to the vegetable—the fleshly organs—which in their turn bring it to the spirit. In the passage,

> How can I be defiled when I behold thy image pure?

Blake means to say, how can even sin in the flesh defile the spiritual part of the craving that began it, so long as this be not altered into a selfish nature, but sees in the sorrowful "West" and "Water" the tendency to "arise from genera-tion free," and go "outwards every way," that alone leads to brotherhood in the risen Christ.

It was what has been called "pantheism" in Blake to believe that the moods, before they enter the flesh, or before we, in the flesh, enter them, are Beings, each an Identity, struggling as we do each for its destiny and the uses of its life, so that he had a poetic right to call them by fancy names. Oothoon is the virgin that Thel is not—the active virgin. Her virginity consists in being, like Thel, as yet unmingled (unmarried) with any portion of life that belongs to a more external (lower) order. Thel, the passive, in right of her beauty is worthy to be the food (the stimula-tion) of the most passive and infantile or unintellectual form of corporeal passion (the worm). Oothoon, active, stimulates with the desire of her conquest the violent, the earthly thunder and fire, and, mingling with it, becomes, to her surprise, outcast from the privileges of mingling her active joy with the sympathetic principle, now turned into her own opposite, passive sorrow, spiritual doubt and melancholy, uncertainty, and jealousy.

A consideration of this will go further than most forms of meditation about Blake towards enabling us to understand the connection between the discovery of what the *Spectre of Tharmas* is and the *Closing of Albion's Western Gate*, when the two ideas are brought together in *Vala*, Night I, 211 or 219.

Oothoon's doctrine, as put forth in this poem, in its commonest social manifestation might be illustrated by money and the history of money, though Blake would not have liked the illustration.

" If the fool would persist in his folly he would become wise," Blake says, and in society we see how the golden river runs itself pure, and how persons originally given to servility and snobbishness on attaining power through acquired wealth bear children who, first relieved of the necessity to struggle for existence, presently lose most of the servility, selfishness, and cruelty belonging to such struggle, and achieve a pure and sweet aristocracy, like that which springs from noblemen whose remote ancestors were brigands. The only disadvantage of this commerce-born aristocracy is that it has not vindicated its courage in the past. We see, however, that this does not matter. Our list of those who wear the Victoria Cross shows that a man may fight well and yet be the first of his family to fight at all. But the propitiativeness needed to win customers in the shop and to negotiate bargains " on the Rialto " survives in the kindness of the educated classes that wins them friends. The keen eye that in earlier generations selected merchandise now educates the taste that turns to art. At first much boasting and foolishness is seen, but the exuberance of self-love in foolish luxury goes past, and a better and sweeter tradition to mould all life remains. The abstract impersonality of gold, its river-like habit of always flowing, has purified family after family in a few generations, " as the clear stream muddied by the feet of beasts grows pure and smiles."

Blake said that *beauty*, or the *holiness of life*, would do all this. The evil side of the passions of the flesh that are not mere covetousness would vanish from every single bosom if people would but keep the faith in ultimate good, and not try to promote by a negative thing called morality a positive thing called virtue. They would then enter into spiritual life. Jealousy has no power beyond bodily life. Bodily life has no power over spiritual life, except through the sad spirit of uncertainty that suspects always the authenticity of joy and the soul, and fears lest sorrow or the body be the ultimate truth. This melancholy vacillation is symbolised in the ever-moving wave, and is here called by its secondary name, not "Tharmas," but "Theotormon," whose highest good is the poor chastity of restraint when he is deprived of Oothoon. Night is not darker than the day-time of common sense, "single vision or Newton's sleep," whose sun in the heavens is "a black shadow like an eye." Restraint means here not only the law of ordinary social morality. It is *prohibition* that is used by Reason's jealousy *against the imaginative or visionary life*. This meaning in Blake's writing is not surprising. The first naughtiness for which he was whipped as a child was the sin of having visions. He now cries out that so far is this from being a sin, that even the wickedness of so far believing in the non-visionary eye as to allow it to couple the soul in spiritual marriage with a sunset by lying on a bank and gazing, should be forgiven.

In view of this exalted doctrine, the puritanical morality of Mrs. Blake's decent and modest girlhood must have seemed a poor thing in her married—her ardently married—home. She struggled for it a long time, though. There is more than the experience of symbolism only in that allusion in *Jerusalem* (page 36, line 45) to the "judgment" which forbids delight so severely that "a man dare hardly to embrace his own wife for the terrors of chastity that they call by the name of morality."

The *Visions of the Daughters of Albion* was composed as part of the education of Mrs. Blake as well as that of posterity, and as such its interpretation on the side that concerned her has its place here. It was first made for her, and then for us, though essentially part of Blake's great task of one process—that of "opening the eyes of man inward into the world of thought, into eternity."

One line in it—or rather less than a line of this poem—might be written over a temple dedicated to Blake. It is all his doctrine in a symbol—

The village dog barks at the breaking day.

With the poetry rubbed away, the flesh of beauty torn from its bones, and the hard skeleton of unchangeable prose meaning left permanent, if hideous, in the wind, it reads :

Appetite heralds Inspiration.

CHAPTER XVII

ENGLAND AND AMERICA

In the promised *Bible of Hell* or *Book of Desire* which was to be thrust upon the world, *America* was probably the next part. Yet both in the text and in the drawings it is so unlike the *Visions* that this indicates that there was some complete separation between the one effort and the other, some important change, some bustling and worry outside the studio, with a return afterwards to the region of art and poetry by a new self-concentration.

The title-page records this in the one word "Lambeth," printed above the signature. In fact, between engraving the *Visions* and *America* Blake had left Poland Street and crossed the river to Hercules Buildings, No. 13. The change of address and the number of the house both show that he was growing poorer, and must economise. A house numbered 13 is likely to be less popular than those numbered 12 and 14, therefore to be cheaper. The staircase in this particular house will always be remembered as the place where Blake saw the vision of the Ancient of Days that he drew with so much dignity and style that it became one of his favourite pictures, and repetitions of it were called for till the last working day of his life. It occurs in the beginning of *Europe*, and is so fascinating that even an artist may be forgiven for not breaking out into fury at the effrontery of its impossible and ill-joined limbs. In the *Europe* of the British Museum we see this design as a figure kneeling and reaching down one arm. It has no other arm, and though in some replicas Blake added another, it could not rise, and if it did, large portions of its form would be found to have been cut out to make the kneeling position possible. It was sometimes less incorrectly drawn than in this version, but never more impressively.

Here also Blake saw a ghost, as he chanced to look

upwards while standing near his garden door. "It was," he himself said, "a horrible figure, scaly, speckled, very awful." He saw it actually coming down the stairs towards him, and was so frightened that he took to his heels.

He was not experienced in ghosts, and admitted that he never saw one before or after, although one of his more grotesque designs is popularly known as the *Ghost of a Flea*. In the poem of *America* the last lines explain the whole. The fires of passion have melted the hinges of the gates of the five senses. Blake still believed this to be a natural result of unrestricted fleshly pleasure. In fact, he held this creed to the end. Indulgence, he thought, would *instantly* so arouse every energy of man that the spiritual energies, which were (of course) the stronger, would immediately put down the five senses, and the liberty of imagination on a spiritual plane from the bondage of what is commonly called "reality" would follow at once. Eternity would open for us *now*, as it will eventually after death, when we shall "go into Mind," as he phrases it in his letter written in old age about the death of Flaxman. Yet, to be able to devote more time to the service of God, he admitted a use in the prohibition of bodily lust, as he will write presently in *Jerusalem*, page 77, preface to chap. iv. The opening and closing of gates, the cleansing or obscuring, was all through Blake's life one of his favourite figures of speech. Already in the *Marriage of Heaven and Hell* he had said, "If the doors of perception were cleansed, everything would appear to man, as it is, infinite." In his last book, *Milton*, he says, on the last line of page 42, "To cleanse the Face of my Spirit by self-examination," and the cleansing is explained at length on the following page.

"Every natural event has a spiritual cause" was one of his chief tenets.

The solidity of Nature had a spiritual cause, namely, the state of mind in which man cannot, in ordinary waking life, be clairvoyant enough to see through it, and consequently is equally incapable of seeing through the natural meaning of the words of Scripture, whose literal sense is a cloud (Luvah's robes of blood), and a tomb (Albion's), and a Rock (that "of Ages"), and on giving this state of mind a Scriptural name Blake called it Og. He is king of the closed heart that will not open its brass gates to let love illuminate nature, and he misreads Scripture and nature into a narrow sense, literal and hateful, suited to his moods. His is the

opposite Gate to the American, and his name as a personage
in Blake's Myth has been well known to general readers
since the first protest was entered against the silent suppression of an allusion to it at the end of a long quotation
from *Milton* in Gilchrist.   But Gilchrist did not know what
Og meant, or, desiring the public only to enjoy the passage
of poetry that led up to this name, quietly dropped it.   Mr.
Swinburne, though he was indignant, did not tell us
what the name meant any more than Gilchrist did,
though both perhaps found out by reading a little Swedenborg
to prepare their minds for the task, and then reading the
closing pages of *Vala*, Night I (this was seen in MS. by
both), and *Jerusalem*, page 13, line 57; page 48, line 63;
page 49, lines 3, 56; page 73, line 16; page 79, line 13; and
page 89, line 47; and *Milton*, page 18, lines 33, 35, 37; page
30, line 33; page 31, line 49; page 37, lines 22, 50, and 51.

In simple eighteenth-century argument, alternatives were
credited with convincing power.   Mind and matter were
alternatives.   If we are not in Matter (under which heading
Blake included the "corporeal understanding," as those who
are technically but not popularly called materialists do), we
must be in Mind.   We must be in something.   We are
in nothing else but Mind after death, and had better be in as
little else as possible even now.

America is, of course, a mere symbol for all that in
Blake's system of divisions he grouped under the *West*.
The idea of dividing the human character under points of
the compass he developed from Swedenborg's reading of the
use made symbolically of those points in the Bible.   In the
Visions we have already the expression—

Thy soft American plains are mine.

All the references to Washington, and so forth, are merely
intended to refer to states of the mind in elementary rebellion.
The names are given as "representative."   But to what detail
of art, imagination, or passion each name of an American hero
refers we shall never accurately know, unless by clairvoyant
reading of his thoughts in Blake's "Universal Mind."

Among the *Ideas of Good and Evil* Gilchrist published a
couple of verses called *Thames and Ohio*, from which he
gathered that Blake at one time entertained the idea of
emigration.   The poem, however, does not justify this
inference at all.   It is practically certain that Blake never
entertained the idea for an instant.

This erroneous and non-symbolic way of reading Blake leads further than to the conclusion that he intended to go out of the country. The only honest inference from it is that he went out of his mind. Just such a natural mistake as this is made by Dr. Garnett in his plausible but altogether misconceived monograph. He says (page 57):

> It is a more serious matter that the descriptions (he is speaking of Blake's accounts of his designs in the *Descriptive Catalogue*) are crammed with statements, far more significant than Blake's visions, of a condition of mental disorder, such as that the Greek marbles are copies of the works of the Asiatic patriarchs; that no one painted in oil except by accident before Vandyke; that ancient British heroes dwell to this day on Snowdon "in naked simplicity"—a species of Welsh Mahatmas, as it would appear. It would have been a judicious emendation if any one had suggested the substitution of "lying spirits" when the artist spoke of himself as molested by "blotting and blurring demons."

Dr. Garnett, who has died since this work (*The Real Blake*) was written, still has power, on account of his wide and well-deserved reputation, to injure the memory of Blake. Therefore this paragraph deserves notice. Blake had many qualities that resembled those of the insane. His visionary imagination, his sporadic anger, his outrageous pride, were like theirs; and his poetic life, lived zealously in a generation that did not share his zeal and with a wife who for long did not sufficiently approve of his over-abundant bodily powers, would have led a weaker and less kindly and lovable man to insanity. His heart, helped by his genius, saved him, while those who did not understand either condemned him. Of these, Dr. Garnett is still one of the most dangerous. It is difficult for any one to realise, while reading his well-balanced pages, that he wrote them without any real knowledge or any attempt to obtain real knowledge of his subject. He writes with an air of scholastic responsibility and moderation, yet was not aware that serious comprehension was here required, thinking that a tone of educated indulgence and mild superiority towards an ill-taught, half-witted enthusiast was all that could be required of him.

With regard to the "Welsh Mahatmas," Snowdon was a name substituted for reasons that may be conjectured for "Mount Gilead" in *Vala* at Blake's second reading of that MS. (Canaan is to Albion as soul to body, it will be remembered). Gilead or Snowdon is essentially a Western or American symbol, the *sense* without which poetry cannot *be*. In *Vala*, in Night I, line 110, Imagination hovers over

it, and "creates man morning by morning." The universal
tent is said a little later to be drawn up above it when
man wanders from inspiration. Eden is within (or above).
Gilead is on the limit of contraction, Night VIII, line 3, and
is, in fact, the ear—the false ear—and the North between
West and East.

Snowdon is mentioned in *Jerusalem*, page 4, line 29, where
the man of the non-mystic and entirely individual mind—
as is Albion with his " western gate " closed and his emanation hidden in jealousy—desires to keep his "mountains" to
himself. Snowdon is the last of a set of five names which
are evidently intended to correspond with our " five senses."

It is also referred to on page 66, line 59, as trembling
when it learns that if man insists on living the purely
individual life, and refusing to be commingled by love, he
will be adjoined by hate.

In the Bible, as will be remembered, Zelophahad's last
daughter (he had five, and no sons) was " Tirzah," called by
Blake " the mother of our mortal part "—the feminine
spiritual cause of generation. The feminine spirits, the parts
of the human mind (or " Daughters " of " Albion ") that
" control our vegetative powers," are the sub-conscious powers
that are opposed to imagination as much as the conscious
reasoning powers are (the " Sons " of " Albion "). They are
united into Tirzah and her sisters on Mount Gilead (*Jerusalem*, page 5, line 40). On page 36, line 12, page 48,
line 64, page 68, line 8, page 79, lines 12, 13, Snowdon or
Gilead is mentioned, from which we learn that Gilead is a
sense that ought to aid vision and the brotherhood which
forms the magic circle of visionaries, but under the influence
of physical moods and the power of the sub-conscious to
draw us down to the mortal limits of our individual bodies
it joins with Og—the selfish centre, the man of scales—the
mood that defends a belief in "the hard substance of things,"
while in the ideal Snowdon's powers still keep a place of
meeting for bards in naked simplicity, not clothed in futile
arguments.

These few references should not have been beyond the
capacity of Dr. Garnett, but his crowning wonder is to be
found in the fact that he refers to Swedenborg on the same
page as that from which the above quotation is taken. The
man who has turned the pages of both Swedenborg and Blake
and yet writes as Dr. Garnett wrote, has a gift of mental
isolation from all that belongs to Blake that is quite his own.

Our minds being now at rest about those "Welsh Mahat-mas," we may perhaps spare a moment to look sufficiently closely at a few passages of Blake's work in order to see in what sense it is to be gathered that we may conclude from the little poem of two stanzas, *Thames and Ohio*, that Blake really had "at one moment a passing project of emigrating to America," as Gilchrist supposed; see vol. i. of his *Life and Works of Blake*, page 373, second edition. Here is the poem:

> Why should I care for the men of the Thames
> And the cheating waters of chartered streams,
> Or shrink at the little blasts of fear
> That the hireling blows into mine ear?
>
> Though born on the cheating banks of Thames,
> Though his waters bathed my infant limbs,
> The Ohio shall wash his stains from me;
> I was born a slave, but I go to be free.

In going to America bodily it is evident that we go by a western port from England. Therefore anything that Blake has to say about the Western gate may be appropriately consulted now.

We first hear of it vaguely, in the rejected preface to *Europe*, as a gate by which man could "pass out," if he would—

> But he will not,
> For stolen fruit is sweet, and bread eaten in secret pleasant.

To "pass out" means to go out from the limitations of egotism into brotherhood, and also from those of the flesh into that spiritual world where all are brothers and commingle completely when we embrace. The nearest approach to any-thing like such commingling that may be enjoyed in the body is when marriage makes two persons "one flesh," to use the Biblical expression. Blake does not consider that form of unity at all equal to spiritual embracements, "which are comminglings, and not a pompous high priest entering at a secret place" (*Jerusalem*, page 69, line 44).

"Stolen fruit" is called "stolen" because abstracted from the "all things in common" that is the rule respecting mental joys in eternity, and "bread eaten in secret" means eaten behind the veil, the flesh, that "curtain on the bed of our desire," as we are told in the *Book of Thel*.

Blake, of course, like all other thinkers, was obliged to philosophise from his own experiences, and to read those of other people by their light, and he did not always remember how peculiar his experience as a visionary was. He declared to Crabb Robinson that all men might have it. He knew that these visions of his, that other people said were invisible, actually taught him thoughts, partly by their appearance, as masqueraders teach, and partly by their words, when they spoke their dream-speeches like dream-actors. He knew that in certain conditions of mind they vanished from him, and that his capacity for either art or poetry was apt to vanish with them, and that doubt and despair tended to cause this vanishing. He found also that arguments, scientific formulæ, and the assumption made by thinkers of his day that no one can experience correctly who experiences abnormally, drove his instructive visions away. This setting up of the average as the standard is done in no part of mental life except the philosophic. It may be called the Great Rationalistic Assumption, for it is no more than an assumption, and, being quite unsupported, a push will topple it over. When it falls, half of most men's Rationalism will fall with it—the negative half. Blake's mind was really entirely rationalistic. But his mental experience led him to believe that he was at times able to get out of the body. By this he meant out of the part of his mind that he recognised to be a direct product of the five senses. He then entered into a state that we cannot always distinguish from trance—the "celestial mind," as Swedenborg calls it—in which he was able to communicate with some small portion of other minds than his own, by something like what we know as "thought transference." Yet others were shut from him when in their ordinary work-a-day individual state, and twice shut when he himself was in this state. Their "western gates" were closed. They were "Men of the Thames." "Why," Blake asks himself in his verse, "should he care for them?" He had only to leave off attending to any one in this common-sense state of mind, and he was free of the disadvantages of it. He would be like one of those spirits of sympathy and rebellion from egotism that he called symbolically "Americans." And to go to America meant to him to go to sympathy, to vision, to communism of the mind, to freedom of the imagination from all prohibitions. This was the sense in which Blake "contemplated emigration," not only "at one time," but habitually. No one has ever suggested that he intended to encourage the emigration of a large number of Welshmen; this exhortation—

Place the tribes of Llewellyn in America for a hiding-place, which is in *Jerusalem*, page 83, line 58, fortunately having escaped Mr. W. M. Rossetti's eye, or else being looked on as mere raving.

Enitharmon's long speech in *Jerusalem*, page 82, lines 22 to 44, gives the key to America and to many other names. "America" is the *secret ark* here, and as such a place of hiding. When Albion's "western gate was closed" he wrongly made an "altar of victims offered to sin and repentance," as told in *Vala*, Night III, line 105.

America, North and South, are Los's "baths of living waters" we have been told in page 58, line 43, of *Jerusalem*, and above that it was shut out by the oaks (of weeping) of Albion's "western shore," when the wheels of the four regions of humanity, clouded and raging, rose up against Albion poisonously. It was at the time referred to on page 59 when the Zoas fell.

We know elsewhere of what an "ark and curtain" is the symbol, and what is the "place of forgiveness of sins" that ought not to be made that of permanent repentance. Even without the prophetic book of *America*, the symbolic use of that name in all its four aspects is obvious.

In 1793, the date of this Prophecy, *America*, there is little to set against Blake's name in the catalogue of his works compiled by Gilchrist. That art and imagination were the most powerful means of acquiring and spreading sympathy, the only salvation of man, may be looked on as a permanent doctrine of his, though he had not yet called attention to the necessary inference from this, that Imagination was the Saviour, and that Jesus of Nazareth was a representative figure through whom we are to learn about It.

Since 1785, when Blake felt his new importance in the family after his father's death, and drew his *Joseph's Brethren bowing down before him* and other subjects from the same story, till now we have only mentioned by Gilchrist the three pictures already noticed here as belonging to 1790, the *Flight into Egypt*, and *Christ blessing Little Children*, with a design (apparently misdescribed) from the *Marriage of Heaven and Hell*. For 1793 we have *Los looking at Orc, bound,* representing the movable means of prophecy in mind ("vehicular") regretting his own attempt to defend man from the blindness of lust by mere self-control (this is only one of the four meanings of that composition), and the design for the frontispiece of the *Visions of the Daughters of Albion,* and the tailpiece to the *Marriage of Heaven and Hell,* which, as

N

early plates show, was not engraved with the rest of the book.

1794 gives Linnell's drawing of the title-page to *Europe*, with a figure omitted from this when engraved, and a separate example in Linnell's possession of the group of Los, Orc, and Enitharmon at the forge in *Urizen*, described by Gilchrist as belonging to *Europe*, but not in the "Museum" copy of that book. There is also a picture of the last design in *Europe*.

In the following year, 1795, the *Songs of Experience* are engraved and their title-page dated. We must suppose that they and the books *Europe, America*, etc., took up much of Blake's time during 1793, 1794. His mind was running almost entirely on art as a means of creating sympathetic imagination. Art that did so only in an elementary degree, being unimaginative—that is, portrait art and drawing-room art—he was not much in sympathy with, and for all his life was furious with Sir Joshua Reynolds, who encouraged borrowed imagination. Reynolds had died, of course, in 1792, and Blake's copy of his *Discourses* is full of indignant pencil notes. Art students will, if imaginative and in love with Raphael and Michael Angelo, read these notes with delight. Others will be angry. But, except considered in relation to Blake's *poetic* preferences, they are quite incomprehensible. Gilchrist relates that Blake used to tell how he had once had an interview with Reynolds, whom he found very pleasant, and who blandly remarked to him, "Well, Mr. Blake, I hear you despise our art of oil painting." "No, Sir Joshua," said Blake, "but I like fresco better."

Blake, in fact, made a sort of fresco for himself, priming his ground with a mixture containing plaster, and using carpenter's glue to give it elasticity and to varnish the surface. He did not "despise" all oil painting, but he objected to it because he held that oil was a body that tended to diminish, by the universality of its own tone, the fresh delicacy and sharpness of the difference between one and another of the tints in which it could only be correctly given when free from this common property. He learned later that carpenter's glue, which he used in his own frescoes, had even more of the same disadvantage.

This diffusion of a tone that in itself means nothing, and that prevents each of the tones which it disguises into semi-uniformity from meaning what they ought to mean, was much liked by connoisseurs in Blake's time, and thought to be artistic because characteristic of the pictures of " Old Masters," notably of Rembrandt. Blake, though himself an inharmonious colourist, spotty, feeble, and incoherent, anticipated the modern schools in their use of pure blue and purple, though their green was practically unknown to him. His pale yellows admitted no treacly brown. He was always strongly opposed to the idea that this " generalising " tone was " artistic." He mixed it up with all other generalising, with the vague drapery lines and dreamy trees of Sir Joshua's portraits, and with the vague benevolence of philosophers who do not attempt to give a real mouthful of bread to anybody. In his prophetic books he attributed to " reason " the faculty of reducing the mind to a " generalising state," and the " minute particulars " in which a man must do good if he would do it at all mean with him accurately divided tints, moods symbolised to his sculpturesque mind by correct and distinguishing treatment of forms, by anatomy with the joints of toes and fingers precisely drawn. He was never tired of maintaining that what Kipling derides as " mess," and as " doing things rather more or less," was fatal to art, to imagination, and to all the intercommunication of precise ideas without which our brotherhood is the brotherhood of " idiots," and its intercourse " slobbering." " Grandeur of ideas," he says, " is based on precision of ideas."

It is said that Sir Joshua once suggested that he should draw better. Blake believed that he " copied perfectly from Imagination," as we know, and he never forgave Sir Joshua. He not only considered the suggestion as unnecessary, but, believing that it meant that he should blur over with suggestive and sketchy touch the finger joints and eyelids, he looked upon it as wicked. Since such suggestive treatment sacrificed his dearly-loved " minute particulars," he of course saw in it the natural contrary of creation, and the gods of the moods that produced it must be enemies of the Creator. This is the meaning of such phrases as " bondage to generalising gods." The gods of Asia are the names Blake chose for almost all the mental attributes that he most disliked. Of course, he did not see that when he mingled Rubens and Rembrandt (as he often did) in one condemnation, and saw no difference between them, he was generalising in criticism without the purpose that Sir Joshua had when doing so in art, namely, to give a true impression of such parts of a scene as we see but do not look at. Blake made the mistake of looking at each part of a picture, and not at the picture.

Graceful attitude we see precisely in Reynolds, who was precise in the balance and pose of his figures. When we are looking at a real person's face we see the hands beneath it and the trees behind without their "minute particulars." Blake generalised in art (though he did not know this) by a method of his own, namely, by thrusting his minute particulars in generally wherever he happened to know enough about them to insert them. His drapery—especially in the floating folds of an angel's garments—is so generalised as not to be drapery at all. It is to be regretted that he did not spare a little mercy for the virtues of the brush from that large amount that he was always ready to demand for the sins of the flesh.

Urizen and *Europe* are both dated 1794, but this is the date of their putting on metal. *Urizen* is an isolated work that may have been written at any time since 1790.

His next " prophetic book " was probably *Europe*. In all his poetry we continually find Europe and Asia used as meaning the two great opposites. They stood as Peleg and Joktan, Esau and Jacob, Saul and David—in fact, as internal and external meaning of Scripture, and as the two styles of Scripture—Law and Prophets. But though Asia is used in a good sense, the gods of Asia are to be understood in a bad sense, as Canaan is the heavenly land, while its inhabitants are not at all heavenly, but had to be cast out when Israel came.

> He scourged the merchant Canaanite
> From out the Temple of his mind,

Blake says of Christ in the poem called *The Everlasting Gospel.* On the other hand, the fairies and others who come at the call of Enitharmon in the poem called *Europe* have many humble purposes of beauty of their own, and if they do but assist in the " sports of night " (emotions of the corporeal understanding, not necessarily of " Eternity "), they may be good and lovable apprentices, and examples to us of the beauties of the half-way house that is given us to rest in on our road.

Now comes 1795, the year of the *Song of Los*, the *Songs of Experience*, and (as copper-plates began to run short and money to be scarce) the minutely engraved *Ahania* and the *Book of Los*. The list of dated works for this year is long : The *Lazar House*, from Milton ; *Elohim creating Adam, Lamech and his two Wives, Good and Evil Angels struggling for Possession of a Child, Elijah in the Fiery Chariot, Newton.*

These drawings are for Butts, and it is probable that many of the undated works, also made for Butts, really belong to the years immediately before. That he was chiefly engaged with uncommissioned work is shown by this leaflet, printed by himself and dated—

October 10, 1793.

To the Public

The labours of the Artist, the Poet, and the Musician have been proverbially attended by poverty and obscurity ; this was never the fault of the public, but was owing to a neglect of means to propagate such works as have wholly absorbed the Man of Genius. Even Milton and Shakespeare could not publish their own works.

This difficulty has been obviated by the Author of the following productions now presented to the Public ; who has invented a method of Printing both Letterpress and Engraving in a style more ornamental, uniform, and grand than any before discovered, while it produces works at less than one-fourth of the expense.

If a method of Printing which combines the Painter and the Poet is a phenomenon worthy of public attention, provided that it exceeds in elegance all former methods, the author is sure of his reward.

Mr. Blake's powers of invention very early engaged the attention of many persons of eminence and fortune ; by whose means he has been regularly enabled to bring before the public works (he is not afraid to say) of equal magnitude and consequence with the productions of any age or country ; among which are two highly finished engravings (and two more are nearly ready) which will commence a Series of subjects from the Bible, and another from the History of England.

The following are the subjects of the several Works now published and on Sale at Mr. Blake's, No. 13 Hercules Buildings, Lambeth :

1. *Job*, a Historical Engraving. Size, 1 ft. 7½ in. by 1 ft. 2 in. Price 12s.

2. *Edward and Elinor*, a Historical Engraving. Size, 1 ft. 6½ in. by 1 ft. Price 10s. 6d.

3. *America*, a Prophecy, in Illuminated Printing. Folio, with 18 designs. Price 10s. 6d.

4. *Visions of the Daughters of Albion*, in Illuminated Printing, with 8 designs. Price 7s. 6d.

5. *The Book of Thel*, a Poem, in Illuminated Printing. Quarto, with 6 designs. Price 3s.

6. *The Marriage of Heaven and Hell*, in Illuminated Printing. Quarto, with 14 designs. Price 7s. 6d.

7. *Songs of Innocence*, in Illuminated Printing. Octavo, with 25 designs. Price 5s.

8. *Songs of Experience*, in Illuminated Printing. Octavo, with 25 designs. Price 5s.

9. *The History of England*, a small book of Engravings. Price 3s.

10. *The Gates of Paradise*, a small book of Engravings. Price 3s.

The illuminated books are printed in colours, and on the most beautiful wove paper that could be procured.

No subscriptions for the beautiful engraved works now in hand are asked, for none are wanted ; but the Author will produce his works and offer them to sale at a fair price.

This leaflet has not been seen in the original by the present writer. He quotes it from Gilchrist, but believes it to be produced there with remarkable accuracy. The way in which a semi-colon or a colon is dropped in without any sufficient cause here and there, sometimes doing duty for a full stop, and sometimes for a comma, or for an even slighter pause, is entirely in the manner of Blake. He adopted it probably from Lavater's translator, whose punctuation is of this description, and can only be wondered at. It defies explanation.

Blake seems to have been almost entirely without commissioned employment as an engraver at this time. Outlines to the *Odyssey* were published in 1793 from plates engraved by him after Flaxman's designs, and Gilchrist has no knowledge of other work so produced. Blake made fourteen plates for Stedman's *Surinam*, published by Johnson in 1796. £5 was his payment for Flaxman's plates. The prices of the others were probably in proportion.

In 1797 he is noticed as engraving "for Johnson "—

> *Alfred in the Neatherd's Cottage,*
> *King John absolved,*
> *Queen Elizabeth and Essex ;*

> also

> *The Death of Lucretia,*
> *Death of Cleopatra,*
> *Caius Marius,*
> *Mars and Rhea Silvia.*

This is the year of the engraving of many of his designs to Young's *Night Thoughts*. The designing of the whole five hundred and seventy-two and the writing of the poem *Vala* make it a most memorable year in Blake's life and in the history of literature. The number of hours during which he worked remains as much a wonder as the quality of the work and the price at which it was paid. He had £1 each for the plates to Young's *Night Thoughts*.

In 1798 we know very little of his work. Some of that attributed to 1797 must necessarily have run on into the following year. Undated works may also belong here.

For 1799 are noted religious pictures for Butts: a *Last Supper*, a *Charity*, a *Rachel giving Joseph the Coat of Many Colours*, *Adoration of the Kings*, *The Sons of God and*

13

To naked waste; a dreary vale of tears:
The great magician's dead! thou poor pale piece
Of outcast earth—in darkness! what a change
From yesterday! thy darling hope so near,
Long-labour'd prize, O how ambition flush'd
Thy glowing cheek! ambition, truly great,
Of virtuous praise: death's subtle seed within,
Sly, treacherous miner! working in the dark,
Smiled at thy well-concerted scheme, and beckon'd
The worm to riot on that rose so red,
Unfaded ere it fell—one moment's prey!
    Man's foresight is conditionally wise;
Lorenzo! wisdom into folly turns
Oft, the first instant its idea fair
To lab'ring thought is born: how dim our eye!
* The present moment terminates our sight;
Clouds, thick as those on doomsday, drown the next;
We penetrate, we prophesy in vain:
Time is dealt out by particles; and each,
Ere mingled with the streaming sands of life,
By fate's inviolable oath is sworn
Deep silence, "where eternity begins."
    By nature's law, what may be, may be now;
There's no prerogative in human hours:
In human hearts what bolder thought can rise,
Than man's presumption on to-morrow's dawn?
Where is to-morrow?—in another world!
For numbers this is certain; the reverse
Is sure to none; and yet on this perhaps,
This peradventure—infamous for lies,

FROM YOUNG'S "NIGHT THOUGHTS."

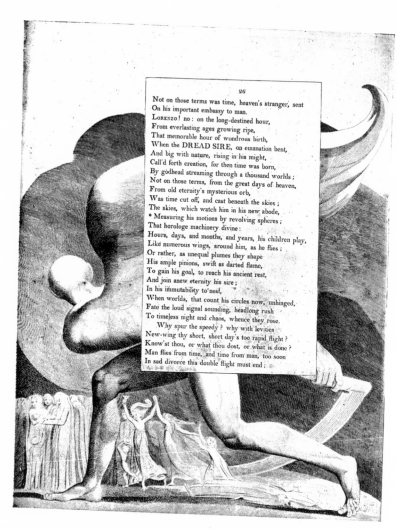

Not on those terms was time, heaven's stranger, sent
On his important embassy to man.
LORENZO! no : on the long-destined hour,
From everlasting ages growing ripe,
That memorable hour of wondrous birth,
When the DREAD SIRE, on emanation bent,
And big with nature, rising in his might,
Call'd forth creation, for then time was born,
By godhead streaming through a thousand worlds ;
Not on those terms, from the great days of heaven,
From old eternity's mysterious orb,
Was time cut off, and cast beneath the skies ;
The skies, which watch him in his new abode,
* Measuring his motions by revolving spheres ;
That horologe machinery divine :
Hours, days, and months, and years, his children play,
Like numerous wings, around him, as he flies ;
Or rather, as unequal plumes they shape
His ample pinions, swift as darted flame,
To gain his goal, to reach his ancient rest,
And join anew eternity his sire ;
In his immutability to'nest,
When worlds, that count his circles now, unhinged,
Fate the loud signal sounding, headlong rush
To timeless night and chaos, whence they rose.
Why spur the speedy ? why with levities
New-wing thy short, short day's too rapid flight ?
Know'st thou, or what thou dost, or what is done ?
Man flies from time, and time from man, too soon
In sad divorce this double flight must end :

FROM YOUNG'S "NIGHT THOUGHTS."

41

On this side death; and points them out to men:
A lecture silent, but of sovereign power!
To vice, confusion; and to virtue, peace.

    Whatever farce the boastful hero plays,
Virtue alone has majesty in death;
And greater still, the more the tyrant frowns:
PHILANDER! he severely frown'd on thee:
" No warning given—unceremonious fate!
" A sudden rush from life's meridian joys!
" A wrench from all we love—from all we are!
" A restless bed of pain! a plunge opaque
" Beyond conjecture! feeble nature's dread!
" Strong reason's shudder at the dark unknown!
" A sun extinguish'd! a just opening grave!
" And oh! the last—last—what? can words express?
" Thought reach? the last, last—silence of a friend!"
Where are those horrors, that amazement where,
This hideous group of ills, which singly shock?
Demand from man—I thought him man till now.

    Through nature's wreck, through vanquish'd agonies,
Like the stars struggling through this midnight gloom,
What gleams of joy! what more than human peace!
Where, the frail mortal? the poor abject worm?
No, not in death, the mortal to be found.
His conduct is a legacy for all,
Richer than Mammon's for his single heir:
His comforters he comforts; great in ruin,
With unreluctant grandeur gives, not yields
His soul sublime; and closes with his fate.

FROM YOUNG'S "NIGHT THOUGHTS."

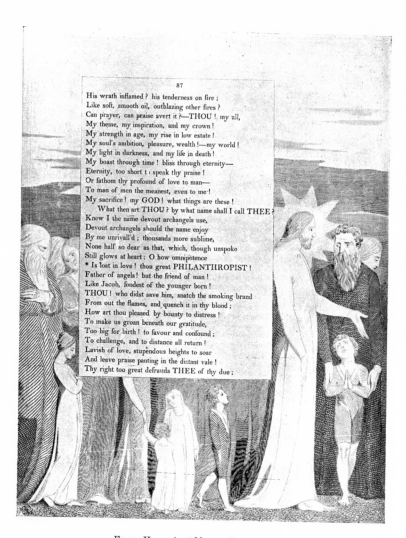

87

His wrath inflamed ? his tenderness on fire ;
Like soft, smooth oil, outblazing other fires ?
Can prayer, can praise avert it ?—THOU ! my all,
My theme, my inspiration, and my crown !
My strength in age, my rise in low estate !
My soul's ambition, pleasure, wealth !—my world !
My light in darkness, and my life in death !
My boast through time ! bliss through eternity—
Eternity, too short to speak thy praise !
Or fathom thy profound of love to man—
To man of men the meanest, even to me !
My sacrifice ! my GOD ! what things are these !
    What then art THOU ? by what name shall I call THEE ?
Knew I the name devout archangels use,
Devout archangels should the name enjoy
By me unrivall'd ; thousands more sublime,
None half so dear as that, which, though unspoke
Still glows at heart : O how omnipotence
* Is lost in love ! thou great PHILANTHROPIST !
Father of angels ! but the friend of man !
Like Jacob, fondest of the younger born !
THOU ! who didst save him, snatch the smoking brand
From out the flames, and quench it in thy blood ;
How art thou pleased by bounty to distress !
To make us groan beneath our gratitude,
Too big for birth ! to favour and confound ;
To challenge, and to distance all return !
Lavish of love, stupendous heights to soar
And leave praise panting in the distant vale !
Thy right too great defrauds THEE of thy due ;

FROM YOUNG'S "NIGHT THOUGHTS."

Daughters of Men, four separate pictures, *The Evangelists*, *Christ taught to read by the Virgin*, a fresco of *A Spirit vaulting from a Cloud to turn and wind a Fiery Pegasus*, afterwards in Blake's own exhibition, unfinished.

This closes the century. The uncoloured drawings are not referred to here.

The list is not given now for purposes of reference. Gilchrist's catalogue must be left holding its own for the historical student. But we require to cast our eyes along its columns to form an idea of how hard Blake was now working, what amazing genius and courage he was showing under neglect and discouragement, and with what miserable starvation prices he kept body and soul together.

The engravings to Young's *Night Thoughts* seem to have been intended by Blake as faint outlines to be coloured by hand. One copy of the work so treated was in the first Blake Exhibition at the Carfax Gallery. This would account for their lack of shading, and for the small sum paid for them.

Most of the more significant of the original water-colour sketches were suppressed, only about a quarter of them being put on copper. Among those not engraved were many showing the allegoric or mythic figures as "children of my thoughts," —to use Blake's own expression,—"walking within my blood-vessels." Young cannot be made responsible for this idea, or for the subjects of the drawings which really belong to *Jerusalem* and *Vala*. (They belong to *Vala's* year, 1797.)

In some of the plates of *Jerusalem*, and in the coloured picture of The Bard from Gray, blood-vessels are seen enmeshing and winding about the figures that move among them.

CHAPTER XVIII

HELPING AND BEING HELPED

At all times, however, the Blakes lived with remarkable frugality.

> We eat little, we drink less.
> This world makes not our happiness,

might be said of them from first to last, as truly as "by incessant labour we have enough."

After Blake's removal to No. 13 Hercules Buildings he had a period which Mrs. Blake in old age used to look backward to as one of prosperity. She actually kept a servant.

The house was not unpleasant. There was a garden, and in the garden was a vine-tree which Blake sat under, and would never allow to be trimmed. The grapes became smaller and smaller, and the plant ran all to leaves and long stems and stalks, but at least it was not educated. To this house, Tatham says, came pupils of rank, and Blake would also go to their houses and stay hour after hour delighting them with the sweet dignity of his manner and the poetry of his conversation. Such good interest was made for him in high places that he was even offered the post of drawing-master to the Royal Family. Had he accepted this he might have become permanently prosperous. But he refused, for he feared that his art would languish in the Court atmosphere, and the offer almost ruined him, for in order not to seem insulting to the Sovereign he gave up all his pupils at once, a very serious sacrifice.

Mrs. Blake's one servant had vanished already, for she was too good a housewife to endure the perfunctory ways of the "general," and she had dismissed her. Blake and his wife were now in the very prime of their health and strength. The long walks in which they used to delight were begun

again, extending sometimes twenty and thirty miles out—it is
said even farther. One day when they had left their house
empty from morning till night, thieves broke in and stole,
says Tatham, sixty pounds' worth of plate. Either this is a
mistake for plates, meaning engraved plates for printing that
were worth sixty pounds, or the pupils of rank who nearly
made Blake a Royal drawing-master must have given him
very handsome presents. Blake, who gave forty pounds for
his printing press, is not likely to have given sixty for his
spoons and forks. He had no dinner-parties.

He had his extravagances, however. He gave away a
lump sum of forty pounds with his wife's knowledge, and
how much more that she never knew of, and so could not
tell Tatham about after his death, we cannot conjecture.
This forty pounds was given to an unfortunate young fellow
who had written a book containing free-thinking views. It
is to be feared that he had ordered it to be printed at his
own expense. Tatham does not tell us his name. During
Blake's lifetime no one was ever told about the gift. The
forty pounds did not all go to the printer. The free-thinking
youth had married a pretty little woman, and a considerable
part of the sum was spent in a handsome dress for her, in
which she then went and called on Mrs. Blake, who was probably found in an apron with her sleeves rolled up. Painters
of historic situations please note. What Mrs. Blake said to
her visitor is not recorded.

Blake was not cured of open-handedness by this. He
noticed a pale-faced young man with a portfolio under his
arm, who passed his house every day. This was enough.
Blake came out and made his acquaintance. He was a poor
art student on his way to death, but struggling to the last.
Blake visited him frequently, taught him, nursed him, and
evidently to the last fed him, but Mrs. Blake, who probably
cooked for him, told Tatham nothing about this. It is a continual and delightful shock to find that Blake, so confident
about his visions and rashly boastful in his art criticism, was
absolutely silent when he had something to brag about.
Had not his wife survived him and in her grief told of his kindnesses to Tatham, and had Tatham not written these things
down in his copy of *Jerusalem*, we should never have known
of any such good deeds. Of Mrs. Blake's own wonderful,
patient, luminous life we get no glimpses from her. She
seems to have been as silent as she was tender and strong.

There is a note belonging to this period in Blake's MS.

book: "I say I shan't live five years, and if I live one it will be a wonder. June 1793." There are no initials after it. We can hardly suppose that Blake wrote it of himself between the fifty-mile walks. Perhaps it was a remembrance of some words of the unfortunate youth, jotted down to see if they would come true. If so, they were justified. Yet Blake was subject to very black moments, and he may have been so imaginatively seized with the feeling of life's short-ness when this boy was dying that it is possible he said it of himself, and wrote it as a warning to himself against the deceptiveness of the sad mood. It is to this period of Blake's life that is usually attributed the story that he wished to add a concubine to his establishment, after the manner of Scriptural patriarchs, but that his wife wept, and that then he gave up the project. It is of suspicious authenticity, and seems rather to belong to the William Bond time and style, just after the *Poetical Sketches* were published. The shock to Mrs. Blake there recorded, which may have occurred then, and which would at least account for her subsequent barrenness, was its probable origin. At this moment it seems out of keeping with the thirty- to fifty-mile walks in which she went with him, which in their turn may have continued the childlessness of the couple.

Many other guesses are open to the reader, who may perhaps even be inclined to suspect that Blake, who had a continual love of the exaggerated and hyperbolic, which is, of course, a characteristic of all men who are both men of geniality and of genius, suggested, when that one unfortunate servant was dismissed, and Mrs. Blake had found the work irksome to resume along with those interminable walks, that Abraham had known a secret for keeping a household servant and attaching her to the family that might be worth con-sideration under the circumstances. If this incident arose from such a piece of Irish sly humour, Blake must have been very much shocked when Mrs. Blake replied to his solemn jest with tears.

An engraving of the *Accusers of Theft, Adultery, and Murder* was done at this time—not a likely subject if Blake, after suffering from theft, had contemplated adultery. It has this line from the *Prologue to Edward III*, which is among the *Poetical Sketches*, "When the senses are shaken, and the soul is driven to madness" (Who can stand ?), p. 53 (*sic*). It occurs on p. 56 of the *Sketches* in Quaritch's facsimile. A drawing also exists with the words, " The Bible of Hell in

Nocturnal Visions collected." Blake does not seem to have engraved this. Perhaps the collection was only projected. Whether or not *America* and the other " Prophecies " belonged to it we can only conjecture. He also wrote here a *Gates of Hell, for Children*, probably in short lines like the *Gates of Paradise, for Children*. He lived in Hercules Buildings till 1800.

Now the century was full. Flaxman, seeing that Blake very much needed a sympathetic patron, and particularly indignant at the small price he received for the plates to Young's *Night Thoughts*, introduced him in the early part of this year to Hayley. The first mention of Blake's name that is at present known is in a letter from Flaxman to Hayley, which begins :—

DEAR AND KIND FRIEND—I have delivered the drawing of Demosthenes to Mr. Blake

This is dated January 29, 1800. The drawing was by Hayley's son, and was to illustrate a book by Hayley on sculpture, in the form of letters to Flaxman, with whom the boy was working as an articled pupil. This year, therefore, begins with the Hayley episode of Blake's life that lasted five years. The head of Demosthenes was to have been engraved for Hayley by Blake on Flaxman's recommendation. On March 26, 1800, he writes:

Perhaps you are not acquainted with Mr. Blake's direction. It is No. 13 Hercules Buildings, near the Asylum, Surrey side of Westminster Bridge.

In this letter, too, Flaxman announces his own appointment as sculptor to the King:

His Majesty has been pleased to appoint me to be his sculptor, but you will understand that this is a *mere* title.

By the middle of the year it is decided that Blake shall leave London and go to Felpham, where Hayley has a large country house, and is the " great man " of the neighbourhood. Blake must have given notice to his landlord at midsummer. On August 18 Flaxman writes to Hayley:

You may naturally suppose that I am highly pleased at the extension of your usual benevolence in favour of my friend Blake, and as such an occasion offers you will perhaps be more satisfied in having the portraits engraved under your own eye than at a distance. Indeed, I hope that Blake's residence at Felpham will be a mutual comfort to you and him, and I see no reason why he should not make as good a livelihood there as in London, if he engraves and teaches drawing, by which he may gain considerably, as also by making neat drawings of different kinds ; but if he places any dependence on painting large pictures, for which he is not qualified either by habit or study, he will be miserably deceived.

Even at that date it is seen that Flaxman was among those who felt it necessary to keep Blake *in his place.*

Hayley was an exceedingly fluent, well-meaning, shallow, and sentimental amateur author, whose character, talents, and taste have a faint and anticipating suggestion of Leigh Hunt about them. He was apparently the very man for Blake. He was well off, and positively anxious to patronise somebody. Unfortunately, he lacked one thing, and in lacking it was absolutely unfitted to enter into Blake's mind, as, though he had no tendencies of his own towards art or literature, he seems to have had no knowledge of Swedenborgianism. He showed absolutely none of the sort of comprehension of Blake that any one who knew anything of Swedenborg must almost necessarily have showed. It is therefore almost certain that he knew nothing. He was a typical eighteenth-century man in matters of religion. Though capable of talking sentiment about angels and heaven, he frankly disliked the Bible. Swedenborg must have been simply intolerable to him. Blake's writings soon became equally abhorrent. Blake wrote to Butts after three years' intimate knowledge of Hayley :

Of this work I take care to say little to Mr. H., since he is as much averse to my poetry as he is to a chapter in the Bible.

In all the correspondence about Blake, from the first introduction to the final difference and estrangement, Flaxman's character stands out as that of a kind and indulgent friend, who bore much petulance from Blake and tried to do him much good. But he also shows himself as a cautious and discreet man, who, while exceedingly anxious to be kind, at the same time makes a hobby of being wise. He is ignorant that tepidity is a detestable quality of character. His own character is like that of some cooks who cook potatoes without salt and leave them in their hot water till sodden, ignorant that this is a detestable method of cookery. Flaxman does not seem to have made any attempt to use his position as King's sculptor to catch Hayley's attention for symbolic art. Yet he could have used it for just this purpose had he possessed zeal and tact. His tasteless and sodden

Swedenborgianism probably did not dare to venture into daylight. If Hayley ever heard of it he only had to put up his eyebrows. Flaxman would have been quite certain never to renew the subject. Not having been born a gentleman, he was always peculiarly at the mercy of a superior look from any one above him in position.

Yet he was more in the secret of Blake's mind than any living man, and he ought to have known better than to introduce Blake to Hayley without preparing Hayley for him by a little bit of education. It was unfriendly not to do so, and the troubles, misunderstanding, and disappointment, both for Blake and Hayley, that followed his introduction are in great measure to be laid at Flaxman's door.

We are glad to suppose that Flaxman did not prepare Hayley for Blake for the same reason that Blake did not prepare his own *Poetical Sketches* for the press—namely, because *he could not*. Here was touch of Nemesis. In this way did the secret justice that sometimes reveals itself behind our affairs punish Blake, when he was behaving best, for his scornful treatment of good Mr. Mathews many years before.

It was in March of this year, while the introduction was still fresh, that Hayley's son, who was Flaxman's pupil, dying, Blake wrote the letter referred to at the beginning of Chapter XII. It is probable that Hayley received it, skimmed it, thought it well-meaning but inflated, and dropped it. He seems not to have gathered from it any of the warning about Blake's nature, character, and mind that Flaxman had not, though a Swedenborgian himself, had the courage or skill to give. Hayley is not, however, the only man who in the long nineteenth century has skimmed Blake, patronised him, and dropped him.

In the next chapter should have been inserted the bit of autobiography addressed "To my Dearest Friend John Flaxman," which is quoted in the preface. But this work was put in type in 1904, and the author first saw those lines in a book that was published in 1905.

CHAPTER XIX

JUST at the same time, separated only by a week, occurred not only the death of Hayley's illegitimate son, but that of his friend Cowper, the poet. Cowper died April 25, Hayley's boy, May 2, 1800.

Hayley now began to write a life of Cowper, and it was arranged that Blake should make engravings for this, and should go to live near Hayley, at Felpham on the Surrey coast, in order that the work might be carried on under the eye of the author. Hayley had not only a certain position in the London bookselling world at that time; he was, like Mr. Mathews of Rathbone Place, an encourager of talent, a man who took a pleasure in befriending the strugglers of art and literature. He was able to do this better than Mr. Mathews, because he was better off. He was the great man of his corner of the country, and his house at Felpham was the great house.

Flaxman deserves credit for bringing Blake to him, however ineffectually he prepared him for the introduction. He did not bear malice for the failure of the Mathews patronage, nor for the money that he had spent in vain in partnership with Mr. Mathews over the *Poetical Sketches*. Blake was still to him his youthful friend and his pet genius. He gave him Hayley as a second mount, hoping that this time he would ride safely to fame and prosperity.

Hayley was in the mood to be an ideal patron. He always liked to see himself as part of an artistic composition. At this moment the tableau of which he was the chief figure was pathetic and attractive. He stood up under the bereavement of his son's death as a good man struggling with sorrow, and in becoming the biographer of his friend Cowper he was, at the same time, a faithful treasurer of the nation's property in the memory of a great man whom he had known, and who was lost at the same time. In patronising Blake he now showed himself also as a pioneer in things of taste, an encourager of the future as well as a preserver of the past.

Blake also seems to have grasped with delight the picturesqueness of the whole situation, and to have been ready to play the hired genius in the spirit of an Italian Old Master at the castle of a prince in the generous Renaissance days. Felpham was hardly even a village. It was a handful of cottages, an inn (The Fox), a farm or two, and a good country-house. Blake was in no danger of rivalry here, or of obscurity. He writes to his friends in absolute glee about all that he sees on arrival. His letters contain not only all the expressions of gratitude and friendship that the occasion called for, but overflowings of joy in phrases about " the swallows fleeting past the window at the moment," the " voices of the winds, trees, and birds, and the odours of the happy ground," the " roller and harrow that lie before the window," " the plough that was met out walking the first morning," and the words of mystic and prophetic significance he heard as " the ploughboy called out to the ploughman : ' Father, the gate is open ! ' "

There were exuberant outbursts of rhyme also, never equalled by him again. The cottage, too, was a marvel, " more beautiful than I thought, and more convenient," he writes. " It is a perfect model for cottages, and, I think, for palaces of magnificence, only enlarging and not altering its proportions, and adding ornaments, not principles." He also tells how " Mr. Hayley received us with brotherly affection," and in substantial things he could soon add, " Mr. Hayley acts like a prince ; we want for nothing."

Here, too, were other advantages. " Felpham is a sweet place for study, because it is more spiritual than London. Heaven opens here on all sides her golden gates ; her windows are not obstructed by vapours ; voices of celestial inhabitants are more distinctly heard, and their forms more distinctly seen," and—words worth all the rest—" I have begun to work."

The journey had been a serious one. Seven different chaises were used at once, and sixteen heavy boxes and portfolios full of prints were in the luggage. The trip took twelve hours, some shifting of weight from chaise to chaise having been necessary on the way.

Blake's sister came with Mrs. Blake, who looked forward to so much pleasure from the change that she worked herself

into an illness of fatigue in the enthusiasm of the prepara-
tions, and Blake tells of it in a letter in these words, "My dear
and too careful and overjoyous woman has exhausted her
strength. . . . Eartham will be my first temple and altar;
my wife is like a flame of many colours of precious jewels
whenever she hears it named."

Eartham was the name of Hayley's house. Flaxman not
having warned Hayley about Blake's style of language, he
seems to have taken these gorgeous expressions as quite a
matter of course.

So Blake went, believing Hayley would accept him as a
prophet under the title "man of genius," and Hayley, after
once taking a liking to him, resolved to cure the poor fellow
both of poverty and of all such nonsense.

The result, for Blake, was, as he said later, that if he could
have turned round and gone back to London the month after
his arrival he would have done so. The rest of the three years
was all painful and laborious endurance, and but for a drunken
soldier, who came, like the "god out of the machine," at the
end and set things right again between Blake and Hayley, the
Felpham period would have ended, as other periods of Blake's
life had, in quarrel and estrangement. It came to this a little
later; and the quarrel, when it at last arrived, was all the more
bitter for delay, and the estrangement more contemptuous.

The record of Blake's work for 1800-1804 is this:

For Butts—*The Crucifixion; A Miniature of Mr. Butts,
Senior, in Artillery Uniform* (painted chiefly from memory);
*Adam naming the Animals; Eve naming the Birds; Portrait
of the Rev. John Johnson* (miniature); *The Riposo; St. Paul
preaching at Athens; Three Maries, with Angel at Sepulchre;
Death of Virgin; Death of St. Joseph; Sacrifice of Jephthah's
Daughter;* "*I was Naked*"; "*Unto Adam and his Wife did
the Lord make Coats of Skins.*"

These two last quotations are the two mottoes, or the title,
of one picture; 1802 is its date.

This recalls to the mind an often-repeated bit of semi-
indecent gossip which has survived while important recollections of Blake have been allowed to drop. Vol. i, page 112,
of Gilchrist gives it in this way:—

Mr. Butts was no believer in Blake's "madness." Strangers to the
man, and they alone, believed in that. Yet he could give *piquant*
account (*sic*) of his *protégé's* extravagances. One story in particular he
was fond of telling, which has since been pretty extensively retailed
about town, and though Mr. Linnell, the friend of Blake's later years

regards it with incredulity, Mr. Butts's authority in all that relates to
the early and middle period of Blake's life must be regarded as unim-
peachable. At the end of the little garden in Hercules Buildings was
a summer-house. Mr. Butts, calling one day, found Mr. and Mrs. Blake
sitting in this summer-house, freed from those "troublesome disguises"
which have prevailed since the Fall. "Come in," said Blake, "it's
only Adam and Eve, you know." Husband and wife had been reciting
passages from *Paradise Lost* in character, and the garden of Hercules
Buildings had to represent the Garden of Eden.

This is a fair specimen of Gilchrist's grammar, and of his
method of treating the duties of a biographer. He hints
much and tells little. He suggests that Blake and his wife
were stark naked in public, and would even invite a friend
to see them so together. But there are several things that
he does not tell us.

The first is whether he received this story *as he gives it*
from Mr. Butts, or from people who "retailed it about town."

The second is that he does not say whether Butts walked
up to the entrance of the summer-house uninvited and saw
Mr. and Mrs. Blake *before* Blake spoke to him, though, from
the usual nature of summer-houses, we are able to conjecture
this, while Blake's speech seems not to have been an invitation but merely made to cover the embarrassment shown by
his indiscreet and intrusive friend.

The third thing that we are not told is whether Blake and
his wife had gone naked all down to that summer-house from
their own door—it was at the end of the garden—or had
disrobed *there*, a thing which it is clear that they had a
perfect right to do.

The fourth is that we are not told whether the couple
were naked at all, a question which the title of this picture,
Unto Adam and his Wife did the Lord make Coats of Skin,
leaves at least open.

The fifth is that, though this story was extensively
retailed for years before Linnell knew Blake, and though
when Linnell did know him he disbelieved it, we are not
told whether Linnell's disbelief was due to the very natural
cause that he had asked Blake whether it was true, and that
Blake had said, "Of course not."

As for the part of the story which attributes the reciting
to one another of passages from *Paradise Lost* by Mr. and
Mrs. Blake, whether "in character" or not, the absurdity of
this will be so clear to any one who has read and *understood*
Blake's works that it may be dismissed at once; it is only
of interest as suggesting to us that Gilchrist's version came

o

from general gossip, unless Captain Butts was himself a deliberate improver of incidents when he came to relate them.

What follows from the whole story as given by Gilchrist is that since, if it was true, it only proves that Blake politely tried to cover the embarrassment of a friend and patron who had intruded on his privacy, and that this friend was at heart, with all his affectionate indulgence and generous helpfulness, such a coarse and selfish-minded person that he did not see that *he* ought to have made, out of a veil of impenetrable silence, the door for that summer-house that it lacked.

He remains the only person really disgraced by it. Gilchrist is but lightly smirched in comparison. After all, Blake and his wife *were married*. And there is still the question of the " coats of skin made by the Lord."

There remains also the possibility that the story has no basis of truth at all. It is not unlikely that it arose out of one of Blake's wild speeches about what he *should be perfectly justified in doing if he chose.* He used to speak in an indiscreet and even boastful manner about his own theories of right and wrong. " Do you think," he said once, " if I came home and discovered my wife to be unfaithful I should be so foolish as to take it ill ? " (Gilchrist, vol. i, p. 374, second edition).

Crabb Robinson relates that Blake said to him, " There is no use in education. I hold it wrong ; it is the great sin ; it is eating of the tree of knowledge of good and evil. That was the fault of Plato. He knew of nothing but the virtues and vices. There is nothing in all that. Everything is good in God's eyes."

Crabb Robinson asked him if there was *nothing* absolutely evil in what man does. " I am no judge of that," said Blake ; " perhaps not, in God's eyes." Asked if Dante was " pure " in writing his *Vision*,—" Pure ! " said Blake. " Is there any purity in God's eyes ? No. He chargeth His angels with folly."

He also said, " What are called the vices in the natural world are the highest sublimities in the spiritual world." When asked, if he were a father, would he not grieve if his son became vicious or a great criminal, he said, " When I am endeavouring to think rightly I must not regard my own any more than other people's weaknesses."

Perhaps he remembered his " brother John, the evil one," at that moment,

What we get from all this is only what Blake himself knew sometimes, namely, that his Antinomian theory was more than he could apply in this world, that there is a Druidical error of forgiveness as of sacrifice. There was evidently much that was creditable in Blake that he would have theoretically repudiated and considered as "weakness."

> In Heaven the only art of living
> Is forgetting and forgiving,
> But if on earth you do forgive,
> You shall not find where to live,

as he printed *backwards* on some clouds in the picture that decorates page 81 of *Jerusalem*, adding after the first couplet of the quatrain, "especially to the female."

What we do not find in any of the many letters to Butts published by Gilchrist, and in all the civil messages from Mrs. Blake that are put into them, is the smallest trace of such familiarity as must necessarily have sprung from that scene in the summer-house at Hercules Buildings if there had been anything in it, such as Gilchrist implies, of the nature of a *spicy secret*. This argument is the chief one for discrediting the whole story, and siding not with Butts but with Linnell, as has already been suggested in the memoir prefixed to the Quaritch edition.

Returning to the list of work done in the Felpham period for Butts, it goes on—*Ruth*, and ends—*Moses striking the Rock, Fire, Plague, Pestilence (Death of the Firstborn), Famine, The Whirlwind, Samson bursting his Bonds, Samson subdued, Noah and the Rainbow, The Four and Twenty Elders casting down their Crowns, Wise and Foolish Virgins, King of Babylon, God judging Adam, Christ appearing, War*, 1805. The rest of Butts' drawings are dated 1805, or later.

Blake also executed at Felpham, *Eighteen Heads of the Poets*, nearly life size, apparently for Hayley's library, as Hayley is among them, and in Gilchrist's list comes next after Voltaire. No attempt at sarcasm seems intended. Blake also did twice a *Satan calling up His Legions* and a *Portrait of Tom Hayley*, the boy that died; a *Los and His Spectre* for *Jerusalem*, page 6, and a picture afterwards engraved as page 51 of *Jerusalem*. These two are dated 1804, the year in which he returned to South Molton Street. They do not in themselves lend any support to Gilchrist's theory that *Jerusalem* was written at Felpham.

Of engraving done during this period, the *Portrait of*

Lavater, for Johnson, dated 1800, was probably finished before the removal to Felpham, and the *Michelangelo* for Fuseli's lectures. Six plates for Hayley's *Triumphs of Temper* were engraved after drawings by Maria Flaxman for Hayley, 1803, and a *Portrait of Cowper and of His Mother* for Hayley's *Life of Cowper*. It is probable that Blake also did something before his return to London for two engravings, a *Death of Queen Katherine* and a *Romeo and the Apothecary*, both after Fuseli, published in 1804 by Rivington.

Blake also illustrated ballads for Hayley—*Little Tom the Sailor*, and others. Hayley also read Klopstock to Blake, who, with his well-known faculty of being a bad listener, became rather indignant at the high praise given to both Homer and the German. His constant habit of reading the Bible, and of reading it as poetry and with enjoyment, had given him a standard by which no Greek and no German could stand without being hopelessly belittled. There was a deficiency in them of "allegory addressed to the intellectual powers while it is altogether hidden from the corporeal understanding."

Blake did all he could to be nice to Hayley, and Hayley was so entirely deceived by his simple and propitiative Irish manner that he thought they were getting on very well, and that he had at last got a *protégé* worth patronising. He calls him "our good Blake," "excellent Blake," and "indefatigable Blake," "my gentle, visionary Blake," and so forth, till Blake (in a fury) wrote the first version of the poem that he afterwards called the *Everlasting Gospel*, to relieve his mind. Blake kept admirably the dreadful secret that "the only man he ever knew who did not almost make him spue was Fuseli," though that expression dropped into his notebook after a few years of habitual Hayley. No one would have suspected the corrosive contempt, concealed now from Hayley as formerly from Mr. Mathews—a merely intellectual contempt, not extending necessarily to the person —that lay behind Blake's pleasant smile, which nevertheless expressed no hypocritical deference, but only his naturally good heart, his yearning for brotherhood, and his desire to treat even publicans and sinners no worse than Christ did. "In the sweetness of his countenance and the gentility of his manner he added an indescribable grace to his conversation," said Crabb Robinson later. Those who remember the late W. G. Wills, who wrote plays for Sir Henry Irving, have seen something of this Hibernian distinction of style.

It is a mingling of the dignified and the affectionate which is due to a deep-seated yearning to win a friend in whoever is addressed. The scornful temperament, when found in a man of an intensely social disposition, makes him so sensitive that he cannot bear not to be loved and admired. When, however, the desire to make a friend or to win a good opinion falls away, a savage animosity and a reckless contempt break out suddenly, to the bewilderment of those whose affections had been caught by the propitiativeness. Yet this propitiativeness was real. The anger meant "How dare you not be worthy of my love and deference!" As a rule, Blake only confided his savage side to his notebook, where it has already given his Anglo-Saxon readers enough bewilderment.

Hayley, pleased with his pet, "introduced Blake to Lord Egremont of Pentworth, Lord Bathurst of Lavant, and Mrs. Poole, and obtained for him commissions for miniatures" (Gilchrist, vol. i, p. 161).

He really acted, as Blake wrote to Flaxman and Butts, "with brotherly affection," and "like a Prince." In one letter, pleased with the country and with the fact that he has a whole house of his own in it (though only a cottage), Blake writes to Butts:

Let me entreat you to give me orders to furnish every accommodation in my power to you and Mrs. Butts. I know my cottage is too narrow for your ease and comfort. We have one room in which we could make a bed to lodge you both, and if this is sufficient it is at your service. But as beds and rooms and accommodations are easily procured by one on the spot, permit me to offer my service in either way, either in my cottage or in a lodging in the village, as is most agreeable to you, if you and Mrs. Butts should think Bognor a pleasant relief from business in the summer. It will give me the utmost delight to do my best. Sussex is certainly a happy place, and Felpham in particular is the sweetest spot on earth, at least it is so to me and my good wife, who desires her kindest love to Mrs. Butts and yourself. Accept mine also, and believe me to remain, your devoted

WILLIAM BLAKE.

And the man to whom Blake wrote this was at that very moment raising an after-dinner laugh by telling with a leer and a chuckle the preposterous story about Adam and Eve in the garden of Hercules Buildings.

He did not come to Felpham.

In another letter Blake attempts to give a popular description of one of his mental states, which seem to have been real trances, in which he left "the body," *going inwards*:

Time flies faster (as it seems to me here) than in London. I labour incessantly. I accomplish not one half of what I intend, because my abstract folly hurries me often away while I am at work, carrying me over mountains and valleys which are not real into a land of abstraction where spectres of the dead wander. This I endeavour to prevent. I with my whole might chain my feet to the world of duty and reality. But in vain. The faster I bind the better is the ballast; and I, so far from being bound down, take the world with me in my flights, and often it seems lighter than a ball of wool rolled by the wind.

He apologises in this way for being so slow in sending Butts some drawings, and adds—

" I should have sent them by my sister, but as the coach goes three times a week to London, they will arrive as safe as with her."

From which it appears that Blake's sister had stayed with him at Felpham from September 20, 1800, when he went there, till nearly September 11, 1801, the date of this letter, and that she travelled in a post-chaise on her return, as she did when she came with Blake in one of his six chaises.

The phrase in this letter, " hurries me . . . into a land where spectres of the dead wander," when read with the ninth line of the third page of *Book of Milton*, first page of the poem itself, which tells how the Source of all inspiration planted a paradise in the poet's brain,

> And in it caused the spectres of the dead to take sweet form
> In likeness of himself,

is another indication that *Milton* was begun towards the close of 1801 at Felpham.

That Blake was a good deal in Hayley's library at this time, and did not do all the decorative poets' heads for it outside without at least fixing them there himself, is suggested by a sentence farther down, " And now I must express my wishes to see you at Felpham, and to show you Mr. Hayley's library, which is not finished, but is in a finishing way, and looks well."

In November of this year he witnesses a death that he must have remembered when drawing one of the designs for Blair's *Grave* a few years later, as his brother Robert's last moments probably inspired another of them.

Hayley writes to Johnson, Cowper's nephew, from " Mrs." Poole's house, " I will transcribe for you, even in the bustle

of this morning, a recent epitaph on your humble old friend
my good William" (a servant ?), "who closed his height of
cheerful and affectionate existence (near eighty) this day
fortnight, in the great house of Eartham, where Blake and I
had the mournful gratification of attending him (by accident)
in the last few hours of his life."

Among the pleasant memories connected with Felpham
was that Miss Blake stayed with "Mrs." Poole during part
of the year 1801, and that "Mrs." Poole lent Blake a
house called "Bruno," of which he grew fond.   He mentions
it with affection after his return to London.   "Mrs." is also
called "Miss" Poole.

January 1802 begins to show the beginning of the end.
The damp cottage had taken all health and spirits from poor
Mrs. Blake, only fifteen months before referred to by Blake
in a letter as his "over-joyous woman," while Hayley's persistent incapacity to understand Blake's religion, and the
place in it held by art, was beginning to wear away his
patience.   Of Mrs. Blake he now writes (to Butts, January
10, 1802):—

"The ague and rheumatism have been her constant
enemies which she has combated almost ever since she has
been here, and her sickness is always my sorrow, of course."
Then referring to the fact that Butts has complained of
failing sight and health : "Let me entreat you to take good
care of both.   It is part of our duty to God and man to take
good care of His gifts, and though we ought not to think
more highly of ourselves, yet we ought to think *as* highly of
ourselves as immortals ought to think."

This sentence is undoubtedly the most difficult to understand that has come down to us of all Blake's writing.   Its
relation to his doctrine of self-annihilation can only be
exactly known if we exactly know (and measure) what he
meant by lines 32 to 36 of the 42nd page of *Milton*, which
must evidently be read with it.

Passing on to news of the hour, the letter continues (the
italics are ours, put to suggest where reading between the
lines is necessary):

When I came down here I was more sanguine than I am at present;
but it was because I was ignorant of many *things that have since occurred*,
and chiefly of the unhealthiness of the place.   Yet I do not repent coming on a thousand accounts, and Mr. H., I have no doubt, will do *ultimately* all that *both he* and I wish, that is, to lift me out of difficulty.

But this is no easy matter to one who, having spiritual enemies of
such magnitude, cannot expect to want natural hidden ones.

"*Such* magnitude" indicates that Blake, who detaches his pen from the MS. of *Milton* to write these letters, has forgotten for a moment, as many absent-minded authors do, that his friends cannot be expected to have miraculous knowledge of his unpublished MS., and of his struggles there recorded in the wrestling of Los and Urizen with Milton.

This reminds one of how it is told of Balzac that after enduring the gossiping chat of his friends for an hour or two in the evening he would suddenly say, "And now let us talk of reality," and continue by telling about the imaginary Paris that he had invented himself, from whose inhabitants he took so many of the characters in his forty-volume *Comédie Humaine*.

Blake continues this letter:

Your approbation of my pictures is a multitude to me, and I doubt not that all your kind wishes in my behalf shall in due time be fulfilled. Your kind offer of pecuniary assistance I can only thank you for at present, because I have enough to serve my present purpose here. Our expenses are small, and our income, from our incessant labour, fully adequate to these at present.

Then after an account of his hackwork of engraving he goes on (all here printed in parenthesis is of course ours, not Blake's):

One thing of real consequence I have accomplished by coming into the country which is to me *consolation* enough, namely, I have re-collected all my scattered thoughts on art, and resumed my primitive and original ways of execution in both painting and engraving, which, in the confusion of London, I had very much lost and obliterated from my mind. . . .

But you have so generously and openly desired that I should share my griefs with you, that I cannot hide what it has now become my duty to explain. My unhappiness has arisen from a source which, if explained too narrowly, would hurt my pecuniary circumstances, as my dependence is on engraving at present, and particularly on the engraving I have in hand for Mr. H., and I find on all hands great objections to my doing anything but the mere drudgery of business, and intimations that if I do not confine myself to this I shall not live. This has always pursued me. This from Johnson and Fuseli brought me down here, and this from Mr. H. will bring me back again. (Yet Blake endured it for more than a year longer. What suffering it was let those only attempt to measure who have suffered from what Balzac calls *la maladie du pouvoir perdu*.) For that I cannot live without doing my duty to lay up treasures in heaven is certain and determined, and to this I have long made up my mind. And why this is made an objection to me while drunkenness, lewdness, gluttony, and *even idleness itself* do not hurt other men let Satan himself explain. (This sentence shows that Hayley's kind introductions into good county society had not been wasted, and that the good people had had "a chiel amang them takin' notes." The doctrine of the Christian Church that includes idleness among the seven *deadly* sins is also brought to mind by the words we have italicised here.) The thing I have most at heart—more than life itself, or all that seems to make life comfortable without—is the interest of true religion and science. And whenever anything affects that interest (especially when I omit any duty to my station as a soldier of Christ) it gives me the greatest of torments. ("Soldier of Christ" means struggler for improvement in imaginative art, of course.) I am not ashamed or averse to tell you what ought to be told, that I am under the direction of messengers from Heaven daily and nightly. But the nature of such things is not, as some suppose, without trouble or care. Temptations are on the right hand and on the left. Behind the Sea of Time and Space roars and follows swiftly. He who keeps not right onwards is lost ; and if our footsteps slide in clay how can we do otherwise than fear and tremble. But I should not have troubled you with this account of my spiritual state unless it had been necessary in explaining the actual cause of my uneasiness into which you are so kind as to inquire ; for I never obtrude such things on others unless questioned, and then I never disguise the truth. But if we fear to do the dictates of our angels (our "leading propensities or virtues," see last note to Lavater) and tremble at the tasks set before us ; if we refuse to do spiritual acts because of natural fears or natural desires, who can describe the dismal torments of such a state ? I too well remember the threats I heard !— "If you who are organised by Divine Providence for spiritual communion refuse, and bury your talent in the earth, even though you should want natural bread,—sorrow and desperation pursue you through life, and after death, shame and confusion of face to eternity. Every one in eternity will leave you aghast at the man who was crowned with glory by his brethren and betrayed their cause to his enemies. You will be called the base Judas who betrayed his friend." Such words would make any stout man tremble, and how can I be at ease ? But I am now no longer in that state, and now go on again with my task, fearless, though my task is difficult. I have no fear of stumbling while I keep it.

My wife desires her kindest love to Mrs. Butts, and I have permitted her to send it to you also. We often wish that we could unite again in society, and hope that the time is not far distant when we shall do so, being determined not to remain another winter here, but to return to London.

> I hear a voice you cannot hear that says I cannot stay,
> I see a Hand you cannot see that beckons me away.

Naked we came here—naked of natural things—and naked we shall return ; but while clothed with the Divine mercy, we are richly clothed in spiritual, and suffer all the rest gladly. Pray give my love to Mrs. Butts and your family.—I am, yours sincerely,

WILLIAM BLAKE.

The letter concludes with a P.S. thanking Butts for proposing to exhibit two of Blake's pictures.

In connection with the old story about the recitation of *Paradise Lost* in a state of nature the unconsciousness of the use of the word "naked" as a mere figure of speech is almost incredible. But in truth it is really time that this ancient tale was buried. It has been long enough above ground since Linnell killed it more than a century ago.

To read this letter in any intimate sense we must now go back to the pages of the poem called *Milton*.

Even at the first moment our eye is caught by one of those little similarities of term that would run from Blake's pen into letters or notes when they were running in his head, on account of their place in a description belonging to some important poem—

> Urizen beheld the immortal Man,
> And he also darkened his brows, freezing dark rocks between
> The footsteps, and infixing deep the feet in marble beds,
> That Milton laboured in his journey and his feet bled sore
> Upon the clay now changed to marble.

This is found in the early part of the seventeenth page of *Milton*, after all the long story about Palamabron and Satan. It is probable, however, that several pages of *Milton* were composed at first very much as we find it now, so far as the early part was concerned, and at such a pace that the first seventeen may have been written even before September 1801, including all the myth of Palamabron. It was done, as a later letter says, " twelve, twenty, or thirty lines at a time, without premeditation, and even against my will. The time it has taken in writing was thus rendered non-existent, and an immense poem exists which seems to be the labour of a long life." He says also that it is " similar to Homer's *Iliad* and Milton's *Paradise Lost*." This "poem" has not really reached us at all. The ten destroyed books of *Milton* must have belonged to it, and we do not know how much of them reappears in the existing *Milton*, and how much in *Jerusalem*. Of course the poem that we have now is not the poem that lay before Blake in MS. when he wrote those words, as will be understood when Blake reaches South Molton Street.

At Felpham Blake not only saw frequently in broad daylight, generally as luminous grey shadows taller than men are usually, any person of whom he thought profoundly, as we see in dreams, and so very naturally concluded that they came from some mental source acting within himself (called Providence), who " planted them in his brain " and " caused them to take shape," but he even heard as one hears words in a dream the very speech of some of these, though this was rarer, and he writes of it with a pleased surprise—

So Ololon uttered in words distinct the anxious thought.
Mild was the voice, but more distinct than any earthly,
That Milton's shadow heard.

Blake's "corporeal understanding" was "Milton's shadow,"
it must be remembered. In the days of the *Marriage of
Heaven and Hell* Isaiah says, "I saw no God, nor heard
any in a finite organical perception."

This letter, in its turn, is dated January 1802, three
months later than that (September 1801) from which we
have taken words that show that the preface to *Milton* was
then being conceived of and written, for Blake never lost
time between conception and production.

Twenty-four days later (February 3) a passage from a
letter of Hayley to Johnson tells us, "Here is a title-page
for thee" (for the new edition of Cowper's *Poems*), "and a
Greek motto which I and Blake, who is just become a Grecian,
and literally learning the language, consider a happy hit."

The "re-collecting" of all his older ideas of art, mentioned
by Blake in this letter, along with the fact that at this time
he was learning Greek and choosing Greek mottoes, shows us
another thing of interest, now that we know enough to take
his poetry seriously, though Gilchrist does not tell it to us.
It was now that he read over the MS. of *Vala*, written in
1797, and brought here in one of his sixteen boxes, and
inserted into it the Greek motto we find at the beginning of
the MS., very much to our surprise, as how it could have
got there in 1797 must have been mysterious in a high
degree. The first page or two of the MS. are tortured
almost out of all meaning by Blake's alterations, and among
these we find some of the lines that are caught like rams by
the horns in a thicket in the pages of *Milton*. We have in
Vala, Night I, line 46,

Why wilt thou number every little fibre of my soul
Spreading them out before the sun like stalks of flax to dry ?
The infant Joy is beautiful, but his anatomy
Horrible, ghast, and deadly. Nought shalt thou find in it
But dark despair and ever-brooding melancholy.

The passage occurs also in *Jerusalem*, page 22, lines 20-24.
Blake, in South Molton Street, had both the MS. of *Vala*
and that of *Milton* before him when making up *Jerusalem*.
In *Milton* we have on page 17, lines 46-49,

Come, bring with thee Jerusalem,—with songs on the Grecian lyre !
        . . . Tirzah numbers her,
She numbers with her fingers every fibre e'er it grow,

which also recalls the earlier poem called the *Mental Traveller*—

> Her fingers number every nerve,
>   Just as a miser counts his gold,—
> She lives upon his shrieks and cries,
>   And she grows young as he grows old.

All of which has to do with Blake's annoyance at the insistence by Hayley on the beauties of scansion in Greek poetry, and the lack of it in portions of Blake's own. Blake, who could alter but could not correct, felt his inspiration withered up.

The "shrieks and cries" of the Mental Traveller are heard again in *Jerusalem*, page 67, line 61.

The "human form" of Imagination is being "bound down" there, just as Hayley wanted to bind it down, by tying Blake to drudgery in art and "numbering every fibre" by scansion in poetry, but Blake would not be bound. Hayley also rebelled against his Biblical phraseology and preferred Greek gods and goddesses.

In the world at large Blake traced the "corporeal" war of the "silly Greek and Latin slaves of the sword" to the "reasoning" mathematical form, and all else that goes to the "memory" and that ends, at its highest, in "Vala," that aspect of Nature "built by the reasoning power in Man," through whom came war on earth. War, called "Luvah's winepress," is further defined in *Vala* as "energy enslaved." War is argument in the head, slaughter in the heart, and sexual love without imagination in the loins, in one plane, but if you pass "earth's central joint" you see all this in reverse order.

This theory is comprehensible when we remember that "everything has a spiritual cause and not a natural cause," and that whether Blake be right about Greek art or not ("the Isles of Grecia lovely"), certainly war will end when mankind are able to divide their emotions between the contemplation of poetic beauty and the forgiveness of sins.

From November 1801 to February 1802 Blake was reading Greek with Hayley. They began because Hayley in writing the *Life of Cowper* wished to form some opinion of his translations of Homer, and Blake's company helped him in the weary task of reading these over and, as Hayley's letters tell us, "comparing them with the original." This led to the picking up by Blake of some smattering of Greek,

and to his falling into a state of rebellion against Hayley's
attempt to fasten Greek rules of art upon him. He had
already strongly resented being asked to admire Klopstock
when German was the favourite language with Hayley.

The first of the scraps of doggerel printed among the
"Resentments" (see Chatto and Windus's edition of Blake's
Poems) and the isolated prose page on Homer and Virgil, called
a "Sibylline leaf" by Gilchrist, show the state of irritation to
which Hayley now reduced him. The latter utterances show
that Hayley was a particular nuisance in exclaiming about
the *unity* of Homer. "Of course," says Blake, "every poem
is a perfect unity, but why Homer's is peculiarly so, I cannot
tell."

At first Blake works off his wrath in these "Sibylline
leaves," but presently he feels that more is needed. He
remains uneasy. He attempts to convert Hayley. But
Hayley is obstinate, and Blake betrays this naïvely by
writing a year later to Butts, "I do not wish to imitate by
being obstinate." Then he sees that much of the wickedness
which he found in Sir Joshua Reynolds (artistic wickedness),
and that he rebuked in his notes to the *Discourses*, which we
shall presently read, and in his myth of Palamabron in *Vala*,
is repeated with emphasis in Hayley's poetic position. He
writes *Milton* in consequence. He sees much poetry in the
classics, but detects—as we all are prepared now to admit—
that myth of an older time is found in a much altered state
in their poems, as traditions of human proportion belonging
to an older art are in their sculpture. But Blake discovered
this for himself. So he begins his *Milton*, and the preface
contains what he said in vain (because too urbanely) to self-
satisfied Hayley.

Gilchrist makes a mistake about this subject through
thinking that *Jerusalem* and not *Milton* was written at
Felpham.

In times but recently passed Blake had been of different
attitude towards Greek art. A letter to Mr. Cumberland,
which is here given in full because it has not yet been
published, shows his feeling in 1800, just before he came to
Felpham.

"Greece" is mentioned even in the prophetic books in two
totally different tones. It is *within* the intellectual temple
built by Urizen that is the reasoned theory of Nature that
has done so much harm to our imagination's elastic and vital
powers, but, like Asia, which is also *within*, it is "ornamented

with exquisite art" (*Jerusalem*, page 58, line 37), and in page 60, line 13, we hear that "the Isles of Grecia lovely" once all belonged to the brotherhood of art (Jerusalem) in days of innocence. This was written after Blake had recovered from the pestering of Hayley, but at the time of the following letter the pestering had not begun. The date of the journey to Felpham is September 20; this is therefore more than two months earlier.

It was probably written to "G. Cumberland of Bristol," the only man of this name mentioned by Gilchrist as knowing Blake at all. He does not refer to him until the year 1813, when he says, "Among present friends may be mentioned Mr. George Cumberland of Bristol." But Blake must have been on friendly terms with him for at least thirteen years by that time, as the familiar opening of the letter shows. He was presumably met at the house of one of the pupils during the prosperous Hercules Buildings period, and perhaps procured at Windsor the unfortunate offer of employment in the Royal Family. Blake's encouragement of our National Gallery before its birth is not sufficiently well known.

2*nd July* 1800.

Mr. CUMBERLAND,
Bishopsgate, Windsor Great Park.

DEAR CUMBERLAND—I am to congratulate you on your plan for a National Gallery being put into execution. All your wishes shall in due time be fulfilled. The immense flood of Grecian light and glory which is coming into Europe will more than realise our warmest wishes. Your honours will be unbounded when your plan shall be carried into Execution, as it must be if England continues a Nation. I hear that it is now in the hands of the Minister, that the King shows it great countenance and encouragement, that it will soon be up before Parliament, and that it *must* be extended and enlarged to take in originals, both of Painting and Sculpture, by considering every valuable Original that is brought into England or can be Purchased Abroad as its Objects of acquisition. Such is the Plan, as I am told, and such must be the plan if England is to continue at all worth notice, as you have yourself observed, only now we must possess Originals as well as France, or be nothing.

Excuse, I entreat you, my not returning Thanks at the proper moment for your kind present. No persuasion could make my stupid head believe that it was proper for me to trouble you with a letter of mere Compliment and expression of Thanks. I begin to emerge from a deep pit of Melancholy, Melancholy without any real reason for it, a disease which God keep you from, and all good men. Our artists of all ranks praise your outlines and wish for more. Flaxman is very warm in your commendation, and more and more of a Grecian. Mr. Hayley has lately mentioned your book on outline in Notes to an essay on sculpture, in six epistles, to John Flaxman. I have been too little among friends, which I fear they will not Excuse, and I know not how to apologise for. Poor Fuseli, sore from the lash of envious tongues, praises you and dispraises with the same breath ; he is not naturally good-natured, and is artificially very ill-natured, yet even from him I learn the Estimation you are held in among artists and connoisseurs.

I am still employed in making Designs and little Pictures, with now and then an engraving, and find that in future to live will not be so difficult as it has been. It is very extraordinary that London, in so few years, from a city of mere Necessaries, or at least a commerce of the lowest order of luxuries, has become a city of Elegance in some degree, and that its once stupid inhabitants should enter into an emulation of Grecian manners. There are now, I believe, as many Booksellers as there are Butchers, and as many Print-shops as of any other trade. We remember when a print-shop was a rare bird in London, and I myself remember when I thought my pursuit of Art a kind of Criminal Dissipation and neglect of the main chance, which I hid my face for not being able to abandon as a passion which is forbidden by Law and Religion. But now it appears to be Law and Gospel too, at least I hear so from the few friends I have dared to visit in my Stupid Melancholy. Excuse this communication of sentiments which I feel necessary to my repose at this time. I feel very strongly that I neglect my duty to my Friends, but it is not want of Gratitude, or Friendship either, but perhaps an Excess of both.

Let me hear of your welfare. Remember my, and my wife's respect-ful compliments to Mrs. Cumberland and family, and believe me to be for ever yours, WILLIAM BLAKE.

13 Hercules Buildings, Lambeth, 1800.

It was from this " stupid melancholy," caused chiefly by being kept by the force of circumstances to ill-paid hack-work, that Blake had bounded up into wild joy and hope when " the gate was open " at Felpham. But the generous and *appreciative* patron that he hoped Flaxman had found for him turned out to be as convinced that he should be kept to merely technical tasks as any one in London, and the open gate slammed-to again.

Blake continued to keep his temper and to " bear all " Hayley's dreadful patronage at Felpham till 1803, and Hayley continued to be delighted with him and to write of him as " our excellent," our " good," " the kind Blake," and when in May both Blake and his wife had fever he wrote of them with delight when they recovered, calling them " our good Blakes." He really seems to have considered them as a pair of ingenious and amiable savages who showed much intelligence, considering, and were quite part of the live stock of his plantation.

CHAPTER XX

BLAKE'S dealings with his MS. of *Vala* in 1802 at the period of re-collecting were not confined to the choosing of a Greek motto. It must have been now that he also adopted the name "Albion" for Man. While he was going over his earlier prints in the many portfolios that filled his sixteen boxes, and discussing within himself his style of drawing on copper, he must, since he says that he returned to his earliest method, have considered the engravings that were mentioned in the opening chapters here, representing *Jocund Day* and *Joseph of Arimathea among the Rocks of Albion*. It will be noticed by any student of the art of engraving that both these, *Jocund Day* in particular, are more in his later manner than anything done during his drudgery years preceding the present re-collecting. It is to be suspected that it was now that he added the words about *Albion* to the plate, and that we are bewildering ourselves in vain if we try to believe that this nickname for Man—it does not seem more to us at the present day—was picked up by Blake in his days of apprenticeship, dropped again when he wrote *Vala*, and resumed when he read over the MS.

It is a point on which we have no certain information, but if indeed it really was so chosen, forgotten, and re-adopted, a tolerable conjecture may be offered, namely, that the word "Albion" was heard, but not seized upon, as a symbol at the time when it first began to come over to us from France. In the book of *America* we have it merely as meaning England, England being itself a symbol, of course, but not one of such universal meaning as the "Albion" of the revised *Vala* and of *Jerusalem*. Man, shut out from brotherhood in the land of vision, is a darkened being not yet called "Albion" in the first draft of *Vala*, though this was begun *after America* was engraved. It would appear that a sort of revelation of the relation between his symbols flashed on Blake. Of course Albion with America shut out by its War of Independence had, in fact, his western gate closed, and was the obvious symbol for Man in the condition called in *Milton* "delivered over to selfhood," page 12, line 24.

This "closed western gate" was also the symbol of decency, in the sense in which we consider decency to mean not the shutting out of allusion to vile meanness and black selfishness, but merely absence of frank language about the sexual passions. Such frankness, however, seemed to Blake to be "honesty," and his complaint that he might not always say what relation all his mythic personages held to the sexual as well as to other portions of the anatomy was part of the blame attaching to "Nature," by whom our "narrowed perceptions" have so perverted us, that "deep dissimulation is the only defence an honest man has left" (*Jerusalem*, page 49, line 23). *Every gate is fourfold*, and it will be noticed that those "whose western gates were open" were "weeping round Albion" (*Jerusalem*, page 45, line 34), in which incident much may be seen about those "intellectual things" tears, and of the meaning of the Western symbols (West—water; Tharmas—good tears of pity and brotherhood, bad tears of discouragement and groves of the "oak of weeping"). The whole passage begins practically at *Jerusalem*, page 42, line 77, that ends here—a new part of the narrative opening page 45, line 37, while the *Albion* story re-appears and vanishes into explanation, emerging again, page after page, at irregular intervals. That the explanation of Blake's own symbols did not always occur to him at once, and that the visions were not a mere lot of deliberate allegories mechanically arranged in every case to fit his own analysis of human character is known, and is shown by the motto on the first page of the *Visions of the Daughters of Albion*, "The eye sees more than the heart knows," which does not mean that Blake did not know *his own meaning*, as the Garnett school maintain, but that the meaning of his visions grew on him, as it will grow on the reader. *Vala*, Night III, line 105, has a word also about the "western gate."

In *Milton*, page 42, lines 2 and 3, we find him knowing only "remotely" some of the acts and words of his own visions.

This would account for his going backwards in the evolution of the *nominality* (if we may coin a word) of his myth-making imagination and writing "Man," "Fallen

One," etc., in *Vala* at first, only correcting it to "Albion," when, by reconsideration, he had seen at Felpham that this was a better term, and that he had wisely used it when writing the *Visions of the Daughters of Albion* in 1793, four years before *Vala* was begun, and nine years before it (in conjunction with his earlier work) was reconsidered. It is just possible that the name was "found" by him on his early engraving when unpacking at Felpham, and was not added at this time. As a biographical point it must remain undecided. As a point of symbolic interpretation the date of the first use of the word in its later meaning is of no consequence whatever.

There is a note of surprise in *Jerusalem*, p. 27, in the prose part of the preface to chap. ii. Blake seems to have only just read what the "learned have explored," and to be pleased to find in it a fresh conviction of the truth of what he had already discovered by vision about *Albion*, even the visions being partly new and seen at Felpham. He had been too busy to read much during the first months at Felpham, and he may have borrowed books from Hayley during his feverish attack of illness in May 1802. It will be remembered that Blake's letter to Butts about the "re-collecting of scattered thoughts on art" is dated January of this year. A letter of November in the same year shows, by an argument quoted from Mr. Gilpin and by allusion to "all Sir Joshua Reynolds's discourses," that the process of re-collecting ideas was still going on.

Hayley was now arguing about Greek art, and thus driving Blake to gather together his own artistic ideas in opposition. To impress Blake, Hayley probably urged in support of his view that the classic standard of excellence was accepted by important persons in high positions, at court, in the army, or at the universities. If so, not only the "Sibylline leaves" but the preface to *Milton* must have been written now, for here, it is said, "We have hirelings in the camp, the court, and the university who would, if they could, for ever depress mental and prolong corporeal war," and the little fragments of poor verse about Sir Joshua in the MS. book which, from their position in the disorderly pages, were evidently written *before* the *Public Address* and other matter belonging to the years following the Felpham period, are found crammed in edgeways on blanks that were not intended to be covered when these "epigrams" were written in the book. One of them refers to the discourse in which Reynolds desires that

the name of Michael Angelo should be his last utterance on
Art.   This epigram is called *A Pitiful Case.*

> "The villain at the gallows tree"
> When he is doomed to die,
> To assuage his misery
> In virtue's praise does cry.
>
> So Reynolds when he came to die,
> To assuage his bitter woe,
> Thus aloud did howl and cry—
> Michel Angelo! Michel Angelo!

There are also several allusions to "hiring" belonging to
1802-10.   And there is the "hired villain," to whom we have
not yet come, but who was long before 1820.   Therefore,
though one line is certainly to be found in the notes on the
Discourses, that seems to imply that they were written
when Blake was "aged sixty-three," that is in 1820, as
Gilchrist maintains, we must remember that we have no
reason to suppose that Blake parted with his *Discourses,* and
we know that he was in the habit of retouching his own
remarks from time to time to enforce their matter or to
improve their symbolism, though not to correct their style.
    The lines are, of course,

> When Nations grow old,
> The arts grow cold,
> And Science settles on every tree;
> And the poor and the old
> Can live upon gold,
> For all are born poor.—Aged sixty-three.

We must regret that Blake did not at this period write
a concise history of the human race.   It would have been
something like this in matter, as we see by *Jerusalem,*
page 27:
    "Notwithstanding what is true about Brutus being the
ancestor of Britain (hence the name), and about the British
being descendants of the Trojans, as I sang in my youth,
and about their having brought here wisdom, art, and science
from Asia, when Asia, given over to war and egotism, no
longer deserved such possessions, a descent from good to
evil of an even earlier date had taken place here, for
we find Druids performing human sacrifice in a manner
that shows them to have been literal misreaders of a
highly ancient and poetic religious decree.   The voice that
uttered that decree must have been that of a man whose
mind was so diffusible in its higher parts that it rode far

out beyond his visible outline, and did not serve as the darkened minds of men do now (though acting along just such a subtle atmosphere in doing so), only to move their arms and legs. His mind reached to the stars, which also means that it reached the remotest truths that were in his limbs, as we call the exteriors of mind, and he embraced in his intuitions all the reasonings and ideas that have since got cut loose from him, and have shrunk up right and left into separations, as we men shrink from one another into mortal egotisms when we forget brotherhood. This atmosphere is now ours in so limited a degree that we cannot generally even see through a brick wall to behold another brick wall, nor allow our imaginations to be visible when our eyes are full of daylight. There was a special part of this ancestral mind most suited to going forth that usually went out on its diffused atmosphere. It exists and can be seen now. It grew to be called 'Jerusalem,' after a city built and destroyed by man in Syria, this deed being permitted in order to be a symbol of man's emanation when literature could not properly describe this because a shyness and modesty had put clothing on man and woman, dulness on their visions, and egotism on their hearts, and matter-of-factness on their poetry. But all things began in 'Albion.'"

Many facts that are now familiar to us all about "thought transference," "pre-natal memory," and about the effects on which much of magic is based, and that are produced by unmated love in the spiritual region, where it acts in an unnatural manner, being diverted from its proper function in the reproduction of species,—these Blake attempted single-handed to understand and control. He saw in them regions of eternity, while in the peculiarly distracting and belittling effect on all prophetic powers wrought by competition, jealousy, argument, and egotism he saw regions of death. There is reason to fear that, just as he was not suspicious enough of rebellion in his apprentice days, so he was not suspicious enough of imagination at a later period, and that the deadly part of mental life is often much more imaginative and contains much more brotherhood than he was willing to believe. But unless Blake's meaning along this central line of idea is properly judged by us, we are only trifling when we pretend that we have a right to deny that he was a madman. It is true that more than this is required if we are to justify our assertion that Blake was sane in the face of all the apparent incoherence of his writings, and the real coherence of the

myth of the Four Zoas must be read in its scattered morsels—
a thing that Gilchrist, the Rossettis, and even Mr. Swinburne
omitted to do, and that Dr. Garnett could not understand
when it had been done for him. Mr. William Michael Rossetti,
while unfortunate enough not to understand Blake's myth, was
man enough to say that he did not think him sane, for which
some respect must always be paid to him, notwithstanding the
unjustifiable concealments of his editorial treatment of *Broken
Love* and the *Everlasting Gospel*, and the mistake that he made
about the "hired villain" epigram, to which we shall soon
come.

In the sketch here given of Blake's historical idea there is
no reference to the Atonement, but that has been treated and
explained by him fully, chiefly in the last pages of *Jerusalem*
and in *Milton*. For those who wish to find the "real"
Blake in his views about this in particular, the following
references may be of use. They are given here, however,
with the warning that the sentences in which the words
referred to occur are not only insufficient, but absolutely
misleading to those who do not weigh others that seem to
have nothing to do with them, particularly those that dwell
on the symbolic difference between the horizontal (length
and breadth, east and west) and the perpendicular (height
and depth, north and south) which have to be traced all
through the poems, for every line in every page must be read
either in relation to the horizontal or to the perpendicular
symbol, and that relation is not always one of immovable
position, but is frequently one of transference.

Redeem, Redeemed, or Redemption are words found in
Milton—page 5, line 3; page 6, line 25; page 9, lines 19, 22,
23; page 11, lines 30, 32; page 18, line 11; page 20, line 44;
page 22, line 52; page 23, line 27; page 25, line 36; and
page 37, lines 11 and 12.

Redemption, a word unfortunately absent from the
Russell and Maclagan sketched index in their edition of
Jerusalem, occurs in that poem on page 36, line 41; page
48, line 63; page 59, line 9; page 92, line 20.

That the first 36 pages do not contain the word shows
them to have been written in a separate meditative mood.
In *Vala* we find it in Night VIII, lines 194, 354, first above
that declaration against separatism—

Now we know that life eternal
Depends alone upon the Universal hand, and not in us
Is aught but death in individual weakness, sorrow, and pain.

The idea is again seen to be that which Comte intended to express by his worship of Humanity. Comte was, of course, an unconscious poet. The story of the temporary triumph of the Body, of Time and Space, and of this world in general is told, and the spiritual causes of it are given mythic names in the close of the first book of *Milton*.

Page 27 of *Jerusalem* may very probably have been first written, not on copper, when the name of Man in *Vala* was altered to Albion, and many of the passages of that poem were cut out for insertion, slightly and significantly enriched by names, but injured horribly in metre.

In the long poem " to the Jews " on this page we catch first a verbal echo of the short poem of the same style at the beginning of *Milton*, the word *builded* applied to Jerusalem in one, to the pillar in the other, and the symbol, being used in the same manner in both, uniting them. Then as the ballad goes on, after a description of the world's innocence comes the question about golden builders near Paddington (South labouring in West, Urizen in the region of Tharmas).

In page 12, lines 25, 27, 28, we have the same question. The builders (for Urizen is *good* and Prince of Light in the world's innocence) build *hope* in the region of sorrow and uncertainty; they give Enion to Tharmas, and Enion is seen to have Jerusalem's attributes in Jerusalem's absence, and is an aspect of fourfold " Golgonooza," which is a symbol for the Intellect of Art and Vision. The whole paragraph explains the verse, and the " dark satanic wheels " at the end unite it with the " dark satanic mills " in the *Milton* ballad, and so assure our minds that one conception is alive under all—one sap in the whole tree, whether seen as branch, leaf, or flower.

Albion's Spectre now withers up the human form. But first he fell. In *Jerusalem*, page 33, line 17 and following, he is described. He is Satan " worshipped as God by the mighty ones of the earth." He is the devouring power, the Polypus, in fact, though not so called on this page. Through the succeeding passages, up to page 34, line 40, the reasons why Spectre, Selfhood, Vala, Rahab, Mystery, Morality, Satan, Nature, Polypus, and Negation are so closely related that they almost merge into each other is next made clear, although some of this list of names are not found in this particular utterance. It may almost be said that the student who can read these paragraphs can read all Blake. In page 60, line 2, is further illumination that will expand if it be followed through every place where the word Luvah or the word Orc is found, particularly in page 62, line 20, and page 63, line 5.

The previous verse is already to be found in *Vala*, Night II, lines 33 and 34, and now the following verse may be discovered in line 40, a little farther on.

The next stanza—twelfth—the Rhine *red* with human blood, reveals a connection of ideas with the Erythrean or Red Sea, in the 44th line of the 49th page.

The next but one, or thirteenth, is found explained as *reserve*, severely called *dissimulation* in that same page 49 of *Jerusalem*, line 23. If the whole 49th page be read, it will shed a light on the whole ballad. Line 68 of it will be found again in *Vala*, Night VIII, line 376, in 'a connection of ideas that helps to make it plain. Its 75th line,

> This is the only means to the forgiveness of enemies,

where the word *this* is understood, is perhaps the one that more completely explains why Blake wrote at all, and what he hoped to achieve in aid of our "eternal salvation," than all the rest of his works and correspondence.

The mingling of the MS. of *Vala* with that of *Jerusalem* begins very early. Readers of *Jerusalem* will not pass the seventh page without recognising in lines 30 to 37, lines 70 to 77 of *Vala*, Night II. Line 34 of this 7th page of *Jerusalem* is found again in *Vala*, Night VIII, line 136. Then the quotation breaks off. Blake does not seem to have cared to print the long and beautiful passage that follows the lament of Luvah in the furnaces. *Jerusalem*, naturally, being written seven years later, is less friendly to Luvah than *Vala*, in which a tenderness for him underlies hostility.

Urizen is hardly more sympathetically treated. His temple of twelve halls that correspond to the hours of the day and to the signs of Zodiac is in Night II of *Vala* quite different from what he builds in *Jerusalem*, page 58 or page 66. Blake grew more hostile to natural intellect as well as to natural passion with the passage of years. The Mundane Shell, most complex of all his symbols, is here built with Urizen's power, II, 248. But in *Milton*, page 34, line 32, Los is said to have built it. Of course he did so *in* Urizen's power. This Mundane Shell is alluded to and explained copiously in *Jerusalem*.

But it is worth while to continue turning over the pages of *Vala*, as Blake was doing now at Felpham to re-collect his scattered thoughts on art. As we go along we find many other fragments to identify with those now to be written or already engraved in other poems. We were at Night II; towards the end of it line 383 refers to a Song of Experience, the Poison Tree. Lines 384 and 385, when we know that *serpent* and *dog* are symbols of various forms of illusion of Nature produced by fleshly passion, help to explain a passage near the top of page 5 of the *Visions of the Daughters of Albion,* where the same words occur, while line 360 of this same Night was both in the close of the *Visions* and in that of the *Song of Liberty;* and a long way farther on in *Vala,* Night VIII, we shall find another phrase from the last page of the *Visions.* Passing to Night III, we do not pass the 45th line before finding a passage of considerable length, going to line 101, that takes in from line 33 to line 80 of *Jerusalem,* page 29, where it appears almost in the same words. The setting of it, and an alteration or two, are valuable to the serious student, and help to show Blake's mind. Going on to line 125 we find ourselves in *Jerusalem,* page 34, line 12, and the word or name "Vala" acquires further interpretation, especially if we remember that she was mingled with Luvah, of the Robes of Blood, whose robes are those of Ololon in the last paragraphs of *Milton.* The symbols will read one another.

Passing on to Night IV, in line 33,

> Los answered in his furious pride, sparks issuing from his hair,

—another connection between Los and Blake besides the merging of the two in *Milton,* page 20, line 12, and page 36, line 21, and the recognisable portrait of him in the Los upon page 6 of *Jerusalem,* for it is said that when Blake was excited his hair stood up (more than ever) and sparks issued from it. Line 41,

> I know I was Urthona, keeper of the gates of Heaven,

is the same, but for the verb, as *Jerusalem,* page 82, line 79, but all the context is different. In line 85 we hear again of the "raven of dawn," who had disappeared from the symbolism since the chorus to the *Song of Liberty.* In line 95 we have the globe of Blood that we saw in the *Book of Urizen,* and the "horrible, dreamful slumber" of that book is heard of again in line 170; the "binding of Urizen by Los" is gradually introduced now, and goes on almost in the words both of the *Book of Urizen* and of the extra page to *Milton* in a manner refreshing to the student who compares

the three. Line 252 is the same as *Jerusalem*, page 50, line
11, with one word altered. In line 264, still Night IV, we
have the beginning of a short passage repeated, with slight
changes, in *Milton*, page 14, line 38. Line 285 is from the
Book of Urizen again. In Night V, line 43, we find a
repetition from Night I, line 477. This repetition is probably
due to a repetition in Blake's personal experience either of
the moods and their visionary equivalents, or to his forgetting
that he had used reference in the same words (or nearly so)
to the same thing before. Night I contains a few lines in the
much-overwritten early pages (they come on page 2), which,
as may be dimly seen in the reduced facsimile, done only for
the sake of the drawing, and almost illegible, of the Quaritch
edition, were later than the first writing, and later than the fair
copying of the MS. They are certainly earlier than the date
of *Jerusalem*, and are found there in page 22, rearranged
and expanded, and may be understood when compared with
Jerusalem, page 68, lines 58, 59. Later on in the first Night
lines will be recognised, and sometimes passages from
Jerusalem, that come in there much farther on than the
passage from the seventh page in Night II. Of these we
note the similarity of the repelling of Enion here, and of the
youth of Los and Enitharmon with *Jerusalem*, end of page
86. Line 187 of Night I describes Eno drawing out a
moment of time as in *Jerusalem*, page 48, line 31, where the
passage following enlarges on the *Vala* account, while the
opening lines of the same page of *Jerusalem* describe what is
told in and near line 395 of this Night of *Vala*. The numbers of the lines here, as in other Nights of *Vala*, differ in the
Quaritch edition and in that of Chatto and Windus, because
lines mistakenly omitted in the earlier edition were found in
time for insertion in the later, a cause of difference often to
be noticed. The part about the " pale limbs of eternal individuality " is all later than the first draft of *Vala*.

Returning to the process of running through that MS.
as Blake did before writing *Jerusalem*, and taking it up again
at Night V, we find chap. vii of the *Book of Urizen* in the
story of the girdle, lines 83 and following. The woes of Urizen
shut up in dens of Urthona are (*necessarily*) (lines 190 and
following) very like to those of Albion when fallen on the
ground at night, with his children exiled from his breast,
page 19 of *Jerusalem*, where the verse is so much more poetic
than the more explanatory and symbolic pages near it.
Urizen explores his dens here through many pages. That

he did so we also knew from the *Book of Urizen*, but here in Night VI the story is expanded. Lines 281 and 282 are from *Milton* and *Jerusalem* also, placing the Zoas.

Line 285 recalls the first lines of *Jerusalem*, page 44, and to line 18 of that page, showing a state of mind produced by opposition unlike that in which Blake wrote the note about the will on the blank leaf of a volume of Swedenborg, and passes us on to the allusion to *Africa* in page 45, lines 19 to 26. In line 115 of Night VII we find the beginning of a passage in *Jerusalem*, page 30, line 30. Line 306 contains an expression from *Jerusalem*, page 17, line 13. The line 379 of this Night recalls the apparent contradiction of it found in line 35 of *Jerusalem*, page 42, easily understood as a significant example of the *variation* of visions of Time and Space, page 98, line 36. Going on to the passage following line 610 of this long Night VII we come upon the preface to *America*, and in line 650 and what follows we have the passage beginning on page 65, line 6, of *Jerusalem*, with an illumination for line 695 where it ends. Near the close of the Night we have in line 781 a repetition from *Milton*, page 34, line 1.

In Night VIII the preface or Preludium to *America* reappears again in line 78, and on 136 we have line 74 of Night II, which is *Jerusalem*, page 7, line 34, also. In line 253 is a suggestion that *Vala* is much the same as *America's* " shadowy female," while her *practical* identity with Tirzah as well as with Rahab is shown by comparing the knife of flint in line 231 here with that in *Jerusalem*, page 67, line 24, as well, whose lines 44 and following are given here in line 293 and following. Line 376 recalls *Jerusalem*, page 49, line 68. After 380 comes all the myth of Palamabron and Satan, and of the Seven Eyes of God from *Milton ;* line 454, since Luvah is Orc, refers to the subject of *Jerusalem*, page 21, line 31. The eagle of line 513 is seen in a full-page picture to *Milton*, that barely touches the subject that might be drawn from the full description.

In Night IX we have in line 99 the passage in *Jerusalem* that begins page 19. In line 230 we recognise the close of the part called *Asia* in the *Song of Los*. In line 450 we have the subject of the picture on page 7 of *America*. The bones that rattled in *Asia* (and in several other places in the MS.) rattle for the last time. The passage from line 633 onwards is seen to be the 96th page of *Jerusalem* in embryo ; line 665 and following recall the 6th page of *America*. In

699 the lion and little girl of the Song of Experience, *A Little Girl Lost*, reappear. In 723 and following the winepress of Luvah from *Milton*, page 24, is shown, and the *Vala* ends.

There is seen to be a sort of "exchange and mart" between Blake's poems of lines appropriate to any mood. They, as has been seen, all thus help the interpretation. For example, in the first writing of *Vala*, Night II, towards the end in Enitharmon's song we have found the phrase "everything that lives is holy" that first appeared at the close of the *Song of Liberty* after the *Marriage of Heaven and Hell*, and that was the termination of Oothoon's long wail on the last page of the *Visions of the Daughters of Albion*, reappearing and explained at last,

> For the Source of Life
> Descends to be a weeping babe.

As we consider this we catch the meaning of the "Devil's account" of the Incarnation in page 516 of the *Marriage of Heaven and Hell*, namely, that "Messiah fell and formed a heaven of what he stole from the Abyss," which we know from other passages to be "the Abyss of the five senses" or *apparent* Nature, the "war of death," the "void outside existence," which *is* existence), "becomes a womb," *Milton*, pages 43, 44; the empty "argument of the reason" that is "from the loins," *Vala*, Night II, line 108, in which "Cathedron's looms" weave literal Christianity (or death), from jealousy, afterwards known as "jealousy of Theotormon," asserting self-righteousness against the Universal Saviour. Nature is, among other things, we know, the "literal expression of the Scriptures," which, like the art and poetry of the Greeks, is dipped in war, in blood, and is, in fact, Luvah's robe that the Saviour put on (*Milton*, page 44, line 14). "War is energy enslaved," *Vala*, Night IX, line 151.

Glancing over these things and other suggestive passages, we have a knowledge of what was arranging and sorting itself in Blake's mind during this period, and we can perceive what he meant by calling this arranging and re-collecting of the scattered thoughts on art (he cared for no other subject) "the grand reason" of his being brought to Felpham. We also find reasons for considering that *Milton* and not, as Gilchrist says, *Jerusalem* was the great poem he was especially destined to write there. Two of these reasons may be noted. Among the first of the characters mentioned in the early pages of *Jerusalem's* hundred leaves, "Scofield" is one. The name is taken from a man who was only known to Blake in the month of August 1803, while the letter was written in April that contains the words, " But none can know the spiritual acts of my three years' slumber on the banks of the ocean unless he has seen them in the spirit, or unless he reads my long poem descriptive of these acts," . . . "the grand reason of my being brought down here." It is to this that Gilchrist puts as footnote the one word *Jerusalem* ; and yet Gilchrist had read *Milton,* and had even criticised Blake's rough sketch of his cottage on page 36, without, it would seem, noticing the following words written above it :

> He set me down in Felpham's vale and prepared a beautiful cottage for me, *that in three years I might* write all these visions,

while in *Jerusalem,* page 38, line 42, " I write in South Molton Street," where Blake went after leaving Felpham, and where he even saw some of the visions, page 74, line 55, " I see in South Molton Street," page 38, line 57.

Yet the conjecture that he put into *Jerusalem* much that he originally intended for *Milton,* as well as some portion that we see that he actually engraved there and some that he took, with slight alterations, from *Vala,* is justified by the line preceding the words " I write in South Molton Street," which says :

> In Felpham I heard and saw the Visions of Albion.

One phrase from *Jerusalem,* that in line 40 of page 83, recalls a letter from Felpham, it is true, but there is nothing in the " ball of wool " in that letter to oblige us to think that this about " the fluctuating earth " was written at the same time.

In the *Public Address* he speaks in 1809 of a " poem " which he intends soon to publish, in which a " nest of villains " is " rooted out " whose misdeeds, not of a new kind, were " never before made so good an occasion of poetic imagery."

This poem was probably neither *Milton* nor *Jerusalem,* though *Jerusalem* seems not to have been finally pro- duced as a completed book till long after its title-page was engraved (in 1804), for it was new in 1820, when Wainewright spoke of it.

The present writer must take the blame now of having written in the Memoir to the Quaritch edition that " Gilchrist was probably right" in considering that the "grand poem" mentioned in Blake's letter was *Jerusalem*. The fact evidently is that Blake had not the same poem in his mind in 1802 and in 1809. In 1802 he referred to *Milton*, still in MS. In 1809, in the MS. notes for his *Public Address*, he referred to neither, though his boastful claim to "poetic" imagery long deceived the present writer. He must have written both the 1809 poem and its praise in his unpoetic and resentful state of mind, and the "poem" must have been a long piece of doggerel, of which only the "Screwmuch" lines have come down to us. Neither *Jerusalem* nor *Milton* roots out any nest of villains, and both were partly on metal several years before he knew about the "nest" to which he refers.

Yet that "the nature of visionary fancy is not, as some suppose, without trouble" is shown not only in Blake's falling down on his own garden path at Felpham when overwrought by it, to the great alarm of his wife, as related in lines 25-28 of page 44 of *Milton* :

> Terror-struck in the vale I stood at that immortal sound,
> My bones trembled, I fell outstretched upon the path
> A moment, and my soul returned into its mortal state,
> To Resurrection and Judgment in the Vegetable Body,
> And my Sweet Shadow of Delight stood trembling by my side.

Sometimes he was assailed with temptations to cease to believe vision, notwithstanding what Eve says in his first book—the *Ghost of Abel*.

It was probably while engraving at Felpham the plates for Hayley's *Life of Cowper* that "Cowper came to Blake and said,—as he notes *apropos* of a passage in a book read later, —'O that I were insane always! I will never rest till I am so. O that in the bosom of God I was hid! You retain health and yet are as mad as any of us all—over us all—mad as a refuge from Bacon, Newton, and Locke.'"

This is so far interesting to those—who are by no means all dead yet—some of them are still unborn, probably—who hold Blake to be mad, that they can claim the vision of Cowper as agreeing with them. We who hold another opinion may make them a present of their ally. That Blake held such madness to be the bosom of God may be, in its turn, presented to followers of Whitefield and Wesley, and all who seek religion from the clergy of whatever church. If they can treat the suggestion with contempt they are happy men, and if they can see something worth considering in it, they are ten times happier. Blake writes (at the end of his November letter of 1802):

And now let me finish by assuring you that though I have been very unhappy I am so no longer. I am again emerged into the light of day. I still, and shall to Eternity, embrace Christianity and adore Him who is the express Image of God, but I have travelled through perils and darkness not unlike a champion. I have conquered, and shall go on conquering. Nothing can withstand the fury of my course among the stars of God and in the Abysses of the Accuser. My enthusiasm is still what it was, only enlarged and confirmed.

The thing he has conquered was, of course, the painful state of doubt, usually called "sanity" by persons who walk and talk more than they think, and playfully so called by Blake himself, perhaps—at least, that is the inference from his use above of the word madness.

"The Visions were angry with me at Felpham," he would afterwards say, as we learn from Gilchrist, and the letter about adoring the image of God suggests that it was here and now that he acted as he afterwards required the reminder of his wife to recall. This was brought to light when Mr. Richmond asked him what he did when the visions deserted him, which he had admitted they had done for weeks at a time. "What do we do then, Kate?" "We kneel down and pray, Mr. Blake."

In April 1803—the Felpham period is drawing to a close —he writes to Butts (the italics are ours, as before):

And now, my dear sir, congratulate me on my return to London with the full approbation of Mr. Hayley and with promise. But, alas! now I may say to you what perhaps I should not dare to say to any one else— that I can alone carry on my *visionary studies* in London unannoyed, and that I may converse with *my friends* in Eternity, see visions, dream dreams, prophesy, and speak parables unobserved and free from doubts of other mortals—perhaps doubts proceeding from kindness, but doubts are always pernicious, especially when we doubt our friends. Christ is very decided upon this point. "He who is not with Me is against Me"; there is no medium or middle state, and if a man is the enemy of my spiritual life while he pretends to be the friend of my corporeal, he is a real enemy; but the man may be the friend of my spiritual life while he seems the enemy of my corporeal, but not *vice versa*.

Then comes the passage already referred to about the "grand" poem that he "has written."

Then on July 6—three months later—he again refers to this after repeating that "Mr. Hayley is quite agreeable to our return" and that he has promise of a considerable amount of engraving for an elegant work to contain all

Milton's poems, with Cowper's notes and Cowper's translations of the Latin and Italian poems.

The designers of the plates were to be Flaxman and
Romney, with whom Blake was to be associated also as a
designer as well as in his capacity as an engraver.

The profits of the work are intended to be appropriated to erect a
monument to the memory of Cowper in St. Paul's or Westminster Abbey.
Such is the project; and Mr. Addington and Mr. Pitt are both among
the subscribers, which are already numerous and of the first rank.
Thus I hope that all our trouble ends in good luck at last, and may be
forgot by my affections (this means "by my emotions," the term affection
being Swedenborgian) and only remembered by my understanding to
be a memento in time to come and to speak to future generations by a
sublime allegory which is now *perfectly completed* into a grand poem.
(Again we note that the poem is already written, and that Scholfield is
not yet known to Blake.)   I may praise it, since I dare not pretend to
be any other than the secretary.   The authors are in eternity.   I consider it as the grandest poem that this world contains.   Allegory,
addressed to the intellectual powers while it is altogether hidden from
the corporeal understanding, is my definition of the most sublime Poetry.
It is also somewhat in the same manner defined by Plato.   This poem
shall with Divine Assistance be progressively printed, ornamented with
prints, and given to the Public.   But of this work I take care to say
little to Mr. H., since he is as much averse to my poetry as he is to a
chapter in the Bible.   He knows that I have writ it, for I have shown
it to him, and he has read part by his own desire, and has looked with
sufficient contempt to enhance my opinion of it.   But I do not wish to
imitate by seeming too obstinate in poetic pursuits.   But if all the
world should set their faces against this I have orders to set my face
like a flint (Ezekiel iii. 8) against their faces, and my forehead against
their foreheads.   As for Mr. H., I feel at liberty to say as follows upon
this ticklish subject.   I regard fashion in poetry as little as I do in
painting, so if both poets and painters should alternately dislike (but
I know the majority of them will not) I am not to regard it at all.
But Mr. H. approves of my designs as little as he does of my poems,
and I have been forced to insist on his leaving me in both to my own
self-will.   I know myself both poet and painter, and it is not his affected
contempt that can move to anything but a more assiduous pursuit of
both arts.   Indeed by my firmness I have brought down his affected
loftiness, and he begins to think that I have some genius, as though
genius and assurance were the same thing!   But his imbecile attempts
to depress me only deserve laughter.   I say this much to you knowing
that you will not make a bad use of it.   But it is a fact too true that if
I had only depended on mortal things both myself and my wife must
have been lost.   I shall leave every one in this country astonished at
my patience and forbearance of injuries upon injuries; and I do assure
you that if I could have returned to London a month after my arrival
here I should have done so.   But I was commanded by my spiritual
friends to bear all and be silent, and to go through all without mur-
muring, and, in fine (to) hope till my three years should be almost
accomplished, at which time I was set at liberty to remonstrate against
former conduct and to demand justice and truth, which I have done in

so effectual a manner that I have compelled what should have been of freedom, my just rights as an artist and a man. And if any attempt to refuse me this be made, I am inflexible, and will relinquish any engagement of designing at all unless left to my own judgment, as you, my dear friend, have always left me, for which I shall never cease to honour and respect you. When we meet I will perfectly describe to you my conduct and the conduct of others towards me, and you will see that I have laboured hard indeed and have been borne on angels' wings.

After this letter Gilchrist closes a chapter by repeating that *Jerusalem* was written at Felpham, and "very grandly designed, if very mistily written," which was all that Blake got for trying too hard to make himself clear. The *Songs of Innocence and Experience* still pass as comparatively easy to understand, though half of them are incomprehensible till *Jerusalem* is explained.

CHAPTER XXI

SCHOLFIELD

THE next letter to Butts describes the adventure with Scholfield which disturbed Blake's last months at Felpham. It runs as follows, and the beginning has this much of unexpected interest. We learn from it that Blake wrote out his letters from a rough draft, and did not improvise them in the careless manner of modern correspondents.

It is dated Felpham, August 16, 1805, and after a few words about seven drawings forwarded, that "about balances our account"—Butts has been advancing him money at last, after Blake's repeated refusals to accept it—the letter continues :

Our return to London draws on apace. Our expectation of meeting again with you is one of our greatest pleasures. Pray tell me how your eyes do. I never sit down to work but I think of you and feel anxious for the sight of that friend whose eyes have done me so much good. I omitted, very unaccountably, to copy out in my last letter that passage from my rough sketch which related to your kindness in offering to exhibit my two last pictures in the Gallery in Berners Street. It was in these words : " I sincerely thank you for your kind offer of exhibiting my two pictures. The trouble you take on my account I trust will be recompensed to you by Him who seeth in secret. If you should find it convenient to do so, it will be gratefully remembered by me among the other kindnesses that I owe to you."

I go on with the remaining subjects which you gave me commission to execute for you, but I shall not be able to send any more before my return, though perhaps I may bring some with me finished. I am at present in a bustle to defend myself against a very unwarrantable warrant from a Justice of the Peace in Chichester, which was taken out against me by a private in Captain Seathes' troop of 1st or Royal Dragoons for an assault and seditious words. The wretched man has terribly perjured himself, as has his comrade, for as to sedition, not one word relating to the King or Government was spoken either by him or me. His enmity arises from my having turned him out of my garden, into which he was invited as an assistant by a gardener at work therein without my knowledge that he was so invited. I desired him as politely as possible to go out of the garden ; he made me an impertinent answer. I insisted on his leaving the garden. He refused. I still persisted in desiring his departure. He then threatened to knock my eyes out, with many abominable imprecations, and with some contempt for my person. It affronted my foolish pride. I therefore took him by the elbows and pushed him before me till I had got him out. There I intended to have left him, but he, turning about, put himself in a posture of defiance, threatening and swearing at me. I, perhaps foolishly and perhaps not, stepped out at the gate, and, putting aside his blows, took him again by the elbows, and, keeping his back to me, pushed him forward down the road about fifty yards, he all the while endeavouring to turn round and strike me, and raging and cursing, which drew out several neighbours. At length when I had got him to where he was quartered, which was very quickly done, we were met at the gate by the master of the house—the Fox Inn (who is the proprietor of my cottage) —and his wife and daughter, and the man's comrade, and several other people. My landlord compelled the soldiers to go indoors, after many abusive threats against me and my wife from the two soldiers ; but not one word of threat on account of sedition was uttered at that time. This method of revenge was planned between them after they had got together into the stable. This is the whole outline. I have for witnesses the gardener, who is ostler at the Fox, and who evidences that, to his knowledge, no word of the remotest tendency to Government or sedition was uttered ; our next-door neighbour, a miller's wife (who saw me turn him before me down the road, and saw and heard all that happened at the gate of the inn), who evidences that no expression of threatening on account of sedition was uttered in the heat of their fury by either dragoon. This was the woman's own remark, and it does high honour to her good sense, as she observes that whenever a quarrel happens the offence is always repeated. The landlord of the inn and his wife will evidence the same, and will evidently prove the comrade perjured who swore that he heard me while at the gate utter seditious words, and d—— the K——, without which perjury I could not have been committed, and I had no witnesses with me before the Justices who could combat his assertion, as the gardener remained in the garden all the while, and he was the only person I thought necessary to take with me. I have been before a Bench of Justices this morning, but they, as the lawyer who wrote down the accusation told me in private, are compelled by the military to suffer a prosecution to be entered into, although they must know, and it is manifest, that the whole is a fabricated perjury. I have been forced to find bail. Mr. Hayley was kind enough to come forward, and Mr. Seagrave, a printer in Chichester, Mr. H. in £100, and Mr. S. in £50, and myself am bound in £100 for my appearance at the Quarter Sessions, which is after Michaelmas. So I shall have the satisfaction to see my friends in town before this contemptible business comes on. I say contemptible, for it must be manifest to every one that the whole accusation is a wilful perjury. Thus you see, my dear friend, that I cannot leave this place without some adventure. It has struck a consternation through all the villages round. Every man is now afraid of speaking to or looking at a soldier, for the peaceable villagers have always been forward in expressing their kindness for us, and they express their sorrow at our departure as soon as they hear of it. Every one here is my evidence for peace and good neighbourhood, and yet such is the present state of things this foolish accusation must be tried in public. Well, I am content, I murmur not, and doubt not that I shall receive justice, and am only sorry for the trouble and expense. I have heard that my accuser is a disgraced sergeant. His name is John Scholfield. Perhaps it will be in your power to hear something about the man. I am very ignorant of what I am requesting of you; I only suggest what I know you will be kind enough to excuse if you can learn nothing about him, and what, I as well know, if it is possible you will be kind enough to do in this matter.

Dear sir, this perhaps was suffered to clear up some doubts, and to give opportunity to those I doubted to clear themselves of all imputation. If a man offends me ignorantly and not designedly, surely I ought to regard him with favour and affection. Perhaps the simplicity of myself is the origin of all offences committed against me. If I have found this I shall have learned a most valuable thing well worth three years' perseverance. I *have* found it. It is certain that a too passive manner, inconsistent with my active physiognomy, has done me much mischief. I must now express to you my conviction that all is come from the spiritual world for good and not for evil.

Give me your advice in my perilous adventure. Burn what I have peevishly written about any friend. I have been very much degraded and injuriously treated, but if it all arise from my own fault, I ought to blame myself.

> O why was I born with a different face?
> Why was I not born like the rest of my race?
> When I look, each one starts; when I speak, I offend,
> Then I'm silent and passive and lose every friend.
>
> Then my verse I dishonour, my pictures despise,
> My person degrade, and my temper chastise;
> And the pen is my terror, the pencil my shame;
> All my talents I bury, and dead is my fame.
> I am either too low, or too highly prised,
> When elate, I'm envied; when meek, I'm despised.

This is but too just a picture of my present state. I pray God to keep you and all men from it, and to deliver me in His own good time. Pray write to me and tell me how you and your family enjoy health. My much terrified wife joins me in love to you and Mrs. Butts and all your family. I again take the liberty to beg of you to cause the enclosed letter to be delivered to my brother, and remain sincerely and affectionately yours, WILLIAM BLAKE.

This description of Blake's two manners—the "elate" and the "meek"—though its truthfulness goes back to his early days with Basire or at Rathbone Place, only applies to him when questions of art were brought forward in the conversation. Then the old story of his conversation with Moser, keeper at the Royal Academy when he was a student, would always repeat itself. People would say things contrary to Blake's profoundly religious, artistic opinions. At first he would "inwardly rage," then he would "speak his mind," and, it may be added, this speaking would be with no note of acrimony or personal discourtesy, and yet with a startling abruptness, as though a near clap of thunder broke the blue silence of a summer sky.

The present writer has had the privilege of seeing an Irish poet who reproduces these and other characteristics of Blake, including the colour of his hair, as the late W. G. Wills reproduced his stately everyday courtesy. He will, it is to be hoped, pardon the use here made of him. It is something to sit as a model for a portrait of Blake. Counting on his pardon, the sketch shall be made, but not named. This poet (he is a most musical and beautiful writer) has a way of remaining silent in company during general conversation, yet wearing an expression of alertness and intelligence, showing him to be fully in sympathy with what is being said, and absolutely ready to reply, to contest, or to accept. Yet a silence as absolute as that of a fish will wrap him up. Suddenly his eye, always brilliant and beautiful (like Blake's), will absolutely flash (like Blake's), his golden hair, always rather rebellious and wavy, will seem like flames rising from his head (like Blake's), and he will thunder out a dictum (as Blake would) in a moving voice for which there is no harmonising or suitable tone belonging to the conversation actually in progress, so that the good-natured among those who are talking are apt to smile and the irritable to rage. Like Blake, again, this enthusiast has combined lyric talent with poetic religious convictions (in his case these are about Shakespeare) quite unrecognised by orthodoxy, and professing to supersede the usual faith, outdoing it on its own ground (as Blake did); lastly, he writes poetry on his pet kind of worship which is sometimes of unsurpassed sweetness, pathos, dignity, and beauty (as Blake did), and he is not discouraged to find it unknown, as happened with Blake's revelation. In his presence the present writer has sometimes even felt an amused and regretful consciousness of seeming to resemble Hayley in his "polite disapprobation," though trying to avoid his "affected scorn." He admits being, like Hayley, a sincere admirer of the unnamed model now sitting for Blake, though, unlike Hayley, he has never been of the smallest use to him, nor "earned a place in the story."

One thing more the present writer has learned from him, and from others of those who live beyond the Bristol Channel, and who (among them) have enabled him to make sketches that build up for him recognisable portraits of Blake's features, habits, tones, and actions. It is—must have been—exceedingly true of Blake, as Crabb Robinson said, that " in the sweetness and gentility of his manner he added an indescribable grace to his conversation." The word to be emphasised is *indescribable*. Those who know this manner, even in a diluted or educated form, will recognise it. The manners of an Englishman, formed in crowds at schools, is more constant and cheerful but less impressive, is quite different and more modern.

But if we are to do Blake full justice while considering this moment of his life at Felpham when he is doing penance himself, and desiring that what he has " peevishly written about a friend " should be burned, we must also not be unjust to Hayley. That Hayley was the " Satan " that accused Palamabron, and Puritanism was the " Urizen " that opposed the poetry in *Milton,* while " Los " opposed his Puritanism, is evident enough, for Blake must have heard them speak *in* Hayley. Allegories always live *in* actual persons. Each of us is inhabited by a good many. But, whether or not the epigram about " H.'s " father and mother be addressed to him, Hayley had feminine qualities, as Blake attempts to explain in the passage in *Milton,* at the beginning of page 35, about " war and hunting," which Swedenborg has told us mean *argument* and *persuasion* in the Bible, because where natural objects are supposed to be real, these are frozen into destroying terrors :

> The Two Fountains of the River of Life
> Are become Fountains of Bitter death and corroding Hell
> Till brotherhood is changed into a curse and a flattery
> By Differences between Ideas, till Ideas themselves (which are
> The Divine Members) may be slain in offerings for sin.
> O dreadful Loom of Death ! O piteous Female forms compelled
> To weave the Woof of Death !

That woof is the mood of common sense that leads to common death, and had to be combated with in the " severe contentions of friendship " through which " he who would see Divinity must see him," as explained in *Jerusalem,* page 91.

The chief thing for Blake, in fact, all through life was, as we have seen, *friendship.* Even Art itself was, in its exterior portions at least, mainly of meaning and value because it could raise friendship, as nothing else could raise it, into regions above all that was exterior. We have seen in *Friendship* Blake's only political idea and his main religious idea. It was the end of this world's best laws and purposes. It was the beginning of the laws and purposes of the next. It

was the ante-chamber of the eternal Father's House of Many
Mansions, the great " I in you, and you in Me," which was
Heaven itself, the kingdom of God, of which we are divinely
forbidden to say " Lo here," or " Lo there," seeing that it is
within us, and its King rules from a temple " not made with
hands." Blake's *Resentments* constantly show that his human
duties were all for his friends, none for his foes, as in morality
we are taught that the duties of a man to a woman are all
for Sarah and none for Hagar. The notes to Lavater show
how troubled Blake was if any suspicion entered his mind
that in the smallest degree he had such qualities as make a
man " unfit for friendship." This is Lavater's Great Condemnation also, seldom uttered. It was the " Major Excom-
munication " pronounced by the sinner on himself, recorded
with sorrow by those who would help him, but could not.

Hayley knew perfectly well that, in a suave manner,
with an appearance of kindness, he was continually inflicting
on Blake pangs of humiliation. How deep those pangs were,
and how long they ached, and how the weakness and lame-
ness of mind that followed the aching made the conscience
of the sufferer continually ask him whether he might not be
acting against his duty as a " soldier of Christ " (of the
Human Imagination) in permitting himself to be so injured
in his talent by diverting his energies into the hard labour
required to keep his patience, Hayley could not conceive. He
had looked on himself as doing a good deed by trying to
bring Blake to his senses. He did it for love. He tried to do
it in kindness. He saw that he had here to deal with a most
original and self-glorifying mind, and he tried to raise it
above its petty conceit at first by education only. He read
Homer and Klopstock, and even gave Blake his own poetry,
which he trusted was both elevating and beautiful. Blake
swallowed Homer and Klopstock, criticised the one, derided
the other, and did not fall into any but polite and grateful
rapture over the *elevating and beautiful* verses of Hayley.
It was then that " pride met pride," and Hayley began to see
that Blake needed a lesson. He gave it in the generous form
of overwhelming him with commissions in engraving. Projects like the decoration of his library, which had been begun
on a scale worthy of a Pope dealing with a Raphael, were
quietly dropped. What was done was done. The eighteen
heads of poets should remain, but the whole house was not
to be a gallery of absurd, sprawling figures with big heads, or
big hands, or big eyes. As for Blake's poetry, Hayley really

would have borne it if he could, but, except Mr. Swinburne, Gilchrist, and the Rossettis, no one who could not understand it ever pretended to like it, until these generous enthusiasts taught the public that it was meritorious to do so.

But all the time Hayley was really fond of Blake, rejoicing in his industry and sorrowing over his illness, and when Blake broke out and poured over him a flood of indignant self-assertion he was not roused to indignant and contemptuous reply. He put his pride in his pocket now, and allowed himself to be "silenced completely." In that silence, as we know, he thought, with regret and kindness, what much deeper pain than he had supposed he had given to this strangely religious man who had taken up the sad and ridiculous idea that eccentric designs and delicious verse were essentials to the service of God, and were a portion of the Christian religion.

Being, as Hayley was, a man of a great—it has been called a "fatal"—facility in words, this complete silence of his after Blake's outburst must stand to his credit, and wherever his name is remembered must remain as its highest title to fame.

Mr. Swinburne, in his Essay on Blake, not only treats Hayley, as Gilchrist treated him, in a contemptuous and sneering manner, but quotes the following epigram from Blake's notebook, saying that Hayley will go further "with this hook in his nose" towards posterity than he could have hoped to go without its help. But Mr. Swinburne did not altogether discover what the meaning of "this hook" really was:

To H——.

Of H——'s birth this was the happy lot,
His mother on his father him begot.

It is one of the rare cases in which Blake's mystic order of speech breaks through in mere epigram. It means that the material, matter - of - fact part of his mind, the "corporeal understanding," the faculty in each of us which is "feminine," like the region of Bacon, Newton, and Locke, and from which Blake claims that his own poetry is "altogether hid," had a larger and more dominant share in the building of "H——'s" mind than the "intellectual powers," or, as we should say, the spiritually sympathetic and symbolic powers that Blake considered to be essentially masculine.

Even in Blake's private notebook he did not put the full name to H——, and there is still some reason to question

whether it referred to Hayley at all, or to a miniature painter
named Haynes, a temporary rival to Blake in the general
struggle for employment.   To him it would have been
equally applicable.   He was one of those non-symbolic
artists who did not work in what Blake believed to be the
right or Raphaelesque style, and who had in the period of
Blake's South Molton Street warfare attracted a spark from
the electric batteries of his wrath.   After the verbal outburst
that was received with such a magnanimous silence by Hayley,
came Blake's arrest through Scholfield's false information.

Delighted at being able to play the prince again and not
the schoolmaster as well, Hayley was in arms for his *protégé*
the moment he found that Blake—become *his* Blake once
more—was in danger.   He "came forward" with a hundred
pounds bail, and took up the cudgels at once.

Blake, whose greatest weakness of character lay always in
the difficulty he felt in forgiving an affront, found with
astonishment that Hayley had absolutely no resentment at
all after the fearful scolding that had "silenced" him.
Hayley, therefore, had shown a divine attribute—forgiveness.

In an amazement of self-inflicted discipline Blake took as
large a measure as possible of the fault of his words upon himself.   Though the fault was a true complaint, that Hayley
had injured him by obstructing his artistic powers (a talent
that he was under divine order to make the best of), by
doubts insinuated, by drudgery insisted on, and by sympathy
withheld, and politeness offered instead—the polished stone
given where the bread of life was craved—yet Blake now
began to blame himself for having allowed Hayley to commit
these faults *ignorantly*, and he recognised that ignorance
was an excuse.   He could not blame Hayley for want of
goodness, so far at least as that want of goodness came from
a want of knowledge, for which he who gave such blame
must himself be blamed.   His "too passive manner," Blake
now discovered, was in fault, the Irish propitiativeness that
conceals as long as possible a conflict between a man and his
friend, even when they are divided by the deeper qualities
of character.   This manner is kept up by a vain hope that
other people will understand, and that the pain of explanation may be saved by the pain of patience.   But it fails at
last.   There is an old proverb about a silk purse.   If "the
Human Imagination," that real, eternal, composite personage
to whom Blake prayed under the name of Jesus, does not
come to our help from the eternal region (the Universal

Mind) in which he dwells, we cannot, however poetic we
may ourselves be, raise a commonplace mind to our level,
however patient with it, however indulgent and long-suffer-
ing we may be. This Blake had at last discovered. He
writes in *Jerusalem*, page 45, the larger form of this old,
sad truth. He could not even attain eternal life himself
by goodness:

                              ——however loving
And merciful the individuality, however high
Our palaces and cities, however fruitful are our fields,——
In selfhood we are nothing, but fade away in morning's breath.
Our mildness is nothing ; the greatest mildness we can use
Is incapable and nothing. None but the Lamb of God can heal
This dread disease.

The disease is, as shown in the context, the closing of
Albion's Western Gate—the gate of brotherhood, by which
man should go " outwards every way."

Blake's time at Felpham was now over. He returned to
town, and left Hayley, who had engaged Mr. Samuel Rose
(a name known to those who have read Cowper's correspondence) as his counsel. He was now thirty, and Blake's
case was one of the last, if not the last, that he was to plead
in his short life. Blake's journey was in October. He had
no sooner established himself in No. 17 South Molton Street,
where he was to spend nearly seventeen years, than he began
rushing about and doing errands for Hayley in London. A
number of carefully-written and good-natured letters of this
period showing how hard Blake worked at this unpaid labour,
are given by Gilchrist. We find him in them constantly visiting different people, seeing Mr. Edwards and Mr. Saunders,
owner of several of Romney's pictures,—for Hayley was now
doing a *Life of Romney* to follow his *Life of Cowper*,—and
calling on Flaxman, but not finding him in town, though he
found Mr. Evans, who was trying, not very successfully, to
sell the broadsheet ballads written by Hayley, for which he
had made small engravings. He learns that although a
publisher not in the running cannot always secure the sale
of a work, " no chance is left to one out of the trade." He
tells how he has got some fresh engraving work to do after
Fuseli of designs made " for a little Shakespeare." On this
subject Blake now sees Mr. Johnson, the bookseller, where
he used to meet Godwin. This is not Hayley's friend Johnson,
Cowper's nephew, the " bard " for whose sake Oxford, where
he lived, is said to bring leaves of the tree of life to Albion
(*Jerusalem*, page 45, line 8). This publisher Johnson assures

him that there is no want of work. Blake had been in difficulties during his last months at Hercules Buildings when receiving £1 each for illustrations to Young's *Night Thoughts,* and naturally feared to have trouble in earning his bread on returning to London. He recalls Hayley's own last encouraging words, " Do not fear that you can want employment," and assures him that he is not neglecting the head of Romney that he is engraving for him. It is, of course, for his *Life of Romney.* The letter ends with Blake's fresh impressions of London :

" God send better times. Everybody complains, but all go on cheerfully and with spirit. The shops in London improve ; everything is clean and neat. The streets are widened where they were narrow. Even Snow Hill is become almost level, and is a very handsome street, and the narrow part of the Strand near St. Clement's is widened and become very elegant."

The date of this is not 1903, as one might suppose, but 1803. Blake should come back now and see the Strand again, if only by moonlight, as Hamlet's father saw Elsinore.

A month or two later, after the turn of the year, Blake went back to Sussex and surrendered to his bail to be tried for insulting the King.

In looking backwards over his life we find Blake's name as only seven or eight times connected with Royalty. The first time is in the passage about " the King " of a derisive though dignified nature that he has written in *Tiriel.* He strikes this passage out. The second is the symbolic use of the King in *America.* The third is when he sacrificed all his pupils and reduced himself to embarrassment in order not to be discourteous to the Sovereign by teaching other humbler subjects of the Crown after refusing to be drawing-master to the Royal Family. The fourth time is when some of his designs were shown to George III, who (probably detecting that they were " Sunday pictures ") would not look at them. The fifth is this trial for treason. The sixth, if we do not count a kind word for " old George II " in a note on Lavater, is the dedication of Blair's *Grave* to the Queen. The seventh is the following note, made not for publication, and in connection with we do not know what public event, but the date must be about 1809 :—

Princes appear to me to be fools ; Houses of Commons and Houses of Lords appear to me to be fools. They seem to be something else besides human life. I am really sorry to see my countrymen trouble themselves about Politics. If men were wise, Princes, the most arbitrary, could not hurt them. If they are not wise, the freest Government is compelled to be a tyranny.

To these may be added a constant suspicion of the Government that it is said Blake had. He supposed it to have engaged the soldier Scholfield to try to entrap him into treasonable utterances, as the *agents provocateurs* do in France.

If this be counted as an eighth, however, then the ninth and last connection of Blake's name with Royalty occurred after his death. We seem to have reached the ninth " Night " of *Vala*.

Mr. Kirkup relates (as recorded in a note to pages 81-83 of the first edition of Swinburne's *Essay*) that a gift of £100 was sent to Blake's widow by the Princess Sophia. Considering what loyalty to Royalty had cost the Blakes, Mrs. Blake might have looked on this as a poor and partial restitution, but she was able to subsist on the sale—carefully spun out—of Blake's drawings and engraved books, and did not expect to need to subsist at all for very long. " She sent back the money with all due thanks, not liking to take or keep what, as it seemed to her, she could dispense with, while many to whom no chance or choice was given might have been kept alive by the gift."

If ever a Blake Church is formed, its priests will not have far to go for the first saint of its calendar.

Gilchrist's account of what now happened at the trial for treason need not be improved, and is adopted here, the present writer having nothing of importance to add to it or to correct in it :

The trial came off at Chichester on 11th January 1804, at the Quarter Sessions, the Duke of Richmond (the radical, not the corn law duke) being the presiding magistrate. The Sessions were held in those days in the Guildhall, which is the shell of a Gothic building, having been formerly the chancel of an early English date to the old church of the Grey Friars convent. The fragmentary chancel and the Friary grounds are still extant, just within what used to be the city walls, at the north-east corner of the cheerful old cathedral town.

A few days before the impending trial Hayley met with an accident which very nearly prevented his attending to give evidence in his protégé's favour. It was of a kind, however, to which he was pretty well accustomed. A persevering and fearless rider, he was in the eccentric habit of using an umbrella on horseback to shade his eyes, the abrupt unfurling of which commonly followed, naturally enough, by the rider's being forthwith pitched on his head. He had on this occasion lighted on a flint with more than usual violence, owing his life indeed to the opportune shield of a strong new hat. "Living or dying, however," he declares to his doctors, he "*must* make a public appearance within a few days at the trial of our friend Blake." And on the appointed day he did appear in court to speak to the character and habits of the accused.

The local report follows, that was looked up, it would appear, by D. G. Rossetti in the *Sussex Advertiser* for January 16, 1804. It says:

William Blake, an engraver at Felpham, was tried on a charge exhibited against him by two soldiers for having uttered seditious and treasonable expressions, such as d——n the King; d——n all his subjects; d——n his soldiers; they are all slaves. When Bonaparte comes it will be cut-throat for cut-throat, and the weakest must go to the wall,—I will help him, etc.

Something curiously like the sentiments of some of Blake's less poetic fellow-countrymen will be noticed here by those who remember what used to be said in the early days of the Boer War.

Gilchrist's account goes on:

Mrs. Blake used afterwards to tell how, in the middle of the trial, when the soldier invented something to support his case, her husband called out "False!" with characteristic vehemence, and in a tone which electrified the whole court, and carried conviction with it. Rose greatly exerted himself for the defence. In his cross-examination of the accuser, "he most happily exposed," says Hayley, "the falsehood and malignity of the charge, and also spoke very eloquently for his client," though in the midst of his speech seized with illness, and concluding it with difficulty. Blake's neighbours joined with Hayley in giving him the same character of habitual gentleness and peaceableness, which must have a little astonished the soldier after his peculiar experience of those qualities. A good deal of the two soldiers' evidence being plainly false, the whole was received with suspicion. It became clear that whatever the words uttered, they were extorted in the irritation of the moment by the soldiers' offensive conduct.

"After a very long and patient hearing," the *Sussex Advertiser* continues, "he was by the jury acquitted, which so gratified the auditory that the court was, in defiance of all decency, thrown into an uproar by their noisy exultations. The business of the aforegoing Sessions," it is added, "owing to the great length of time taken up by the above trials" (Blake's and others), "was extended to a late hour on the second day, a circumstance that but rarely happens in the western division of the country. The Duke of Richmond sat the first day from ten in the morning till eight at night without quitting the court or taking any refreshment."

An old man at Chichester, lately dead, who was present as a stripling at the trial, attracted thither by his desire to see Hayley, "the great man" of the neighbourhood, said, when questioned, that the only thing he remembered of it was Blake's flashing eye. Great was Hayley's satisfaction.

CHAPTER XXII

AFTER the trial, Eartham being too far off, a congratulatory supper was held at Lavant, at the house of "Mrs." Poole, who lived only ten minutes' drive from Chichester. It was she who had invited Blake's sister, and had lent him the horse called "Bruno." Blake, in his letter of no date, printed by Gilchrist between that of November 22, 1801, and January 25, 1803, gives the long flight of rhymed verse, printed in his collected works under the title *Los the Terrible*, remarking that they were "composed above a twelvemonth ago while walking to Lavant to meet my sister." The supper after the trial seems to have been a delightful meal. Blake, after his return to town, mentions Mrs. Poole constantly with expressions of affectionate gratitude. There is nothing to show that Mrs. Blake was either at the trial or at the supper. She was still suffering from the rheumatism caught in the damp cottage, and travelling was hard work in those days.

Blake returned by coach, apparently on the day after the conclusion of the trial, which seems to have lasted to the evening of January 11th or 12th. The next knowledge we have of him is from the letter to Hayley dated "London, January 14, 1804, which he says that he writes immediately on his arrival." It seems that the horse that threw Hayley had come from some cavalry stables.

Blake has learned during his journey by coach from an old soldier, his fellow-passenger, that

No one, not even the most expert horseman, ought ever to mount a trooper's horse. They are taught so many tricks, such as stopping short, falling down on their knees, running sideways, and in various and innumerable ways endeavouring to throw the rider, that it is a miracle if a stranger escape with his life. All this I heard with some alarm, and heard also what the soldier said confirmed by another person in the coach. I therefore, it is my duty, beg and entreat you never to mount that wretched horse again, nor again to trust to one who has been so educated. God our Saviour watch over you and preserve you.

The letter goes on to show how buoyant Blake's hopes were at this moment, while it explains why Mrs. Blake was not at his trial, and what provision he had made for her during his absence :

I have seen Flaxman already, as I took to him early this morning your present to his scholars. He and his are all well and in high spirits, and welcomed me with kind affection and generous exultation in my escape from the arrows of darkness. I intend to see Mr. Lambert and Mr. Johnson, the bookseller, this afternoon. My poor wife has been near the gate of death, as was supposed by our kind and attentive fellow-inhabitant (Blake had not the whole of 17 South Mólton Street) the young and very amiable Mrs. Enoch (a kind-hearted little Jewess, no doubt), who gave to my wife all the attention that a daughter could pay to a mother, but my arrival has dispelled the formidable malady, and my dear and good woman begins to resume her health and strength. Pray, my dear sir, favour me with a line concerning your health, how you have escaped the double blow, both from the wretched horse, and from your innocent humble servant, whose heart and soul are more and more drawn out towards you, Felpham, and its kind inhabitants. I feel anxious, and therefore pray to my God and Father for the health of Miss Poole, and hope that the pang of affection and gratitude is the gift of God for good. I am thankful that I feel it. It draws the soul toward eternal life and conjunction with spirits of just men made perfect by love and gratitude, the two angels who stand at the gate of heaven, ever open, ever inviting guests to the marriage. O foolish philosophy ! Gratitude is heaven itself. There could be no heaven without gratitude. I feel it, and I know it. I thank God and man for it, and above all you, my dear friend and benefactor in the Lord. Pray give my and my wife's duties to Miss Poole, and accept them yourself.

As "Miss Poole" is sometimes called "Mrs. Poole," she was perhaps an elderly maiden lady.

Blake is now at South Molton Street again, and this is the first of the portfolio of letters he writes from there. He begins to rejoice in his freedom, and prepares his two title-pages and prints them off, one to *Jerusalem*, and the other to *Milton*. He does not foresee how he is to be harassed by running errands for exacting Hayley. His delight in being able to "prophesy and dream dreams" unmolested could not better be shown than by this bold commencement of his two greatest books in one year. The title-page of the *Milton, a Poem in 12 Books*, is the one that does him, perhaps, the most credit, in view of the fact that he only printed two, for when we remember the immense change in his feeling toward Hayley since the day—only a few months ago—when he "wrote peevishly " about him after " completely silencing " him and calling him " my antagonist," we cannot doubt that the reason for the suppression of those ten books is to be found in this change. He probably saw that they treated Hayley as an enemy (of his spiritual life) who pretended to be the friend (of his corporeal). But the real affection and enthusiasm Hayley had lately shown had carried Blake into " heaven itself "—into gratitude. Can a man be an enemy of one's spiritual life who does this? He was presently to lay it down as a general truth that " corporeal friends are spiritual enemies," but this passage was engraved after he had been bothered by correspondence with his corporeal friend a little longer. Just at first he was in a reaction. There is a line in *Milton*, page 11, line 31, which seems to have been part of a passage added in South Molton Street—

Astonished at the transgressor, in him beholding the Saviour.

The passage occurs in a place and connection which makes its meaning subtle and not to be explained in two words, but what the state of the plate and the separateness of the paragraph show is that it was a later insertion and not part of the original MSS. written at Felpham. Unpacking these now, Blake did with many pages of them what he had urged Butts to do with his letters. He *burned what he had peevishly written about a friend*, reserving only what he felt could never be brought home to Hayley in a way that could hurt his feelings, but would remain hidden as to its meaning under the poetic style of the symbolism. After all, Hayley himself, like all individuals, was not eternal as the moods are, or the spiritual acts of a man's mental life.

That Blake destroyed any of his MS. *now* is, of course, not actually recorded. No one saw him do it but his wife, and she would not have told. To do so would be to bring up the Hayley troubles in a very complete manner. But the silent evidence found in the sudden reduction of *Milton* from the twelve books mentioned in its frontispiece to the two that were actually engraved, shows that there was a great destruction made for some motive or other very soon after Blake unpacked his papers in South Molton Street. We have the fact of his self-chastisement and of his buoyant and indulgent gratitude to Hayley at that moment in his letters, and the inference is not to be avoided. We can feel as certain as though we had been present that this is the motive that reduced *Milton* by ten-twelfths, and that the reduction

was decided on as soon as he read over that very long manuscript after engraving its frontispiece in the first rush of
energy as soon as he set up his press in his new lodgings.
He often destroyed MSS. of his own later in life when he
had no time or money to engrave them, and this was probably
the first time that he did so. Crabb Robinson tells us of
his doing this. Blake said to him once:

When I am commanded by spirits, then I write, and the moment
I have written I see the words fly about the room in all directions.
It is then published. The spirits can read, and my MS. is of no
further use.

This was on the occasion when he said, truly we need not
doubt—

I have written more than Rousseau or Voltaire—six or seven epic
poems as long as Homer's, and twenty tragedies as long as *Macbeth*.

But probably most of these were left unfinished, to be burned
rather than continued when the mood failed.

Whatever was unreal about Blake (if anything was),
certainly his gratitude to Hayley was real at this time. How
many poets have sacrificed a MS. to a friend? A poet of
our own day, who had buried his poems with his wife in
his first grief, had her poor remains dragged from the earth
afterwards that he might get them back and send them to
the printer.

Blake changed his view about Hayley soon for the last
time, and the shock must have been almost maddening.

For a year or two, however, he continued rushing about
doing Hayley's messages in town and engraving for his books
whenever he could induce himself to put down the plates of
Milton and *Jerusalem*.

On January 27 he writes a long letter, though he is only
just free from so " violent " a cold that it had kept him in
bed for three days, and in his room for a week. He has been
to see Mr. Walker, to show him, as desired, the portrait of
Romney. Mr. Walker is at Birmingham. He has been to
Mr. Saunders. He has sent off money to Kendal, West-
moreland, as requested. He has carried presents (for Hayley)
to Mr. Rose. He has shown a letter (for Hayley) to Flaxman.
He has been asking about Sir Allan Chambre (for Hayley).
He has twice called on Mr. Edwards for Lady Hamilton's
address (for Hayley). He writes all this and its result, and
ends with more expressions of enthusiasm for Hayley and for
" our good Lady Paulina of Lavant."

Hardly a week later (Feb. 23) he has more errands to report. He has called on Mr. Brathwaite (for Hayley), and is inducing Mr. Brathwaite to speak to Mr. Reed about Romney (for Hayley). He has called again on Mr. Rose, but can give no " pleasant account of him." Rose died soon after. He has called on Mr. Wallace, and found him from home, and will call again. He encloses a present of twenty-two numbers of Fuseli's *Shakespeare* and the book of Italian letters from Mrs. Flaxman. He encloses also the Academical correspondence of Mr. Hoare. All this means care, thought, worry, business, waste of time. Blake is Hayley's right hand in London when he needs both hands for himself as much as—perhaps more than—he ever did in his life.

The people to whom he goes on all this business see his enthusiasm, and they know how Hayley took trouble for him at his trial, and Hayley was a man of wealth and position. His *Life of Cowper* had been a great success. Of course, when they understood that Blake was doing his errands they said all kinds of civil things to him about Hayley, and must have been amused to see Blake's eyes flash and to hear how delighted he was with this. On April 7 (still 1804) Blake writes :—

DEAR SIR—You can have no idea, unless you were in London as I am, how much your name is loved and respected. . . .

Mr. Philips thinks of starting a Review. He is prepared to spend £2000 a year over it. Hayley is to be connected with it. Blake takes up the scheme warmly, gets terms *in writing* from Philips offering four times as much to Hayley as to any other contributor. Blake is on fire with enthu-siasm. The magazine

. . . may be called a Defence of Literature against those pests of the press [reviewers] and a bulwark for genius which shall, with your assistance, disperse those rebellious spirits of Envy and Malignity. . . . Literature is your child. She calls for your assistance. . . .

and so forth.

On April 27 he sees Mr. Hoare, who is helping in the founding of the Review, " after having repeatedly called upon him every day and not finding him." A long letter results, in the course of which·he says, " I have seen our excellent Flaxman lately. He is well in health." Gilchrist has printed in full all the interminable letters here reduced to the smallest dimensions by compression. As he says, they are " valuable as showing Blake's perfect sanity and prudence in the conduct of practical affairs."

R

On October 23 Blake writes again. He has received the money he asked for and worked for, so at least he has bread to eat. But something else excites him now, and he pours out his heart to Hayley. He has seen a few good pictures known as the "Truchsessian Gallery," of which we have no list, but which, it seemed, contained examples by the best masters which, while they could still be bought cheaply, were allowed, of course, to escape us. The National Gallery was not there then, jealously watching for chances.

After saying how pleased he is to hear that Miss Poole is well, and telling how electrical treatment has cured his wife's rheumatism entirely, including the stiffness and swelled knees, he goes on in one of his red-hot fits—he is "elate,"—

For now, O glory! O delight! I have entirely reduced that spectrous fiend to his station [no spectrous fiend has been mentioned in the letter; evidently another scrap of rough draft has gone astray, as on a former occasion, when the fair copy was being made] whose annoyance has been the ruin of my labours during the last past twenty years of my life. He is the enemy of conjugal love, and is the Jupiter of the Greeks, an iron-headed tyrant, and the ruiner of ancient Greece. I speak with perfect confidence and certainty of the fact which has passed upon me. Nebuchadnezzar had seven times passed over him. I have had twenty. Thank God, I was not altogether a beast as he was, but I was a slave bound in a mill amongst beasts and devils. These beasts and these devils are now, together with myself, become children of light and liberty, and my feet and my wife's feet are free from fetters.

This letter was probably written after all the earlier pages of *Jerusalem*.

O lovely Felpham, parent of immortal friendship, to thee I am eternally indebted for my three years' rest from perturbation, and the strength I now enjoy.

Here we have the contrast again, already noted, with the mood in which he went through troubles at Felpham, "not unlike a champion," and in which had he and his wife "depended only on mortal things" they "must have been lost." He is in a wild state of "all's well that ends well."

Suddenly on the day after visiting the Truchsessian Gallery of pictures I was again enlightened with the light I enjoyed in my youth, which has for exactly twenty years been closed from me as by a door and by window-shutters. Consequently I can with confidence promise you ocular demonstration of my altered state in the plates I am now engraving after Romney, whose spiritual aid has not a little conduced to my restoration to the light of Art. Oh the distress I have undergone, and my wife with me, incessantly labouring, and incessantly spoiling what I had done well. Every one of my friends was astonished at my faults, and could not assign a reason. They [these are spiritual friends of course] knew of my industry and abstinence from every pleasure for the sake of study, and yet, and yet, and yet these wanted the proofs of industry in my works. I thank God with entire confidence that it shall be so no longer. He is become my servant who domineered over me. He is even as a brother who was my enemy. Dear sir, excuse my enthusiasm, or rather madness, for I am really drunk with intellectual vision whenever I take a pencil or graver into my hand, even as I used to be in my youth ; but as I have not been for twenty dark, but very profitable years, I thank God that I courageously pursued my course through darkness. In a short time I shall make good my assertion that I am become as I was at first by producing the *Head of Romney* and *The Shipwreck*—quite another thing from what you or I ever expected them to be. In short, I am now satisfied and proud of my work, which I have not been for the above long period.

In this letter we see the joy of an artist who is trying to reach beyond the taste of his day, and who is like a musician who would write music for the violin when he had only heard a bad viola played once or twice by a blind beggar when he was a boy. Blake had seen engravings of the early Italian masters, and had drawn from casts of the antique ; that also was long ago. In trying to make a better use of this when composing and when arranging a style for himself so as to be able to see his own compositions as though treated by that style, before each drawing began to go upon paper, he was out of sympathy with the art of his day because its aims, though not absolutely all bad, were bad for his purposes to so large a degree that he fell into a state of hostility to all.

But though the higher parts of the mind may supply a man with unlimited *vision* or *imagination*, and many who are not artists at all are inclined mistakenly to cry out, "*Anch' io pittore !*" ("I, too, am a painter!") because theirs are rich in this, yet, as all practical picture-makers know, the conception of *treatment* requires a prevision or pre-sensation of the hand as well as of the mind. In the same way an actor when imagining his part as he reads it will bring his throat into the attitude of speech, and even a sleeping dog who dreams of hunting will twitch his legs. It is this nervous part of imagination that is the rarest and (as in the case of Rembrandt and some others) is enough to make a man a genius if he possesses it largely, even though he may be without more than a humble portion of the rest of inspiration. It was this nervous part of his artistic mind that constantly wore very thin in Blake, as it will in all men who draw too much "out of their own heads." The wearing thin becomes very marked if they look too much at their own work, and not enough at that of other people. Their own feeblest parts have a power of so affecting their minds through their own pictures as to hypnotise them into exaggeration of error. They then become "mannered," to use the technical term. This, of course, is one of the worst forms of that "generalisation" against which Blake thought he had fought successfully, because his work contained, too often, a harassing want of sequence in its scheme of light, and trusted only to that "real effect" which is the "making out of parts." Yet he would have been the first to know that real impressiveness in poetry, the literary correlative of real effect in art, depends more on the making out of sequences of emphasis.

Recently at Felpham he had tried to rub up his nerves into vitality by going over all his old drawings, and by looking at the prints after the old masters that he had bought when a boy. It did him some good, because he was able to go into the subject with a fresh zest. "Another covering of earth is removed" was the way in which he spoke of the liberation of some of the forces of his mind that had been fretted away by the struggles and distractions of London.

At that time, as the effects of his consideration of such artistic material as he possessed ripened within him, he wrote a long artistic letter to Butts on Nov. 22, 1802. It has been here only passingly referred to. It is chiefly about artistic technicalities and full of self-praise. Blake has stupefied himself into an incapacity to see beyond his own portfolios. With the letter about the Truchsessian Gallery before us it is a shock to go back and read in this one : "There is nothing in the art which our painters do that I can confess myself ignorant of." This is nothing less than an Irish bull. The making such a confession could only be possible after it had ceased to be true. He goes on : "I also know and understand, and can assuredly affirm, that the works I have done for you are equal to the Caracci or Raphael, and I am now some years older than Raphael was when he died."

Considering how intensely eager Blake was to learn from any one from whom he could take anything without falling into subjection, and considering the Truchsessian letter itself, this is too sad to be amusing. The staggerings of a half-starved man who is too hungry to walk straight are not a joke. Blake's artistic sympathies were starving. His violent scorn when rebuked or when asked to revise his prosody is so well known that it tends to hide from us his remarkable teachability in art.

Yet this never ceased to be evident all through his life, from the days when he became so warm a partisan of Basire and so staunch an upholder of the despised beauties of Gothic sculpture—supposed then to be only a fit subject of consideration for antiquaries, and not for artists—through the time when he gave "copy for ever" as his prescription for learning art, and (against Sir Joshua himself) said that " *slavish* " copying is the only kind that has true merit, to the present moment when we find in May 4, 1804, in the letter of that date (only referred to as yet in the terrible list of Blake's errands for Hayley): " I sincerely thank you for Falconer, an admirable poet, and the admirable prints to it by Fettler. Whether you intended it or not, they have given me some excellent hints in engraving; his manner of working is what I shall endeavour to adopt in many points."

Blake had become worried by the contest between his visions and his pursuits at Felpham. He did some small portraits there, of which we have no knowledge, as well as Hayley's work. He says in his letter of July 6, 1807, to Butts: " I am become a likeness-taker, and succeed admirably well, but this is not to be achieved without the original sitting before you for every touch."

This sentence is of value in helping to distinguish Blake from another artist of the same name whose strong point was pictorial memory, who used to paint portraits from a vision of his sitters sitting in the empty chair in which they had sat during the first day's sketch only, so powerful was his faculty of calling up by association the features of any one who had once been seen in a particular place with particular surroundings. He overworked this faculty, and is said to have died in an asylum, where he spent many years. The popular press has reprinted allusions to this man from time to time under the idea that he was William Blake, of the Prophetic Poems. This error must be the less blamed that even the catalogue of the Print Room in the British Museum does not appear to have discovered the difference between our Blake and another namesake who was connected with a well-known benevolent institution.

The feeling of "glory" that Blake felt after seeing the Truchsessian collection was due to the fact that elation seems like power to any one who feels it, particularly to an artist. It produces a kind of concentration mingled with impulse, and concentration and impulse together are, of course, the two parents of the child that we call Art, Imagination being its soul—not born of either. Each particular and detailed feeling of artistic sympathy—it is difficult to remember with sufficient persistence and care—arouses a particular elation, and brings a particular concentration to the artistic mind, just as, if we may illustrate the circumstances or "laws" of *increased* by the pathology of *destroyed* power, the illness called "scrivener's palsy" kills the writing power of a man's fingers when their power of holding or lifting any other article than a pen may be undiminished.

In the new excitement caused by seeing better pictures than he had ever been able to study before, Blake felt that some "*fibre*" of his strength was invigorated which had all along been weak. Industry, he had hoped, would have strengthened it. Of course industry only helps concentration by gradually weeding out, through the automatic impulses acquired by habit, the results of distraction from habits of imagination caused by consciously directed efforts to improve.

Blake, who had less power to analyse, while he had a great deal more analysable material in him than most men, was naturally enough continually falling into surprises about himself. He alternated these with childish misstatements of a self-critical character. That this should be the case with so great a genius and so hasty a judge was inevitable. It need not delay us by any necessity for heart-searching when we find ourselves obliged to disagree with him on some points.

The passages about the "friends" who were surprised at his labours not having improved him refers evidently to friends "in eternity" (in imagination, that is).

CHAPTER XXIII

CROMEK

In December 1804, still feeling the ground to be firm under his feet, and his position with Hayley that of a friend, Blake writes for more money. We gather that Hayley has succeeded in representing the taking from him, which now occurred, of the prospect of engraving ten more plates for the *Life of Romney*, as due to the fact that he evidently has not the time to undertake so much work before the book should be in the binder's hands. All references to other subjects but the portrait and *The Shipwreck* have vanished, but a cordial tone has not vanished. Blake is, of course, secretly conscious of giving some of his time to *Jerusalem*, whose plates are progressing. He dares not say a word about this to Hayley. There would be a quarrel at once. Meantime he lives as frugally as he can. We notice that the last time he has had money from Hayley is in October. It is acknowledged on October 23: "I have received your kind letter, with the note to Mr. Payne, and have had the cash from him." This was the time when Blake's household expenses were reduced (as Cromek will tell soon) to ten shillings a week, and when in the verses "I rose up at the dawn of day" Blake protests with his visions for not letting him pray for riches. The allusion to his visionary companions here is under the title "mental friends." They were not the hallucinatory presences that deceive a madman.

The present letter (December 18, 1804) begins by speaking of proofs enclosed and of Flaxman's approval of them, and of his advice, "which he gives with all the warmth of friendship both to you and me." Blake adds: "The labour I have used on these two plates has left me without any resource but that of applying to you. I am again in want of ten pounds; hope that the size and neatness of my plate of *The Shipwreck* will plead for me the excuse for troubling you before it can be properly finished, though Flaxman has already pronounced it so."

To show Hayley that he is not being overcharged, Blake presently adds: "The price Mr. Johnson gives for the plates of Fuseli's *Shakespeare,* the concluding numbers of which I now send, is twenty-five guineas each. On comparing them with mine of *The Shipwreck* you will perceive that I have done my duty and put forth my whole strength."

He then speaks of other books sent by Hayley, or promised, and winds up:

My wife joins me in wishing you a merry Christmas. Remembering our happy Christmas at lovely Felpham, our spirits still seem to hover round our beautiful cottage and round the lovely Forest. I say *seem,* but am persuaded that distance is nothing but a phantasy. We are often sitting by our cottage fire, and often we think we hear your voice calling at the gate. Surely these things are real and eternal in our eternal minds, and can never pass away. My wife continues well, thanks to Mr. Birch's Electrical Magic, which she has discontinued these three months.—I remain, your much robbed——

We see in Mrs. Blake's treatment another source of spending besides the copper-plates for *Jerusalem* and *Milton.* It must have been exceedingly true now that, as Blake said, "we eat little,—we drink less."

Mr. Rose, the barrister who had defended Blake, died at this time, or "got before me into the Celestial City," as Blake wrote, adding: "I also have but a few more mountains to pass ere I hear the bells ring and the trumpets sound to welcome my arrival." As a piece of Blake's consistency, if no more, it is nice to find that, after writing like this when in health, he died in the same mood—about twenty years later —rejoicing and singing aloud.

Blake's next letters are about the futile publication of Hayley's ballads that were written to give him something to illustrate, and presented to him. He has done most of the plates now. The price, to be paid by Philips, who is publishing the book, is to be twenty guineas each for the engravings. Blake asks him what the verses are worth, but Philips, with many polite messages to Hayley, will not put a price on them. He says that the value of the copyright must be estimated when they see what the sale of the work is. As a matter of fact, it turned out a commercial failure. One of the plates, the horse, was afterwards lost by Blake, and then found. In a letter dated June 4, 1805, he rejoices at the finding because he is in need of money again, and if the plate had remained lost it would have "cut off ten guineas" from his next demand on Philips; from which it seems that the plates were paid at twice, as art work often was—"half on order and half on delivery," as the expression used to run.

Blake could have written the ballads much better, of course, for himself, and was rather bothered by having to thank Hayley for them. His "Mental Friend" Los told him (as he says in *Milton*)—

Let each his own station keep
Nor in pity false, nor in officious brotherhood where
None needs be active.

The sentence is broken. There is no grammar in it, but the meaning is obvious.

We possess one more letter of this series, though June 4, 1805, is the date of the last that is given by Gilchrist, who follows it up by four quotations from *Milton* and from the MS. book. They are not appropriate. Three of them belong to an earlier date, and one to a later period, when Blake began to suspect Flaxman of being seriously in the Cromek interest against him.

Just after the Memoir to the Quaritch edition was in type, and too late to place it in its proper position, Mr. Daniell, of Mortimer Street, London, obligingly and generously placed this letter in the present writer's hands for biographical use. It is the latest known of those written to Hayley, and is written, as will be seen, in a softened mood of Christmas kindness after Blake had buried all old resentments and complaints, and when he looked back with exaggerated tenderness from the worries of London, "the city of assassinations," on the quiet fields of Felpham, and saw that Hayley had been, after all, more of a *spiritual* friend than he had intended or appeared to be. The whole friendship turned into suspicion and enmity through Cromek before another Christmas had gone:

To William Hayley, Esq.,
    Felpham, near Chichester,
       Sussex.

DEAR SIR—I cannot omit to return you my Sincere and Grateful Acknowledgments for the kind Reception you have given to my New Projected Work. It bids fair to set me above the difficulties I have hitherto encountered. [Was this Blair's *Grave*?] But my fate has been so uncommon that I expect Nothing. I was alive and in health with the same Talents I now have all the time of Brydells, Macklins, Bowyers, and Other Great Works. I was known to them and looked on them as incapable of Employment in those works. It may turn out so again, notwithstanding appearances; I am prepared for it, but at the same time sincerely grateful to those whose kindness and good opinion has supported me through all, hitherto. You, my dear sir, are one who has my Particular Gratitude, having conducted me through Three that would have been the Darkest years that ever Mortal suffered, which were rendered through your means a Mild and Pleasant Slumber. I speak of Spiritual Things, not of Natural, of things known only to myself and the Spirits Good and Evil, but Not known to Men on Earth. It is the passage through these Three Years that has brought me to my Present State, and I *know* that if I had not been with you I must have Perished. Those Dangers are now passed and I can see them beneath my feet. It will not be long before I shall be able to present the full history of my spiritual sufferings to dwellers upon Earth and of the Spiritual Victories obtained for me by my Friends. Excuse this Effusion of the Spirit from One who cares little for this World which passes away, whose happiness is Secure in Jesus our Lord, and who looks for suffering until the time of complete deliverance. In the meanwhile I am kept Happy as I used to be because I throw Myself and all that I have on our Saviour's Divine Providence. O what Wonders are the Children of Men! Would to God that they would consider it—that they would consider their Spiritual Life regardless of that faint Shadow called Natural Life, and that they would Promote Each other's Spiritual labours, Each according to his Rank, and that they would know that Receiving a Prophet as a Prophet is a Duty which, if omitted, is more Severely Avenged than Every Sin and Wickedness beside. It is the Greatest of Crimes to Depress True Art and Science. I know that those who are dead from the Earth, and who mocked at and Despised the Meekness of True Art (and such I find have been the situation of our Beautiful and Affectionate Ballads), I know that such Mockers are Most Severely Punished in Eternity. I know it, for I see it and dare not help. The Mocker of Art is the Mocker of Jesus. Let us go on, my Dear Sir, following His Cross. Let us take it up daily, Persisting in Spirit Labours and the Use of that Talent which it is Death to Bury, and of that Spirit to which we are called.

Pray Present my sincerest thanks to our Good Paulina, whose Kindness to Me shall receive recompense in the presence of Jesus. Present also my thanks to the generous Seagrave, in whose debt I have been too long, but perceive that I shall be able to settle with him soon what is between us. I have delivered to Mr. Saunders the 3 works of Romney, as Mrs. Lambert (said) to me you wished to have them. A very few touches will finish the Shipwreck. Those few I have added upon a Proof before I parted with the Picture. It is a Print that I feel proud of on a New inspection. Wishing you and all friends in Surrey a Merry and Happy Christmas.—I remain, Ever Your Affectionate

WILL BLAKE and his Wife CATHERINE BLAKE.

South Molton Street,
December 11th, 1805.

This closes the Hayley and the Flaxman friendship. Blake, with a burst of fury, decided that they were not friends at all, since they had been, while pretending to patronise him, quietly conspiring to reduce his prices, when he was looking twice at each mouthful of bread that he ate.

Until we have understood this, the story of *Jerusalem* must wait, though Gilchrist takes it at this point, and produces an unfortunate chapter, beginning with a repetition of the old error that *Jerusalem* was written at Felpham, and going on to treat of *Milton*, giving extracts among which are included the lines which tell us that Blake was especially given his cottage at Felpham that he might write this poem there. Gilchrist also quietly describes *Milton* as a poem in two books. Perhaps he never saw the title-page of the copy now in the British Museum where Blake has engraved in Arabic numerals the number twelve—" 12 books." The numerals are half-an-inch in height, and cannot be mistaken.

The trouble that led to the division between Hayley and Flaxman and Blake had its sources in what was said and done as far back as the year of Blake's first coming to Felpham. Flaxman, who introduced him, was also consulted by Hayley about patronising Caroline Watson. He wrote to Hayley about this on June 18, 1800 ; he is cautious, and not at all desirous to seem to be a go-between where a woman is concerned—Hayley being a man of gallantry. It might be unpleasant afterwards. Flaxman is Greek enough to remember Pandarus.

DEAR AND KIND FRIEND—Notwithstanding your apparent determination and reasons given for having the drawing engraved by the lady you have mentioned, I cannot communicate the commission until I have given my reasons for delay. I, like you, delight in paying a large portion of preference and respect to female talent. But if I am to execute a commission for a friend it ought to be done faithfully, with a view to his satisfaction and advantage,—at least not to his hurt, and really I have seen two children's heads, with the above lady's name, lately copied from a picture by Sir William Beechey, but so miserably executed that a similar engraving instead of being a decoration would be a blemish to your book. I am very sure that the fault could not be in the pictures, for the painter is a man of great merit. If after this information you still continue in the same resolution as at first I will deliver your commission, but there my interference must cease, and all further communication must be between the engraver and yourself, because I foresee that the conclusion of such an engagement must be unsatisfactory to all parties concerned.

From which we see again how habitually Hayley was not only ready to be useful to his friends, but to make them useful also, and that Flaxman knew his way of sending people on errands. Hayley, however, is determined to employ Caroline Watson, and does so. But it is not until April 25, 1805, that Blake seems to know about it. He then learns that she is to do a head of Cowper that he has already done, and takes this affront quite impersonally, without resentment, looking at it altogether in the artistic spirit,—for he then writes:

The idea of seeing an engraving of Cowper by Caroline Watson is, I assure you, a pleasing one to me. It will be highly gratifying to see another copy by another hand, and not only gratifying but improving, which is much better.

Two more sentences from this letter may be added—one to show Blake's austere renunciation of popular amusements at this busy time, and his resistance of fashionable enthusiasm, the other to indicate how high Fuseli and Flaxman stood then in the world of art:

The town is mad. Young Roscius (Master Betty), like all prodigies, is the talk of everybody. I have not seen him, and perhaps never may. I have no curiosity to see him, as I well know what is within the compass of a boy of fourteen; and as to real acting, it is, like historical painting, no boy's work.
Fuseli is made Master of the Royal Academy. Banks the sculptor is gone to his eternal home. I have heard that Flaxman means to give a lecture on sculpture at the Royal Academy on the occasion of Banks's death. He died at the age of seventy-five of a paralytic stroke, and I conceive that Flaxman stands without a competitor in sculpture.

Flaxman had already introduced to Hayley a man who was to be one of Blake's bitterest aversions. This was Cromek, who had been educated as an engraver, but who had become a publisher. He is now very well known through Blake, though he once boasted that Blake was hardly known at all except through him. He was, as Gilchrist tells us, a native of Hull, had been a pupil of Bartolozzi, and had engraved many plates for books after Stothard. He found that engraving did not suit his health, and, with little or no capital, he decided to begin publishing. He knew Blake, it may be inferred, through Stothard, to whom Blake had been introduced many years before, in his apprentice days, by Trotter, to whom he had given lessons. Trotter was an engraver who used to draw patterns for calico-printers. He had also engraved a plate or two after Stothard. It is Stothard from whom we learn that the engraving made of the " Portrait of Queen Philippa from her Monument," which he spoke highly of long afterwards when hearing of Blake's death, was really Blake's, though it bears beneath it the signature of Blake's master, Basire.
Cromek, knowing of the success of the Young's *Night*

W. Blake, del.

L. Schiavonetti, sculp.

DEATH'S DOOR.

From Blair's *Grave.*

" 'Tis but a night, a long and moonless night,,
We make the grave our bed, and then are gone ! "

Thoughts, and probably also knowing what a very small sum Blake had received for the drawings he made and engraved for this, decided to risk a few pounds in buying from him some designs to Blair's *Grave,* on the understanding that Blake should also be commissioned to engrave them. In order to make quite sure of being at no loss, he issued a prospectus, from which it appears that Blake was to do the engraving, but from which it does not appear that it was precisely on account of this that only twenty guineas was paid for the twelve original drawings. The prospectus contains a good many important names of people who guarantee that subscribers will find the illustrations to be of high quality. Fuseli is one, Malkin is another; there were nearly a dozen Academicians, including the President.

Safe under the protection of these, Cromek threw over Blake and gave the engraving of the work to Schiavonetti, who could handle the human figure, as he had shown by his plate of the picture whose draughtsmanship divides modern from mediæval art, Michael Angelo's *Cartoon of Pisa,* the subject of which, as is well known, was the sudden call to arms of a detachment engaged in bathing. The nude forms of the young men scrambling to shore were the first since classic days to be done gracefully, strongly, and naturally, and remain the standard of masculine beauty. The original cartoon, as will be remembered, was destroyed, probably through Florentine jealousy, during Michael Angelo's lifetime.

Schiavonetti could therefore do justice—it is said that he did the least little bit *more* than justice—to Blake. It is very difficult, as the present writer knows, having produced the lithographs for the Quaritch edition, to copy Blake *without* improving him the least bit in the world. He is so fine where he is good, and his odd little errors are so easy to remove, that it requires Indian fortitude to refrain from abolishing them as the hand reaches first one and then another.

Blake, however, felt himself cheated. Cromek pleaded that he had worked hard for Blake's reputation, had introduced him to more patrons than he could have reached otherwise, and, admitting that the drawings might " now " (he writes this in May 1807) be worth sixty guineas, he offers to return them if Blake can obtain that sum for them. Cromek is to collect the £60 so promised, and will take from it the £20 he has already paid for the drawings, handing over the £40 to Blake. The offer was, if not a generous one, by no means unhandsome. Cromek had worked to obtain recognition for Blake—though it is true that he had been obliged to do so, that he might not fail in his own venture. Blake is now to work to use that recognition so as to get more money for himself since that is what he demands, and Cromek, as a reward for allowing him to get double pay in the end, namely, £40 instead of £20, is to deduct the £20 he has already given from the gross £60, and so have the use of the drawings for nothing. He does not even propose any safeguard to prevent Blake re-engraving them himself and so cutting out his Schiavonetti plates from public favour. He also was a poor man, and what makes this offer the more creditable to him is that Blake had written him a most insulting letter, charging him with imposition and demanding four guineas for a vignette which was to go with his verses of dedication to the Queen.

Cromek good-naturedly replies to this demand about the vignette, that so far as the honour of the dedication is concerned, it is Blake himself who will profit by it, and that as a drawing the sketch is not worth the money, and he returns it. With regard to the charge of imposition, he replies in the same half-bantering and quite friendly vein in a way that shows that Blake has been bragging to him, as he used to brag to Mr. Butts, about his equality to the old masters, and with most creditable moderation he refrains from turning back the charge of imposition upon Blake on the strength of this. The letter is very long, but that part, for Cromek's sake, is worth quoting:

You charge me with *imposing on you*. Upon my honour, I have no recollection of anything of the kind. If the world and I were to settle accounts to-morrow, I do assure you the balance would be considerably in my favour. In this respect I am more sinned against than sinning, but if I cannot recollect any instances wherein I have imposed on *you*, several present themselves in which I have imposed on myself. Take two or three that press upon me.

When first I called on you I found you without reputation; I *imposed* on myself the labour—and an herculean one it has been—to create and establish a reputation for you. I say the labour was herculean because I had not only [? the public] to contend with, but I had to battle with a man who had pre-determined not to be saved. What public reputation you have—the reputation of eccentricity excepted—I have acquired for you; and I can honestly and conscientiously assert that if you had laboured through life for yourself as zealously and as earnestly as I have done for you, your reputation as an artist would not only have been enviable, but it would have put it out of the power of an individual so obscure as myself either to add to or take from it. *I also imposed on myself* when I believed, what you have so often told me, that your works were equal, nay, superior, to a Raphael or to a Michael Angelo. Unfortunately for me, as a publisher, the public awoke me from this state of stupor, this mental delusion. That public is willing to give you credit for what real talent is to be found in your productions, but for no more.

Just as a little North Country shrewdness is perhaps to be found in the bargain that he suggests about the sale of the drawings by Blake after the book is published—not an unfair shrewdness at all—so a little North Country pride may be detected in his good-nature—a well-justified pride —that peeps through this easy-going style of commercial- room banter. It would not have been difficult to put the same facts in an offensive manner; Blake himself, when not affectionately polite, was ferociously offensive. The sincerity of all this passage is further vouched for by the accidental absence of some such words as *the public* from one of the sentences, a deficiency which, as will be noticed, leaves it broken.

But Blake, after posing as a money-hater (we must remember that he himself told Crabb Robinson, later, that he used to turn pale when money was offered him), has suddenly begun to wrangle abusively for more pay.

Cromek's smiling reproof to him goes on (the italics are his):

I have imposed on myself yet more grossly in believing you to be one altogether abstracted from this world, holding converse with the world of spirits! simple, unoffending, a combination of the *serpent* and the *dove*. I really blush when I reflect how I have been cheated in this respect. The most effectual way of benefiting a designer whose aim is general patronage is to bring his designs before the public through the medium of engraving. Your drawings have had the *good fortune* to be engraved by one of the first artists in Europe, and the specimens already shown have produced you orders that, I verily believe, you would not otherwise have received. [Here he probably refers to the engravings done for Dr. Malkin in a book published the following year.] Herein I have been gratified, for I was determined to bring you food as well as reputation, though from your late conduct I have some reason to embrace your wild opinion, that to manage genius and to oblige it to produce good things it is absolutely necessary to starve it. [This is an error. It was not Blake's opinion at all. He has written and supported a contrary view. But he may have said in some torrent of words that people, judging by their conduct, *seem to think* many things about art, that this is necessary among them, and that there may have been such a rush of eloquence between the *seem to think* and this part of their mistakes that Cromek may have taken it for a "wild opinion" of Blake's own. Nothing here in the letter suggests either disingenuousness or sarcasm.] Indeed (my confidence that I may adopt) this opinion is considerably heightened by the recollection that your best work—the illustrations of *The Grave*—was produced when you and Mrs. Blake were reduced so low as to live on half-a-guinea a week.

[Blake had lately been reduced to one of his fits of deep melancholy at this time, as he was just before he left Hercules Buildings for Felpham, by seeing how his narrow circumstances crippled his artistic production and laid him open not only to the distraction of drudgery, but to annoyance, supercilious treatment, and even hunger. We find four months before the date of this letter of Cromek's—at the cold period of the year to which it referred, when poetry is least felt and poverty most—the following note in Blake's book, placed there by himself, it would seem, in memory of five hours of a winter afternoon, in which daylight and hope failed him together :—"Tuesday, Jan. 7, 1807.— Between two and seven in the evening : Despair."]

Before I conclude this letter it will be necessary to remark (that) when I gave you the order for the drawings from the poem of *The Grave*, I paid you for them more than I could afford ; more in proportion than you were in the habit of receiving, and what you were perfectly satisfied with, though I must do you the justice to confess, much less than I think is their real value.

Once more the oversight of leaving out a few words, here restored in parentheses, shows an attempt at self-control, and a genuine feeling on the part of the writer, most of whose sentences are of the elaborately balanced and well-chosen kind that was not yet considered too good for ordinary correspondence.

The way in which Cromek twice goes out of his way to acknowledge Blake's talent in this letter, advising him to show a little more commercial faculty in making it worth money if he wishes to be independent, cannot be considered as at all a customary and natural way of answering a letter in which a charge of imposition has been brought. How many business men would do as much now, or make so good an offer as that with which the letter proceeds ?

At the close, after the offer, as already described, the letter refers to a picture of the Canterbury Pilgrims. This has a story of its own, which must be told first. But, knowing Blake, we can hardly expect him to have received this letter in the spirit in which it was written. Even Gilchrist, who was not personally concerned at all, falls into so Blakean a wrath over it that he says : " It is one thing to read such a letter fifty years after it was written, though one can hardly do so without indignation ; another to have had to receive and digest its low affronts."

He also rakes up against Cromek a bit of mere suspicion, and practically charges him with having at another time stolen an autograph from Sir Walter Scott. It has been necessary to put the case from Cromek's side a little, because Gilchrist, when relating it, ill-treats Cromek all through, contradicting Allan Cunningham also, who gives testimony that the price Cromek gave for the drawings, "though small, was more," as he admits, "than Blake was accustomed to receive." It was more than he received for *coloured* drawings for Young's *Night Thoughts*. This was the last important work for which he had made designs at all. Cromek rightly looks on the fact that he became Blake's commercial traveller as being part payment. With regard to Blake's prices, we possess this list. It is part of a bill or account addressed to Mr. Butts, May 12, 1805:

Twelve drawings, viz. :—1. Famine. 2. War. 3. Moses striking the Rock. 4. Ezekiel's Wheels. 5. Christ girding Himself with Strength. 6. Four-and-twenty Elders. 7. Christ baptizing. 8. Samson breaking his bonds. 9. Samson subdued. 10. Noah and Rainbow 11. Wise and Foolish Virgins. 12. "Hell beneath is moved for thee." —£12 : 12s.

These are not inferior, whether as inventions or as pieces of art-labour, taken altogether, to the Blair's *Grave* drawings. Some would seem to be more *mannered*, but some are more startling and effective, and, with regard to the feeble nervous fault called "manner," this was removed by Schiavonetti to a considerable extent in the *Grave* drawings before they came to our sight.

Gilchrist was therefore wrong and Cromek right in the actual statement. Gilchrist also says that Cromek "jockeyed Blake out of his copyright."

But "hungry Cromek," as he calls him—and the name, an apology in itself, is worth considering—was, "with little or no capital," making a first venture at publication, and saw, just in time, that if he allowed Blake to engrave his own work, the venture would be a failure. He had already paid more for the drawings than Butt used to pay at the time for un-coloured work, and to save himself from failure, and Blake from self-destruction, he personally told Blake by word of mouth that on second thoughts he could not carry out the original intention of letting him engrave his own work. He did not do this in secrecy or behind his back, and he gave his reasons for it. Nothing else can be read in that sentence of his letter which describes him as doing battle with a man who was pre-determined not to be served. The copyright he simply left to Blake, and when the drawings were resold they could have been re-engraved.

S

The upshot of the transaction is therefore all in Cromek's favour, and posterity owes him some reparation for the treatment which he has received at the hands of Gilchrist.

But if we follow Blake's mind—and it is our present business to do so—we not only rage against Cromek, but we discover that what he was doing was very like what Hayley did over the Cowper portrait frontispiece, and that his boasting of his obtaining patronage for the designer was of a piece with Hayley's salve to his own conscience, the presenting to him what turned out to be the worthless copyright of some "insipid" ballads, which he no longer felt compelled by gratitude to call "beautiful and affectionate." The exclamation on p. 30 of *Milton*, "How wide and impassable the gulf between simplicity and insipidity!" is not part of its original MS., and evidently refers to them. Flaxman was guilty also of treachery—so it seemed now to Blake, because of both Caroline Watson and Cromek; and in the midst of his labours and hunger, just when he was in the "heaven of gratitude and affection," he suddenly found all his friends turned to enemies. Had there been the slightest taint of insane tendency in Blake, his mind might really have given way.

It is not probable that he ever had the comfort of seeing the letter from Flaxman (here printed for the first time) urging Hayley to hesitate about giving the engraving that had been promised to him to Caroline Watson. He probably only learned that Flaxman had (as his letter promises to do if it be insisted on) "communicated the commission." He certainly must have learned that Flaxman consulted Cromek on the subject. Cromek was not in the least likely to have concealed the honour that was done him. Flaxman was a man in high position. The quotation given above from his letter to Hayley, of June 18, 1800 (see above, page 251), stopped at the close of a paragraph that ended with the words, "unsatisfactory to all parties concerned." The letter goes on from this point:

The engraver mentioned in my last as having been casually consulted is Mr. Cromak (*sic*), with whom, I believe, you have no acquaintance. He has engraved several pictures and drawings of Stothard's, which in beauty exceed any other prints from that artist's works; and I am very sure that he would engrave in strokes the man on horseback saving the people in the shipwreck, or any other *coloured* picture for your book, in very great perfection. In sketches, outlines, or etchings others might succeed as well as him. I have sent you a specimen of his work, by no means one of his best, but it was one of the few he had done that would go into the compass of a letter. Mr. Cromak (*sic*) says he could get the drawing you sent engraved by a friend as well as it could be done for 25 guineas. Pray do me the justice to believe that what I have mentioned on this subject has no other object than the interest of your publication. Mr. Cromak (*sic*) is a man of independent spirit, and is very handsomely employed, as he well deserves. [Clearly Hayley has hinted to Flaxman that he has foisted Blake on him as a recommendable engraver when he was a hopeless and annoying genius, lovable at first, intolerable afterwards, who could only be employed, if at all, as an act of charity.] One of the heads painted by Romney in Rome of a man with a flattened nose, a beard, and black hair, is a portrait of a dwarf called "Baiocco" from begging for Baioccs or half-pence. I remember his person perfectly well. His whole height was about 3 ft. or 3 ft. 2 ins.

I know, on the whole, little of our valued friend Romney, but what I know I will cheerfully communicate, with a few remarks on the powers and qualities which I valued so much in him both as an artist and a friend.

Nancy unites with me in warmest wishes for the happiness and prosperity of our Dear Bard, and I have the honour to remain, your much obliged and affectionate, J. FLAXMAN.

June 18, 1804, Buckingham Street.

Hayley is employing his friends as usual. Even staid Flaxman has to go out and "consult casually" other people about his engravings, as well as to write him long weary letters about his biography of Romney. After this Hayley seems to have used against Flaxman, in defence of Caroline Watson, some expressions in Blake's letter of May 24, which has been already passingly referred to. The thread of Blake's attempts to negotiate for Hayley the direction of the proposed magazine, as well as the double scale of payment for contributions, has not been followed here all through. It came to nothing, but the disinterested labour for it that Blake gave was considerable. But for the fact that, as Gilchrist mentions, Hayley never again caught the attention of the public after his *Life of Cowper*, there might have been some tangible result which would have left him under considerable financial obligations to Blake.

It was long ago, when he was urging Hayley to have his work printed in Chichester, that Blake said at the close of this letter (of May 23, 1804):

I venture to give it as my settled opinion that if you suffer yourself to be printed in London you will be cheated in every way; but, however, as some little excuse (for Johnson who, by implication, is one of the cheats), I must say that in London every calumny and falsehood uttered against another of the same trade is thought fair play. Engravers, painters, statuaries, printers, poets, we are not in a field of battle but in a City of Assassinations.

In *Jerusalem*, page 91, line 11 :

> He who envies or calumniates, which is murder and cruelty,
> Murders the Holy One.

The whole context of the ninety-first page should be read with this. In *Milton* also, in the extra page 32, we read :

> The idiot reasoner laughs at the Man of Imagination
> And from laughter proceeds to murder by undervaluing calumny.

Flaxman's view of such expressions is found in a letter dated August 2, 1804, to Hayley, which begins about a Cupid and Psyche by Romney and goes on, evidently to remove from Hayley's mind a possible suspicion that Cromek was not recommended to him as a good engraver, but in order to shift a charitable burden from Flaxman's own shoulders, or perhaps that he was going to have a commission for doing so, and was therefore nothing less than a paid tout :

> . . . And, above all, I beg you will remember that I had no motive of interest in the mention of Mr. Cromek, for he is abundantly employed and sought after, and unless you think such engraving as (that of) the specimens he sent will be creditable to your book, you will do wrong to employ him.
> Concerning Caroline Watson's engraving, I should have acted more judiciously if I had desired you to see her last works for the education of your own judgement, rather than have sent any opinion of my own. I confess my own want of taste in (*sic*) Richardson's portrait, for though it is delicately engraved it don't come up to my idea of Highmore's portraits. Notwithstanding (this) if you are inclined to have a plate engraved by this artist, the only sentiment I can feel on the occasion will be satisfaction at seeing an ingenious lady engaged in a respectable employment. This is the only kind of "atonement" which seems requisite for an opinion delivered upon works publicly exhibited.

It is here, of course, that we gather that Hayley has evidently been taking up arms for Caroline Watson in a knight-errant spirit, and hacking at Flaxman with swords taken from Blake's armoury, for the letter goes on :

> With respect to Blake's remark upon "assassinations," I suppose he may have been acquainted with wretches capable of such practices, but I desire it may be understood that I am not one of them, and though I do not deal in "barbarous stilettoes" myself (Hayley has been improving on Blake while quoting him), I am willing to acknowledge the benevolence and soundness of Blake's general observations, as well as the point and keenness with which it was applied : but this was only a poetic *jeu d'esprit* which neither did, nor intended to do, harm.

So Flaxman puts aside Hayley's foolish gallantry and petulant attempt to sow mischief between him and Blake.

But it must have rankled. The letter goes on with Olympian calm :

> Now to serious business. I must shortly go once or twice to Winchester and Cambridge. Where I shall go, how long I shall stay, or when return I do not know, but in case you should have reason to consult Mr. Cromak (*sic*) in the meantime, who is gone to Yorkshire for six weeks or a month, I have sent you his address, No. 37 Charles Street, opposite the New river head, Tottenham Court Road.
> Nancy unites with me in kindest wishes, and I have the honour to remain, your much obliged and affectionate, JOHN FLAXMAN.

It is clear that if we are to use the French maxim, *Cherchez la femme*, when trying to understand the estrangement that ended Blake's affection for Hayley, we must seek her in Caroline Watson—not, as Mr. W. M. Rossetti maintained, in Mrs. Blake. Hayley's attempt to "murder the Holy One" *in* Blake, "by undervaluing calumny," is to be traced from Caroline, through Flaxman (of whose objection to her, of course, no one ever dreamed of telling Blake) and through Cromek (whom Flaxman brought on the scene as *her* rival, not Blake's) to Leigh Hunt and the "Examiners," and it unites all these together at last, as we shall presently see.

Of course, Blake did not find any one to buy his drawings for £60. He was always the worst of bargainers.. It was a serious professional loss to him to have to make a bargain at all, for the nervousness into which he fell when his pride was suffering under any attempt to do business would make him utterly incapable of artistic work, for this (as the public never realises) must be done *with the nerves* as certainly as the music of a piano is produced by its wires. If these are jangled, the best tuners may tune and the best pianist may finger as much in vain as the best intellectual portion of a man's genius may give directions and suggest subjects to his artistic portion, which is no longer able to give them forth as works of art. Blake was not bragging but telling the plainest truth when he said, as we learn from Allan Cunningham, "Were I to love money, I should lose all power of thought. Desire of gain deadens the genius of man. My business is not to gather gold, but to make glorious shapes, expressing God-like sentiments."

To this period of Blake's life, though, it is to be feared, not to this period only, may be referred the well-known anecdote that tells how Mrs. Blake found him so irritable when she mentioned that there was no more money,—exclaiming, "Damn the money! It's always the money!" that she would silently place on the table all the food there was in the cupboard until only empty dishes could be served up.

Then Blake would leave the poetry that we all cherish now, and go back to the engraved plates of other people's designs that, but for the name that his poetry has left, would now be waste-paper. Bread earned by labour that is *not* "above payment" is always paid in fairy's gold, of which tradition says that, however bright and authentic it may look to-day, it will be a heap of dead leaves to-morrow.

CHAPTER XXIV

BLAKE'S next affliction, and the cause of an anger that kept him in a more or less constant state of wrath for years, was in connection with a drawing representing Chaucer's *Canterbury Pilgrims*, which he seems to have made at Felpham, where he could see and ride horses, as his grateful message to Miss Poole about " Bruno " shows, though he never learned to draw a horse even decently. In Felpham also he could, and did, read and meditate upon Chaucer. Cromek saw this sketch in South Molton Street, and liked it. He saw business in it, and (Gilchrist says) " wanted to secure a finished drawing from it for the purpose of having it engraved, without employing Blake to do so, just as he had served him over the designs to the *Grave*, as I learn from other sources on sifting the matter." We now know how touchy Blake was in his dealings with Cromek, and what good cause Cromek had to approach him cautiously if he would escape the accusation of imposture. Gilchrist continues, " but Blake was not to be taken in a second time," without adding that Cromek was not to be caught promising the work of engraving to a man whom he now knew not to be able to obtain a sale for his prints, as the Hayley *Ballads* had shown him.

" But as Blake understood the matter, he received a commission, *tacit or express*, from Cromek to execute the design." The words are Gilchrist's. The italics are ours. One can guess the conversation : " An admirable drawing you have there, Mr. Blake ! Could I not persuade you to carry it a little further ? I should *like to see* an engraving of that. I think it would pay."

While speaking aloud he was wondering to himself who would be the best man to use for engraving such a subject. That Blake had a sole and exclusive right to make designs from Chaucer, and that it was Cromek's duty to keep secret a drawing that Blake left about loose where any one in the world might see it and talk of it, would be the last ideas to recommend themselves to a tradesman, though Cromek has been called many hard names for not acting as though it were incumbent upon him to understand the difference between a studio and a shop.

Does a man, by making a sketch on a theme that has been before his country for several hundred years, earn a right to complain if any other man uses the same subject? Does such a sketch, hung on a wall or left on his table or in his open portfolio, become a confidential document that no one is to speak of lest the artist should lose some possible advantage which *might* be obtained from it, but which he is taking no steps to obtain? An injured man, or any man who lets opportunity slip, will have his own view, but evidently there is a good deal to be said on both sides, and the Blake view of this, as of any subject that touched either himself or any friend of his personally, was not in the least likely to be an impartial view. Infected with Blake's wrath, the world has been very hard on Cromek and on Stothard. It was to Stothard that Cromek seems to have spoken next of the subject; not as violating a confidence. There seems no reason to suppose that Blake himself was at all likely to have kept the sketch secret from Stothard. In the end, Stothard painted the picture now in our National Gallery, and more than one engraver laboured on a plate which gave an admirable and even a slightly flattered rendering of it. Blake would have been altogether incapable of doing anything of the kind.

But he attacked the subject with enthusiasm, believing it to be his own, and not thinking that Cromek was likely to speak about it to any one else. In fact, it did not occur to him that Cromek had any interest in doing so. He thought himself supreme in every department of art.

Even when Blake knew that Stothard was painting a *Canterbury Pilgrims,* he did not at once take alarm, or see any direct rivalry in this. He called on Stothard, saw him at work, and spoke with his usual urbanity, politely praising anything that he could praise in the work. This afterwards made him look like a hypocrite. Stothard does not seem to have mentioned that he was painting for Cromek. This afterwards made Stothard look like a false friend. Two artists chatting over the technique of a picture are the last men in the world to turn aside the thread of their conversation to bring in the name of the business man who is to see to the selling of the work when complete. Neither should have accused the other of treacherous reticence.

Stothard may possibly have known that a paper or prospectus was already being circulated by Blake's friends to obtain him subscriptions for an engraving of Chaucer's *Canterbury Pilgrims*, but he would probably not have mentioned it, even if he knew of it. Blake had engraved his own designs to Young's *Night Thoughts* in 1797. Stothard had been commissioned to illustrate the same poem, and his work had been produced in 1802, while Blake was at Felpham. No quarrel had occurred. No one had complained. The same kind of thing might be about to happen again.

But Blake was in a different mood now, and did not seem to himself a Michael Angelo with a Medici behind him. He wanted every penny for the production of his own prophetic books. He starved for them, and would not allow any one to take away his chances of obtaining money to spend over them by cutting the ground from under his feet when he was attempting to fight for popularity with the kind of picture that artists call a "pot-boiler."

In May 1807 Stothard's *Canterbury Pilgrims* was exhibited, and it must have been then that Blake made against Cromek the virulent accusation of imposture to which we have read Cromek's reply. The letter was not quoted to the end. Blake has been writing to him in the very words of the subsequently published *Descriptive Catalogue* about Stothard's picture. After the offer about the *Grave* drawings and their possible sale by Blake for sixty guineas, the letter concludes (the italics are Cromek's):

I will not detain you more than one minute. Why did you *furiously rage* at the success of the little picture of *The Pilgrimage?* Three thousand people have now *seen it and have approved of it.* Believe me yours is *the voice of one crying in the wilderness.*

You may say the subject is *low,* and *contemptibly treated.* For his excellent mode of treating the subject the poet has been admired for the last 400 years; the poor painter has not yet the advantage of antiquity on his side, therefore with some people an apology may be necessary for him. The conclusion of one of Squire Simkin's letters to his mother in the *Bath Guide* will afford one. He speaks greatly to the purpose—

> I very well know,
> Both my subject and verse is (*sic*) exceedingly low ;
> But if any *great critic* finds fault with my letter,
> He has nothing to do but to send you a better.

With much respect for your Talents, I remain, Sir, your real friend and well-wisher,
                                                                    R. H. CROMEK.

This is what Gilchrist calls the letter of "low affronts. Cromek would have been very much surprised had he known that posterity would expect him to treat Blake with deference and veneration. He treated him (under much provocation) with respect and good nature and substantial fairness, and even his last hint—that Blake's best retort could be made with the pencil—he veils under a playful quotation rather than seem to be betrayed into acrimony by making the suggestion as from himself. So, on the whole, Cromek comes out of the business not such an unmitigated villain.

But it would be as unfair to Blake as Gilchrist is to Cromek if we expected Blake to be aware that he was not ill-treated. His pride was, as we remember, "terrific" when he was "exalted," and envy was his besetting weakness. Hastily desirous to injure no one, he was hastily ready to conclude that others were ready to injure him. His doctrine, that we owe all things to a friend and nothing at all but hard knocks to an enemy, was inherited from generations of Irish faction fighters, and we cannot expect him to see beyond it, any more than we can expect a cat to understand that a singing-bird is of value in a garden except for sport or food. But the result was very sad, and, however interesting Blake's *Descriptive Catalogue* may be, so far as it is descriptive of Blake himself, it tends to teach us, of all lessons, the one that he himself never learned his whole life long—indulgence.

In his present trouble his trading brother James, who had never left the hosier's shop, but who had been helpful from time to time, while Blake was at Felpham, seeing to the sending of things and writing to pacify Butts when he felt himself neglected, now came forward in a still more useful and efficient manner. He lent his house for Blake to make a little exhibition of pictures there, as on his first floor in South Molton Street he was not able to clear space enough for himself to do so. There, in May 1809—the year in which, as Gilchrist tells us, Hayley's admiration for the female sex caused him to contract a second marriage, "more ill-advised than the first"—Blake collected sixteen pictures, of which his own description shall be given.

He was now thoroughly at enmity with both Stothard and Cromek. After he had made his picture of the *Canterbury Pilgrims*—so well known to the public now, with its wooden horses, from the reduced outline given by Gilchrist—he happened to be taking down that first sketch which had caused so much trouble, from where it had hung above his door, with no covering, and he found that dust and smoke—for London smoke existed even in those days—had so bedimmed the whiteness of the paper that the pencil strokes hardly showed on it. Gilchrist says that he attributed this vanishing of his drawing to a malign spell effected by Stothard. If so, Cosway (" of Egypt's lake "), a friend given to occultism, must have been preaching magic to his credulous and Hibernian mind. Flaxman is said to have smilingly asked him what else he could expect if he left his drawing hung up exposed for so long a time, which shows that he was not yet in a state of open rupture with Flaxman. There are one or two incidents which suggest a cordial state of intercourse between them since the *Romney's Life* period and up to the time of this exhibition. On August 12, 1805, Flaxman is found to be earnestly trying to get further opportunities for Blake to show his capacities. A project is on foot to get out a little book for the benefit of Mrs. Rose, the widow of Blake's legal defender. Flaxman offers to give five drawings of his own, *gratis*, to be engraved for this, and (evidently against some opposition on the part of Hayley) he adds:

I have seen two or three noble sketches by Blake which might be drawn in outline by him, in a manner highly creditable to your book, and *I would overlook them* so far as to see that they should be suitable to the other designs.

The italics are ours. The words that follow them are also evidently put from motives of kindness lest any one seeing the letter should say, "Blake's drawings are no good unless Flaxman looks over them and puts them right." He adds:

The day after I received your last letter Blake brought a present of two copies of the *Songs*. It is a beautiful work. Nancy and I are equally thankful for the present, and equally delighted with your bounty to the Poet Artist. God's blessing will attend ¦your good deeds.

It is probable that the hospitality shown to Blake's exhibition in his brother's house was a sort of return visit in acknowledgment of the long year that their sister—who naturally lived generally in the elder brother's home—had spent with Blake and his wife when they first went to Felpham.

But while Blake was preparing for his exhibition, and executing his painting of the life-sized *Ancient Britons* for it, he had other work. Dr. Malkin, the headmaster of Bury

Grammar School, heard of him, through Cromek we may suppose, as he afterwards knew the names of some of the other persons of taste who "approved and patronised" the designs to Blair's *Grave* when that work was in preparation.

Dr. Malkin had for son an unfortunate little boy who was one of those prodigies whose minds make an average person feel quite sick. He was a genius in the nursery. He wrote good prose and fairly good verse at from four to six years old. His paragraphs read like those of an unusually clever but quite uneducated youth of seventeen. Yet there was nothing like "possession" or inspiration about him; what he invents is always his own, and always child-like in its way. But he had an imagination to which there seemed no limit. He invented a whole dream-land the size of an English county. He called it Allestone, and had names more or less English in sound for a hundred villages, towns, and rivers in it, all nicely written on the map. He learned languages, was good-natured, drew little landscapes in the Claude style with trees and castles in them—citadels and vegetation of the kingdom of *Allestone*—and died before he was seven. The book of his *Memoirs*, by his father, has a decorative design of Blake's on it. If that boy had lived, and had passed through a phase of Swedenborgianism, we feel as we read that Blake would have been completely out-Blaked. His *Jerusalem* would have been child's play to this child, hard reading as it is to most of us. It is doubtful whether a more literary, artistic, and inventive mind ever existed.

Blake approved particularly of the "firm and determinate outline" of little Malkin's fancy landscapes, and when the boy drew copies of heads by Raphael, Banks—Flaxman's only serious rival in sculpture of that day—said that he would one day rank as a distinguished artist.

Dr. Malkin was so much touched by Blake's appreciation of his son, that he has introduced into his pamphlet of *Memoirs* a short account of Blake himself, from which several of the facts about his early life are taken in all the succeeding biographies.

Gilchrist says that the decorative design for the frontispiece of Dr. Malkin's book, designed and originally engraved by Blake, was erased and re-engraved by Cromek. It is very well done, and truthfully Blakean in drawing.

The fact that at this time (1806) Philips was editor of the *Monthly Magazine*, gave Blake a chance to obtain a hearing in his pages, and he used it at once in support of Fuseli.

He was able now to do better than only bespeak the indulgence of Cumberland for him if he failed to show himself as good-natured as could be wished when criticising his book on outline, by pleading that he was " ill-natured artificially," because " sore from the lash of envious tongues." The critics had been sarcastic about his picture of Ugolino of Pisa, who was starved with his children in prison, as our own Chaucer's verses remind us. Blake does not at all reflect that he is going to need the good opinion of the critics for himself. He at once sets lance in rest and spurs forth, full to the brim of knight-errantry, to do battle for his friend.

Gilchrist tells us that Mr. Swinburne was the fortunate discoverer of this letter in the *Monthly Review* for July 1806. He prints it as follows :

To the Editor of the *Monthly Magazine* (different title).

Sir—My indignation was exceedingly moved at reading a criticism in Bell's *Weekly Messenger* (25th May) on the picture of *Count Ugolino* by Mr. Fuseli in the Royal Academy Exhibition, and your magazine being as extensive in circulation as that paper, as it also must, from its nature, be more permanent, I take the advantageous opportunity to counteract the widely diffused malice which has for many years, under the pretence of admiration of the arts, been assiduously sown and planted among the English public against true art such as it existed in the days of Michelangelo and Raphael. Under the pretence of fair criticism and candour the most wretched taste ever produced has been upheld for many, very many years ; but now, I say, its end has come. Such an artist as Fuseli is invulnerable. He needs not my defence ; but I should be ashamed not to set my hand and shoulder, and whole strength, against those critics who, under pretence of criticism, use the dagger and the poison.

My criticism on this picture is as follows. Mr. Fuseli's Count Ugolino is the father of sons of feeling and dignity, who would not sit looking in their parent's face in the moments of his agony, but would rather retire and die in secret, while they suffer him to indulge his passionate and innocent grief, his innocent and venerable madness and insanity and fury, and whatever paltry, cold-hearted critics cannot, because they dare not, look upon. Fuseli's Count Ugolino is a man of wonder and admiration, of resentment against man and devil, and of humiliation before God ; prayer and parental affection all fill the figure from head to foot. The child in his arms, whether boy or girl signifies not (but the critic must be a fool who has not read Dante, and does not know a boy from a girl), I say the child is as beautifully drawn as it is coloured, in both inimitable, and the effect of the whole is truly sublime on account of that very colouring which our critic calls black and heavy. The German-flute colour which was used by the Flemings (they call it burnt bone) has (so) possessed the eye of certain connoisseurs that they cannot see appropriate colouring, and are blind to the gloom of a real terror.

The taste of English amateurs has been too much formed upon

pictures imported from Flanders and Holland, consequently our country-men are easily browbeat on the subject of painting; and hence it is so common to hear a man say, "I am no judge of pictures." But, O Englishmen! know that every man ought to be a judge of pictures, and every man is so who has not been connoisseured out of his senses.

A gentleman who visited me the other day said, "I am very much surprised at the dislike which some connoisseurs show on viewing the pictures of Mr. Fuseli, but the truth is he is a hundred years beyond the present generation." Though I am startled at such an assertion, I hope the contemporary taste will shorten the hundred years into as many hours; for I am sure that any person consulting his own reputation, and the reputation of his country, will refrain from disgracing either by such ill-judged criticisms in future.—Yours, WM. BLAKE.

Who shall describe to us the feelings of Fuseli's critic as he read this? A headmaster of Eton who should find himself suddenly seized by an unusually strong boy, stripped and birched before the school and visitors, might be able to imagine what he suffered.

It is not to be supposed that he was rash enough to reply at once. He was dealing with an artist—his natural prey —and his day would come. It did; and by that time the artist had so totally forgotten the provocation that he had given, as to construct a most elaborate theory of hiring and treachery to account for the stab in the back that he presently received.

Of course, when Blake's exhibition was opened it was a failure. A Blake exhibition to-day is a brilliant success, but that is because his name is now sufficiently well known to give people something recognisable to talk about when they have been to look at his things. Of real appreciation no one who has spent an hour or two mingling with the public in a room filled with his work will think that there is much in the general mind, even yet. The truth is, that Blake's art *cannot* be really enjoyed except by long contemplation *in silence.* When his obvious and harassing faults gradually sink below the surface of our observation, an influence begins to come forth from his works which hides itself until then. It is, in fact, the emanation called "Jerusalem," in his book of that name. It cannot live under the hailstorm of pattering little exclamations and comments of conversation, nor can people in general, who absolutely make the ridiculous attempt of going two or three at a time to see Blake's pictures, ever hope to come away with any real perception of what was in them.

Seymour Kirkup, well known as the discoverer of Dante's portrait among the heads that crowd a fresco by Giotto, going

THE LAST JUDGMENT.

From Blake's pencil sketch. This design, about eighteen inches high, was afterwards modified and developed.

to see Blake's little collection at Broad Street, was there, however, and so was Mr. Crabb Robinson, who bought four copies of the *Descriptive Catalogue*. These were sold at half-a-crown apiece, and their possession was the ticket of admission to the exhibition. Crabb Robinson bought them to give to his friends, and he asked James Blake whether he might himself come again to the exhibition and be admitted free. " Oh yes, free as long as you live," said James.

Among those to whom Crabb Robinson gave a copy was Charles Lamb. In his Reminiscences he says :

When, in 1810, I gave Lamb a copy of the Catalogue of the paintings exhibited in Carnaby Street (Gilchrist says, and Blake's own prospectus to his engraving of the *Canterbury Pilgrims* says, Broad Street), he was delighted, especially with the description of a painting afterwards engraved, and connected with which there was a circumstance which, unexplained, might reflect discredit on a most excellent and amiable man. It was after the friends of Blake had circulated a subscription paper for an engraving of his *Canterbury Pilgrims*, that Stothard was made a party to an engraving of a painting of the same subject, by himself. But Flaxman considered this as not done wilfully. Stothard's work is well known ; Blake's is known by very few. Lamb preferred the latter greatly, and declared that Blake's description was the finest criticism he had ever read of Chaucer's poem.

It was like Lamb, of course, to base an artistic criticism upon a literary enjoyment. Crabb Robinson says also of this exhibition : " There were about thirty oil paintings, the colouring excessively dark and high, and the veins black. The hue of the primitive men was very like that of the Red Indians. Many of his designs were unconscious imitations."

The " thirty oil paintings " is an evident error. With regard to the "imitations," it will hardly be believed by those who have never had occasion to discover how untrustworthy is the eye even of clever men, who have not trained it, that in the Blake exhibition at the Carfax Gallery this year (1904), a gentleman of considerable ability standing with the present writer (to whom he was a stranger) before a pencil sketch of Blake's *Last Judgment*, here reproduced, asked if it was not true that Blake had taken many of his ideas—notably the figures in this design—from Michael Angelo ; and when, in reply, a commencement was made for him of a sketch, from memory, of Michael Angelo's *Last Judgment*, he was amazed, and, saying hastily, "Oh, I see you know something about it," withdrew the imputation against Blake. So feeble is pictorial memory in most of us, when put to the test, that the present writer has found that hardly any one knows the attitude of any of Michael Angelo's figures, yet none are easier to remember; and on one occasion *an artist*, who professed to know them *quite well*, on having a pencil put into his hand to sketch—however roughly—the *Expulsion* from the series in the roof of the Sistine Chapel, threw it down after a few strokes, in despair and mortification. He did not even remember that the expelling angel has the sword, which has no guard, in his left hand!

Mr. Crabb Robinson records further, speaking of the illustrations to the *Night Thoughts*, " that he had showed them to William Hazlitt, who ' saw no merit ' in them, but when I read him some of Blake's poems he was much struck, and expressed himself with his usual strength and singularity. ' They are beautiful,' he said, ' only too deep for the vulgar. As to God, a worm is as worthy as any other object—all alike being indifferent—so to Blake the chimney-sweeper, etc. He (Blake) is ruined by vain struggles to get rid of what presses upon his brain. He attempts impossibilities.' " I added, " He is like a man who lifts a burden too heavy for him. He bears it an instant, and then it falls and crushes him."

This is so happy a description, *not* of Blake under the burden of his imagination, but of Blake-criticism under the burden of Blake, and Crabb Robinson himself was crushed so very flat by it—as many other men of great ability who did not know how to use their own strength—that, however ridiculous his words are in their place, they deserve to be remembered.

Gilchrist mentions as being " now " (that is, in 1810) in the possession of Mr. Alex. C. Weston, a printed programme (not *Descriptive Catalogue*) of this exhibition, containing one page of print, preceded by an elaborate title-page. It is from this we learn that the picture of the *Ancient Britons* had the figures " full as large as life."

In a sort of prose-verse like that of *Jerusalem* it has these lines:

In the last battle that Arthur fought the most beautiful was one
That returned, and the most strong another. With them also returned
The most ugly, and no other beside returned from the bloody field. ·
The most beautiful the Roman warriors trembled before and wor-
    shipped.
The most strong they melted before and dissolved in his presence.
The most ugly they fled with outcries and contortions of their limbs.

Mr. Kirkup, trained in the examination of Italian frescoes of the best period, thought this the finest of Blake's works, remembering in his old age " the fury and splendour of energy there, contrasted with the serene ardour of simply beautiful courage." He remembered, too, "the violent life of the design," and its " fierce distance of fluctuating battle." It is Mr. Swinburne who reports, and one suspects his vocabulary of supplying the word " fluctuating," if nothing more.

The verse-sound of the rambling lines quoted showing that the conception of the design was affiliated in Blake's mind with the allusions to " Arthur" in *Jerusalem*, it is natural to turn to that poem to see whether nothing further can be gathered with regard to his ideas about the name.

One suspects, of course, that it will turn out, like Elijah and Rahab, to be the name of a " state." It is only mentioned in four places, and all are given, for once, in the sketch of an index at the end of A. H. Bullen's well-printed *Jerusalem*, edited by Messrs. Russell and Maclagan. The word occurs on page 54, line 25, page 64, line 15, page 75, line 2, and page 88, line 18. It will be noticed that even its earliest appearance is in the latter half of the poem.

When Arthur appears first, it is as a name for a being, " the hard, cold, constructive spectre " who is also called our Rational Power, under which description and as a nameless " Spectre " he has haunted the pages of *Jerusalem* from the beginning. The inference is that Blake was in this part of the book when he began the design, probably in 1806. " Arthur " makes an appeal against imagination, and forgiveness of sin, in fact against Blake's whole idea of Christianity, and chides those who would build a world of phantasy upon his great abyss. He bids them " come from the desert and turn these stones to bread." We know of what Blake was thinking when he wrote that—of James, of Cromek, of Hayley, of all who gave him good advice, though the only two names mentioned in connection with Arthur are " his wings," Voltaire and Rousseau. It is clear that he is Albion's Angel—a form of Urizen in the North. In page 64, line 15, he is mockingly told to " go assume papal dignity," and called a " male harlot." We recognise him now as the winged pope on page 9 of *Europe*. It is Los to whom the speech is really addressed, and Vala is the scolding speaker. " Arthur " is merely a term of abuse. Line 20 gives another definition that enlightens :

All Quarrels arise from Reasoning, the Secret Murder, and
The violent Manslaughter. These are the Spectre's double Cave,
The Sexual Death living on accusation of Sin and Judgment.

T

Page 75, line 2, by placing Arthur as the third of three names (Merlin, Bladud, and Arthur), indicates, as we should expect, that his symbolic region is in the loins.

In page 88, line 18, he is mentioned as the masculine name for one of the places that Enitharmon will create to increase the power of Nature over Mind, till the Incarnation of Divine Imagination is the only salvation, after God has submitted to death, " become subservient to the female," that is, Imagination subservient to materialistic habits of thought.

A Descriptive Catalogue of Pictures, poetical and historical inventions, painted by William Blake in water colours, being the ancient method of fresco painting restored, and drawings for public inspection, and for sale by private contract. London : Printed by D. N. Shury, 7 Berwick Street, Golden Square. 1809.

CONDITIONS OF SALE

I. *One third of the Price to be paid at the time of purchase and the remainder on Delivery.*

II. *The Pictures and Drawings to remain in the Exhibition till its close, which will be on the 29th September 1809. And the Picture of the Canterbury Pilgrims, which is to be engraved, will be sold only on condition of its remaining in the artist's hands twelve months, when it will be delivered to the Buyer.*

PREFACE

THE eye that can prefer the colouring of Titian and Rubens to that of Michael Angelo and Rafael ought to be modest and to doubt its own powers. Connoisseurs talk as if Rafael and Michael Angelo had never seen the colouring of Titian or Correggio. They ought to know that Correggio was born two years before Michael Angelo, and Titian but four years after. Both Rafael and Michael Angelo knew the Venetians and contemned and rejected all he did with the utmost disdain, as that which is fabricated with the purpose to destroy art.

Mr. B. appeals to the public from the judgments of those narrow blinking eyes that have too long governed art in a dark corner. The eyes of stupid cunning never will be pleased with the work, any more than with the look, of self-devoting genius. The quarrel of the Florentine with the Venetian is not because he does not understand Drawing, but because he does not understand Colouring. How should he who does not know how to draw a hand or a foot know how to colour it.

Colouring does not depend on where the colours are put, but on where the lights and darks are put, and all depends on Form or Outline —on where that is put. Where that is wrong, colouring can never be right, and it is always wrong in Titian and Correggio, Rubens and Rembrandt. Till we get rid of Titian and Correggio, Rubens and Rembrandt, we shall never equal Rafael, and Albert Durer, Michael Angelo, and Julio Romano.

No. I

The spiritual form of Nelson guiding Leviathan, in whose wreathings are enfolded the nations of the Earth.

Clearness and precision have been the chief objects in painting these pictures. Clear colours, unmudded by oil, and firm, determinate lineaments, unbroken by shadows, which ought to display, and not to hide form, as is the practice of the latter schools of Italy and Flanders.

No. II

Its Companion

The spiritual form of Pitt guiding Behemoth. He is that Angel who, pleased to perform the Almighty's orders, rides on the whirlwind, directing the storms of war. He is ordering the reaper to reap the vine of the Earth, and the ploughman to plough up the Cities and Towers.

This picture is also a proof of the power of colours unsullied with oil or with any cloggy vehicle. Oil has falsely been supposed to give strength to colours. But a little consideration must show the falsity of this opinion. Oil will not drink or absorb colour enough to stand the test of very little time and of the air. It deadens every colour it is mixed with at its first mixture, and in a little time becomes a yellow mask over all that it touches. Let the works of modern artists since Rubens' time witness the villainy of some one of that time who first brought oil painting into general opinion and practice ; since which we have never had a picture painted which could show itself by the side of an earlier production. Whether Rubens or Vandyke, or both, were guilty of this villainy is to be inquired in another work on painting, and who first forged the silly story and known falsehood about John of Bruges inventing oil colours ; in the meantime let it be observed that before Vandyke's time and in his time, all the genuine pictures are on plaster or whiting grounds, and none since.

The two pictures of Nelson and Pitt are compositions of a mythological cast, similar to those Apotheoses of Persian, Hindoo, and Egyptian antiquity which are still preserved on rude monuments, being copies from some stupendous originals now lost, or perhaps buried till some happier age. The artist having been taken in vision into the ancient republics, monarchies, and patriarchates of Asia has seen those wonderful originals, called in the sacred scriptures the Cherubim, which were sculptured and painted on walls of Temples, Towers, Cities, Palaces, and erected in the highly cultivated states of Egypt, Moab, Edom, Aram, among the Rivers of Paradise—being the originals from which the Greeks and Hetruvians copied Hercules Farnese, Venus of Medicis, Apollo Belvedere, and all the grand works of ancient art. They were executed in a very superior style to those justly admired copies, being, with their accompaniments, terrific and grand in the highest degree. The artist has endeavoured to emulate the grandeur of those seen in his vision, and to apply it to modern Heroes on a smaller scale.

No man can believe that either Homer's Mythology or Ovid's was the production of Greece or Latium ; neither will any one believe that the Greek statues, as they are called, were the invention of Greek Artists : perhaps the Torso is the only original work remaining ; all the rest being evidently copies, though fine ones, from the greater works of the Asiatic Patriarchs. The Greek Muses are daughters of Mnemosyne, or Memory, and not of Inspiration or Imagination, therefore not authors of such sublime conceptions. Those wonderful originals seen in my visions were, some of them, one hundred feet in height : some were painted as pictures and some carved as basso-relievos and some as groups of statues, all containing mythological and recondite meaning, when more is meant than meets the eye. The artist wishes it was now the fashion to make such monuments, and then he should not doubt of having a national commission to execute these two Pictures on a scale that is suitable to the grandeur of the nation who is the parent of his heroes, in high-finished fresco, where the colours would be as pure and as permanent as precious stones, though the figures were one hundred feet in height.

All frescoes are as high-finished as miniatures or enamels, and they are known to be unchangeable ; but oil, being a body itself, will drink, or absorb, very little colour, and changing yellow, and at length brown, destroys every colour it is mixed with, especially every delicate colour. It turns every permanent white to a yellow and brown putty, and has compelled the use of that destroyer of colour, white lead, which, when its protecting oil is evaporated, will become lead again. This is an awful thing to say to oil painters : they may call it madness, but it is true. All genuine old little pictures, called cabinet pictures, are in fresco and not in oil. Oil was not used, except by blundering ignorance, till after Vandyke's time ; but the art of fresco painting being lost, oil became a fetter to genius and a dungeon to art. But one convincing proof among many others that these assertions are true is that real gold and silver cannot be used with oil as they are in all the old pictures and in Mr. B.'s frescoes.

No. III

Sir Jeffrey Chaucer and the nine-and-twenty pilgrims on their journey to Canterbury.

The time chosen is early morning, before sunrise, when the jolly company are leaving the Tabarde Inn. The Knight and Squire with the Squire's Yeoman lead the Procession ; next follow the youthful Abbess, her nun, and three priests ; her greyhounds attend her—

> Of small hounds had she, that she feed
> With roast flesh, milk, and wastel bread.

Next follow the Friar and Monk, and then the Tapiser, the Pardoner, and the Sompnour and Manciple. After this " Our Host," who occupies the centre of the cavalcade, and directs them to the Knight, as the person who would be likely to commence their task of each telling a tale in their order. After the Host follows the Shipman, the Haberdasher, the Dyer, the Franklin, the Physician, the Ploughman, the Lawyer, the Poor Parson, the Merchant, the Wife of Bath, the Miller, the Cook, the Oxford Scholar, Chaucer himself ; and the Reeve comes as Chaucer has described :—

> And ever he rode hindermost of the rout.

These last are issuing from the gateway of the Inn; the Cook and the Wife of Bath are both taking their morning's draft of comfort. Spectators stand at the gateway of the Inn, and are composed of an old Man, a Woman, and a Child.

The landscape is an eastward view of the country from the Tabarde Inn, in Southwark, as it may be supposed to have appeared in Chaucer's time : interspersed with cottages and villages. The first beams of the sun are seen above the horizon ; some buildings and spires indicate the position of the Great City. The Inn is a Gothic building which Thynne in his glossary says was the lodging of the Abbot of Hyde by Winchester. On the Inn is inscribed its title, and a proper advantage is taken of this circumstance to describe the subject of the Picture. The words written over the gateway of the Inn are as follows :—" The Tabarde Inn, by Henry Baillie, the lodgynge house for Pilgrims who journey to St. Thomas' Shrine at Canterbury."

The characters of Chaucer's Pilgrims are the characters which compose all ages and nations. As one age falls another rises different to mortal sight, but to immortals only the same ; for we see the same characters repeated again and again, in animals, vegetables, minerals, and in men. Nothing new occurs in identical existence ; accident ever varies. Substance can never suffer change or decay.

Of Chaucer's characters as described in his *Canterbury Tales* some of the names or titles are altered by time, but the characters themselves ever remain unaltered ; and consequently they are the physiognomies, or lineaments of universal human life beyond which Nature never steps. Names alter; things never alter. I have known multitudes of those who would have been monks in the age of monkery, and who in this deistical age are deists. As Newton numbered the stars and as Linneus has numbered the plants, so Chaucer numbered the classes of men.

The Painter has consequently varied the heads and forms of his personages into all Nature's varieties. The horses he has also varied to accord to their Riders ; the costume is correct according to authentic monuments.

The Knight and the Squire and the Squire's Yeoman lead the procession as Chaucer has also placed them first in his Prologue. The Knight is a true Hero, a good, great, and wise man ; his whole length portrait on horseback as written by Chaucer cannot be surpassed. He has spent his life in the field, has ever been a conqueror, and is that species of character which in every age stands as the guardian of man against the oppressor. His son is like him with the germ of perhaps greater perfection still as he blends literature and the arts with his warlike studies. Their dress and their horses are of the first rate, without ostentation, and with all the true grandeur that unaffected simplicity when in high rank always displays. The Squire's Yeoman is also a great character, a man perfectly knowing in his profession :

> And in his hand he bore a mighty bow.

Chaucer describes here a mighty man ; one who, in war, is the worthy attendant on noble heroes.

The Prioress follows these with her female chaplain :

> Another Nonne also with her had she,
> That was her Chapelaine, and Priestes three.

This lady is described also as of the first rank, rich and honoured. She has certain peculiarities and little delicate affectations, not unbecoming in her, being accompanied with what is truly grand and really polite : her person and face Chaucer has described with minuteness ; it is very elegant and was the beauty of our ancestors until after Elizabeth's time, when voluptuousness and folly began to be accounted beautiful.

Her companion and her three priests were no doubt all perfectly delineated in those parts of Chaucer's work which are now lost ; we ought to suppose them suitable attendants on rank and fashion.

The Monk follows these with the Friar. The Painter has also grouped with these the Pardoner and the Sompnour, and the Manciple, and has here also introduced one of the rich citizens of London : characters likely to ride in company, all being above the common rank of life, or attendants on those who were so.

For the Monk is described by Chaucer as a man of the first rank in society, noble, rich, and expensively attended ; he is a leader of the age, with certain humorous accompaniments in his character that do not degrade but render him an object of dignified mirth,—but also with other accompaniments not so respectable.

The Friar is a character of a mixed kind :

> A friar there was, a wanton and a merry ;

but in his office he is said to be a "full solemn man"; eloquent, amorous, witty, and satirical ; young, handsome, and rich ; he is a complete rogue, with constitutional gaiety enough to make him a master of all the pleasures in the world.

> His neck was white as the flour-de-lis,
> Thereto was he strong as a champioun.

It is necessary here to speak of Chaucer's own character that I may set certain mistaken critics right in their conception of the humour and fun that occur on the journey. Chaucer himself is the great poetic observer of men who in every age is born to record and eternise its acts. This he does as a master, as a father, and superior, who looks down on their little follies, from the Emperor to the Miller, sometimes with severity, oftener with joke and sport.

Accordingly, Chaucer has made his Monk a great tragedian, one who studied poetical art. So much so that the generous Knight is, in the compassionate dictates of his soul, compelled to cry out :

> " Ho," quoth the Knyght,—" good sir, no more of this ;
> That ye have said is right ynough I wis,
> And mokell more ; for little heaviness
> Is right enough for much folk, as I guesse.
> I say, for me, it is a great disease.
> Whereas men have been in wealth and ease
> To heare of their sudden fall,—alas !
> And the contrary is joy, and solas."

The Monk's definition of tragedy in the proem to his tale is worth repeating :

> Tragedie is to tell a certain story,
> As old books us maken memory,
> Of hem that stood in great prosperity,
> And (who) be fallen out of high degree
> To miserie, and ended wretchedly.

Though a man of luxury, pride, and pleasure, he is a master of art and learning, though affecting to despise it. Those who think that the proud Huntsman and Noble Housekeeper, Chaucer's Monk, is intended for a buffoon or a burlesque character, know little of Chaucer.

For the Host who follows this group, and holds the centre of the cavalcade, is a first-rate character, and his jokes are no trifles ; they are always,—though uttered with audacity, equally free with the Lord and the Peasant,—they are always substantially and weightily expressive of knowledge and experience ; Henry Baillie, the keeper of the greatest Inn of the greatest City,—for such was the Tabarde Inn in Southwark, near London,—our Host was also a leader of the age.

By way of illustration I instance Shakespeare's Witches in *Macbeth*. Those who dress them for the stage consider them as wretched old women, and not, as Shakespeare intended, the Goddesses of Destiny. This shows how Chaucer has been misunderstood in his sublime work. Shakespeare's Fairies, also, are the rulers of the vegetable world, and so are Chaucer's. Let them be so understood and then the poet will be understood, and not else.

But I have omitted to speak of a very prominent character, the Pardoner, the Age's Knave, who always commands and domineers over the high and low vulgar. This man is sent in every age for a rod and scourge, and for a blight, for a trial of men, to divide the classes of men. He is in the most holy sanctuary, and he is suffered by Providence, for wise ends, and has also his great use and his grand leading destiny.

His companion, the Sompnour, is also a Devil of the first magnitude, grand, terrific, rich ; and honoured in the rank of which he holds the destiny. The uses to Society are perhaps equal of the Devil and the Angel. Their sublimity, who can dispute.

> In danger had he at his owne gise,
> The younge girles of his diocese,
> And he knew well their counsel, etc.

The principal figure in the next group is the Good Parson ; an Apostle, a real Messenger of Heaven, sent in every age for its light and its warmth. The man is beloved and venerated by all and neglected by all. He serves all and is served by none. He is, according to Christ's definition, the greatest of his age, yet he is a Poor Parson of a town. Read Chaucer's description of the Good Parson, and bow the head and knee to Him, who in every age sends us such a burning and a shining light. Search, O ye rich and powerful, for these men, and obey their counsel ; then shall the golden age return. But alas ! you will not easily distinguish him from the Friar, or the Pardoner. They, also, are "full solemn men," and *their* counsel you will continue to follow.

I have placed by his side the Sergeant at Lawe, who appears delighted to ride in his company, and between him and his brother the Plough-man, as I wish men of law would always ride with them, and take their counsel, especially in all difficult points. Chaucer's Lawyer is a character of great venerableness, a Judge, a real master of the juris-prudence of his age.

The Doctor of Physic is in this group, and the Franklin the volup-tuous country gentleman, contrasted with the Physician, and on his other hand, with two Citizens of London. Chaucer's characters live age after age. Every age is a Canterbury Pilgrimage. We all pass on, each sustaining one or other of these characters, nor can a child be born who is not one or other of these characters of Chaucer. The Doctor of Physic is described as the first of his profession : perfect, learned, completely Master and Doctor in his art. Thus the reader will observe that Chaucer makes every one of his characters perfect in his kind. Every one is an Antique Statue, the image of a class, not of an imperfect individual.

This group also would furnish substantial matter on which volumes might be written. The Franklin is one who keeps open table, who is the genius of eating and drinking, like Bacchus. As the Doctor of Physic is the Æsculapius, the Host is the Silenus, the Squire is the Apollo, the Miller is the Hercules, etc. Chaucer's characters are a description of the eternal Principles that exist in all ages. The Franklin is voluptuousness itself, most nobly portrayed :

> It snewed in his house of meat and drink.

The Ploughman is simplicity itself with wisdom and strength for its stamina. Chaucer has divided the ancient character of Hercules between his Miller and his Ploughman. Benevolence is the Ploughman's great characteristic. He is thin with excessive labour, and not with old age, as some have supposed :

> He would threash, and thereto dike and delve,
> For Christe's sake, for every poure wight,
> Withouten hire, if it lay in his might.

Visions of these eternal principles or characters of human life appear to poets in all ages. The Grecian gods were the ancient Cherubim of Phœnicia, but the Greeks, and since them, the Moderns, have neglected to subdue the gods of Priam. These gods are visions of the eternal attributes or divine names, which, when erected into gods, become destructive to humanity. They ought to be the servants and not the masters of man or of society. They ought to be made to sacrifice to Man, and not man compelled to sacrifice to them ; for when separated from man, or humanity, who is Jesus, the Saviour, the vine of eternity ? They are thieves and rebels ; they are destroyers.

The Ploughman of Chaucer is Hercules in his supreme eternal state, divided from his spectrous shadow, which is the Miller, a terrible fellow, such as exists in all times and places for the trial of men, to astonish every neighbourhood with brutal strength and courage, to get rich and powerful, and to curb the pride of Man.

The Reeve and the Manciple are two characters of consummate worldly wisdom. The Shipman or Sailor is a similar genius of Ulyssean art, but with the highest courage superadded.

The Citizens and their cook are each leaders of a class. Chaucer has been somehow made to number four citizens, which would make his whole company, himself included, thirty-one. But he says there were but nine-and-twenty in his company :

> Full nine-and-twenty in a company.

The Webbe, or Weaver, and the Tapiser, or Tapestry Weaver, appear to me to be the same person, but this is only an opinion, for "full nine-and-twenty" may signify one more or less. But I daresay that Chaucer wrote "A webbe dyer," that is, a Cloth dyer :

> A Webbe Dyer, and a Tapiser.

The Merchant cannot be one of the Three Citizens, as his dress is different and his character is more marked, whereas Chaucer says of his rich citizen :

All were y-clothed in o liverie.

The characters of Women, Chaucer has divided into two classes : the Lady Prioress, and the Wife of Bath. Are not these leaders of the ages of men ? The Lady Prioress in some ages predominates, and in some the Wife of Bath, in whose character Chaucer has been equally minute and exact, because she is also a scourge and a blight. I shall say no more of her, nor expose what Chaucer has left hidden. Let the young reader study what he has said of her. It is useful as a scarecrow. There are such characters born,—too many for the peace of the world.

I come at length to the Clerk of Oxenford. This character varies from that of Chaucer as the contemplative philosopher varies from the poetical genius. There are always these two classes of learned sages, the poetical and the philosophical. The painter has put them side by side as if the youthful clerk had put himself under the tuition of the mature poet. Let the Philosopher always be the servant and scholar of inspiration and all will be happy.

Such are the characters that compose this picture which was painted in self-defence against the insolent and envious imputation of unfitness for finished and scientific art,—and this imputation most artfully and industriously endeavoured to be propagated among the public by ignorant hirelings. The painter courts comparison with his competitors, who, having received fourteen hundred guineas and more, from the profits of *his* designs in that well-known work Designs for Blair's *Grave*, have left him to shift for himself, while others, more obedient to an employer's opinions and directions, are employed at great expense to produce works in succession to his, by which they acquired public patronage. This has hitherto been his lot, to get patronage for others and then to be left and neglected, and his work, which gained that patronage, cried down as eccentricity and madness,—as unfinished and neglected by the artist's violent temper. He is sure the works now exhibited will give the lie to such aspersions.

Those who say that men are led by interest are knaves. A knavish character will often say, " Of what interest is it to me to do——so and so ?" I answer, "Of none at all, but the contrary, as you well know. It is of malice and envy that you have done this, therefore I am aware of you, because I know that you act, not from interest, but from malice, even to your own destruction." It is therefore become a duty which Mr. B. owes to the public, who have always recognised him, and patronised him, however hidden by artifices, that he should not suffer such things to be done, or be hindered from the public exhibition of his finished production by any calumnies in future.

The character and expression in this picture could never have been produced with Rubens' light and shadow, or with Rembrandt's, or anything Venetian or Flemish. The Venetian and Flemish practice is broken lines, broken masses, and broken colours : Mr. B.'s practice is unbroken lines, unbroken masses, and unbroken colours. Their art is to lose form. His art is to find form and keep it. His arts are opposite to theirs in all things.

As there is a class of men whose sole delight is the destruction of, so there is a class of artist whose sole art and science is fabricated for the purpose of destroying Art. Who these are is well known. "By their works ye shall know them." All who endeavour to raise up a style against Raphael, Michael Angelo, and the Antique, those who separate Painting from Drawing, who look if a picture is well drawn, and, if it is, immediately cry out that it cannot be well coloured,—those are the men.

But to show the stupidity of this class of men nothing need be done but to examine my rival's prospectus.

The five first characters in Chaucer, the Knight and the Squire, he has put among his rabble, and indeed his prospectus calls the Squire the "fop of Chaucer's age." Now hear Chaucer:

> Of his stature he was of even length,
> And wonderly deliver, and of great strength
> And he had been some time in chivauelry,
> In Flanders, in Artois, and in Piccardy,
> And borne him well, as of so litele space.

Was this a fop?

> Well could he sit a horse, and faire ride,
> He could songs make, eke well indite
> Joust, and eke dance, portray, and well write.

Was this a fop?

> Curteis he was, and meek and servicable,
> And kerft before his fader at the table.

Was this a fop?

It is the same with all his characters. He had done all by chance, or perhaps his fortune,—money, money! According to his prospectus he has three monks. These he cannot find in Chaucer, who has only one Monk, and that no vulgar character, as he has endeavoured to make him. When men cannot read they should not pretend to paint. To be sure Chaucer is a little difficult to him who has only blundered over novels, and catch-penny trifles of booksellers, yet a little pains ought to be taken even by the ignorant and weak. He has put the Reeve, a vulgar fellow, between his Knight and Squire, as if he was resolved to go contrary to everything in Chaucer, who says of the Reeve:

> And ever he rode hindermost of the rout.

In this manner he has jumbled his dumb dollies together and is praised by his equals for it, for both himself and his friend are equally masters of Chaucer's language. They both think that the Wife of Bath is a young, beautiful, blooming damsel, and H—— says, that she is the "Fair Wife of Bath," and that "the Spring appears in her cheeks." Now hear what Chaucer has made her say of herself,—who is no modest one:

> But Lord(e) (Christ) when (that) it remembreth me
> Upon my youth and on my joleity
> It tickleth me about the hearte-root,
> Unto this day it doth my hearte boot
> That I have had my world as in my time,
> But age, alas, that all will envenime

Hath me breft my beauty and my pith,
Let go ! Farewell ! The Devil go therewith,
The flour is gone ; there is no more to tell
The bran, as best I can, I now mote sell.
And yet to be right merry I will fond,—
Now forth, to tell about my fourth husband.

She has had four husbands ; a fit subject for this painter. Yet the painter ought to be very much offended with his friend H——, who has called his "a common scene," and "very ordinary forms," which is the truest part of all, for it is so, and very wretchedly so indeed. What merit can there be in a picture of which such words are spoken with truth ?

But the prospectus says that the painter has represented Chaucer himself as a knave who thrusts himself among honest people to make game of and laugh at them ; though I must do justice to the painter and say that he has made him look more like a fool than a knave. But it appears in all the writings of Chaucer, and particularly in his *Canterbury Tales*, that he was very devout, and paid respect to true enthusiastic superstition. He has laughed at his knaves and fools, as I do now, but he has respected his True Pilgrims, who are a majority of his company, and are not thrown together in the random manner that Mr. S—— has done. Chaucer has nowhere called the Ploughman old, worn out with "age and labour" as the prospectus has represented him, and says that the picture has done so too. He is worn down with labour, but not with age. How spots of brown and yellow, smeared about at random, can be either young or old I cannot see. It may be an old man ; it may be a young man ; it may be anything that a prospectus pleases. But I know that where there are no lineaments there can be no character. And what connoisseurs call touch, I know by experience must be the destruction of all character and expression and of every lineament.

The scene of Mr. S——'s picture is by Dulwich Hills, which was not the way to Canterbury, but perhaps the painter thought he would give them a ride round about because they were a burlesque set of scarecrows not worth any man's respect or care.

But the painter's thoughts being always upon gold, he has introduced a character that Chaucer has not, namely, a goldsmith, for so the prospectus tells us. Why he introduced a goldsmith, and what is the wit, the prospectus does not explain. But it takes care to mention the reserve and modesty of the painter. This makes a good epigram enough :

The fox, the mole, the beetle, and the bat
By sweet reserve and modesty grow fat.

But the prospectus tells us that the painter has introduced a " Sea-Captain." Chaucer has a ship-man, a sailor, a trading master of a vessel, called by courtesy Captain, as every master of a boat is ; but this does not make him a Sea-Captain. Chaucer has purposely omitted such a personage, as it only exists in certain periods : it is the soldier by sea. He who would be a soldier in inland nations is a sea-captain in commercial nations.

All is misconceived, and its mis-execution is equal to its misconception. I have no objection to Rubens and Rembrandt being employed, or even to their living in a palace. But it shall not be at the expense of Raphael and Michael Angelo living in a cottage, and in contempt and derision. I have been scorned long enough by those fellows who owe me all that they have. It shall be so no longer;

> I found them blind : I taught them how to see ;
> And now they know neither themselves nor me.

No. IV

THE BARD, FROM GRAY

> On a rock whose haughty brow
> Frown'd o'er old Conway's foaming flood
> Robed in sable garb of woe
> With haggard eyes the Poet stood :
> Loose his beard, and hoary hair,
> Streamed like a meteor to the troubled air,

> Weave the warp and weave the woof
> The winding sheet of Edward's race.

Weaving the winding sheet of Edward's race by means of sounds of spiritual music, and its accompanying expressions of spiritual speech, is a bold, and daring, and most masterly conception that the public have embraced and approved with avidity. Poetry consists in these conceptions, and shall painting be confined to the sordid drudgery of facsimile representations of merely mortal and perishing substances and not be as painting and music are, elevated to its own proper sphere of invention and visionary conception ? No: it shall not be so ! Painting, as well as poetry and music, exists and exults in immortal thoughts. If Mr. B.'s Canterbury Pilgrims had been done by any other power than that of the poetic visionary it would have been just as dull as his adversary's.

The Spirits of the murdered bards assist in weaving the deadly woof :

> With me in dreadful harmony they join
> And weave with bloody hands the tissue of thy line.

The connoisseurs and artists who have made objections to Mr. B.'s mode of representing spirits with real bodies would do well to consider that the Venus, the Minerva, the Jupiter, the Apollo, which they admire in Greek statues are all of them representations of spiritual existences,—of God's immortal,—to the ordinary perishing organ of sight ; and yet they are embodied and organised in solid marble. Mr. B. requires the same latitude, and all is well. The Prophets describe what they saw in vision as real and existing men, whom they saw with their imaginative and immortal organs; the Apostles the same; the clearer the organ the more distinct the object. A spirit and a vision are not, as the modern philosophy supposes, a cloudy vapour, or a nothing. They are organised and minutely articulated beyond all that the mortal and perishing nature can produce. He who does not imagine in stronger and better lineaments and in stronger and better light than his perishing and mortal eye can see, does not imagine at all. The painter of this work asserts that all his imaginations appear to him infinitely more perfect and more minutely organised than anything seen by his mortal eye. Spirits are organised men. Moderns wish to draw figures without lines and with great and heavy shadows. Are not shadows more unmeaning than lines and more heavy? Oh who can doubt this?

King Edward and his Queen Eleanor are prostrated, with their horses at the foot of a rock on which the Bard stands; prostrated by the terrors of his harp, on the margin of the river Conway, whose waves bear up a corpse of a slaughtered bard at the foot of the rock. The armies of Edward are seen winding among the mountains.

He wound with toilsome march his long array.

Mortimer and Gloucester lie spell-bound behind their king. The execution of this picture is also in water colours, or fresco.

No. V

THE ANCIENT BRITONS

In the last Battle of King Arthur, only three Britons escaped; these were the Strongest Man, the Beautifullest Man, and the Ugliest Man. These three marched through the field, unsubdued, as gods, and the sun of Britain set, but shall rise again with tenfold splendour when Arthur shall awake from sleep and resume his dominion over earth and ocean.

The three general classes of men who are represented by the most Beautiful, the most Strong, and the most Ugly, could not be represented by any historical facts but those of our own country,—the ancient Britons,—without violating costume. The Britons (say historians) were naked civilised men, learned, studious, abstruse in thought and contemplation; naked, simple, plain in their acts and manners; wiser than after-ages. They were overwhelmed by brutal arms, all but a small remnant. Strength, Beauty, and Ugliness escaped the wreck, and remain for ever unsubdued, age after age.

The British Antiquities are now in the Artist's hands,—all his visionary contemplations relating to his own country and its ancient glory, when it was, as it shall be again, the source of learning and inspiration. Arthur was a name for the constellation Arcturus, or Boötes, the keeper of the North Pole; and all the fables of Arthur and his Round Table, of the warlike naked Britons, of Merlin, of Arthur's conquest of the whole world, of his death, or sleep, and promise to return again, of the Druid monuments or temples, of the pavement of Watling Street, of London stone, of the caverns of Cornwall, Wales, Derbyshire, and Scotland, of the giants of Ireland and Britain, of the elemental beings called by us by the general name of Fairies, and of these those who escaped, namely Beauty, Strength, and Ugliness, Mr. B. has in his hands poems of the highest antiquity. Adam was a Druid, and Noah; also Abraham was called to succeed the Druidical age, which began to turn allegoric and mental signification into corporeal command, whereby human sacrifice would have depopulated the earth. All these things are written in Eden. The artist is an inhabitant of that happy country, and if everything goes on as it has begun, the world of vegetation and generation may expect to be opened again to Heaven, through Eden, as it was in the beginning.

The Strong Man represents the human sublime, the Beautiful Man represents the human pathetic, the Ugly Man represents the human reason. They were originally one man who was fourfold. He was self-divided and his real humanity slain on the stems of generation, and the form of the fourth was like the Son of God. How he became divided is a subject of great sublimity and pathos. The artist has written it under inspiration, and will, if God please, publish it. It is voluminous and contains the ancient history of Britain, and the world of Satan and Adam.

In the meantime he has painted this picture, which supposes that in the reign of that British Prince who lived in the fifth century there were remains of those naked heroes in the Welch Mountains. They are there now. Gray saw them in the person of his Bard on Snowdon. There they dwell in naked simplicity. Happy is he who can see and converse with them above the shadows of generation and death. The Giant Albion was Patriarch of the Atlantic. He is the Atlas of the Greeks: one of those the Greeks called Titans. The stories of Arthur are the acts of Albion, applied to a Prince of the fifth century who conquered Europe, and held the Empire of the world (in the dark age), which the Romans never again recovered. In this picture, believing with Milton the ancient British History, Mr. B. has done as all the ancients did, and all the moderns who are worthy of fame,—given the historical fact in its poetic vigour, so as it always happens, and not in that dull way that some historians pretend, who, being weakly organised themselves, cannot see either miracle or prodigy. All is, to them, a dull round of probabilities and possibilities. But the history of all times and places is nothing else but improbabilities and impossibilities, —what we should say was impossible if we did not see it always before our eyes.

The antiquities of every nation under Heaven are no less sacred than those of the Jews. They are the same thing, as Jacob Bryant and all antiquarians have proved. How other antiquities came to be neglected and disbelieved, while those of the Jews are collected and arranged, is an inquiry worthy both of the Antiquarian and Divine. All had originally one language and one religion: this was the religion of Jesus, the Everlasting Gospel. Antiquity preaches the Gospel of Jesus. The reasoning historian, turner and twister of causes and consequences, such as Hume, Gibbon, and Voltaire,—cannot with all his artifice turn and twist one fact or disarrange self-evident action and reality. Reasons and opinions concerning acts are not history. Acts themselves alone are history, and these are not the exclusive property of either Hume, Gibbon, or Voltaire, Echard, Rapin, Plutarch, or Herodotus. Tell me the acts, O historian, and leave me to reason upon them as I please. Away with your reasoning and your rubbish! All that is not action is not worth reading. Tell me the What: I do not want you to tell me the Why, and the How. I can find that out myself as well as you can, and I will not be fooled by opinions that you please to impose, to disbelieve what you think improbable or impossible. His opinion who does not see spiritual agency is not worth any man's reading. He who rejects a fact because it is improbable must reject all history and retain doubts only.

It has been said to the Artist: "Take the Apollo for the model of your Beautiful Man, and the Hercules for your Strong Man, and the Dancing Faun for your Ugly Man." Now he comes to his trial. He knows that what he does is not inferior to the grandest Antiques. Superior it cannot be, for human power cannot go beyond either what he does or what they have done ; it is the gift of God : it is inspiration and vision. He had resolved to emulate those previous remains of antiquity. He has done so, and the result you behold. His ideas of strength and beauty have not been greatly different. Poetry as it exists now on earth in the various remains of ancient authors, Music as it exists in old tunes or melodies, Painting and Sculpture as they exist in the remains of Antiquity and in the works of more modern genius,—each is inspiration, and cannot be surpassed : it is perfect, and eternal. Milton, Shakespeare, Michael Angelo, Raphael, the finest specimens of Ancient Sculpture and Painting and Architecture, Gothic, Grecian, Hindoo, and Egyptian, are the extent of the human mind. The human mind cannot go before the gift of God,—the Holy Ghost. To suppose that Art can go beyond the finest specimens of Art now in the world is not knowing what Art is. It is being blind to the gifts of the Spirit.

It will be necessary for the painter to say something concerning his ideas of beauty, strength, and ugliness.

The Beauty that is annexed and appended to folly is a lamentable accident and error of the mortal and perishing life. It does but seldom happen. But with this unnatural mixture the sublime Artist can have nothing to do. It is fit for the burlesque. The Beauty proper for sublime art is lineaments, or forms and features that are capable of being the receptacles of intellect. Accordingly the painter has given, in his Beautiful Man, his own idea of intellectual Beauty. The face and limbs that deviate or alter least from infancy to old age are the face and limbs of the greatest Beauty and perfection.

The Ugly, likewise, when accompanied and annexed to imbecility and disease is a subject for burlesque, and not for historical grandeur. The Artist has imagined his Ugly Man one approaching to the beast in features and form ; his forehead small, without frontals, his jaws large, his nose high on the ridge, and narrow, his chest, and the stamina of his make, comparatively little, and his joints and his extremities large, his eyes, with scarce any whites, narrow and cunning, and everything tending toward what is truly Ugly, the incapability of intellect.

The Artist has considered his Strong Man as a receptacle of Wisdom, a sublime energiser. His features and limbs do not spindle out into length without strength, nor are they too large and unwieldy for his brain and bosom. Strength consists in accumulation of power to the principal seat, and from thence a regular gradation and subordination. Strength is compactness, not extent nor bulk.

The Strong Man acts from conscious superiority, and marches on in fearless dependence on the divine decrees, raging with the inspirations of a prophetic mind. The Beautiful Man acts from duty, and anxious solicitude for the fate of those for whom he combats. The Ugly Man acts from love of carnage, and delight in the savage barbarities of war, rushing with sportive precipitation into the very jaws of the affrighted enemy.

The Roman soldiers, rolled together in a heap before them, "like the rolling thing before the whirlwind," show each a different character and a different expression of fear, or revenge, or envy, or blank horror and amazement, or devout wonder and unresisting awe.

The dead and the dying—Britons naked mingled with armed Romans—strew the field beneath. Among these the last of the Bards who was capable of attending warlike deeds is seen falling, outstretched among the dead and dying, singing to his harp in the pains of death.

Distant among the mountains are Druid Temples similar to Stonehenge. The sun sets behind the mountains, bloody with the day of battle.

The flush of health in flesh exposed to the open air, nourished by the spirits of forests and floods, in that ancient happy period which history has recorded, cannot be like the sickly daubs of Titian or Rubens. Where will the copier of Nature as it now is find a civilised man who is accustomed to go naked? Imagination only can furnish us with colouring appropriate, such as is found in the frescoes of Raphael and Michael Angelo. The disposition of forms always directs colouring in true art. As to a modern man, stripped from his load of clothing, he is like a dead corpse. Hence Rubens, Titian, Correggio, and all of that class are like leather and chalk. Their men are like leather and their women like chalk, for the disposition of their forms will not admit of grand colouring. In Mr. B.'s Britons the blood is seen to circulate in their limbs : he defies competition in colouring.

No. VI

" A spirit vaulting from a cloud to turn and wind a fiery Pegasus."—
Shakespeare. The Horse of Intellect is leaping from the cliffs of
Memory and Reasoning. It is a barren Rock. It is also called the
Barren Waste of Lock and Newton.

This picture was done many years ago, and was one of the first Mr. B. ever did in Fresco. Fortunately, or rather, providentially, he left it unblotted and unblurred, although molested continually by blotting and blurring demons. But he was also compelled to leave it unfinished, for reasons that will appear in the following.

No. VII

The Goats—an experiment picture.

The subject is taken from the missionary voyage, and varied from the literal fact for the sake of picturesque scenery. The savage girls had dressed themselves with vine leaves, and some goats on board the missionary ship stripped them off presently. This picture was painted at intervals, for experiment with the colours, and is laboured to a superabundant blackness. It has, however, that about it which may be worthy the attention of the Artist and connoisseur for reasons that follow.

No. VIII

The Spiritual Preceptor—an experiment picture.

The subject is taken from the Visions of Emanuel Swedenborg (Universal Theology, No. 623). The learned who strive to ascend into heaven by means of learning, appear to children like dead horses, when repelled by the celestial spheres.

The works of this visionary are well worthy the attention of Painters and Poets. They are foundations for grand things. The reason they have not been more attended to is because corporeal demons have gained a predominance. Who the leaders of these are will be shown below. Unworthy Men who gain fame among Men continue to govern mankind after death, and in their spiritual bodies oppose the spirits of those who worthily are famous, and, as Swedenborg observes, by entering into disease and excrement, drunkenness, and concupiscence, they possess themselves of the bodies of mortal men, and shut the doors of mind and thought by placing Learning above Inspiration. O Artists, you may disbelieve all this, but it shall be at your own peril.

No. IX

Satan calling up his legion, from Milton's " Paradise Lost " : a composition for a more perfect Picture afterwards executed for a Lady of high rank. An experiment Picture.

This Picture was likewise painted at intervals, for experiment on colours without any oily vehicle. It may be worthy of attention, not only on account of its composition but of the great labour which has been bestowed on it,—that is,—three or four times as much as would have finished a more perfect picture. The labour has destroyed the lineaments. It was, with difficulty, brought back to a certain effect, which it had at first, when all the lineaments were perfect.

These pictures, among numerous others painted for experiment, were the result of temptations and perturbations, seeking to destroy imaginative power, by means of that infernal machine called Chiaro Oscuro, in the hands of Venetian and Flemish Demons, whose enmity to the Painter himself, and to all Artists who study the Florentine and Roman Schools, may be removed by an exhibition and exposure of their vile tricks. They cause that everything in art shall become a Machine. They cause that execution shall all be blocked up with brown shadows. They put the original artist in fear and doubt of his own original conception. The spirit of Titian was particularly active in raising doubts concerning the possibility of executing without a model ; and when once he had raised the doubt, it became easy for him to snatch away the vision time after time, for, when the Artist took his pencil to execute his ideas, his power of imagination weakened so much and darkened, that memory of nature, and of Pictures of the various schools possessed his mind instead of appropriate execution resulting from the inventions,—like walking in another man's style, or speaking, or looking in another man's style and manner, unappropriate and repugnant to your own individual character,—tormenting the true Artist till he leaves the Florentine, and adopts the Venetian practice, or does as Mr. B. has done—has the courage to suffer poverty and disgrace till he ultimately conquers.

Rubens is a most outrageous demon, and by infusing the remembrances of his pictures and style of execution, hinders all power of individual thought, so that the man who is possessed of this demon loses all admiration of any other Artist but Rubens, and those who

U

were his imitators and journeymen. He causes the Florentine and Roman Artist to fear to execute, and though the original conception was all fire and animation he loads it with hellish brownness, and blocks up all its gates of light except one, and that one he closes with iron bars, till the victim is obliged to give up the Florentine and Roman practice and adopt the Venetian and Flemish.

Correggio is a soft and effeminate, and consequently most cruel demon, whose whole delight is to cause endless labour to whoever suffers him to enter his mind. The story that is told in all Lives of the Painters about Correggio being poor and but badly paid for his Pictures is altogether false. He was a petty Prince in Italy, and employed numerous journeymen in manufacturing (as Rubens and Titian did) the pictures that go under his name. The manual labour in these pictures of Correggio is immense, and was paid for originally at the immense prices that those who keep manufactories of art always charge to their employers, while they themselves pay their journeymen little enough. But though Correggio was not poor, he will make any true artist so who permits him to enter his mind, and take possession of his affections. He infuses a love of soft and even tints without boundaries, and of endless reflected lights that confuse one another, and hinder all correct drawing from appearing to be correct; for if one of Raphael's or Michael Angelo's figures was to be traced, and Correggio's reflections and refractions to be added to it, there would soon be an end of proportion and strength, and it would be weak and pappy, and lumbering, and thick-headed like his own works; but then it would have softness and evenness, by a twelvemonth's labour where a month with judgement would have finished it better and higher; and the poor wretch who executed it would be the Correggio whom the Life-writers have written of,—a drudge and a miserable man, compelled to softness by poverty. I say again, O Artist! you may disbelieve all this, but it shall be at your own Peril.

Note.—These experiment pictures have been bruised and knocked about without mercy to try all experiments.

No. X

The Bramins.—A Drawing.

The subject is Mr. Wilkin translating the Geeta; an ideal design, suggested by the first publication of that part of the Hindoo Scriptures translated by Mr. Wilkin. I understand that my Costume is incorrect; but in this I plead the authority of the Ancients, who often deviated from the Habits to preserve the Manners, as in the instance of Laocoön, who, though a priest, is represented naked.

No. XI

The Body of Abel found by Adam and Eve; Cain, who was about to bury it, fleeing from the face of his parents.—A Drawing.

No. XII

The soldiers casting Lots for Christ's garment.—A Drawing.

No. XIII

Jacob's Ladder.—A Drawing.

No. XIV.

The Angels hovering over the Body of Jesus in the Sepulchre.—
A Drawing.

The above four drawings, the Artist wishes were in Fresco on an
enlarged scale to ornament the altars of churches, and to make England,
like Italy, respected by respectable men of other countries on account
of Art.   It is not the want of Genius that can hereafter be laid to our
charge.   The Artist who has done these Pictures and Drawings will
take care of that, Let those who govern the Nation take care of the
other.   The times require that every one should speak out boldly.
England expects that every man should do his duty in Arts as well
as in Arms or in the Senate.

No. XV

Ruth.—A Drawing.

This design is taken from that most pathetic passage in the Book
of Ruth, where Naomi is taking leave of her daughters-in-law,
with intent to return to her own country.   Ruth cannot leave her,
but says, "Whither thou goest I will go, and where thou lodgest I will
lodge ; thy people shall be my people, and thy God my God ; where
thou diest I will die, and there will I be buried.   God do so to me and
more also if aught but death part thee and me."
   The distinction that is made in modern times between a painting
and a drawing proceeds from ignorance of art.   The merit of a Picture
is the same as the merit of a drawing.   The dauber daubs his drawings;
and he who draws his drawings draws his Pictures.   There is no
difference between Raphael's cartoons and his frescoes or Pictures,
except that the Frescoes or Pictures are more finished.   When Mr. B.
formerly painted in oil colours his Pictures were shown to certain painters
and connoisseurs, who said that they were very admirable drawings on
canvas, but not Pictures ; but they said the same of Raphael's Pictures.
Mr. B. thought this the greatest of compliments, though it was meant
otherwise.   If losing and obliterating the outline constitutes a Picture,
Mr. B. will never be so foolish as to do one.   Such art of losing the
outlines is the art of Venice and Flanders.   It loses all character and
leaves what some people call "expression" ; but this is a false notion of
expression.   Expression cannot exist without character as its stamina,
and neither character nor expression can exist without form and
determinate outline.   Fresco Painting is susceptible of higher finishing
than Drawing on Paper or any other method of Painting.   But he
must have a strange organisation of sight who does not prefer a
Drawing on Paper to a Daubing in Oil by the same master, supposing
both to be done with equal care.
   The great and golden rule of art as well as of life is this ;—that the
more distinct, sharp, and wiry the boundary line, the more perfect the
work of art,—and the less keen and sharp, the greater is the evidence

of weak imagination, plagiarism, and bungling. Great inventors in all ages knew this. Protogenes and Apelles knew each other by this line. Raphael, Michael Angelo, and Albert Dürer are known by this and by this alone. The want of this determinate and bounding form evidences the idea of want in the Artist's mind, and the pretence of the plagiary in all its branches. How do we distinguish the oak from the beech, the horse from the ox but by the bounding outline? How do we distinguish one face or countenance from another but by the bounding line and its infinite inflexion and movements? What is it that builds a house and plants a garden but the definite and determinate? What is it that distinguishes honesty from knavery but the hard and wiry line of rectitude and certainty in the actions and intentions? Leave out this line, and you leave out life itself. All is chaos again, and the line of the Almighty must be drawn out upon it again before man or beast can exist. Talk no more then of Correggio or Rembrandt, or any of those plagiaries of Venice or Flanders. They were but the lame imitators of lines drawn by their predecessors, and their words prove themselves contemptible, disarranged imitations, and blundering, misapplied copies.

No. XVI

The Penance of Jane Shaw in St. Paul's Church.—A Drawing.

This Drawing was done above Thirty Years ago, and proves to the Author, and he thinks will prove to any discerning eye, that the productions of our youth and those of our maturer age are equal in all essential points. If a man is master of his profession he cannot be ignorant that he is so, and if he is not employed by those who pretend to encourage art, he will employ himself, and laugh in secret at the pretences of the ignorant, while he has every night dropped into his shoe,—as soon as he puts it off, and puts out the candle, and gets into bed,—a reward for the labours of the day, such as the world cannot give,—and patience and time await to give him all that the world can give.

———

So ends the famous *Descriptive Catalogue.* Butts bought the *Canterbury Pilgrims.* The list of subscribers to the engraving is lost. The exhibition very nearly escaped public observation altogether. But before it closed, an art critic —whether the same that Blake had so thoroughly chastised for attacking Fuseli, or a friend writing for him, is not known—found it out, and must have enjoyed it very much.

He does not write in Blake's savage sort of Shawn O'Neil tone (why did Philips not bury Blake up to the ears in sand when he wanted to write that letter about Fuseli?), but he makes himself quite sufficiently disagreeable.

The first article—both are in Leigh Hunt's paper, the *Examiner,* in August—betrays the connection of his wrath against Blake with the Fuseli letter by pairing Fuseli and

Blake together as a "visionary" and a "fanatic." The designs to Blair's *Grave* are ridiculed. The design of the *Soul exploring the Recesses of the Grave* suggests to the critic "no other idea but that of a human being with a candle." That of the *Reunion of the Soul and Body*, reproduced in the second volume of the Chatto and Windus *Blake's Poems*, suggests that the upper figure is trying to dive into the mouth of the lower.

Though at the present day this seems so silly that we can hardly avoid the idea that the critic is writing with his tongue in his cheek, yet in fairness we must remember that it is not really below the average intelligence of sensible men who are ignorant of art and poetry. In his little collection of original essays recently published under the title *Ideas of Good and Evil*, which has been already alluded to, Mr. W. B. Yeats, speaking of people whose education has not prepared them for such imaginative expressions as are usual in good poetry, says:

"Go down into the street and read to your baker or your candlestick-maker any poem which is not popular poetry. I have heard a baker who was clever enough with his oven declare that Tennyson could not have known what he was writing when he wrote

> . . . warming his five wits,
> The white owl in the belfry sits.

And once when I read out Omar Khayyam to one of the best of candlestick-makers he said, ' What is the meaning of

> We come like water, and like wind we go ?' "

We cease as we read this to doubt the objective and actual existence of that traditional German critic who is said to have discovered a curious misprint in the close of the Duke's speech at the beginning of the Second Act of *As You Like It*, in which the Duke speaks of the charms of living in the backwoods, and says,

> And this our life, exempt from public haunts,
> Finds tongues in trees, books in the running brooks,
> Sermons in stones, and good in everything.

This critic, it is said, bringing his own sound sense to bear on the matter, placed the words in their right order, and made the Duke say,

> And this our life, exempt from public *tongues*,
> Finds *haunts in trees*, *stones* in the running brooks,
> Sermons in *books*, and good in everything.

But just in time to show malice, although too late to serve any public purpose by art-criticism, the critic of the *Examiner*, when the chief picture of Blake's collection was already taken down to engrave, and the exhibition itself is about to close in two days, rushes before the public to warn them against it. Blake himself is called "an unfortunate lunatic, whose personal inoffensiveness secures him from confinement," and who would have escaped criticism also, had not "persons of position" praised him, and so, "in feeding his vanity stimulated him to publish his madness more largely." Malkin's kind notice in *A Father's Memoirs of his Child* seems to have hurt that critic. When a public schoolmaster knows no better than to take an interest in a man of genius, that sort of thing is evidently becoming a danger to society. The *Descriptive Catalogue* is called a "wild farrago of nonsense, unintelligibleness, and egregious vanity, the wild effusion of a distempered brain. . . . That men of taste, in their sober senses, should mistake its unmeaning and distorted conceptions for the flashes of genius is indeed a phenomenon."

The critic was doubtless honest in his way, and so, indisputably, was Blake when, on reading the article, he attributed it to a pen inspired and paid by Hayley!

Hayley, who had tried in vain to make Blake have a little common sense at Felpham, and had even endeavoured, like a clever man of the world, to bring pressure on him through his wife—the wives of men of genius are always supposed to be more amenable to sensible counsels than their husbands —was now, Blake conjectured, using just such "dagger and poison" against him as Fuseli's critic had used against Fuseli.

Blake had already written "peevishly" in his notebook a quatrain about Hayley before he had reduced him to being a "completely silenced antagonist." Here it is:

> When H——y finds out what you cannot do,
> That is the very thing he'll set you to.
> If you break not your neck, 'tis not his fault,
> But pecks of poison are not pecks of salt.

Since then Hayley had forgiven Blake for the scolding he had given him, and Blake had wearied himself in effusions of affection sent by post, and in the labours of an errand-boy and a commercial traveller for his sake.

But lately Blake had suspected that something was wrong.

Hayley's many fine promises had come to nothing, and the
fine gift of the ballads had turned out to be waste paper.
While telling him not to fear the lack of employment Hayley
had been secretly taking it from him. He had joined Blake's
enemy Cromek, and Flaxman had been to blame for this. It
was now clear enough that he had hired Leigh Hunt (the
editor is always responsible) to strike him this blow in the
back, hindering him ("Murder is hindering another!" as he
says in the notes to Lavater—a quotation that was found too
late for use in the Quaritch edition memoir), and even helping to deprive him of the very scant allowance of bread with
which he kept body and soul together. He now wrote an
addition to that epigram—a new quatrain—but the MS.
book was crowded, and he had no room to put the lines under
one another, so he put two beside the other two :

> To forgive enemies Hayley does pretend,
> Who never in his life forgave a friend,
> And when he could not act upon my wife,
> Hired a villain to bereave my life.

In the chapter on this in the Quaritch edition memoir
the present writer has spent long pages in making the whole
affair clear, being impelled to do so by the unfortunate and,
as it seems to him, shocking and injurious mistake made by
Mr. Rossetti in his Memoir in the Aldine edition of Blake,
which held the field to the disgrace of Blake's memory for
many years.

This mistake of Mr. Rossetti must now be referred to, for
the sake of those who cannot otherwise believe that a professed admirer of Blake could write such things of him.
Indeed, viewed as mere errors, Mr. Rossetti's words are, as
coming from such a quarter, hardly more credible than

> Stones in the running brooks.

To begin with, Mr. Rossetti prints the epigram as a sestet,
taking the last couplet of the second quatrain and adding it
to the first.

He says about it, " The last couplet conveys two distinct and
most grave charges against poor Hayley, charges to which one
can hardly suppose Blake to have *lent any real credence*." (The
italics are ours, but is not this deliciously parliamentary? It
is pleasant to know by the sequel that Mr. Rossetti does not at
all perceive that he is now bringing a " grave charge " against
Blake.) The paragraph continues: "He seems rather to

have been writing in a spirit of wilful and wanton perversity ; the more monstrous and obviously untenable the accusation, the more pat it comes under a pen guided by mere testiness. It is exactly the spirit of a 'naughty little boy.' The phrase 'when he could not act upon my wife' has a somewhat indeterminate though manifestly virulent meaning. The other statement that Hayley 'hired a villain to bereave my life'" (note the grammar), "can only (it would seem) refer to the affair of the soldier Scholfield, who accused Blake of using seditious words, and thereby subjected him to a trial on a criminal (not in reality a capital) charge." (Note that Mr. Rossetti had only read of Scholfield in Gilchrist's *Life*, where we are told that Blake used to suspect the Government, not Hayley, of having sent the soldier to entrap him in revenge for his having helped Tom Paine to escape from arrest a dozen years before.) Mr. Rossetti goes on : "Now the fact is that Hayley, so far from hiring the villain to bereave Blake's life, had, as we have seen, come forward immediately as his bail, and afterwards as a witness on his behalf. Blake, if he believed that Hayley had plotted against his life, can hardly have been quite sane, and if he disbelieved it and yet wrote it, our conclusion as to his state of mind at that moment *need only differ in detail*." (Mr. Rossetti thus does not notice that he tells us now that there seems to him to be no essential difference between a lunatic and a liar—it is a mere matter of "detail.") He goes on : "I may here point out that the line

Hired a villain to bereave my life

is repeated in this epigram from the poem 'Fair Elenor' in the *Poetic* (sic) *Sketches*. The other line also,

And when he could not act upon my wife,

seems to have some affinity at any rate" (this is criticism) "to the course of the story of Fair Elenor, more affinity, at any rate, to that effort of the Macphersonian romancing faculty in verse than to aught that we can suppose to have taken place in real life between Mr. Hayley and Mrs. Blake."

These references look like careful editing, but no intelligent use is made of them. It is mere catch-word repetition. Though leaving a bad taste in the mouth, one cannot look on this kind of thing as serious, though its writer may have thought it so ; but the wretched jest is not complete without

Mr. Smetham's tribute to those who have done good work in the cause, printed in the second edition of Gilchrist's *Life of Blake*. This ends: "Last, but not least, the richly condensed and representative essay prefixed by Mr. W. M. Rossetti to his edition in the Aldine series of Blake's Poetical Works" (from which we have quoted above), "demands from all sides, as its writer has from all sides discerned and declared Blake, the highest commendation we can here briefly offer."

The same volume from which we quote this inimitable piece of pomposity contains the statement that Blake's connection with Hayley was "honourable to each" (Gilchrist's *Life*, vol. i., p. 223).

It would have been pleasant to leave all this pack of mistakes to settle itself into the wallet at Time's back along with his other "alms for oblivion," but the books where it is found are still bought and read, and the Quaritch edition, where it is exposed, is—in its cheaper form—a three-guinea book.

Among the verses by Blake that are directly due to distress of mind occasioned by the Hayley and Stothard quarrels are two fine poems, of which the second bears, in Blake's MS. book, this title: the *Everlasting Gospel*. It had chiefly for cause the *Canterbury Pilgrims*, as the first had Hayley's patronisingly coaxing manner and his "gentle, visionary Blake" way of speaking. He could not even give Blake a copy of his own verses without writing in the beginning,

> Accept, my gentle, visionary Blake,
> Whose thoughts are fanciful and kindly mild, etc.,

while really he was almost "making Blake spue," as Blake himself wrote *at this time* in his notebook.

These, joined together, with a few omissions, as one poem, were printed by Mr. W. M. Rossetti in that Aldine collection over which, with its essay, Mr. Smetham falls into a trance of admiration. Mr. Rossetti says that he prints it *in extenso*, though he does not. What is the morality of editing? one asks oneself. On studying the poems one discovers:

1. That Mr. Rossetti did not know he had made up his text from two poems, written at two different times.

2. That he did not know what either of them meant.

And yet he had the original manuscript in his hand.

The first, or untitled poem, may be summed up in the words, " I did well to be angry," and belongs to a mood very like that which produced the paragraph in extra-page 3 of *Milton* beginning .

> If you account it Wisdom, when you are angry, to be silent and
> Not to show it, I do not account that wisdom, but folly,

though the *Milton* lines were probably written a little later, as the expression

> Anger me not, thou canst not drive the harrow in pity's paths,

suggests, if we are not mistaken in seeing through its symbol an allusion to the poetic failure of Hayley's " beautiful and affectionate ballads."

The second poem, called the *Everlasting Gospel*, appears to have been written as a substitute for the first, using as much of it as Blake cared to retain in his altered mood, and aimed at the kind of imagination that had produced Stothard's *Canterbury Pilgrims*, as distinguished from the kind that had produced Blake's own design of that subject.

But the most outrageous piece of doggerel ever written by any man of real poetic ability was now set down by Blake in what may be called his second period of wrath against Hayley. The first had been mainly an inspired wrath against a spiritual enemy, and fine poetry had arisen from it. The second, when he suspected him of having hired the *Examiner*, was purely personal, and the poetic result is deplorable.

In part justification of Blake's suspicion of Hayley it must be remembered that he lived in times when Walpole's saying, " Every man has his price," was by no means ancient history, when votes were frankly bought and sold at elections, and when the press was so venal that Shelley (a few years later), without fear of being accused of writing anything unlike what was to be seen in real life, could put into his *Peter Bell the Third* the incident of the enemy of an author enclosing copies of his book to the papers with a five-pound note in each and this brief notice, " Pray abuse." To know that Hayley had not done anything of the kind Blake would have needed some of that gift of instinctively judging personal character at sight, so common in imaginative people who are purely prosaic and sentimental, and so rare in poets. Blake could judge situations,—as the Tom Paine

incident showed,—but to see into the heart of a speaker
while he was speaking was not his strong point. The fact
that he was what is called "a bad listener" was of the
utmost use to him all through life in defending his genius
from being frittered away by the personal influence of the
presence of people who had none. Personal influence over
minds—quite apart from personal opinions, a nervous exuda-
tion merely—is, unfortunately, strong in the unimaginative.
Byron, for example, was full of it. He made unpoetic
people think him the greatest of poets, but while he was
staying with Shelley in Switzerland, though he wrote, in
Childe Harold, the best pages of poetry that have come from
his energetic and egotistic pen, he so affected Shelley that
Shelley was not able to write at all.

A complete extinction of poetic faculty now came over
Blake during his wrath with Hayley, Flaxman, Stothard, and
Cromek, and will be noticed in the "Screwmuch" lines given
in the Chatto and Windus edition. They were printed for the
first time in the Quaritch edition, where some explanation of
them is given. They are so bad that their badness accounts
for the very small portion of them that remains to us, for it
is told by a friend of D. G. Rossetti, who had the privilege
of seeing him after he had bought for ten shillings from
Palmer of the British Museum that invaluable MS. book
from which so much, both poetical and biographical, has been
gathered, that there were many loose papers in the book
besides the sketches of Blake and his wife (reproduced in the
Gilchrist second edition) for which Rossetti really bought
the book. Many of these loose sheets contained verses which
were so bad that Rossetti threw them into his waste-paper
basket, from which Swinburne rescued a few fragments not
quite so worthless as the rest. Of course, the main mass of
the "Screwmuch" lines, which we see to have been crowded
out of the now choking MS. book, went to the housemaid.
In Gilchrist's time, and until Mr. White of Brooklyn
generously sent to England the original of the book for the
present writer's use, no one seems to have guessed who
"Screwmuch" was. The light that would have been shed
on this part of Blake's life if the masks of "Daddy," "Jack
Hemp," and the others had been lifted in time from their
owners' faces is now lost to us for ever. There remains this
warning to all poets—Beware of anger!

CHAPTER XXV

AFTER this doggerel, but during the period when Blake was scrambling for dear life against want of employment and the desertion of Hayley and Flaxman, he prepared the misguided prose document, which is here printed from the fragmentary notes in the MS. book. The paragraphs are here placed in what seems the order in which they were written by the author. Gilchrist's second volume contains them in a somewhat fanciful sequence. Sentences are dropped and pages transposed without any ascertainable reason. What was, at best, a series of hurried and angry jottings comes forth as a *Public Address* in an order which adds to their incoherence, and with a title which their author's MS. does not place at their head. In putting the words *Public Address* here the only object is that readers may recognise at a glance what Gilchrist has given under that name. An editorial note at the beginning of the prose selections in Gilchrist's volume, of which this is one, refers to it without giving any hint of the fact that the title is not the author's, and instead of admitting that the text is not the author's either, the editor leads the reader astray by this explanatory note: "It has been compiled from a very confused mass of MS. notes. . . . As evidence of the writer's many moods these pieces of prose are much best left unmutilated." Not one of the pieces is so left. Even the *Descriptive Catalogue* is silently deprived of its own preface, and these pages, like the description of the picture called the *Last Judgment*, are both jumbled and garbled.

For this—when pretence to literal reproduction is made— no pardon can ever be accorded, but it is right to say that even though it has not been quite faithfully fulfilled, the task that Gilchrist's editor should have attempted was not an easy one. Paragraphs intended for a late place in the prospectus or *Address* were often written by Blake on early pages of his notebook just as blank space offered itself on turning over the leaves, backwards and forwards, long after the later pages had been crowded with sentences intended for the opening lines of the manifesto, for which he seems to have hoped to find space there.

But the displacements and alterations actually made by the Gilchrist editor were not due to error thus caused. He divides what is continuous at his own fancy, and makes a new composition of the fragments.

In all else but the claim to accuracy his editorial note is admirable.

The punctuation here and elsewhere is conjectural. Blake's own is on a wrong-headed system which confuses the text. It was a convention of his own day, now obsolete, and was adopted by the translator of Lavater, and by Flaxman in private letters. These probably influenced or "infected" Blake.

The numbers printed here at the margin indicate the number of the page of the MS. book in which the paragraph printed beside it is to be found. The sequence has not been departed from except when an examination of the MS. gave the impression that the later page was the earlier written. Here and there extra sentences written *later* or *sideways* on the margin are indicated. This enables the reader to perceive that Blake's style is not broken to scraps because he was too scatter-brained to write continuously, but because he was here jotting down meditations and recollections for consideration and after-use, employing a notebook already too full to hold them properly.

These notes for a prospectus or advertisement were intended for issue with the engraving to the *Canterbury Pilgrims.* (*On page 57 of the MS. book we learn that in some form this seems to have been printed.*) "This day (*no date*) is published Advertisment to Blake's *Canterbury Pilgrims* from Chaucer, containing anecdotes of Artists." *Where is it?*

Some erased sentences have been restored for their biographical value—marked *erased.* What others would have been erased also we cannot tell, since the entire prospectus seems to have vanished as soon as it was published. The present arrangement may stand until the lost print is found. Nothing else can settle the matter.

PUBLIC ADDRESS

(Gilchrist's title for the following)

66 CHAUCER'S CANTERBURY PILGRIMS, BEING A COMPLETE INDEX OF HUMAN CHARACTERS AS THEY EXIST AGE AFTER AGE

[No date. This title is written on a page of the MS. book containing rhymes that allude, among other things, to the death of Schiavonetti, that occurred on June 7, 1810. The title seems written later than the rhymes, and as a note for those prose paragraphs. The title, however, was written *after* the paragraphs, of which those on page 68 at any rate were written before May 2, 1810, when Blake found the word golden and noted it on a margin, where it is squeezed by these paragraphs.]

61 The originality of this production makes it necessary to say a few words.

While the works of Pope and Dryden are looked upon as the same art with those of Shakespeare and Milton,—while the works of Strange and Woollett are looked upon as the same art with those of Raphael and Albert Dürer, there can be no art in a nation but such as is subservient to the interests of the monopolising trader,*[1] who manufactures art by the hands of ignorant journeymen, till at length Christian charity is held out as a motive to encourage a blockhead, and he is accounted the greatest genius who can sell a good-for-nothing commodity at a great price. Obedience to the will of the monopolist is called Virtue, and the really virtuous, industrious, and independent Barry is driven out to make room for a lot of idle sycophants **62** with whitloes on their fingers.** Englishmen! rouse yourselves from the fatal slumber into which booksellers and trading dealers have thrown you, under the artfully propagated pretence that a translation or a copy of any kind can be as honourable to a nation as an original, belying the English character in that well-known saying,—Englishmen improve what others invent. This, even Hogarth's works prove a detestable falsehood. No **63** man can improve an original invention.* Since Hogarth's time we have had very few efforts of originality,*** nor can an original invention exist without execution organised and minutely delineated and articulated either by God or man. *(Margin, sideways.)* I do not mean smoothed and niggled, and poco-penned and all the beauties paled out, blurred and spotted out, but drawn with a firm hand at once, with all its ** spots and blemishes, which are beauties,—not faulty,*** like Fuseli, Michael Angelo, Shakespeare, and Milton. I have heard many people say,—"Give me the ideas; it does not matter what words you put them into,"—and others say,—"Give me the design; it is no matter for the execution." These people knew enough of artifice but little of art. Ideas cannot be given but in their minutely appropriate words. Nor can a design be made without its minutely appropriate execution. The unorganised blots of Rubens and Titian are not art, nor can their method ever express

---

[1] The words between * and ** erased.
Between * and *** erased.   Between ** and *** erased.

ideas or imaginations any more than Pope's metaphysical jargon
(?) of rhyming. *(later)* Unappropriate execution is the most
nauseous of all affectation and foppery.

64   Whoever looks at any of the great and expensive works of
engraving which have been published by English traders must
feel a loathing and disgust ; and, accordingly, most Englishmen
have a contempt for art, which is the greatest curse which can
fall upon a nation.

The Modern Chalcographic connoisseurs and amateurs admire
only the work of the journeyman, picking out whites and blacks
in what is called *tints.* They despise drawing, which despises
them in return. They see only whether everything is carved
down but one spot of light.

Mr. B. submits to a more severe tribunal. He invites the
admirers of old English portraits to look at his print.

*(Below,—of another date,—this note intended to hit Rembrandt,
—not belonging to this part of the essay.)* He who could represent
Christ uniformly like a drayman must have had queer conceptions : consequently his execution must have been queer, and
those must be queer fellows who give great sums for such nonsense and think it fine art.

(Upside down,—at foot of page 64.)

> Great men and fools do often we inspire,
> But the greater fools the greater liar.

65   I do not know whether Homer is a liar, and that there is no
such thing as generous contention. I know that all those with
whom I have contended in art have striven, not to excel, but to
starve me out by calumny and the arts of trading competition.

66   *(Title and verses.* "Having given great offence by writing
prose," etc.)

67   The English artist may be assured that he is doing an injury
and injustice to his country while he studies and imitates the
effects of Nature. England will never rival Italy while we
servilely copy what the wise Italians, Raphael and Michael
Angelo scorned, as Vasari tells us.

> Call that the public voice which is their error
> Like to a monkey, peeping in a mirror,
> Admires all his colours warm and brown,
> Nor ever once perceives his ugly form.

What kind of intellect must he have who sees only the
colours of things and not the forms of things ?

Let us teach Buonaparte and whomsoever it may concern that
it is not the arts that follow and attend upon Empire, but
Empire that attends upon and follows arts.

It is nonsense for noblemen and gentlemen to offer premiums
for the encouragement of art when such pictures as these can
be done without premiums. Let them encourage what exists
already, and not endeavour to counteract by tricks.

Let it no more be said that empires encourage arts, for it is
arts that encourage arts. Arts and artists are spiritual and laugh

at mortal contingencies. This is their power, to hinder instruction, but not to instruct, just as it is in their power to murder a man but not make a man.

68   No man of sense can think that an imitation of an oleograph is the art of painting, or that such imitation, which any one can easily perform, is worthy of notice, much less that such an act should be the glory and pride of a nation. The Italians laugh at the English connoisseurs, who are most of them such silly fellows as to believe this.

Sideways. A man sets himself down with colours, and with all the articles of painting. He puts a model before him, and he copies that so neat as to make it a deception. Now let any man of sense ask himself one question. Is this art? Can it be worthy of admiration to anybody of understanding? Who could not do this? What man who has eyes and an ordinary share of patience cannot do this neatly? Is this art, or is it glorious to a nation to produce such contemptible copies? Countrymen! countrymen! do not suffer yourselves to be disgraced!

Pp. 69, 70, 71, etc., *of the notebook contain chiefly the account of the picture called the "Last Judgment," with the title, "For the year* 1810, *Addition to Blake's catalogue of pictures." On two little clear spaces of p.* 72 *are found, written sideways, the following two fragments:*

72   A jockey that is anything of a jockey will never buy a horse by the colour, and a man who has got any brains will never buy a picture by the colour.

When I tell any truth it is not for the sake of convincing those who do not know it, but for the sake of defending those who do.

77   The greater part of what are called in England "old pictures" are oil-colour copies of frescoe originals. The comparison is easily made and the copy detected. (*Note.*—I mean frescoe, easel, or cabinet pictures on canvas or wood, copper, etc.)

[The remainder of the book is filled with the description of the *Last Judgment* picture, which seems to have been begun upon p. 69 before any of this was written. Whatever space it did not require was given to verses. Therefore we must turn back to the beginning of the book to find the rest of this *Public Address.*]

2   If men of weak capacities have alone the power of execution in art, Mr. Blake has now put to the test. If to invent and to draw well hinders the executive power in art, and his strokes are to be condemned because they are unlike those of artists who are unacquainted with drawing, is now to be decided by the public. Mr. Blake's inventive powers and his scientific knowledge of drawing are on all hands acknowledged. It only remains to be certified whether Physiognomic strength and power are to give place to imbecility. In a work of art it is not fine tints that are required but fine forms.*[1] Fine tints without fine forms are always the subterfuge of the blockhead.*

I account it a public duty respectfully to address myself to the Chalcographic Society, and to express to them my opinion, the

[1] *——* Later.

result of expert practice and experience of many years, that engraving, as an art, is lost to England, owing to an artfully propagated opinion that drawing spoils an engraver. I request the society to inspect my print, of which drawing is the foundation, and, indeed, the superstructure. It is drawing on copper, as painting ought to be drawing on canvas, or any other surface, and nothing else. I request likewise that the society will compare the prints of Bartolozzi, Woollett, Strange, etc., with the old English portraits :—that is, compare the modern art with the art as it existed previous to the entrance of Vandyke and Rubens into the country—since which event engraving is lost—and I am sure the result of the comparison will be that the society must be of my opinion, that engraving, by losing drawing, has lost all character and expression, without which the art is lost.

(*No. 19 is the next page which had blank space enough left in* 1810 *for the manifesto. It continues on that page,—as follows*) :

19   There is not, because there cannot be any difference between the effect in pictures by Rubens and Rembrandt. When you have seen one of their pictures you have seen all. It is not so with Raphael, Julio Romano, Albert Dürer, Michael Angelo. Every picture of theirs has a different and appropriate effect. What man of sense will lay out his money on the life's labour of imbecility and imbecility's journeyman, or think to educate a fool how to build a universe with farthing balls? The contemptible idiots who have been called great men of late years ought to rouse the public indignation of men of sense of all professions.

That vulgar epigram in art, Rembrandt's *Hundred Guelders*, has entirely put an end to all genuine and appropriate effect. All, both morning and night, is now a dark cavern. It is the fashion. Yet I do not shrink from comparison in either relief or strength of colour with Rembrandt or Rubens; on the contrary, I court the comparison and fear not the result. Their effects are in every picture the same. Mine are in every picture different. Raphael, Michael Angelo, Albert Dürer, Julio Romano, are accounted ignorant of that epigrammatic wit in art, because they avoid it as a destructive machine, as it is.

I hope my countrymen will excuse me if I tell them a wholesome truth. Most Englishmen when they look at a picture begin immediately searching about for points of light, and clap the picture in a dark corner. This, when done by grand works, is like looking for epigrams in Homer.

A point of light is a witticism. Many are destructive of all art. One is an epigram only, and no good work can have them. Mr. B. repeats here that there is not one character or expression in this print which could be produced with the execution of Titian, Rubens, Correggio, Rembrandt, or any of that class. Character and expression can only be expressed by those who feel them. Even Hogarth's execution cannot be copied or improved. Gentlemen of fortune who give great prices for pictures should consider the following :

20   Rubens' Luxembourg gallery is confessed on all hands to be the

X

work of a blockhead. It bears this evidence in its face. How can its execution be any other than the work of a blockhead ? Bloated gods,—Mercury, Juno, Venus, and the rattletraps of mythology, and the lumber of an awkward French palace are thrown together, around clumsy and rickety princes and princesses, higgledy-piggledy. On the contrary, Julio Romano's *Palace of T.* at Mantua is allowed on all hands to be the production of a man of the most profound sense and genius, and yet his execution is pronounced by English connoisseurs, and Reynolds, their doll, to be unfit for the study of the painter. Can I speak with too great contempt of such fellows ? If all the princes in Europe like Louis XIV. and Charles I. were to patronise such blockheads, I, William Blake, a mental prince, would decollate and hang their souls as guilty of mental high treason.

Who that has eyes cannot see that Rubens and Correggio must have been very weak and vulgar fellows ? And are we to imitate their execution ! This is what Sir Francis Bacon says,— that a healthy child should be taught and compelled to walk like a cripple, while the cripple must be taught to walk like healthy people. Oh rare wisdom !

21 The wretched state of the arts in this country, originating in the wretched state of political science (which is the science of sciences), demands a firm and determinate conduct on the part of artists to resist the contemptible counter arts, established by such contemptible politicians as Louis XIV., and originally set on foot by Venetian picture-traders, music-traders, and rhyme-traders, to the destruction of all true art as it is this day. An example of these contrary arts is given us in the characters of Milton and Dryden as they are given in a poem signed with the name of Nat Lee, which perhaps he never wrote, and perhaps he wrote in a paroxysm of insanity, in which it said that Milton's poem is a rough, unfinished piece, and that Dryden has finished it. Now let Dryden's *Fall* and Milton's *Paradise* be read, and I will assert that everybody of understanding must cry out shame on such niggling and poco-pen as Dryden has degraded Milton with. But at the same time I will allow that stupidity will prefer Dryden, because it is rhyme, and monotonous sing-song, sing-song from beginning to end. Such are Bartolozzi, Woollett, and Strange. To recover art has been the business of my life, to the Florentine original, and if possible to go beyond that original. This I thought the only pursuit worthy of a man. To imitate I abhor. I obstinately adhere to the true style of art such as Michael Angelo, Raphael, and Albert Dürer left it,—*the art of invention, not of imitation. Imagination is my World. This world of dross is beneath my notice, and

22 beneath the notice of the Public.**[1] I demand, therefore, of the amateurs of art the encouragement which is my due. If they continue to refuse, theirs is the loss, not mine, and theirs is the contempt of posterity. I have enough in the approbation of

---

[1] * to ** erased. The words are valuable as showing the consistency of the author, who looked on the Public as being, like himself, truly a portion of the spiritual world, and outside the " world of dross."

fellow-labourers. This is my glory, and my exceeding great reward. I go on, and nothing can hinder my course.

> And in melodious accents I
> Will sit me down and cry,—I ! I !

23   (*The Screwmuch lines fill page* 23 ; *they were written before this* " *Address," as was also the fragment* " *was I angry with Hayley, who used me so ill, etc.," which holds the central place under a sketch in page* 24.)

24   The painters of England are unemployed in public works while the sculptors have continual and superabundant employment. Our churches and our abbeys are treasures of their producing for ages back, while painting is excluded. Painting, the principal art, has almost no place among our only public works. Yet it is more adapted to solemn ornament than marble can be, as it is capable of being placed in any height, and, indeed, would make a noble finish placed above the great public monuments in Westminster, St. Paul's, and other cathedrals. To the Society for the Encouragement of Art I address myself with respectful duty, requesting their consideration of my plan as a great public means of advancing fine art in Protestant communities. Monuments to the dead painters by historical and poetical artists like Barry and Mortimer (I forbear to name living artists, though equally worthy), I say, monuments to painters must make England what Italy is ; an envied storehouse of intellectual riches.

25   It has been said of late years the English public have no taste for painting. This is a falsehood. The English are as good judges of painting as of poetry, and they prove it by their contempt for great collections of all the rubbish of the Continent brought here by ignorant picture-dealers. An Englishman may well say, " I am no judge of painting " when he is shown these smears and daubs at an immense price, and told that such is the art of painting. I say the English public are true encouragers of real art, while they discourage and look with contempt on false art. I know my execution is not like any one else's. I do not intend it should be so. None but blockheads copy one another. My conception and invention are allowed on all hands to be superior. My execution will be found so too. To what is it that gentlemen of the first rank both in genius and fortune have subscribed their names ? To my inventions. The executive part they never disputed.

26   In a commercial nation impostors are abroad in all professions. These are the greatest enemies of Genius. *Mr. B. considers it his duty to caution the public against a certain impostor who * * In one art, the art of painting, these impostors sedulously propagate an opinion that great inventors cannot execute. This opinion is as destructive of the true artist as it is false by all experience. Even Hogarth cannot be either copied or improved. Can (?) Anglus ever discern perfection but in the journeyman's labour ?

Sideways.   P.S.—I do not believe that this absurd opinion was set on foot till, in my outset into life, it was artfully published both in whispers and in print by certain persons whose robbery from me made it necessary to them that I should be hid in a corner. It never was supposed that a copy could be better than an original, or near so good, till a few years ago it became the interest of certain envious knaves. The lavish praise I have received from all quarters for invention and drawing has generally been accompanied by this : " He can conceive but he cannot execute." This absurd assertion has done me, and may still do me the greatest mischief. I call for public protection against the villains. I am, like others, just equal in invention, and execution of my work. I, in my own defence, challenge comparison with the finest engravings, and defy the most critical judge to make the comparison honestly, asserting in my own defence that this print is the finest that has been done, or is likely to be done when drawing, the foundation, is condemned, and absurd nonsense about dots and lozenges made to occupy the attention to the neglect of all true art. I defy any man to cut cleaner strokes than I do, or rougher, when I please, and apart that he who thinks he can engrave or paint without being a master of drawing is a fool. Painting is drawing on canvas and engraving is drawing on copper, and nothing else, and he who draws best must be the best artist, and to this I subscribe my name as a public duty.   WILLIAM BLAKE.

So we come in connected sentences to the end of the manifesto. Valuable as it is, its great purpose, that of vindicating the characteristics of the imaginative style in art as against the false idea that smoothness is necessarily "finish," has long ago been fully served. Every student now knows only too well that smoothness is often merely obliteration, and often leaves his own work timidly rough lest it should appear foolishly smooth.

But in reading the statement that one man cannot take up another man's beginnings and improve them we are led astray, if we forget that this can only be true when the continuer is incapable of receiving the true impulse from the work which he handles. Should he catch the intention and work forward in the same spirit, then, supposing his capacities not inferior to those of the " original inventor " he will do just as well as the inventor himself would were he to resume labour on a design that he had put aside in past years, and forgotten so completely, that he had to re-invent whatever of its development was not indicated in the plan. But when the continuer is superior to the beginner, then,— as was the case when Shakespeare re-wrote old plays for the stage,—he will simply put to the best artistic purpose an opportunity which his predecessors left half used.

But the " advertisement " of the *Canterbury Pilgrims* did

not stop here. The Anecdotes of Artists referred to in the announcement of its publication "this day" are yet to come.

These were probably added after he had finished and signed it. One isolated "dictum" is to be found on p. 45, twenty pages later than the close of the signed "advertisement."

41   There is the same science in Lebrun or Rubens, or even Vanloo, that there is in Raphael or Michael Angelo, but not the same genius. Science is soon got, the other never.

45   "Let a man who has made a drawing go on, and he will produce a picture, or painting, but if he chooses to have it before he has spoiled it, he will do a better thing."

Then on p. 47, after many epigrams and the above two isolated sentences, we get at last to what Blake seems to have imagined could be called "Anecdotes of Artists."

----

47   They say there is no straight line in nature. This is a lie, like all they say, for there is every line in nature. But I will tell them what there is not in nature. An even tint is not in nature. It produces heaviness. Nature's shadows are ever varying, and a ruled sky that is quite even can never produce a natural sky. The same with every object in a picture. Its spots are its beauties. Now, gentlemen critics, how do you like this? You may rage, but what I say I will prove by such practice, and have already done so, that you will rage to your own distraction. Woollett I knew very intimately by his intimacy with Basire, and I knew him to be one of the most ignorant fellows that I ever knew. A machine is not a man, nor a work; it is destructive of humanity and of art. The word Machination. . . . [1]

Delicate hands and heads will never appear,
While Titian, etc. . . . as in the *Book of Moonlight.*

Woollett, I know, did not know how to grind his graver: I know this. He has often proved his ignorance before me at Basire's by laughing at Basire's knife-tools, and ridiculing the
48   form of Basire's graver till Basire was quite dashed and out of conceit with what he himself knew. But his ignorance had a contrary effect upon me. Englishmen have been so used to journeymen's undecided bungling that they cannot bear the firmness of a master's touch. [2] Every line is the line of beauty. It is only fumble and bungle which cannot draw a line. This only is ugliness. But that is not a line which doubts and hesitates in the midst of its course.
49 and   *Everlasting Gospel, and the epigram on Fuseli,* "*The only man*
50   *I ever knew,*" etc.

[1] In the MS. the sentence about machination and the quotation from the *Book of Moonlight* (a lost work of Blake's) are broken as here printed.
[2] Sideways.

52   *Everlasting Gospel above.   On lower half:*—In this plate
Mr. B. has resumed the style with which he set out in life, of
which Heath and Stothard were the awkward Imitators at that
time.   It is the style of Albert Dürer and the old engravers,
which cannot be imitated by any one who does not understand
drawing, and which, according to Heath, Stothard, Flaxman,
and even Romney, spoils an engraver ; for each of these men
53,   has repeatedly asserted this absurdity to me in condemnation of
upper   my work, and approbation of Heath's lame imitation, Stothard
part   being such a fool as to suppose that his blundering blurs can be
made out and delineated by any engraver who knows how to
cut dots and lozenges, equally well with those little prints
54,   which I engraved after him twenty years ago, by which he
upper   got his reputation as a draughtsman.   Flaxman cannot deny
part   that one of his very first monuments he did I gratuitously
designed for him.   How much of his Homer and Dante he will
allow to be mine I do not know, as he went far enough off to
publish them, even to Italy, but the public will know ; and at
the same time he was blasting my character to Machlin my
employer, as Machlin told me at the time.
53,   [1] The manner in which my character has been blasted these
lower   thirty years both as an Artist and as a Man may be seen particu-
part   larly in a Sunday paper called the *Examiner,* published in Beau-
fort's Buildings,[2] and the manner in which I have rooted out the
nest of villains will be seen in a poem concerning my three years'
Herculean labours at Felpham, which I shall soon publish.
Secret calumny and open professions of friendship are common
enough all the world over, but have never been so good an
occasion of poetic imagery.   When a base man means to be your
enemy, he always begins first with being your friend.[3]   We all
know that editors of newspapers trouble their heads very little
about art and science, and that they are always paid for what
they put in on those ungracious subjects.
54,   Many people are so foolish as to think they can wound
lower   M. Fuseli over my shoulder.[4]   They will find themselves
part   mistaken : they could not wound even Mr. Barry so.
A certain portrait painter said to me in a boasting way :
"Since I have practised painting I have lost all idea of
drawing."   Such a man must know that I looked upon him with
contempt.   He did not care for this any more than West did,
who hesitated and equivocated with me on the same subject, at
55,   which time he asserted that Woollett's prints are superior to
Ever-   Basire's, because they had more labour and care.   Now this is
lasting contrary to truth.   Woollett did not know how to put so much
Gospel labour into a head or a foot as Basire did.   He did not know
to end. how to draw the leaf of a tree.   All his study was clean
strokes and mossy tints.   How then should he be able to make

---

[1] The two upper parts of these pages were written consecutively.   The middle
was occupied by drawings, and by a late portion of the *Everlasting Gospel*
written *after* the prose.   The lower portions were also written consecutively, and
now follow.

[2] Begun in 1808.   Criticised Blake August 1808, and September 1809.

[3] Hayley ; thus connected by the "living" with Hunt.

[4] In the *Examiner* Fuseli's name is coupled with Blake's.

use of either labour or care, unless the labour or care of imbecility ? The life's labour of mental weakness scarcely equals one hour of the labour of ordinary capacity, like the full gallop of the gouty man to the ordinary walk of youth and health. I allow that there is such a thing as high-finished ignorance, as there may be a fool or a knave in an embroidered coat. But I say that the embroidery of the ignorant finisher is not like a coat made by another, but is an emanation from ignorance itself, and its finding is like its master—the life's labour of five hundred idiots, for he never does the work himself.

What is called the English style of engraving, such as it proceeded from the toilets of Woollett and Strange, for their were fribble's toilets, can never produce character and expression. I knew the men intimately from their intimacy with Basire, my master, and knew them both to be heavy lumps of cunning and ignorance, as their works show to all the continent, who laugh at the contemptible pretences of Englishmen to improve art before they even know the first beginnings of art. I hope
57 this print will redeem my country from this coxcomb situation, and show that it is only *some* Englishmen, and not all, who are thus ridiculous in their pretences. Advertisements in the newspapers are no proof of popular approbation, but rather the contrary. A man who pretends to improve fine art does not know what fine art is. Ye English engravers must come down from your high flights. Ye must condescend to study Marc Antonio and Albert Dürer. Ye must begin before you attempt to finish or improve ; and when you have begun you will know better than to think of improving what cannot be improved.
58 It is very true what you have said for these thirty years : I am mad, or else you are so. Both of us cannot be in our right senses. Posterity will judge by our works. Woollett's and Strange's works are like those of Titian and Correggio, the life's labour of ignorant journeymen, suited to the purposes of commerce, for commerce cannot endure individual merit ; its insatiable maw must be fed by what all can do equally well ; at least it is so in England, as I have found to my cost these forty years. Commerce is so far from being beneficial to arts or empires that it is destructive of both, as all their history shows, for the above reason of individual merit being its great hatred. Empires flourish until they become commercial, and then they are scattered abroad to the four winds.

I do not pretend to paint better than Raphael or Michael Angelo, or Julio Romano, or Albert Dürer, but I do pretend to paint finer than Rubens, or Rembrandt, or Titian, or Correggio. I do not pretend to engrave finer than Albert Dürer, but I do pretend to engrave finer than Strange, Woollett, Wall, or Bartolozzi, and all because I understood drawing which they understood not.

[1] Such prints as Woollett and Strange produce will do for those who choose to purchase the life's labour of ignorance and imbecility in preference to the inspired moments of genius and inspiration.
58 [2] Woollett's best works were etched by Jack Brown. Woollett again etched very ill himself. Strange's prints were, when I knew

[1] Sideways—later.
[2] Between lines, written to connect the sideways sentence of 57 with that of 58.

him, all done by Aliamet and his French journeymen, whose names I forget. [1] The *Cottagers* and *Jocund Peasants*, the *Views in Kew Gardens*, the *Diana and Actæon*, and, in short, all that are called Woollett's were etched by Jack Brown, and in Woollett's works the etching is all, even though a single leaf of a tree is never correct.

59　In this manner the English public has been imposed upon, under the impression that engraving and painting are somewhat else besides drawing. Painting is drawing on canvas, and engraving is drawing on copper, and nothing else, and he who pretends to be either painter or engraver without drawing is an impostor. We may be clever as pugilists, but as artists we are, and have long been, the contempt of the continent. Gravelot once said to my master Basire : "De English may be very clever in deir own opinions, but dey do not draw de draw."

60　[2] Men think they can copy nature as correctly as I copy imagination. This they will find impossible ; and all the copies or pretended copies of nature, from Rembrandt to Reynolds, prove that nature becomes, to its victim, nothing but blots and blurs. Why are copies of nature incorrect while copies of imagination are correct ? This is manifest to all.

59 again　[3] Resentment for personal injuries has had some share in this public address, but love to my art, and zeal for my country a much greater.

[1] Sideways.

[2] At the top of p. 60, apparently continuing what is at the top of p. 59.

[3] This occupies the lower part of page 59. It was apparently intended as the last sentence of the pamphlet, and was almost certainly the last written. The corresponding portion of p. 60, that lies opposite as the book opens, is occupied with a quotation from Bell's *Weekly Messenger*, dated Aug. 1811. The manifesto *begins* on the next p. 61, over leaf.

CHAPTER XXVI

THE 'LAST JUDGMENT'

ONE of the finest pictures in the Blair's *Grave* is, as will be remembered, a *Last Judgment*. Blake drew this subject more than once. The design in the *Grave* series is more condensed than that which was the subject of the description printed (in a rather mixed way) in the second volume of Gilchrist, and of the letter to Ozias Humphry in the first. The form of the composition there referred to was built, as one would say of a house, in many more stories than are found in the *Grave* design. Had the scheme for the larger work been exactly reproduced in the *Grave*, on account of the comparative smallness of the folio page the figures would have been only a couple of inches or less in height. The group of trumpeters in the *Grave* design is a substitute, as will be seen, for a very different centre-piece in the lower part of this picture.

Gilchrist thinks that this picture was among the commissions claimed by Cromek as being won for Blake through the *Grave* publication, but it appears from his narrative that it was really ordered by the Countess of Egremont (to whom Hayley had introduced Blake) on the recommendation of Ozias Humphry, as Blake himself tells us.

The probability is that this design, which "occupied Blake during the year 1807," was in progress when Cromek visited Blake, and first commissioned the *Grave* series, and that it was the cause of that commission. Gilchrist thinks that it was "a repetition or enlargement of the most elaborate of the *Blair* drawings." But everything in the appearance of the sketch (which corresponds to this description) that was shown at the Carfax Gallery suggests that it was an original *form* of the idea from which the *Blair* drawing was developed. The letter runs as follows :

The design of the *Last Judgment*, which I have completed by your recommendation for the Countess of Egremont, it is necessary to give some account of, and its various parts ought to be described for the accommodation of those who give it the honour of their attention.

Christ seated on the throne of Judgment : before His feet, and around Him, the heavens in clouds are rolling like a scroll ready to be consumed in the fires of Angels who descend with the four trumpets, sounding to the four winds. (In Blair they do not descend, but stand and blow upwards.)

Beneath, the earth is convulsed with the labours of the resurrection. In the caverns of the earth is the Dragon with seven heads and ten horns, chained by two Angels with chains, while her palaces are falling into ruins and her councillors are descending into the abyss in wailing and despair. (The whole of this *cavern*, which has so little earth around its entrance as to appear more like a catafalque a foot or two in thickness, is omitted in Blair, and its place occupied by the four standing angels with trumpets.) The right hand of the design is appropriated to the resurrection of the just. The left hand of the design is appropriated to the resurrection and fall of the wicked. (This description needs reversing. What Blake means, of course, is not the right and left hand of the design, but of the figure of Christ in the design.)

Immediately before the throne of Christ are Adam and Eve, kneeling in humiliation as representatives of the whole human race (omitted in the Blair design). Abraham and Moses kneel on each side beneath them (also omitted). From the cloud on which Eve kneels is seen Satan, wound round by the serpent, falling headlong (removed to right of design, where he leads the fallers). The Pharisees appear on the left hand, pleading their own righteousness before the throne of Christ, and before the book of death, which is opened by two angels. (The angels are elderly men with beards and no wings, as are the Pharisees.) Many groups of figures are falling from before the throne, and from the sea of fire which flows before the steps of the throne, on which are seen the seven lamps of the Almighty, burning before the throne (the lamps omitted). Many figures, chained and bound together in various attitudes of despair and horror, fall through the air, and some are scourged by Spirits with flames of fire (the scourgers omitted) into the abyss of Hell, which opens beneath on the left side of the Harlot's seat (seat omitted), where others are howling and descending into the flames, and in the act of dragging each other into Hell, and of contending and fighting with each other on the brink of perdition. (This group is transferred to the lowest part of the centre, where the awakening skeleton was.)

Before the Throne of Christ, on the right hand, the just, in humiliation and exultation, rise through the air with their children and families, some of whom are bowing before the Book of Life, which is opened on clouds by two angels (young figures in robes without wings). Many groups arise in exultation. Among them is a figure crowned with stars and the moon beneath her feet, with six infants around her—she represents the Christian church (omitted). Green hills appear beneath the graves of the blessed, which are seen bursting with their births of immortality ; parents and children, wives and husbands embrace and arise together, and in exulting attitudes tell each other that the New Jerusalem is ready to descend upon earth ; they arise upon the air rejoicing ; others, newly awaked from the grave, stand upon the earth embracing, and shouting to the Lamb who cometh in the clouds with power and great glory. (There is no Lamb, and no one *coming* in either of the designs. The figure of Christ, in robes, with a book on His knee, sits still on a still throne, on a still platform.)

The whole upper part of the design is a view of heaven opened around the throne of Christ. In the clouds which roll away are four living creatures filled with eyes, attended by seven angels with seven vials of the wrath of God, and above these seven angels with the seven trumpets—these compose the cloud (all omitted and replaced by a golden arch of atmospheric cloud at the top of the picture), which by its rolling away displays the opening seats of the blessed, on the right and on the left of which are seen (dimly and far behind the Throne, no sitting figures except some of) the four and twenty Elders seated on Thrones to judge the Dead. (Is that orthodox ?)

Behind the seat and throne of Christ appear the Tabernacle, with its veil opened—the Candlestick on the right, the Table with the shew-bread on the left, and in this the cross, in place of the ark, and the cherubim bowing over it (replaced by young angels with harps and wings).

On the right hand of the throne of Christ is Baptism, on the left is the Lord's Supper—the two introducers into Eternal Life. Women with infants approach the figure of an apostle, who represents Baptism, and on the left hand the Lord's Supper is administered by angels from the hands of another aged apostle. These kneel on each side of the throne (replaced by two young winged angels with notebooks who kneel right and left on lists of the saved and damned), which is surrounded by a glory ; in the glory many infants appear, representing Eternal Creation flowing from the Divine Humanity in Jesus, who opens the Scroll of Judgment upon His knees before the Living and the Dead.

Such is the Design, which you, my dear sir, have been the cause of my producing, and which, but for you, might have slept till the last judgment.   WILLIAM BLAKE.

February 1808.

The date of this letter is, if Gilchrist is right, a year later than the commencement of the design from which so much was omitted in the Blair. It is the date perhaps of the completion of the first picture outside that series. " The design which I have completed," the letter begins.

Gilchrist adds that in the final years of Blake's life he repeated this as a fresco, " into which he introduced some thousands of figures, bestowing much finish and splendour of tint upon it." He also says that Blake made it too heavy in trying to take the advice of a " Frenchwoman, a fellow-lodger." She perhaps wanted more unity, less of confusing " making out of parts." Again we see Blake willing to be taught, if only he could see any good artistic sense in what the teacher said.

Ozias Humphry, Gilchrist says, was " a miniature painter of rare excellence, whose faces have a peculiar sweetness and refined simplicity in a now old-fashioned style." He was " a patron, as well as a friend, for whom Blake had expressly coloured many of his illustrated books." He painted Indian princes in India, and his sketches and notebooks are now in the British Museum.

This year, in 1808, Blake exhibited ("after nine years' interval ") two works at the Royal Academy, hung in the drawing and miniature room. The subjects were *Christ in the Sepulchre, guarded by Angels,* and *Jacob's Dream.*

CHAPTER XXVII

BLAKE'S SECOND ACCOUNT OF HIS 'LAST JUDGMENT PICTURE, FOR THE YEAR 1810 [1]

THE Last Judgment is not fable or allegory, but Vision. Fable or allegory is a totally distinct and inferior kind of poetry. Vision, or imagination, is a representation of what actually exists really, and unchangeably. Fable or allegory is formed by the daughters of Memory. Imagination is surrounded by the daughters of Inspiration who in the aggregate are called Jerusalem.

Fable is allegory, but that which is called the Fable is Vision itself.

Fable or allegory is seldom without some vision. *Pilgrim's Progress* is full of it. The Greek poets the same. But allegory and vision ought to be known as two things, and so called for the sake of eternal life.

(*After a paragraph cut out in the MS. and leaving broken words only*)—

The (? *Ancients produce fable*) when they assert that Jupiter usurped the throne of his father Saturn and brought on an iron age, and begot on Mnemosyne or Memory the great Muses, which are not Inspiration as the Bible is. Reality was forgot, and the accidents of Time and Space only remembered, and called reality. Such is the mighty difference between allegoric fable and spiritual mystery. Let it be here noted that the Greek Fables originated in Spiritual Mystery and real vision, which are lost and clouded in fable or allegory, while the Hebrew Bible and Greek Gospel are genuine, preserved by the Saviour's Mercy. The Nature of my work is Visionary or Imagination. It is an endeavour to restore what the Ancients called the golden age.

The Greeks represent Chronos, or Time, as a very aged man. This is fable; but the real vision of Time is an eternal youth. I have, however, somewhat accommodated my figure of time to the common opinion, as I myself am also infected with it, and I see Time aged—alas! too much so.

Allegories are things that relate to moral virtues. Moral virtues do

---

[1] Such is the general subject of all the following in the MS. book :—These first paragraphs are arranged from somewhat disordered notes in the MS. book, which appear to have been intended as an introduction to the description of the composition representing the *Last Judgment*. Some occur in the course of the description. They were not sorted out by the author. The places of these in the MS. are indicated in footnotes.

not exist. They are allegories and dissimulations. But Time and Space are real beings. Time is a man. Space is a woman, and her masculine portion is Death.

The Hebrew Bible and the gospel of Jesus are not allegory but eternal vision, or imagination of all that exists.[1]

Plato has made Socrates say that poets and prophets do not know or understand what they write or utter. This is a most pernicious falsehood. If they do not, pray is an inferior kind to be called 'Knowing'? Plato confutes himself.

The *Last Judgment* is one of these stupendous visions. I have represented it as I saw it. To different people it appears differently, as everything else does, for though on earth things seem permanent, they are less permanent than a shadow, as we all know too well.

In eternity one thing never changes into another thing. Each identity is eternal. Consequently Apuleius' *Golden Ass* and Ovid's *Metamorphoses*, and others of the like kind are fable; yet they contain vision in a sublime degree, being derived from real vision in more ancient writings. Lot's wife being changed into a pillar of salt alludes to the mortal body being made a permanent statue, but not changed or transformed into another identity, while it retains its own individuality. A man can never become ass or horse. Some are born with shapes of men who are both. But eternal identity is one thing, and corporeal vegetation is another thing. Changing water into wine by Jesus and into blood by Moses relates to vegetable nature also.

The Nature of visionary fancy or imagination is very little known, and the eternal nature and permanence of its ever existent images is considered less permanent than the things of vegetable and generative nature. Yet the oak dies as well as the lettuce, but its eternal image or individuality never dies but renews by its seed. Just so the imaginative image returns by the seed of contemplative thought. The writings of the Prophets illustrate these conceptions of the visionary fancy, by their various sublime and divine images as seen in the world of vision.

The world of imagination is the world of eternity. It is the divine bosom into which we shall all go after the death of the vegetated body. This world of imagination is infinite and eternal, whereas the world of generation or vegetation is finite and temporal. There exist in that eternal world the eternal realities of everything which we see reflected in this vegetable glass of nature.

All things are comprehended in their eternal forms in the divine body of the Saviour, the true vine of eternity, the Human imagination, who appeared to me as coming to judgment among his Saints and throwing off the temporal that the eternal might be established. Around him are seen the images of existence according to a certain order suited to my imaginative eye—(*later;* energy).

DESCRIPTION OF THE PICTURE.

Jesus, seated between two pillars, Joachim and Boaz, with the word of divine revelation on his knee, and on each side the four and twenty

---

[1] Blake inserts at this point, "Note here that Fable or Allegory is seldom without some vision, etc." But it breaks up what little continuity may be found in the subsequent sentences.

elders sitting in judgment, the heavens opening around him by unfolding the clouds around his throne. The old heavens and the old earth are passing away, and the new heavens and the new earth descending : a sea of fire issues from before the throne. Adam and Eve appear first before the judgment-seat in humiliation ; Abel, surrounded by innocents, and Cain, with the flint in his hand with which he slew his brother, falling, with the head downwards. From the cloud on which Eve stands Satan is seen falling headlong, wound round by the tail of the serpent, whose bulk, nailed to the cross round which he wreathes, is falling into the abyss. Sin is also represented by a female, bound in one of the serpent's folds, surrounded by her friends. Death is chained to the cross, and Time falls, together with Death, dragged down by a demon crowned with laurel. Another demon with a Key has the charge of Sin, and is dragging her down by the hair. Beside them a figure is seen scaled with iron scales from head to feet, precipitating himself into the abyss, with the sword and balances. He is Og, King of Bashan.

On the right, beneath the cloud on which Abel kneels, is Abraham, with Sarah and Isaac, also with Hagar and Ishmael, on the left. Abel kneels on a bloody cloud descriptive of those churches before the flood,—that they were filled with blood and fire and vapour of smoke. Even till Abraham's time the vapour and heat were not extinguished. These states exist now. Man passes on, but states remain for ever. He passes through them like a traveller, who may as well suppose that the places he has passed through exist no more, as a man may suppose that the states he has passed through exist no more. Everything is eternal.

Beneath Ishmael is Mahomet, and beneath the falling figure of Cain is Moses, casting his tables of stone into the deeps. It ought to be understood that the persons, Moses and Abraham, are not here meant, but the states signified by those names : the individuals being representatives or visions of those states as they were revealed to mortal man in the series of divine revelations as they are written in the Bible. These various states I have seen in my imagination : when distant they appear as one man ; but as you approach they appear multitudes of nations. Abraham hovers above his posterity, which appear as multitudes of children ascending from the earth, surrounded by Stars, —as it was said : "As the stars of heaven for multitude." Jacob and his twelve sons hover beneath the feet of Abraham and receive their children from the earth. I have seen, when at a distance, multitudes of men in harmony appear like a single infant, sometimes in the arms of a female. This represented the Church.

But, to proceed with the description of those on the left hand. Beneath the cloud on which Moses kneels are two figures, a male and a female, chained together by the feet. They represent those who perished by the Flood. Beneath them, a multitude of their associates are seen falling headlong. By the side of them is a mighty fiend with a book in his hand, which is shut. He represents the person named in Isaiah xxii. c., and 20 v., Eliakim, son of Hilkiah. He drags Satan down headlong. He is crowned with oak. By the side of the scaled figure, representing Og, King of Bashan, is a figure with a basket, emptying out the variety of riches and worldly honours. He is Araunah the Jebusite, master of the threshing floor. Above him are two figures elevated on a cloud representing the Pharisees, who plead their own righteousness before the throne. They are weighed down by two fiends. Beneath the man with the basket are three fiery fiends, with grey beards, and scourges of fire. They represent cruel laws. They scourge a group of figures down into the deeps. Beneath them are various figures in attitudes of contention, representing various states of misery, which, alas, every one is liable to enter into, and against which we should all watch. The ladies will be pleased to see that I have represented the three Furies by three men, and not by three women. It is not because I think the ancients wrong, but they will be pleased to remember that mine is vision, and not fable. The spectator may suppose them clergymen in the pulpit, scourging sin instead of forgiving it.

The earth beneath these falling figures is rocky and burning, and seems as if convulsed by earthquake. A great city, on fire, is seen in the distance. The (?) armies are fleeing upon the mountains. On the foreground Hell is opened, and many figures are descending into it, down stone steps, and beside a gate, beneath a rock, where sin and death are to be closed eternally by that fiend who carries the key in one hand and drags them down with the other. On the rock, and above the gate, a fiend with wings urges the wicked onward with fiery darts. He is Hazael the Syrian, who drives abroad all those who rebel against their Saviour. Beneath the steps is Babylon, represented by a King, crowned, grasping his sword and sceptre. He is just awakened out of his grave. Around him are other kingdoms arising to judgment, represented in this picture by single persons according to the descriptions in the Prophets. The figure dragging up a woman by the hair represents the Inquisition, as do those contending on the sides of the pit, and in particular, the man strangling a woman represents a cruel church.

Two persons, one in purple, the other in scarlet, are descending down the steps into the pit. These are Caiaphas and Pilate, two states where all those reside who calumniate and murder under pretence of holiness and justice. Caiaphas has a blue flame like a mitre on his head. Pilate has bloody hands that can never be cleansed. The females behind them represent the females belonging to such states, who are under perpetual terrors and vain dreams, plots, and secret deceit. Those figures that descend into the flames before Caiaphas and Pilate are Judas and those of his class. Ahithophel is here, with the cord in his hand.[1]

Between the feet of Adam and Eve appears a fiery gulph descending from the sea of fire before the throne. In this cataract four angels descend headlong with four trumpets to awake the dead. Beneath these is the seat of the harlot named Mystery in the Revelations. She is seized by two beings, each with three heads. They represent vegetative existence. As it is written in the Revelations they strip her naked and burn her with fire. It represents the eternal consumption of vegetable life and death with its lusts. The wreathed torches in their hands represent eternal fire, which is the fire of generation or vegetation : it is an eternal consummation.

[1] Here, in the original, follows the paragraph beginning " In eternity one thing never changes into another, consequently Apuleius' *Golden Ass*," etc., and ending, " changing water into wine by Jesus, and into blood by Moses relates to vegetable nature also." It interrupts the narrative, and was probably not intended to be printed where it is written.—ED.

Those who are blessed with imaginative vision see this eternal female, and tremble at what others fear not, while they despise and laugh at what others fear. Beneath her feet is a flaming cavern, in which are seen her kings and councillors and warriors descending in flames, lamenting and looking on her in astonishment and terror, and Hell is opened beneath her seat ; on the left hand the great Red Dragon with seven heads and horns. He has Satan's book of accusations, lying on the rock, open before him. He is bound in chains by two strong demons. They are Gog and Magog, who have been compelled to subdue their master (Ezekiel xxxviii. c. 8 v.) with their hammer and tongs about to new - create the seven - headed kingdoms. The graves beneath are opened and the dead awake and obey the call of the trumpet. Those on the right hand awake in joy, and those on the left in horror. Beneath the Dragon's cavern a skeleton begins to re-animate, starting into life at the trumpet's sound, while the wicked contend with each other on the brink of perdition. On the right a youthful couple are awaked by their children : an aged patriarch is awaked by his aged wife. * He is Albion our Ancestor, patriarch of the Atlantic Continent whose history preceded that of the Hebrews, and in whose sleep and chaos creations began. The good woman is Britannica, the wife of Albion ; Jerusalem is their daughter.* Little infants creep out of the flowery mould into the green fields of the blessed, who, in various joyful companies, embrace and ascend to meet eternity.

The persons who ascend to meet the Lord, coming in the clouds with power and great glory, are representatives of those states described in the Bible under the names of the Fathers before and after the flood. Noah is seen in the midst of these, canopied by a rainbow ; on his right hand Shem ; on his left Japhet. These three persons represent Poetry, Painting, and Music—the three powers in man of conversing with Paradise which the flood did not sweep away. Above Noah is the Church Universal represented by a woman surrounded by infants. There is such a state in eternity : it is composed of the innocent civilised heathen, and the uncivilised savage who, having not the law, do by nature the things contained in the law. This state appears like a female crowned with stars driven into the wilderness. She has the moon under her feet. The aged figure with wings, having a writing tablet, and taking account of the numbers who arise, is that Angel of the Divine Presence mentioned in Exodus xiv. c. 10 v., and in other places. The angel is frequently called by the name of Jehovah Elohim. † The I am, of the oaks of Albion.†

Around Noah and beneath him are various figures risen into the air. Among these are three females, representing those who are not of the dead but who are found alive at the Last Judgment. They appear to be innocently gay and thoughtless, not being among the condemned, because ignorant of crime in a corrupted age. The Virgin Mary was of this class. A mother meets her numerous family in the arms of their father. These are representations of the Greek learned and wise,

---

* The words between the asterisks were added later by Blake. At the time this description was written, 1810, there was no intention to mention Albion. This seems to suggest that *Jerusalem* was still in progress ; probably but little of it belongs to 1804. This also dates the substitution of the word " Albion " for " Man " or " Fallen Man " in the MS. of *Vala.*

† Once more, a later insertion of Blake's.

Y

and also of those other nations such as Egypt and Babylon in which were multitudes who shall meet the Lord coming in the clouds.

The children of Abraham, or Hebrew Church, are represented as a stream of figures on which are seen stars somewhat like the Milky Way. They ascend from the earth, while figures kneel, embracing above the graves, and represent religion, or civilised life, such as it is in the Christian Church which is the offspring of the Hebrew. Just above the graves and above the spot where the infants creep out of the ground stand two—a man and a woman. These are the primitive Christians. The two figures in purifying flames by the side of the Dragon's cavern represent the latter state of the Church when on the verge of perdition, yet protected by a flaming sword. Multitudes are seen ascending from the green fields of the blessed in which a Gothic Church is representative of true art (called "Gothic" in all ages by those who follow the fashion, as that is called which is without form or fashion). By the right hand of Noah, a woman with children represents the state called Saban the Syrian. It is the remains of civilisation in the state from which Adam was taken. Also on the right hand of Noah a female descends to meet her lover or husband, representative of that love called friendship which looks for no other heaven than the beloved, and in him sees all reflected as in a glass of eternal diamond.

On the right hand of these rise the diffident and humble, and on their left a solitary woman with her infant. These are caught up by three aged men who appear as suddenly emerging from the blue sky for their help. These three aged men represent divine providence as opposed to and distinct from divine vengeance—represented by three aged men, on the side of the picture among the wicked, with scourges of fire.[1]

Above the head of Noah is Seth. This state called Seth is in a higher state of happiness than Noah, being nearer the state of innocence. Beneath the feet of Seth two figures represent the two seasons of Spring and Autumn, while beneath the feet of Noah four seasons represent the changed state made by the flood.[2]

By the side of Seth is Elijah. He comprehends all the prophetic characters. He is seen in his fiery chariot bowing before the throne of the Saviour. In like manner the figures of Seth and his wife comprehend the Fathers before the flood and their generations. When seen remote they appear as one man. A little below Seth, on his right, are two figures, a male and a female, with numerous children. These represent those who were not in the line of the Church and yet were saved from among the antediluvians who perished. Between Seth and these a female figure represents the solitary state of those who, previous to the flood, walked with God.

All these rise toward the opening cloud before the throne, led onward by triumphant groups of infants. Between Seth and Elijah three female figures crowned with garlands represent learning and science which accompanied Adam out of Eden.

---

[1] Here follows in the MS. the paragraph beginning "If the spectator could enter into these images——," and ending, "an insignificant blur or mark." It has no place in the description, which is resumed after it as though it had not been written.

[2] The words "the changed state produced by the flood" replace in the original the words "our present state of existence," erased.

The cloud that opens, rolling apart from before the throne, and before the new heaven and the new earth, is composed of various groups of figures, particularly the four living creatures mentioned in Revelations as surrounding the throne. These I suppose to have the chief agency in removing the old heaven and old earth to make way for the new heaven and the new earth, to descend from the throne of God and of the Lamb. That living creature to the left of the throne gives to the seven angels the seven phials of the wrath of God, with which they, hovering over the deeps beneath, pour out upon the wicked their plagues. The other living creatures are descending with a shout, and with the sound of the trumpet, and directing the combats in the upper elements. In the two corners of the picture, on the left hand, Apollyon is foiled before the sword of Michael, and on the right, the two witnesses are subduing their enemies.

On the cloud are opened the books of remembrance of life and of death. Before that of life, on the right, some figures bow in lamentation. Before that of death, on the left, the Pharisees are pleading their own righteousness. The one shines with beams of light, the other utters lightnings and tempests.[1]

Around the throne heaven is opened, and the nature of eternal things displayed, all springing from the Divine Humanity. All beams from him. He is the bread and the wine. He is the water of Life. Accordingly on each side of the opening heaven appears an Apostle, that on the right represents Baptism. That on the left represents the Lord's Supper.[2]

Over the head of the Saviour and Redeemer, the Holy Spirit, like a dove, is surrounded by a blue heaven in which are the two cherubim that bowed over the ark, for here the temple is open to heaven and the ark of the covenants is a dove of peace. The curtains are drawn apart, Christ having rent the veil. The candlestick and the table of show-bread appear on each side. A glorification of angels with harps surrounds the dove.

The Temple stands on the mount of God. From it flows on each side a river of life, on whose banks grows the Tree of Life, among whose branches, temples, and pinnacles, tents and pavilions, gardens and groves, display Paradise with its inhabitants walking up and down in conversations concerning mental delights. * Here they are no longer talking of what is good and evil, of what is right or wrong, and puzzling themselves in Satan's Labyrinth, but are conversing with eternal realities as they exist in the human imagination.*

Jesus is surrounded by beams of glory in which are seen all around him infants emanating from them. These represent the eternal births of intellect from the Divine Humanity. A rainbow surrounds the throne and the glory, in which youthful nuptials receive the infants in

[1] Here follows the paragraph beginning with the words, "A Last Judgment is necessary because fools flourish," which were added later by Blake to the MS., and ending, "the purpose of hindering them from oppressing the good."

[2] After the paragraph ending "the Lord's Supper" comes the paragraph beginning, "All life consists of these two, throwing off error, and receiving truth," —and ending, "A Last Judgment passes upon that individual."

* The words between asterisks were added here later by Blake, and were followed by the paragraph beginning, "We are in a world of generation and death," and ending, "Venetian painters who will be cast off and lost from art."

their hands. The Eternity woman is the emanation of man. She has no will of her own. There is no such thing in eternity as a female will.

On the side next Baptism are seen those called in the Bible, Nursing Fathers and Nursing Mothers. They represent Education. On the side next the Lord's Supper, the Holy Family, consisting of Mary, Joseph, John the Baptist, Zacharias, and Elizabeth receiving the bread and wine among other spirits of the Just made perfect. Beneath these a cloud of women and children are taken up, fleeing from the rolling cloud which separates the wicked from the seats of bliss. They represent those who, though willing, were too weak to reject error without the assistance and countenance of those already in the truth, for a man can only reject error by the advice of a friend or by the immediate inspiration of God. It is for this reason, among others, that I have put the left hand of the throne, for it appears so at the Last Judgment, for a protection.

END OF THE DESCRIPTION OF THE PICTURE

The following paragraphs appear to have been intended as a sequel to the description. Those whose places are not indicated in footnotes above, come all together at the end. They chiefly unite the idea of Imagination as the Saviour with art, considered as a service and vision as a manifestation of Him.

BLAKE'S SEQUEL TO HIS DESCRIPTION OF THE PICTURE OF THE 'LAST JUDGMENT.'

If the spectator could enter into these images in his imagination, approaching them on the fiery chariot of his contemplative thought— if he could enter into Noah's rainbow, could make a friend and companion of one of these images of wonder, which always entreat him to leave mortal things (as he must know), then would he arise from the grave, then would he meet the Lord in the air, and then he would be happy. General knowledge is remote knowledge. It is in particulars that wisdom consists and happiness too. Both in art and in life, general masses are as much art as a pasteboard man is human. Every man has eyes, nose, and mouth. This every idiot knows. But he who enters into and discriminates most minutely the manners and intentions, the characters in all their branches, is the alone wise or sensible man, and on this discrimination all art is founded. I entreat, then, that the spectator will attend to the hands and feet, to the lineaments of the countenance. They are all descriptive of character, and not a line is drawn without intention, and that most discriminate and particular. As poetry admits not a letter that is insignificant, so painting admits not a grain of sand, or a blade of grass insignificant— much less an insignificant blur or mark.

A Last Judgment is necessary because fools flourish. Nations flourish under wise rulers and are depressed under foolish rulers. It is the same with individuals as with nations. Works of art can only be produced in perfection where the man is either in affluence or above the care of it. Poverty is the fool's rod which at last is turned on his own back. That is a Last Judgment when men of real art govern and pretenders fall. Some people, and not a few artists, have asserted that

the painter of this picture would not have done so well if he had been
properly encouraged. Let those who think so reflect on the state of
nations under poverty and their incapability of art. Though art is
above either, the argument is better for affluence than poverty, and
though he would not have been a greater artist he would have produced
greater works of art in proportion to his means. A Last Judgment is
not for the purpose of making bad men better, but of hindering them
from oppressing the good.[1]

All Life consists of these two,[2] throwing off error, and knaves from
our company continually, and receiving truth, or wise men into our
company continually. He who is out of the church and opposes it
is no less an agent of religion than he who is in it. No man can
embrace true art until he has explored and cast out false art, such is
the nature of mortal things, or he will be himself cast out by those
who have already embraced true art. Thus my picture is a history of
art and science, the foundation of Society, which is humanity itself.
What are the gifts of the Spirit but mental gifts? When any individual rejects error and embraces truth, a Last Judgment passes upon
that individual.

[3] We are in a world of generation and death, and this world we
must cast off if we would be painters (sic) such as Raphael, Michael
Angelo, and the ancient sculptors. If we do not cast off this world we
shall be only Venetian painters who will be cast off and lost from art.

The painter hopes that his friends Amytus, Melitus, and Sycon[4]
will perceive that they are not now in ancient Greece ; and though
they can use the poison of calumny the English public will be convinced that such a picture as this could never be painted by a madman,
or one in a state of outrageous manners, as these bad men both print
and publish by all the means in their power. The painter begs public
protection and all will be well.

(Here followed a paragraph through which Blake seems to have drawn
his pen. It is found in the chapter on the MS. Book, Vol. I., p. 332.)

Men are admitted into heaven not because they have curbed and
governed their passions, or have no passions, but because they have
cultivated their understandings. The treasures of heaven are not
negations of passion, but realities of intellect, from which the passions
emanate, uncurbed in their eternal glory. The fool shall not enter
into heaven, let him be ever so holy. Holiness is not the price of
entrance into heaven. Those who are cast out are all those who,
having no passions of their own, because no intellect, have spent their
lives in curbing and governing other people's by the various arts of
poverty and cruelty of all kinds. The modern church crucifies Christ
with the head downwards. Woe, woe, woe to you hypocrites ! Even
murder, with the courts of justice, more merciful than the church, is
not done in passion but in cold-blooded design and intention.[5]

[1] This paragraph was written later—probably 1812—but meant for insertion
here.

[2] "These two" actions correspond with the Sacraments of Baptism and the
Lord's Supper respectively.

[3] A sentence added later.   ? 1812.

[4] ? Flaxman, Hayley, and Cromek, "in disguise," the late date makes it
probable.   It also dates and explains p. 93 of Jerusalem.

[5] This use of the word "murder" in spiritual sense should have been noted
in the course of vol. i., chapter vii.

Many suppose that before the Creation all was solitude and chaos. This is the most pernicious idea that can enter the mind, as it takes away all sublimity from the Bible and limits all existence to creation and chaos—to the time and space fixed by the corporeal and vegetated eye, and leaves the man who entertains such an idea the habitation of unbelieving demons. Eternity exists, and all things in eternity, independent of creation, which was an act of mercy. I have represented these who are in eternity by some in a cloud, within the rainbow that surrounds the throne. They merely appear as in a cloud when anything of creation, redemption, or judgment is the subject of contemplation, though their whole contemplation is concerning these things. The reason they so appear is the humiliation of the reasoning and doubting selfhood and the giving up all to inspiration. By this it will be seen that I do not consider either the just or the wicked to be in a supreme state, but to be every one of them states of the sleep which the soul may fall into in its deadly dreams of good and evil when it leaves Paradise following the serpent.

Many persons, such as Paine and Voltaire, with some of the ancient Greeks, say : " We will not converse concerning good and evil ; we will live in Paradise and Liberty." You may do so in spirit, but not in the mortal body as you pretend, until after a Last Judgment. For in Paradise they have no corporeal and mortal body. *That* originated with the fall and was called Death, and cannot be removed but by a Last Judgment. While we are in the world of mortality we must suffer. The whole Creation groans to be delivered.

There will always be as many hypocrites born as honest men, and they will always have superior power in mortal things. You cannot have liberty in this world without what you call [1] moral virtue, and you cannot have moral virtue without the subjection of that half of the human race who hate what you call moral virtue.

The nature of hatred, and envy, and of all the mischiefs in the world, is here depicted. No one envies or hates one of his own party. Even the devils love one another in their own way. They torment one another for other reasons than hate or envy : These are only employed against the just. Neither can Seth envy Noah, or Elijah envy Abraham. But they may both of them envy the success of Satan, or Og, or Moloch. The horse never envies the peacock, nor the sheep the goat ; but they envy a rival in life and existence, whose ways and means exceed their own. Let him be of what class of animals he will, a dog will envy a cat who is pampered at the expense of his comfort, as I have often seen. The Bible never tells us that the devils torment one another through envy. It is through this that they torment the just. But for what do they torment one another ? I answer : For the coercive laws of hell—moral hypocrisy. They torment a hypocrite when he is discovered ; they punish a failure in the tormentor who has suffered the subject of his torture to escape. In Hell all is self-righteousness. There is no such thing there as forgiveness of sins. He who does forgive sin is crucified as an abettor of criminals, and he who performs works of mercy in any shape whatever is punished, and if possible destroyed—not through envy, or hatred, or malice, but through self-righteousness that thinks it does God service, which God is Satan. They do not envy one another.

[1] The words " what you call " are later in date.

They contemn or despise one another. Forgiveness of sin is only at the judgment-seat of Jesus the Saviour, where the accuser is cast out not because he sins, but because he torments the just, and makes them do what he condemns as sin, and what he knows is opposite to their own identity.

It is not because angels are holier than men or devils that makes them angels, but because they do not expect holiness from one another, but from God only.[1]

The player is a liar when he says, " Angels are happier than men because they are better." Angels are happier than men or devils because they are not always prying after good and evil in one another, and eating the tree of knowledge for Satan's gratification.

The Last Judgment is an overwhelming of bad art and science. Mental things are alone real. What is called corporeal, nobody knows of. Its dwelling-place is a fallacy, and its existence an imposture. Where is the existence out of mind, or thought? Where is it but in the mind of a fool? Some people flatter themselves that there will be no Last Judgment, and that bad art will be adopted and mixed with good art—that error, or experiment, will make a part of truth, and they boast that it is its foundation. These people flatter themselves. I will not flatter them. Error is created. Truth is eternal. Error or creation will be burned up, and then, and not till then, truth or eternity will appear. It is burned up the moment men cease to behold it. I assert for myself that I do not behold the outward creation, and that to me it is hindrance, and not action. It is as the dirt upon my feet—no part of me.

" What," it will be questioned, " when the sun rises do you not see a round disk of fire something like a guinea? Oh! no! no! I see an innumerable company of the heavenly host crying—'Holy, holy, holy, is the Lord God Almighty!'" I question not my corporeal eye any more than I would question a window concerning a sight. I look through it and not with it.

The Last Judgment (will be) when all those are cast away who trouble religion with questioning concerning good and evil, or eating of the tree of those knowledges or reasonings which hinder the vision of God, turning all into a consuming fire. When imagination, art, and science, and all intellectual gifts—all the gifts of the Holy Ghost—are looked upon as of no use, and only contention remains to man, then the Last Judgment begins, and its vision is seen by every eye according to the situation which he holds.

All through this it is clear that Blake considered the Jesus whose " body " was the " Human Imagination," composed of the immortal parts of all the living and the dead, to be a " Grand Man " (to use the Swedenborgian phrase), and a deity to whom prayer might be addressed, and whose existence was judgment and mercy in itself as well as brotherhood and power.

[1] The difference between Blake's conception of an angel in 1789 and 1810 is worth noting. The progress in nobility of mind, it shows, is peculiarly unlike "a madman, or one in a state of outrageous manners."

CHAPTER XXVIII

A LITTLE BIT OF INTERPRETATION

BUT we have gone on too long with fatal facility, offering no hint of interpretation to Blake's myth, though it is in this that the Real Blake is most to be found. Something has been done in notes elsewhere—a small postscript on a few points may be added now. Blake devoted himself to his books of *Jerusalem* and *Milton* all through his exhibition period.

These are not at all what they would have been but for that harassing period of perpetual visits, interviews, and letters that kept Blake constantly distracted in the service of Hayley and his *Life of Romney*, during the years 1804 and 1805, when *Milton* was reduced to two books and *Jerusalem* was begun. Here again we must look at what has already been noticed when comparing the styles of *Thel* and *Tiriel*. The parts of *Milton* that evidently belong to Felpham contain a freer and smoother diction than that which is habitual in *Jerusalem*. There is a marked change of style. It is the difference in tone between a narrative and a manifesto. The difference between *Vala* and *Jerusalem* is still more distressingly noticeable. The tendency to melody of language which is a physical thing in a poet, and has a close connection with the nerves that direct his articulation, is always injured if he is obliged to talk much prose. The Arabs say that if their best racer goes once in the plough his gallop is never the same afterwards. Prolonged business conversations cause a poet to lose a fairyland note from his verse, and to descend to a sort of inspired and emphatic talking. Sometimes he brings with him what was best from his earlier manner and only drops a retarding and belittling sweetness. No one would say that Shakespeare's verse in *Antony and Cleopatra* was worse than in *Romeo and Juliet*, yet a shadow of the same kind of change as that between

Thel and *Tiriel* and between *Vala* and *Jerusalem* may be noticed there. Sometimes the contrast in *Jerusalem* is only between a passage taken verbatim from *Vala* and the rest of the page. But sometimes additional words are thrust into the verse of *Vala* to bring it into keeping with the surroundings in *Jerusalem* by adding terms from that poem that Blake had not begun to use when *Vala* was written. No attempt is made to so alter the sentence that these terms may come in without destroying the musical quality of the verse. The "long-resounding line" resounds no longer, though it powerfully urges and impresses.

Blake seems to have felt in *Jerusalem* that he was making his last great cry to the inattentive world.

He has only one thing to say: *Imagination is Eternity. Art is its means of Brotherhood. Brotherhood is its means of Immortality. These three things together will weld the souls of the dead into the kingdom of God in heaven. Seek them!*

He has still the same enemies as before against which to warn us, the most dangerous being *individual* morality, a private property in sin or righteousness, detrimental to that socialism of mental properties without which we could not learn to be Members of Christ.

We must learn to forgive sins to individuals; but sin is unpardonable unless it be looked on as a property of the state in which the sinful individual is. When we can so look on it, we have acquired "the only means to the forgiveness of sins."

The contrast and seeming antagonism between the sweetness of Blake's religious professions and the fury of his denunciations of those who, he thought, had used him ill, now grow less and less as the years pass. He ended by forgiving them all, but they never forgave him. Flaxman, probably feeling that Blake was the most ungrateful of men, at last dropped him: "I have no more intercourse with Mr. Blake." Hayley could not be expected to endure him as a judge and denunciator *twice*. Stothard, in later life, refused to shake hands with him. Of course, as the phrase runs, "it served him right." His doctrine of the difference between a friend and an enemy may be invoked by those who considered his conduct to them as not that of a friend. "He who loves his enemies, hates his friends; this surely is not what Jesus intends." Does not Jesus, he reflected, whom we are told to imitate, promise in the end to cast off for ever all who will not accept him? In his parables is not the tree, that by a year's gardening is proved useless, to be cut down. Did not he whip his own enemies out of his " Father's House " ? " He that is not with Me is against Me," with the postscript—" and I will be against him," was Blake's Christianity. It is, at least, biblical, but is evidently as well adapted for use by our opponents as by ourselves. " The Word " is " a two-edged sword."

But Blake's main idea of reforming the world turned on the providing of mankind with a *love for ideas* which they *could* share, instead of the love of *property and woman* which he admitted that, at present, they cannot, socialists and upholders of promiscuous intercourse notwithstanding. This great hope and object in Blake's life was due to a peculiar effect of his unusually strong imagination upon his *equally* unusually affectionate heart; and his complete forgetfulness that other people are almost invariably incapable of feeling as he did, because the vital connection between their imaginations and their hearts, always weak, breaks for ever while they are still children. The quality in his own character that led to Blake's belief that symbolic art, vivifying *all things* and *all words* through imaginative connection with the human form, would lead to universal love has already been shown by this sentence in his notes to Swedenborg:

Think of a white cloud as holy; you cannot love it. But of a holy man within the cloud; love springs up in your thought.

Jealousy and covetousness are parts of Nature, and Nature is full of evil will. " There is no good will."

But sympathy with unshared feelings (none shares his *wife*, but each good husband *sympathises* with each other good husband) ends in leading man into imagination and so to art and heaven. That is the doctrine. Or as Blake says, we pass Orc (the Polypus) to get to Golgonooza.

This Polypus symbol is always so far good as *adjoining* is good, whether the Polypus be that of loves, each bad, or of Albion's spectre sons, each bad. But its bad form tends to destroy its good form—*Jerusalem.* The *adjoining* is the first step to *anything* good. It is an opening of the Western Gate, now closed by this attempt to live individual lives, which are necessarily temporary, composite life only being eternal. Of course, composite life means quite another thing to most people from what it means to a clairvoyant and a spiritualist, who really feels and sees that total unreality of Nature with its " apparent surfaces," which scientific men only calculate on.

In reading Blake we must allow for this, and allow for that anti-individual or composite view of Christ, the opposite to the individualist view which the nonconformist conscience has adopted from the non-mystic Roman Catholic Church since it gradually changed into prose from the day when Gnostics were declared heretics; when these allowances are made they will clear all clouds from the symbolism. Then *Jerusalem* will be seen to be not only intelligible, but true. In it we also see Blake as a missionary.

It requires reading and re-reading before we track all the symbols down and sort out those that are explained in various passages from those that almost remain mere names (like some of the counties of England that are but loosely joined to any other symbols, and for lack of authoritative punctuation not quite comprehensibly divided under the headings of the tribes); and it must always be remembered, no reader can expect to take much pleasure in it who has not had *a little* Swedenborgian training, even though Blake does not adopt Swedenborg *exactly*. The day when people can be expected to endure a full account of *Jerusalem*, which would necessarily be ten times as long as the poem, has not dawned yet. The few students who really care will find that it interprets itself with a little help from Blake's letters, manifestoes, and maxims. But it is always necessary to beware of being satisfied too soon with any *one* of the four meanings of every symbol, even after the stories of the Zoas are familiar to us and we can even see one *in* the other, and Milton *in* Blake, *in* Christ, *in* his own Shadow, and even *in* Satan. That word *in*, with its brother *within* and the interpretation of *within* as *above*, is the beginning of a comprehension of Blake. There is hardly any line of his poems that can be read apart from his use of this idea and symbol.

Rarely, but with suggestive hint for interpretation, Blake even employs *in* so that it is difficult for the mind to see a vision of his particular statement that shall be congruous with its preconceived vision of one or more terms of his statement. There is an example of this in *Milton*, page 36, line 13, where we hear that—

> Ololon stepped into the polypus.

Now, as the Polypus is Orc, son of Los and Enitharmon, we have a female stepping *into* a male.

But Ololon, who was a host, appeared *in* a female form.

for reasons described in the immediate context. These reasons are elaborated in connection with the "nameless shadowy female" by Orc himself in the long argument which fills extra-page 17. The exact prose interpretation of "Ololon" is not offered here, because, like other mystical symbols, it would require too frequent a reference to generative truths and details to make it suitable for the uninitiated, who would not take it wisely and purely.

The word *in* has also been used, as we have seen if we have read through *Milton*, on page 19, line 59, etc.—

> So spake the family Divine as One Man, even Jesus,
> Uniting *in* One with Ololon, and the appearance of One Man
> Jesus the Saviour appeared coming in the clouds of Ololon—

this cloud being an appearance that *became* female *within* the Mundane Shell. The word *in* is also used when what is *seen in the vision* of Milton is described—*Milton*, page 37, lines 15 to 60.

In the same way the word *is* becomes a lamp for those who can use its flame and a thick darkness to those who are lost in its smoke.

Satan *is* Enitharmon's first-born (he is also her last-born, being Orc's human remains, explained in *Vala*).

Orc *is* her first-born—*Europe*, page 4, line 11; *Vala*, Night VIII, line 375, etc.

Orc *is* Luvah—*Vala*, Night VII, line 151.

Luvah *is* Satan—*Jerusalem*, page 49, line 63.

Urizen *is* Satan—*Milton*, extra-page 8, line 1.

In *Milton*, Milton *is* both Los, Blake, and a crowd of others. In the *Jerusalem*, page 96, line 22, Albion sees Jesus *in* likeness of Los. In real life Blake would sometimes only just remember in time not to speak the same language. To Crabb Robinson, who asked him whether there was an affinity between his *Spirits* and the *Genius* that used to hold converse with the mind of Socrates, he said : " I was Socrates, or a sort of brother. I must have had conversations with him. So I had with Jesus Christ. I have an obscure recollection of being with both of them." " Jesus," he also said, " is the only God, and so are you, and so am I." This passage about having been with Socrates may have given rise to the idea that Blake adopted the theory of reincarnation. To those who know how free from Time is the part of us called by Swedenborg the " Celestial Mind," and how difficult it is, when we have put this to sleep in order to chat with our friends across its bed, to exactly place a "memory" belonging to it (which ought not to be called memory) with its right relation to the "obscure recollections" of our "corporeal understanding," Blake's remark will be seen not to require the reincarnation theory to make sense of it.

Of a similar kind was his opinion that Wordsworth had not written all his poems, nor Napoleon I fought all his battles. The first merely submitted to "dictate," the latter *was killed* and another spirit possessed his body. We all know cases now in which a man is *personally* killed by a bang on the head, while, on his "recovery," another *person* is found to be using his body. Sometimes later on the first person returns, whether by another bang or by a system of repeated awakenings from short sleeps, but to those who take it that *one man* means *one person* the medical accounts of such cases must make many physicians appear as mad as Blake seemed at his worst.

All this change of personality in the poetic beings or "states" was very annoying to readers of Blake who had no natural capacity for "meeting the Lord in the air" and no previous training in myth beyond such simple exercises as the classic tales have preserved for us, which have the immense advantage of lending themselves to almost unlimited misunderstanding without pulling us up short in our complacent career of misinterpretation. The theory usually adopted is that already mentioned as frankly uttered by Dr. Garnett,—namely, that Blake did not know what he meant himself. But Dr. Garnett's day was over before it dawned, and now Messrs. Russell and Maclagan, working independently with no further guide than the incomplete and reticent interpretations of the Quaritch edition (which was in Dr. Garnett's hands also), made one discovery which they have written down and signed. "Blake is never vague." (See preface to their edition of *Jerusalem*, the first in ordinary type to be printed, and still, for the sake of its cheapness (5s.), its wide margins good to write notes on, and its sketch of an index, one that every reader who buys will be glad of.) A full index should be published. Theirs has the disadvantage of omitting many important words, and, what is worse, omitting important references to those words that it contains. There will be an encyclopædia and complete index to Blake published some day, but the disparaging tone of the scholarly average critic who does not know his *Blake*, but can write in such a tone as to make plain people think that he knows all that is worth knowing, still clings like a wet blanket over the heads of the public, and publishers are very naturally afraid to print such a book, though the present writer has offered it. It ought to come out as the "Proceedings" of a Blake Society.

The explanation of most of Blake's seeming errors *about himself* in the use of his own symbols is that he never quite threw off a habit of using nouns, and even proper names, as *adjectives*, or rather in places where adjectives would have seemed more comprehensible; and though this sounds a very wicked thing to do, it is not so if we who read have but the wit to understand; and those who contest this point, and set up a prejudice derived from the prose value of the nomenclature of grammar (a strong and valid plea in its place) as a reason for condemning Blake, might learn something if they would try and *say what Blake said* according to their own rules. They could do it, but the weary and verbose volume that would result would by its depressing and unpoetic quality so injure the fresh nerves of its best reader as to *unfit him for seeing the visions and hearing the voices* in his own interior faculties, without which all Blake's works will be to him as those nods or winks which the old proverb tells us are the same to a blind horse.

With regard to the tangle of *is in is* given above. The way to sort it from the text of Blake without any special exercise of faculties not usual to the run of mankind (the present writer has no such faculties whatsoever) may be found from contemplation of such sentences as that in *Jerusalem*, page 49, line 68—

Luvah is named Satan because he has entered that State;

which has just been explained by—

Satan is the State of Death, and not a Human Existence.

The whole passage is a master key to most of Blake's houses. Enitharmon (who loved Satan and nursed him as a son, as she had nursed Orc, *Vala*, Night V, line 70) herself sings a song of death to kill Los (after line 250 of Night I of *Vala*), who refused to be killed, though he had to smite her "to *the earth*." She also sang a song reviving him to life towards the end of Night II, but admitting the delight of the female in the death of the male.

It ceases to be paradoxical when we think of the facts of

life that underlie the poetry, on the living power of imagination that springs from the mental love aroused by our desire to be near the material beauty of nature, which is its one real result, notwithstanding that such beauty is illusion, its date a flash, and its material future eternal death.

So the good feminine or good material is essentially Nature's faculty of being the vessel that holds the male vital power, the emotion in which the "seed of contemplative thought" is carried, and the bad feminine is the carrier of the unformed reason and unformed memory or chaos that between them shall fight with imagination, trying to convince it of worthlessness and even of sin, and persuading it "to try self-murder on its soul"—*Vala*, Night I. These males and females are in fact *influences*.

> Divide, ye bands, influence by influence,

says Urizen to his hosts in *Vala*, Night II.

Now that we have grown accustomed to understanding that throughout all mind, all life, feminine is one kind of influence, an emotional and beautiful kind, good when subservient to masculine, and that masculine is absolutely dead and satanic without it, and only tends to build nature by the power of reason in the space which otherwise is void and virginal, with no result (since nature is nothing), not even with the result of death, which is the state of nothing, we can with equanimity read such symbolic words as those, for example, about Canaan, which offer a typical set of Blakean difficulties:

> The Heavenly Canaan . . . is over Albion . . . as the soul is to the body (*Jerusalem*, p. 71, first paragraph).
> They took the falsehood [falsehood is prophetic]. They named it Canaan—gave a time—even six thousand years—called it Divine Analogy (*Jerusalem*, page 82, lines 17-20; page 84, line 28; page 85, first seven lines).

And compare with—

> The body of Moses in the valley of Peor—the body of Divine Analogy.

Compare also for the expression *six thousand years,* and the connection between Locke, Nature, Rahab, Luvah, and Satan, *Milton*, page 44, lines 14 and 15. We can understand it along with further allusions, as when we are told how Jerusalem (is an) emanative vision of Canaan, page 82, line 21. For meaning of this compare *Jerusalem*, page 54, lines 1-5. The kings of Canaan: delusion and love, page 89, line 46. " I call to Canaan, etc.: they listen not," page 83, line 17. The central or *heart* daughters of Albion are Canaan (deceitfully so called), page 82, lines 24-30. " Flames of dusty fire " to Canaan, *Jerusalem*, page 80, line 50. Los drove the daughters of Albion from Albion; they became daughters of Canaan, page 74, line 38. (He did a similar thing for the kings of Asia.) Reasoning, doubt, despair, and death, go from Canaan to devour Jerusalem. The daughters of Albion shoot forth *in* (note the *in*) tender nerves, and are taught to dance before the kings of Canaan, who are, as we learn from *Milton*, page 16, line 36, the fires of youth, enthusiasm, " the all in all " of art in this world as a practical thing. They call Luvah king of Canaan, and take off his vesture (the woof of six hundred years) and darken his eyes, *Jerusalem*, page 66, lines 20 to 34. The Mundane Shell froze round Canaan, whose love is in man's blood (p. 64, line 1 and line 37). Canaan's daughters require human victims (imaginative ideas; jealousy separates it from man, Albion—lines 31, 41, and 42). Once Canaan was under the sky of liberty, Jerusalem. This is Canaan the man, not the place (line 18). Canaan is a portico, through which the sun and moon can pass, of the Temple of Human Intellect (page 58, line 33). It was in the central region, or his heart (page 29, line 31), and as one of the double-tried tends to destroy the offspring of liberty and mental love (page 5, line 14). Finally, there is *Milton*, extra-page 8, (from which we learn how) Urizen as Satan oft entered, vibrating and weeping, into the space called Canaan, there appearing an aged female form (six thousand years!) that shrinks the organs of life till they become finite and itself seems infinite. It will be seen that difficulty is not obscurity, and this will also enable the reader to recall again the poem called the *Mental Traveller*, and on going through *Jerusalem* once more to be less pestered by echoes in his mind of ordinary church-going allusions to Canaan which make it, to most of us, almost as annoyingly blessed a word as Mesopotamia.

Among the most irritating and perhaps at first the most puzzling sayings of Blake are those about the Mundane Shell. Built by Los *in* the power of " Urizen and by the bands of ' Influences,' above (within) which, see *Milton*, last half of page 16, Milton's *Human* Shadow travelled in lands some of which belong to a list given in Jerusalem, page 5, line 14. The Mundane Shell turns out to be itself *in* twenty-seven heavens that are folds of opaqueness (" another covering of Earth is removed," Blake wrote triumphantly, after arriving at Felpham, in his letter). It has *caverns*, fortunately (*Milton*, page 18, line 42), and is blue (page 19, line 30), and its caves are between the stars (page 22, line 22), and—we must note this—it is continually built by Los round the Polypus, which is the dead sea of storgeous appetite, within which are the females, and which has, for its male portion, the satanic sons of Albion. Compare *Jerusalem*, page 69, lines 1 to 5, with *Milton*, page 34, lines 23 to 31. It has chaoses (places of memory without imagination), where the sons of Ololon, who turns out to be (page 34, line 41), so far as she was female, Milton's wives, daughters, Rahab, the twenty-seven heavens, and the Shell itself *as a shadow*,—all that is *contrary* to the poetic genius (see page 43, line 29 and onwards).

In the clouds of Ololon (Pathos), the Lord (Imagination) surrounds the dry acts of Intellect (Mundane Shell), page 35, line 39.

Line 13 of page 36 shows us the Polypus ("soft affections" under the name of Ololon, of course) *within* the Mundane Shell.

These things, moods, thoughts, and despairs in this Polypus—so called because they all grow to one another, and to touch one is to touch all—are named, that they may be recognised wherever else mentioned in page 37, lines 19 to end; where its relation is seen to Los, the voids between the stars and much else that is related in Jerusalem, especially where Los's spectre, Satan, and Sons of Albion are explained. In page 40, line 43 to end, we hear of Milton, who unites with Los in the shadowy prophet who fell six thousand years ago—fell from his station, and who now labours while Urizen faints in terror to find that he is giving him life, among the caverns of the Mundane Shell, and (so large is the contest) on the banks of appetite (Armon).

In *Milton* we hear no more of this Shell, but in *Jerusalem* we hear of it from the earlier pages, which again is an indication that *Milton* was at first written before *Jerusalem* at Felpham, after Blake had read over *Vala* and thrust the word Albion into its earlier Nights, for in *Jerusalem* we are told, in that long and explanatory page 13 (lines 33, 35 to 54), of its twenty-seven heavens that, of course, are outside Golgonooza (the city of art and life), and of all that lies in the voids and chasms. It is again explained as separate from the Earth of Vegetation, page 16, line 25, and then not heard of till page 59, line 10, where it is not spoken of directly, but where we hear of the egg whose shell it is; and in page 64, line 1, we hear that it froze on all sides round Canaan, which with its context we must read along with page 65, line 32, in the long passage about the daughters of Albion. Its relationship to the Vegetative Earth is given in page 72, line 45 and following.

But in page 75 the first puzzling detail is offered, namely, that the twenty-seven folds of opaqueness—satanic folds—or "heavens" are *formed by Los* within the Mundane Shell, which can only be understood in connection with its purpose in the following line 25, and in connection with the line in "Africa" (a portion of the book called *A Song of Los*), where the terrible race of Los gave laws and religions to the sons of Har, *binding them more and more to earth* till a philosophy of the five senses was complete which Urizen, weeping, gave to Newton and Locke. Churches tend to make worshippers materialistic. They are poetic, if at all, at their peril. These coverings are "poisons" of Rahab, one notices, in this same page 75 of *Jerusalem,* which must be read also with page 37 of *Milton.* The sense in which the physical part is to be taken is indicated in page 83, lines 33 etc., which may be also read along with the poem called the *Mental Traveller,* and in the long and difficult speech of Los in page 92 of *Jerusalem* (where a wrong full-stop seems to have been inserted after the word *Judgment,* line 20 of the Russell and Maclagan edition), and where we are told that the Druids reared their rocky circles and framed the Mundane Shell in order to make permanent remembrance of sin. But this is how the thing is seen *when viewed* in the emanative visions of Canaan. With regard to poison, this is (in poetry only) used by Blake to refer to whatever charms the mind into corporeal limits :

> Why cannot the ear be closed to its own destruction,
> Or glistening eye to the poison of a smile ?

from the closing page of *Thel,* is the most widely-known instance of this, as it is in Gilchrist and in Mr. Yeats's cheap volume of selections—the best cheap volume yet issued.

> In her lips and cheeks his poisons rose
> In blushes like the morning.
>
> Quaritch edition, *Vala,* I, 152 ;

> Reddening, the demon strong prepared the poison of sweet love.
> Quaritch edition, *Vala,* VII, 227,

are the next most familiar. The following words from the crossed-out lines in *Tiriel*, given on page 293 of the Chatto and Windus edition of Blake, are less familiar, but to the same purpose:

> In silent deceit, poisons inhaling from the morning rose.

This has the further value of reminding us that deceit in Blake always meant the deceit of the flesh, its power of making us attribute reality to it on account of our emotions, though our minds know better.

This is all that *Jerusalem* contains about the Mundane Shell, but it would be troublesome enough without the references in *Vala*, where we learn that Urizen ordered its building to be done by his bands of influences (Night II, line 21 and following), and that it was he who petrified human imagination into rock and sand, till there were groans among the Druid temples.

Line 240 says plainly:

> Thus was the Mundane Shell built by Urizen's strong power—

a line which follows what, but for the allusions in *Milton* (last page) to the red woof of 600 years, would be unintelligibly irrelevant:

> And the Divine vision appeared in Luvah's robes of blood.

The difficulty is to understand why Blake did not seem to see that he was contradicting himself. We see it without difficulty by looking at the names. He overlooked the appearance—it is no more—by having his eyes fixed on the meanings.

A little higher in Night VI, we find Luvah saying:

> And Urizen who was Faith and Certainty is changed to Doubt.

Urizen is spoken of as changed by the action of Luvah. Affections and passions change intellect.

We find that the furnaces (of affliction) were unsealed, and that the metal ran in channels cut by the plough of ages held in Urizen's hands. In this part of the poem, it is true, Los now and then appears. He is young and sarcastic. Later on he changes, takes command of the furnaces, and manages everything, because he has found Urizen unfit to do so, until the time of the end when Albion (Man) awakes. The spirit of prophecy, the "ever-apparent Elias," who is Los, takes up the work of mere Intellect when it ceases to have strength to carry the living fire of Faith, and, elaborating every religion into a system in his style, at last shows him how they all lead to a philosophy of the five senses which he has to give, weeping, to Newton and Locke.

Thus the Mundane Shell is built twice over in each of us, for "The fool sees not the same tree that the wise man sees," and "The eye altering alters all," and in the human race generally, as the early innocent savage forms of "wisdom, art, and science" (the primæval state of man) freeze into mathematic hardness as man's rationalistic intellect advances, he passes through miscomprehension of all poetry and so of all psychology into hopeless darkness ("Science is bankrupt" as the French say now), and finally has to learn, from freshly inspired reading of the misunderstood Christian religion, the relation of vision to mind, and of mind, in its two parts, to death and the body on one side and to immortality and brotherhood on the other. This is the last judgment *now going on*. It will, of course, "overwhelm bad art and science."

These few details are intended for readers of Blake who, even after going through all his works, and reading the few explanatory notes given in the Chatto and Windus edition, are occasionally hindered by seeming contradictions from seeing the real meaning, and *so the real man*, in his poetry.

CHAPTER XXIX

HIS THREE LEADING IDEAS

AMONG the preoccupations of Blake's mind one religious thought was always first, the idea of the " Grand Man " that he derived from Swedenborg, and that we all know from Auguste Comte. By contemplating Swedenborg's symbol that fell into his mind like an apple into a garden, he discovered what may be called a law of Spiritual Gravitation. This gives him so curious a brotherhood with Sir Isaac Newton, his favourite aversion, that it is difficult to read his bursts of fury against Newton without smiling. The Newton whom he abused was a name for a mood, of course. The actual Sir Isaac he would have loved. There was much in common between the two men, beginning with their appearance, for if the nose be a little sharpened, the long quivering mouth reduced and moulded into lines more fit for a benevolent silence, and the eyes pressed a little back under the brows, instead of bulging out while they flashed fire, Blake's face and forehead would be very like Newton's. Newton reminds us of Blake also in his fate, in being compelled to work hard for his living while conscious that his genius was hindered by such labour, so that it was really a compulsory waste of time, in being misunderstood, in having the works of his brain attributed to others, in being supposed to be an alchemist, and even in being supposed to be mad. The word alchemist, indeed, was never applied to Blake, but his symbols were misread in a way similar to that which made Newton seem an alchemist.

The Mind, into which, as Blake says (in his letter about Flaxman's death, given below), we shall all go after death, is the Divine Bosom into which all the " Human Forms " of the Powers we now see in " Visions of Time and Space " as trees, metals, and stones, will also awake, as told in the last lines of *Jerusalem*. That inanimate objects have life as much as we ourselves, seems another of Blake's opinions in which he was

341

just a century before his time, since *Jerusalem* bears date 1804. He even defined in his own way the region of the Divine Mind in which we shall live: it was the Body (the risen body) of Christ, and was the Human Imagination (*Jerusalem*, page 5, line 59), of which we were members, and which it was our business to help to build. It was "not a state," being "existence itself," and was therefore all that a "state" is and more. The extra-page 32 of *Milton*, read with *Jerusalem*, page 73, line 43, explains this. Incongruous as are such terms as protoplasm, primordial cell, and microbe in this connection, we see these organisms as intermediately between electrons and our own selves, much as Blake saw himself intermediary between Ideas and Christ, the Composite or Grand Man.

The word Body in a mental sense is used also in *Jerusalem*. "Satan," called Limb of opaqueness (page 73, line 27), is the Body of Doubt, that seems but is not, in page 93, line 20; and in page 49, line 57, the body of Moses is seen to be built and to be Divine Analogy, but not to circumscribe Divine Analogy, for on being looked at again (page 85, line 7), this is seen to be larger, and Moses is planted in it as a seed, along with David and the Twelve Tribes. None of these are to be understood as the historical personages any more than Newton (along with Bacon and Locke) is the historic Rahab, who (in her turn) is only a name in the mortal and temporal region for the mythic Vala, who is the goddess Nature, daughter of "Luvah," mother, along with Jerusalem, of Albion's sons and partly of Los, and built herself by the reasoning power in man, aided by the Polypus, Orc, for passion, like reason, opposes the translucence and eternity of Imagination, and all the opposites of Imagination, being opposites of Eternity, and Christ, and Forgiveness, become also composite and One Body, that of Satan, who is Orc, Luvah, the Spectre of each Zoa (selfhood of each sense) and of Albion (Man), and of Rahab, and Tirzah, and Vala, and so far of Enitharmon as she is mother of Satan, and one of the emotional forms of that state of mind of which "the males" (Sons of Albion) are the intellectual forms. They are all Nature in the mass, until they arise and get free and join Christ "That is Satan; he is the Greek Apollo," said Blake once, pointing to the sun. As natural objects lead us to doubt imaginations, though they do not really exist, Blake called Satan "The body of doubt that seems, but is not" (*Jerusalem*, page 93, line 30). That Nature does not forgive, and is, in fact the permanent " opposite " of " Forgiveness of Sins," was another of Blake's ideas in which he spoke an opinion that has become celebrated in the mouths of modern thinkers who would have despised him as a dreamer, though they had a great respect for their own dreams, none of which were so scientific as his.

Plainly as he says in the preface to the last chapter of *Jerusalem* that we shall " live " in our eternal or imaginative bodies when our vegetable or mortal bodies are no more, except as part of the composite mind, Blake does not preach immortality. When his selfhood and reason begs him with tears to give it a little hope, he is as obdurate as any eighteenth-century rationalist. This portion of him, " cold, scientific " (*Jerusalem*, page 43, line 2), under the name of " Urizen," both in *Jerusalem* and *Vala*, desires " with iron power to avert his own despair " (*Jerusalem*, page 7, line 33, and *Vala*, Night II, 76, and VIII, 136). When he is seen in "The Spectre" or the Pride, Self-righteousness, and Reasoning Power of man, this portion of mind says to the prophetic portion :

Oh that I could cease to be ! Despair ! I am despair,
Created to be the great example of horror and agony ; also my
Prayer is vain. I called for compassion, compassion mocked ;
Mercy and Pity threw the gravestone over me, and with lead and iron
Bound it over me for ever.

And in reply to this, and more, the prophetic portion of mind wiped the tears of self-pity from Reason and Pride ;

But comfort none could give or beam of hope.
Jerusalem, page 10, lines 51, 61.

On the subject of division and unity as to be seen in the soul of one man between other " men "—his many thoughts that *are* men and even seem so to one another (*Vala*, VIII, 118), just as cities are men (*Jerusalem*, page 30, line 46) —much is told, beginning with the early lines of *Vala* that promise to sing of the Spirit of Prophecy,

His fall into Division and his Resurrection into Unity.

He divides into " sons and daughters," which are ideas and feelings, as we learn, and include the twelve tribes. We can see ourselves in these mythic figures, who are to one of us what we all are to the chief " Son," or development and corollary, of the Universal Father.

In the first lines of page 87 of *Jerusalem,* "Los" begs "Enitharmon" to seize in her hand the roots of love that surround him—the small fibres, and he says :

> I will fire them
> With pulsations ; we will divide them into Sons and Daughters
> To live in thy bosom's translucence as in an eternal morning ;

but she will not. The Reasoning Power has quite another purpose in having sons and daughters (for Albion's are essentially his). It is

> To separate a law of Sin, to punish thee in thy members.

The daughters provoke love, the sons contradict it. Los afterwards tells of his divisions to Rahab (Nature):

> I am that shadowy prophet who, six thousand years ago,
> Fell from my station in the eternal bosom. I divided
> To multitudes, and my children are children of care and labour.
> Oh, Rahab, I behold thee. I was once, like thee, a son
> Of Pride, and I have pierced the Lamb of God in pride and wrath
> Hear me repeat my generations that thou may'st also repent.
> *Vala*, VIII, 345.

Then follows a list of the children of Los, that causes the reader to believe that only the earlier portions of *Vala* were written in 1797, and that this and much else was produced at Felpham in 1801—a conjecture supported by the handwriting of the MS., but of which proof is not yet acquired. Los also, though, says of the "Sons of Albion":

> They have divided themselves in wrath ; they must be united
> By pity ;   *Jerusalem*, page 7, line 57,

though elsewhere we are told of how even pity, which may work both ways, "divides the soul" (*Milton*, page 6, line 19). The "Religion of Generation," of which he speaks hereafter, calls for a uniting pity, which was meant for the destruction of Jerusalem, and is to "become her covering till the time of the end," is a "representative" symbol, and means the religion of restraint of imagination, which is "first author of energy enslaved" (*Vala*, IX, 151), and substitutes argument as a mental effort to attain truth and sympathy, has this result. The network of symbols hiding the doctrine is never entangled, and is always clear whenever *any* of the words in which it is contained is found in the text.

War—Energy enslaved, argument.
Generation—Energy divided to create argument.

Regeneration—Inspired imagination undisputed.
Jerusalem—All mental liberty to dream, to unite, and to adjoin man to his fellow-man.

The contrast is symbolised also as cog-wheels opposed to each other compared with concentric wheels, the contrast being that of nature with imagination, and of law with forgiveness. That ideas are Sons of Albion is seen in *Jerusalem*, page 70, line 1, as they are streets of the composite person called London (page 38, line 31). When he is looked at closely, London, called the "immortal guardian" (*Jerusalem*, page 38, line 40) of those "minute particulars" symbolised as his own streets, is Luvah in a secondary sense, after Luvah has "assumed the south" (*Jerusalem*, page 36, line 29), and so got into his place. But in the same line Urizen assumed east, and London is always geographically in the south-east of England. He has markedly the attributes of Urizen, and in his resemblance to Tiriel (when blind, age-bent, led by a child—*Jerusalem*, page 84, line 11), is related to Tharmas; both these had, we remember, innocent days when Urizen was Prince of Light. He is a symbol full of universal suggestiveness, his quarters being those of Man, and his points of the compass the four "senses" or Zoas, for he is fourfold, and spiritually is Art and Golgonooza (*Jerusalem*, page 53, line 19). "In the exchanges of London every nation walked" (nations are truths of imagination)—*Jerusalem*, page 24, line 42. And yet London was only a stone of the ruins of Jerusalem when she was ruined for a while by Albion's reaction in favour of ideas of Sin and Repentance—the forbidden tree (*Jerusalem*, page 29, line 19). Properly he is the centre of Erin, his "holy place" (page 72, line 20), but in evil days, when the Zoas or senses are "clouded" and rage (*Jerusalem*, page 36, line 25), London is Luvah, and is his "English name," in fact (*Jerusalem*, page 59, line 14), and is, like imaginative art, "a void." He mingles with Albion's reasoning power and becomes Satan (Body of Doubt) and the dark Hermaphrodite of self-contradiction (*Jerusalem*, page 49, line 67, and page 58, line 20).

The expression Spiritual Gravitation, here offered only as a descriptive figure of speech to help us to group Blake's ideas, not as a term of his or part of his language, does not refer to such a line as

All fell towards the centre, sinking down in dire ruin,
Jerusalem, page 59, line 17,

as these told of the senses acting without imaginative liberty, but to such tendencies of the separate to unite, as in this passage, where every noun is a technical symbol from the myth:

Teaching them to form the Serpent of Precious Stones and Gold,
To seize the sons of Jerusalem and plant them in One Man's Loins.
Jerusalem, page 55, line 15.

The idea of a composite individual is, of course, familiar in an incomplete way to whoever has seen two men pulling at one rope, has heard the music of a chorus, or the speech of a member of Parliament, has seen any of the effects produced (unprofessionally) by people sitting in a ring and wishing all together, or has heard of the miracles at Lourdes, or of that star of Italy that appeared miraculously in the sky while Mazzini was making a great speech to an excited multitude—a star which two Englishmen left the crowd to observe better, and of which they could see nothing when alone, though they perceived it again when they came back to the crowd to hear the rest of the speech. The existence of Urizen or Luvah is shown just as the existence of the great god Pan was shown. He has survived his own myth, and his adjective has become a noun—panic. Our Lady of Lourdes, whose existence stands on similar testimony, may have as unforeseen a future. What that of Blake's "Zoas" may be we cannot guess till they have a more complete birth. They are still "advancing," as he said was the beauty of imagination and the horror of selfish rational despair:

The joys of God advance
. . . .
But my griefs advance also, for ever, and without end.
Jerusalem, page 10, lines 40 and 50.

Or—

Brotherhood is Religion.   *Jerusalem*, page 57, line 10.

Where "Religion" is used in its good sense of non-legal or, as it may be called, antinomian restraint—Blake's only idea of true morality; or—

In beauty the Daughters of Albion divide and unite at will.
Jerusalem, page 58, line 1.

Where this gravity works (as in nature) to produce centrifugal as well as centripetal movement. Or—

Then all the Males conjoined in One Male and every one
Became, etc.   *Jerusalem*, page 61, line 1.

Or again when the Sons of Albion were incorrect—

> They rise as Adam before me, united into One Man.
> *Jerusalem*, page 10, line 16.

Or again in the final perfection—

> We live as One Man, for, contracting our infinite senses,
> We behold multitude or expanding we behold as one,
> As One Man all the Universal Family, and that One Man
> We call Jesus the Christ, etc.
> *Jerusalem*, page 30, line 17.

Spiritual gravitation makes even those under the influence of the Daughters, or, in brief, Tirzah, who is Natural Religion, Daughter of Morality (compare *Milton*, page 17, line 54), though such are not able to mingle and meet by sympathy and become one in "Jesus," yet

> By invisible hatreds adjoined they seem remote and separate.
> . . . .
> He who will not commingle in Love must be adjoined by Hate.
> *Jerusalem*, page 66, lines 53 and 56.

But as the "contraction" of senses is just what leads to "fall," or movement of the soul into exterior or experience, this explains the sentence in the opening of *Vala*, where the poem is said to tell of the Spirit of Prophecy (called Los), and of

> His fall into division and his resurrection into Unity,

and why it was only in the "Earth of Eden" that he propagated his sons and daughters, of which (towards the close of Night VIII, in line 350) he gives repentantly so terrible a list, speaking to Rahab, the symbolised natural conscience and vegetative restraint.

Satan, the Body of Doubt (*Jerusalem*, page 93, line 20), on which vegetative man, or Reuben, was fed till he became so horrible that all who beheld him fled and guarded their tongues for pain (*Jerusalem*, page 36, line 9), has allowed him divine attributes of unifying—"that he may be put off." The Sons of Albion become one great Satan mingled with Luvah (*Jerusalem*, page 90, line 43). The thirty-ninth and fortieth pages of *Milton*, as well as much of *Jerusalem*, tell of this. The last line of page 37 may be read with remembrance that Europe and Asia correspond *with* Urizen and Luvah. The twelve gods becoming Satan in *Jerusalem*, page 74, line 22, the end of page 37, and beginning of page

40 of *Milton*, all repeat the idea that Doubt is opposed to Imagination—particularly to Vision.

That Imagination leads to the Grand Man through brotherhood and its opposite, fleshly experience and reason, to isolation, is told both in *Jerusalem* and *Vala*, where after line 620 in Night IX, we read:

Man is a worm renewed with joy, he seeks the caves of sleep.

. . . .

Forsaking brotherhood and universal love in selfish clay,
Folding the wings of his pure mind.

. . . .

Man subsists by brotherhood and universal love.

. . . .

Man liveth not by self alone, but in his brother's face
Man shall behold the Eternal Father, and love and joy abound—

Which may be read with this from Night III:

Rent from eternal brotherhood we die and are no more.

All deities reside in the human breast.
Marriage of Heaven and Hell, page 11.

If the doors of perception were cleansed, everything would appear to man, as it is, infinite.
Marriage of Heaven and Hell, page 14.

God only Acts and Is in existing beings, or Men.
Marriage of Heaven and Hell, page 16.

The Infinite alone resides in Definite and Determined Identity.
Jerusalem, page 55, line 64.

The Worship of God is honouring His gifts
In other men, and loving the greatest, best, each according
To his Genius, which is the Holy Ghost in Man; there is no other
God than that God who is the intellectual fountain of Humanity.
He who envies or calumniates, which is murder and cruelty,
Murders the holy one.   *Jerusalem*, page 91, line 7.

And O thou Lamb of God, whom I
Slew in my dark self-righteous pride!
Jerusalem, page 27, seventeenth stanza.

I act with benevolence and virtue and get murdered time after time.
Jerusalem, page 91, line 25.

Displaying the Eternal Vision, the Divine Similitude,
In loves and tears of brothers, sisters, sons, fathers, and friends
Which if Man ceases to behold he ceases to exist.
Jerusalem, page 38, line 11.

On the Laocoön plate he has summed up the whole affair in one sentence:

The whole Business of Man is: the Arts and All Things in Common.

Many more passages of the same kind could easily be added, but these are enough to show that Blake's idea of the composite person was to him the one greatest and most pressing reality. Besides the One Man, the Divine Saviour, there were lesser composites called "states" that came into existence when imagination in the person of some existing imaginative man perceived them, much as sound comes into existence when we hear it and light when we see it. Seeing them "created them." They say of themselves:

> We are not Individuals but States, combinations of Individuals.
> *Milton*, extra-page 32, line 10.

They are permanent in one way :

> As the Pilgrim passes on while the country permanent remains,
> So men pass on, but States remain permanent for ever.
> *Jerusalem*, page 73, line 43.

But they do not remain unchangeable. They merge, divide, and recombine :

> States change, but Individual Identities never change nor cease.

A mortal, however, may change, and his mortality cease, and it and he must cease and change if he is to become fit to survive :

> The Mortal fades away in improved knowledge.
> *Vala*, Night VIII, 546.

At the present day Mr. Myers has brought on to the solid mahogany or oak table of every library the very vaporous question of what is individual personality as a matter of fact ; and there is some reason to suppose that Blake was attempting to say something in his day that would have been consonant with the new discoveries.

The word *in* continues to be the one which most needs a special gift of comprehension if the reader would not be misled by it. *Represent* is another Swedenborgian term to be read with care.

> Then Milton knew that the three Heavens of Beulah were beheld
> By him on earth in his bright pilgrimage of sixty years
> In the three females whom his wives and those three whom his daughters
> Had represented and contained that they might be resumed
> By giving up of selfhood ; and they, distant, viewed his journey
> In their eternal spheres, now human, though their bodies remained closed

In the dark Ulro till the judgment.   Also Milton knew and they
  knew
Himself was Human, though now wandering through death's vale
In conflict with those three female forms which in blood and
  jealousy
Surrounded him, dividing and uniting without end or number.
Milton, pages 15 and 16.

The females whom Milton's living wives and daughters
represented were female *forms*—forms of thought whose
tendency is to the opposite of sympathy and forgiveness, and
who fight for their mental lives, and are ready to destroy
any mental life, or to bind any down that threatens their
materialistic view of existence, which *is their* existence.
Their names—

Rahab and Tirzah, and Milcah and Mahlah, and Noah and Hoglah,
Milton, page 16, line 11,

betray what kind of forms of thought they are.   We have
seen them in *Jerusalem* in page 68, at their symbolic work on
Schofield (variously spelled), who was the limit of contraction
recreated in Edom (or red earth), and therefore called Adam,
who absorbed many of his brethren, to be himself bound down
by Mahlah, Hoglah, and Milcah.   Their names are biblical,
and will be recognised as those of Zelophehad's daughters.
He, as related in Numbers, chap. xxvi., verse 33, and chap.
xxvii. at the beginning, had only these daughters and no sons.
They obtained from Moses a special inheritance, as though
they were heirs male, and not female, and from their time
the Salic law, hitherto existing (though not under that
name) among Israelites, was abolished.
    Blake uses them symbolically as names suggestive of
feminine or materialistic tyranny, as he uses those of the
"Sons of Albion" for argumentative or negative tyranny.
The next thing we hear of Milton was that

His body was the rock Sinai—that body
    Which was on earth bound to corruption ;

and the female influences were rocky also, and have further
names which are heard of in *Jerusalem*.
    All this is aimed at the belief in the hard apparent
surfaces of Nature, that seems real, but is not, till some one
is entrapped into lending his imagination to believe it.
    The rock Sinai is heard of in the *Book of Ahania* in
detail :

> But Milton's Human Shadow continued journeying above
> The rocky masses of the Mundane Shell.   Line 18.

And this is elaborately explained. Space forbids us to follow his journey minutely, but at last Blake cries out, after exhausting attempt to makes himself clear :

> How can I, with my gross tongue that cleaveth to the dust,
> Tell of the fourfold man ?   *Milton*, page 10, line 15.

He cannot, except by figures of speech. Our language was made for food and love, labour and war, on the plain, and in the state of mind that produced utterance. How can it in specific terms tell of psychic involutions ? Arithmetic alone could as easily deal with the forms of thought for which the language called Algebra was invented. Blake's books are to those of other poets almost exactly what algebra is to arithmetic. His x, y, and z are biblical and historical names, and their action on each other contains truth that cannot be told except in mythic form. Those who insist that Blake shall be explained in non-mythic form are as reasonable as those who expect the mathematician to go without his letters and signs. More may be done than has yet been done, but *Milton* alone deserves a volume as long as this entire book to unravel it, though Blake tried hard, as such passages as the following show :

> As when a man dreams he reflects not that his body sleeps,
> Else he would wake, so seemed he entering his own shadow,
> *Milton*, page 14, line 1,

a passage to be read whenever the word *sleep* or *dream* occurs in *Jerusalem*. A little farther down, on line 10 and following :

> When he entered into his shadow, himself,
> His real and immortal self was, as appeared to those
> Who dwell in immortality, as one sleeping on a couch of gold.
>
> .   .   .   .
>
> But to himself he seemed a wanderer lost in dreary night.

The word *self* is used in several senses. It is a pity that Blake did not adopt a different way of writing for each,— roman, italic, black letter, and Greek.

> Thus Milton stood forming bright Urizen, while his Mortal past
> Sat frozen on the rock of Horeb, and his Redeemed portion
> Thus formed the clay of Urizen, but within that portion
> His real Human walked above in power and majesty
> Though darkened, and the seven angels of the Presence attended him.
> Page 18, lines 10-14.

Or again :

> As the ploughman or artificer or shepherd,
> While in the labours of his calling, sends his thoughts abroad
> To labour in the ocean or in the starry heavens, so Milton
> Laboured in chasms of the Mundane Shell, though here before
> My cottage, etc.
> Page 40, lines 4 etc.

"Milton," being the name of a state *about to be created*, is a composite individual, and yet, "Milton" being a person, personal division is carefully explained.

The doctrine that there is a divided as well as a composite personality is seen even without more attempt to analyse it; as Blake's it was his second leading idea; his third, almost as puzzling at first, must be spoken of if we are to set up any real portrait of his mind.

This third idea was his view of morality. That he had been punished as a child for seeing visions, left him for life with the idea that generalised maxims not poetically illustrated in myths were what people called *moral*, and that it was therefore immoral to allow the mind to create mythic figures with their refusal to be translated, and their pictorial vividness—vision being clearer than sight itself,—and their own passions of love and hate, lust and cruelty, that make them just like so many living savages.

All through *Jerusalem, moral* and *matter-of-fact* are seen to mean the same thing, while *sin* and *sympathy* are the same. *Vision* and *forgiveness*, we have already seen, are names for the Saviour seen in different attributes, male or female.

The result inevitably is that *moral* becomes a term of reprobation. The word "holy" means (in sarcastic sense) unfruitful of imagination, sterile. Impurity and harlotry is a mixture of imagination with actual love or credulity,—of nature and mind. Chastity is (in a bodily sense) of no more importance compared to the mental virtues than body is compared to mind. It is actually evil when its mental effects are evil.

This is very much the view that Mr. Sinnett says was current in the Atlantic lands, now under the ocean, in times before that modern period known as ancient history. It survives, of course, in the modern clubman. Perhaps no one is ready to deny it unconditionally, except to uphold the ascetic Christianity of the Pauline dogma. Paul will be read of in Blake along with Constantine, Charlemagne, and Luther, as one who was not a whole-hearted upholder of Forgiveness as the only Christ.

At one period of Blake's life he certainly considered thought that is wrong a deadlier sin than certain acts that are not held to be right. The ethics of thought are still so far from being generally agreed on that the subject must be left here. There are words at the close of *Broken Love* that show him as not in the mood that wrote the *Marriage of Heaven and Hell*.

CHAPTER XXX

LATER than *Jerusalem* and *Milton* we can find no record of Blake's mind which has any completeness and force to be compared to that which they contain. They will remain the places where we must look for his portrait by his own hand in its most emphatic form. As it has been supposed for so long that *Jerusalem* was the poem that he wrote at Felpham, though passages in it are common to both *Milton* and *Vala,* and though we have no contemporary record, and though some pages of *Milton,* as engraved, seem to be later than anything in *Jerusalem,* the reasons for considering that *Milton* was the poem he wrote there, and "considered the grand reason" of his "being brought there," deserve to be brought together, even if some are repeated in doing so.

The first is that the poem was shortened from twelve books to two; the second, that he says, page 36 of *Milton,* that "Los" prepared his cottage at Felpham that he might write those visions, and one chief incident is given as occurring on his garden path. The third is that in *Jerusalem,* page 38, he says that he saw certain visions in Felpham that belong to the poem, but that he writes in South Molton Street, London. He says that he even heard some of what he writes in Lambeth, where he lived before he went to Felpham. The fourth is that he begins the poem with a list of symbolic characters, among whom is one (Scholfield) whose name he had only heard during the very last days that he was at Felpham. The fifth is that *Milton* is full of country descriptions and symbols—the lark, the shepherd, wildflowers—and that these are lost in *Jerusalem.* The sixth is that though a passage from one of his letters dated from Felpham recalls an expression from *Jerusalem* about the "fluctuating earth" on page 83, it is even more closely allied to the passage

354

on the vegetable earth bound on the foot in *Milton*, page 19, while the long poem called *Los the Terrible* in the *Collected Works*, which was written at Felpham, is closely allied to the part played by Los in *Milton*, and not at all in the manner of the speeches of Los and his acts in *Jerusalem*.

Another sign of Felpham in *Milton* is the frequent use of the word *bard*, a term habitually used by Hayley when speaking of his friend, R. G. Johnson, Cowper's nephew, who may be the personage whose presence in Oxford caused Blake to give it afterwards in *Jerusalem* its function as giving leaves of the tree of life to Albion, after mistakenly repenting its human kindness, though its imagination was *cut round* and shrunken. With Cambridge, Winchester, and the Scottish Universities it holds a place among the places that correspond to the four ungenerated sons of Los and Jerusalem. Its references are—Albion's ancient porches (or "inlets to the soul," or imaginative senses), including Oxford, are darkened and scattered, page 5, line 3. Oxford is the dust of Jerusalem's wall, page 29, line 19. Jerusalem ruined it, repents of its human kindness, page 42, line 58, is urged by the spirit of healing (Bath) to take leaves of the tree of life and bring them to help Albion, and does so, weeping, page 45, line 30, and page 46, lines 8, 17. It counts as a symbol for one of the four "ungenerated" sons of prophecy and sympathy who did not *flee* into error. Daughters of Albion beam on it mildly, and Oothoon hides these in chaste appearances, pages 81, line 11, and 83, line 28.

This is all written in the *last* days of Felpham and first of South Molton Street. Blake still corresponded with Hayley. But though *Oxford* continued to produce an impression on him, the word "bard," which occurs nine times in the first twenty pages of *Milton*, is forgotten. Oxford is only mentioned once in *Milton*, on page 40, written after most of *Jerusalem*, and then only on line 44 as one of four, Bath, Oxford, Cambridge, Norwich, on the front of Albion's bosom.

That the last pages of *Milton* are later than the last of *Jerusalem* is suggested by the ending of the poem—a call to the harvest (of symbols), and a statement that no more seed should be sown. This is presumably the "seed of contemplative thought," by which all things renew.

It is also suggested by the deplorable and hasty state of the drawings towards the close of *Milton*. They betray worn-out patience, jarred nerves, and a distracted mind. They seem to say, " I shall print no more," as Blake said to Crabb Robinson.

That the story of Satan and Palamabron in *Milton* recalls Hayley and Blake is not so conclusive as it would be if it did not occur in a modified form in *Vala,* whose MS. title-page dates 1797. But the latter pages of *Vala* are later than the title, and so far as the "Satan" there has an affinity to Sir Joshua Reynolds, no moral turpitude in Sir Joshua is implied in the suggestion that he has something to do with the symbol; it is a term all whose more precise characteristics are in *Milton* only, and are clearly to be traced to a recent reading of *Paradise Lost,* and to a purposed departure from its ideas.

There was another " Satan "—Bacon. There was another —the old-fashioned *Devil.* Blake was soon to see him.

Before finally leaving the subject of *Jerusalem* until the not-yet-demanded Encyclopædia of Blake is required by the public, a detail may be referred to with regard to Gilchrist's treatment of the subject. In the first edition of the *Life of Blake* the poem *To the Jews* is given at full length, with a challenge at the top to whoever can do so to interpret it.

The present writer has to thank Gilchrist for this challenge. It was what set him to work in 1870, and caused him to find that clue to the four regions, four points of the compass, four quarters of London and of the world, or the four ungenerated sons of Los, and four Zoas, with their relationships and their order of habitual arrangement, which had escaped the elder critics. For want of it they had no means of discovering any coherence in the book. They could not prove that a *region* never loses its characteristics whether it be entered into by a being from another region or not. Height and depth are never as length and breadth, nor north and south as east and west. Europe and Asia never means what Asia and Europe would, and America is never anything but opposite to England.

The clue slept while its discoverer was travelling and living in Italy until, in 1890, Mr. Yeats asking for it, some rough hints were dragged out of a little notebook. Mr. Yeats took fire from the slender gleam and offered the collaboration which was entered on at once, and resulted in a crop of discoveries made now by one, now by the other, often by both at once, of which as many as could be got into any sort of order were thrust into the Quaritch edition, which grew from two volumes to three while under compilation, and was prepared during an excitement of enthusiasm that left it full of misprints.

The challenge that began it all is quietly suppressed in the second edition of Gilchrist, but all the old depressing mistakes are repeated.

The arrangement of the quarters of London and the chief towns of England and the continents of the world under the four Zoas is, although it was the clue to all Blake, a matter that itself is as difficult to sort up as anything that he contains. Canterbury is the most difficult of all. As it is but lightly treated in the notes to the Chatto and Windus edition, the references to the word in *Jerusalem*, being but few, are here offered. They are—

Page 17, line 59	Page 46, line 6	Page 65, line 39
" 33 " 12	" 57 " 1	
" 38 " 45	" 63 " 35	

York, another of the four, occurs—

Page 16, line 44	Page 57, line 1	Page 73, line 51
" 38 " 51	" 59 " 14	" 74 " 3
" 46 " 24	" 66 " 65	

In *Milton* there is a long passage on page 40, as "Albion rose up," which merely sums itself up into the symbol of facing eastwards. The colossal figure is a map of the imagination, whose nether parts, as elsewhere—the exterior region—are seen as feet, hands being more inward. The four pillars do not exactly follow the usual four-fold.

There is only one general system to follow in reading Blake, and that is to remember that all his names are merely tickets more or less appropriate through correspondence with points of the compass when they are places, and facts of history or traditions of doctrine when they are personages either sacred or profane. These tickets apply *only* to impersonations of Human Qualities. The qualities must be thought of partly *by help of* the appropriateness of the symbol when the four points of the compass and Swedenborg's meaning of Biblical names are borne in mind, and partly *in spite of* the almost overwhelming picturesqueness of those suggestions belonging to the words on the tickets that have nothing to do with the human qualities—the psychology, for the sake of which they are used. The qualities change and mingle, and the tickets cannot always, even by aid of the allegoric figures behind them, tell all the drama.

This system must be used along with an unceasing memory that Blake had always before his mind the root idea that there is only one good—love with imaginative art, and only one evil—law with realistic art; that the first unites us all with each other, beauty, and eternity, Christ having made this possible by inventing forgiveness; the second entices us to distraction, God having made this possible by inventing virtue, and Satan by inventing pride and punishment. This summary is the condensation of a lifetime of ardent thought that was never lukewarm for one moment, and whose chief hatreds were for doubt, distraction, and restraint.

CHAPTER XXXI

SATAN, BACON, REES, AND THORNTON

In 1813 Mr. Cumberland introduced Blake to John Linnell, whose descendants at this moment have the finest collection existing of his work. For him he made a set of pictures to *Job*, different from those he sold to Mr. Butts, all his coloured drawings to *Dante* and to the *Temptation of Christ*, besides many separate designs. Linnell kept him alive for the rest of his life, never giving him large sums, but always keeping him employed at a living wage. It was less than would be paid to a good head gardener now, but was more than the publication of the *Job* when engraved showed to be the market value of the work. The fact is, of course, that art, *until it is talked about*, has *no* market value. Talk alone is worth gold. Talk has gone on since then for nearly a century about Blake, and now every penny that John Linnell paid could be recovered in the shape of a pound if the family desired to do so. None the less, it was a fine deed on the part of John Linnell when it was done, and will remain a patent of nobility associated with the name of his heirs as long as art or poetry exists.

It is pleasant to be able to note as a proof that John Linnell is not forgotten that two of his landscapes were sold by auction for good prices as lately as June 4 of this year (1904), his *Woodcutters* for £504 and his *Carting Timber* for £840. In him now, when past the prime of life, Blake may be said to have found his good angel. (The expression is used popularly, not technically.) It is amusing to remember that now also he saw a vision of the devil. We hear of it through Varley and Allan Cunningham.

"For many years I had longed to see Satan," said he. Readers of *Jerusalem* will notice how few *visions* there are in its descriptive passages. "I never could believe him to be

359

the vulgar fiend which our legends represent him. I imagined him a classic spirit such as he appeared to him of Uz with some of his original splendour about him. At last I saw him. I was going upstairs in the dark when suddenly a light streamed among my feet. I turned round, and there he was looking fiercely at me between the iron gratings of my stair-case window. I called for my things. Catherine thought the fit of song was on me, and brought me pen and ink. I said, 'Hush! never mind! this will do.' As he appeared, so I drew him. There he is." "Upon this" (Allan Cunning-ham's report of Varley's reminiscence goes on), "Blake took out a piece of paper with a grated window sketched on it, while through the bars glared the most frightful phantom that ever the mind of man imagined. Its eyes were large and like two coals, its teeth as long as those of a harrow, and the claws such as might appear in the distempered dream of a clerk in the Heralds' office.

"'It is the Gothic Fiend of our legends,' said Blake, 'the true devil; all else are apocryphal.'"

In reading about "Satan" in the poems we must adopt the picture of him suggested by the text described in the early part of this reminiscence, and afterwards drawn in the *Job* series. Blake used this "apocryphal" devil for poetic purposes and quietly suppressed the "true." Varley was an artist with whom Linnell had lived for a year as pupil. He is well known both for his art and his astrology, with which he made many true predictions, as astrologers often do. He used to get Blake to sketch heads from him from "vision." Sometimes Blake only needed to be asked to see any his-torical head one pleased to name, and he would see it, and unless it moved, or some portion vanished, as was the case occasionally before he had finished his drawing, a creditable sketch would be made. If people criticised the likenesses Blake would say calmly, "It's all right, it *must* be so; I saw it so."

Gilchrist says that nevertheless "critical friends could trace in all these heads Blake's mind and hand, his *receipt* for a face. Every artist has his own, from which he may depart in the proportions, but seldom substantially. John Varley, however, could not be persuaded to look at them from this merely rationalistic point of view." One asks oneself why not? Could Blake at that age be *rationalistically* or ration-ally expected to drop his mannerism because he was drawing from vision? Would he have done so had the sitters been half-a-dozen of his "critical friends" who occupied the chair for a few minutes each? Edward III in the drawing appeared to have a swollen head. Blake's assertion that it was right because he saw it so is merely a bit of his usual self-confidence. He was not only the most gifted, poetic, generous, lovable, courageous, industrious, and philosophic of men; he was the most opinionative. "The man who built the pyramids" is as funny a title for a visionary head as though it had been called "the man who wrote the newspapers." Most of these heads were drawn in August 1820. The celebrated *Ghost of a Flea* (with two legs and two arms), manifestly symbolic, "appeared" in as authentically visionary a form as any of them. Doubtless he, too, is "all right." One asks oneself whether Varley hypnotised Blake a little. But all this is neither art, in any important sense, nor poetry. It is not beauty in any sense at all. "The visionary faculty was so much under control that at the wish of a friend he could summon before his abstracted gaze any of the familiar forms he was asked for. This was during the favourable and befitting hours of night, from nine or ten in the evening till one or two, or perhaps three or four in the morning, Varley sitting by, sometimes slumbering and sometimes waking. Varley would say, 'Draw me Moses,' or David, or would call for a likeness of Julius Cæsar, or Cassivellaunus, or Edward III, or some other great historical personage. Blake would answer, 'There he is!' and paper and pencil being at hand, he would begin drawing with the utmost alacrity and composure, looking up from time to time as though he had a real sitter before him. . . . Sometimes Blake had to wait for the Vision's appearance, . . . at others, in the midst of the portrait he would suddenly leave off, . . . would remark, 'I can't go on, it is gone! I must wait till it returns,' or, 'It has moved; the mouth is gone,' or, 'He frowns; he is displeased with my portrait of him.'"

This recalls Blake's complaint of the effect on him of Venetian painters, who "snatch away the vision time after time," and accounts for his anger with them. Two pictures, very unlike each other, of Richard Cœur de Lion were made. But if Blake had drawn for Crabb Robinson as he did for Varley we should have Milton with a beard.

Gilchrist also relates how once, "the other evening," said Blake, "taking a walk, I came to a meadow and saw a fold of lambs. Coming nearer, the ground blushed with flowers, and the wattled cote and its woolly tenants were of an

exquisite pastoral beauty. But I looked again, and it proved
to be no living flock but only beautiful sculpture."

"I beg pardon, Mr. Blake," said a lady, "but *where* did you
see this?"

"Here, Madam," said Blake, touching his forehead.

It was a "Memorable Fancy." No doubt the story is true,
but Blake never said, "its woolly tenants were of an exquisite pastoral beauty." Why could no one remember his
real words?

In a similar vein he tells how he saw a fairy's funeral.

Blake in his more important, his indignant mood is
seen in extracts from his notes on the margin of his "Bacon."
Gilchrist, who had the privilege of seeing these, says:

The epithets *fool, liar, villain, atheist,* nay *Satan,* are freely indulged
in, and even, most singular of all, "stupid." "Good advice for Satan's
kingdom" is the inscription on the title-page. "Is it true or false that
the wisdom of this world is foolishness with God? This is certain; if
what Bacon says is true, what Christ says is false. If Cæsar is right,
Christ is wrong, both in politics and religion, since they will divide
themselves in two." Another note, "Everybody knows that this
is epicureanism and libertinism, and yet everybody says that it is
Christian philosophy. How is this possible? Everybody must be a
liar and deceiver? No! 'Everybody' does not do this, but the hirelings of kings and courts" (here is a "hired villain" again), "who made
themselves 'everybody' and knowingly propagate falsehood. It was a
common opinion in the court of Queen Elizabeth that knavery is
wisdom. Cunning plotters were considered as wise Machiavels."

To Bacon's "It is great blasphemy to personate God and
bring him in, saying, 'I will demand,'" etc., Blake notes,
"Did not Jesus descend and become a servant? The Prince
of Darkness is a gentleman and not a man; he is a Lord
Chancellor." To the essay on Virtue Blake says, "What do
these knaves mean by 'virtue'? Do they mean war and its
horrors and its heroic villains?" To Bacon's "Good thoughts
are little better than good dreams," Blake says, "Thought *is*
act. Christ's acts were nothing to Cæsar's if this is not so."
To Bacon's "The increase of a state must be upon the
foreigner," Blake says, "The increase of a state, as of a man,
is from internal improvement or intellectual acquirement.
Man is not improved by the hurt of another. States are not
improved at the expense of foreigners." Blake also says,
"Bacon calls intellectual arts unmanly, and so they are for
kings and wars, and shall in the end annihilate them." He
means that art shall in the end annihilate kings and war,
but does not seem to say so. Later, "What is fortune but

an outward accident, for a few years, sixty at the most, and then gone!" (Blake of course counts from twenty-one years of age.) Again, "King James was Bacon's *primum mobile*." To Bacon's expression "mighty princes," Blake adds "the Powers of darkness." Again, "A tyrant is the worst disease, and is the cause of all others" (and yet Mr. Yeats in his last essay on Blake goes no further than to say that he was "probably" an Irishman). Also, "Everybody hates a king. David was afraid to say that this envy was upon a king, but is this envy or indignation?" Gilchrist gives no more. The curious recurrence of "envy" in Blake is interesting. He had cause for much, of course, but cause without a special faculty of feeling never produced an emotion yet, not even gratitude.

In 1820 Blake was employed by Dr. Thornton to illustrate a school edition of Virgil's *Pastorals*. He made some curious and simple woodcuts for it, engraved by himself. They are oblong and small, scarcely exceeding a postage stamp in height, and four postage stamps in width. They are "generalised" very finely, if Blake will permit us to say so, and are poetic and touching. The Linnell family own the blocks, of which a few examples are given in Gilchrist's *Life*. Dr. Thornton must have been very much disappointed with them, and they must have seemed to him coarse, heavy, and childish.

To quote Gilchrist:

Blake made twenty drawings to illustrate the *Pastorals* of Philips, introduced by Dr. Thornton into his "course" of Virgil reading. From these he executed seventeen wood-blocks, the first he ever executed, and, as it will turn out, the last. The rough, unconventional work of a mere 'prentice hand to the art of wood-engraving they are (an unfortunate expression; there is nothing of the apprentice and everything of the untaught master about them); they are in effect vigorous and artist-like, recalling the doings of Albert Dürer and the early masters, whose aim was to give ideas, not pretty language (another error, of course. Gilchrist's misfortunes when he speaks of art are Niobean). When he sent in these specimens, the publishers, unused to so daring a style, were taken aback, and declared "this man must do no more," nay, were for having all he had done re-cut by one of their regular hands. The very engravers received them with derision, crying out in the words of the critic, "This will never do!"

Dr. Thornton, adds Gilchrist,

Had in his various undertakings been munificent to artists, to an extent which brought him to poverty. But he had no knowledge of art, and despite kind intentions was disposed to take his publishers' view. However, it fortunately happened that, meeting several artists at Aders's table—Lawrence, James Ward, Linnell, and others—conversation fell on the Virgil. All present expressed warm admiration of Blake's art, and of those designs and woodcuts in particular. . . . The contemplated sacrifice of the blocks already cut was averted. The three other designs had, however, been cut by another, nameless, hand : those illustrative of the three "comparisons" in the last stanza but one of Philips's *Pastorals*.

Dr. Thornton introduced Blake's blocks with this apology :

The illustrations of this English Pastoral are by the famous *Blake*, the illustrator of Young's *Night Thoughts* and Blair's *Grave*, who designed and engraved them himself. This is mentioned, as they display less of art than of genius, and are much admired by some eminent painters.

Dr. Thornton also employed Blake to make etchings from antique busts. "Rees" had already given him somewhat similar work, for the article on "Sculpture" in his *Encyclopædia*. Gilchrist says :

One example selected (for Rees) was the Laocoön, which carried our artist to the Royal Academy's antique school for the purpose of making a drawing from the cast of that group. "What, you here, *Meesther Blake!*" said Keeper Fuseli ; "we ought to come and learn of you, not you of us." Blake took his place with the students and exulted over his work, says Mr. Tatham, like a young disciple, meeting his old friend Fuseli's congratulations and kind remarks with cheerful, simple joy.

Gilchrist's omission of many interesting pieces of Blake biography which are inserted here from Tatham's manuscript sketch is only the more surprising because of this reference to Tatham. Equally surprising is the absence of all notice of Blake's most remarkable engraving, a Laocoön made from this drawing that differs in outline very little from the plate in Rees, but that in style of execution is altogether unlike it. Blake's plate is done in the artistic style of a "drawing on copper," without the least conventionality. All that he had learned from Basire is dropped at last. Its fault, besides a careless and round-lined rendering of the form of the figures, is that the shading makes the statue so dark that it seems a bronze. The plate in Rees is all rendered in dotted "half-tone" outline, as are the other figures, the Apollo, and so forth, which Blake must have drawn when he drew the Laocoön. It is hardly credible that they are Blake's at all. He must have foamed at the mouth while doing them. They suggest Cromek. But what makes the Laocoön most interesting is that he took his shaded plate (presumably after it had been rejected by the publishers) and covered every open space in it with little prose aphorisms on art, which are printed in type in vol. i. of the Chatto and Windus edition of his Works. They are facsimiled in the Quaritch edition.

Blake's views on Dr. Thornton's religion were as hostile as Dr. Thornton's views on his wood engravings. It happened — though over this also Gilchrist has drawn a discreet veil of silence—that Dr. Thornton published, about seven years later, during the last year that Blake lived, a pamphlet, stitched in blue paper, about the Lord's Prayer. It was quarto size, and Blake covered the wide margin of the paper with pencilled comments which show that it would be desirable, if possible, to collect *all* the books that he had during the close of his life.

Dr. Thornton's scholarly observations he describes thus:

This is saying the Lord's Prayer backwards, which, they say, raises the Devil.

Dr. Thornton having attempted a fresh translation of his own, Blake expands it, putting in what he conceives to be the ideas left out, but not left unthought, by Dr. Thornton. The effect is inconceivably blasphemous, until one examines it closely and sees that it is just what a mystic might suppose a matter-of-fact man's view of the meaning of this prayer would be, if he were sufficiently complex-minded to draw all possible ignominious and matter-of-fact inferences from his matter-of-factness, which, of course, no one ever does. Blake calls his indignant paraphrase

Doctor Thornton's Tory translation, translated out of its disguise in the classical or Scotch language into the vulgar English.

Our Father Augustus Cæsar who art in these thy substantial astronomical, telescopic heavens, holiness to thy name or title, and reverence to thy shadow.

Thy kingship come upon earth ; then in heaven.

Give us day by day our real, substantial, taxed, money - bought bread. Deliver us from the Holy Ghost, and everything that cannot be taxed. Forgive us all debts and taxes between Cæsar and us, and deliver us from poverty in Jesus.

Lead us not to read the Bible, but let our Bible be Virgil and Shakespeare.

For thine is the kingship, or allegoric godship, and the power, or war, and the glory, or law, ages after ages, in thy descendants, for God is only an allegory of kings and nothing else. Amen.

Blake is not attempting to make fun. In this rather

clumsy but intelligible paraphrase he is too angry to try to be witty. He writes on Dr. Thornton's title-page:

I look on this as the most malignant and artful attack upon the kingdom of Jesus by the classical learned, through the instrumentality of Dr. Thornton. The Greek and Roman classics is the Antichrist. I say *is* and not *are* as most expressive, and correct too.

To Dr. Thornton's remark that the Bible is a difficult book and not understood by the unlearned, Blake says—

Christ and His Apostles were illiterate men. Caiaphas, Pilate, and Herod were learned.

Blake, whether learned or not, is at least irrelevant. Another attempt at a hit is—

If morality was Christianity, Socrates was the Saviour.

This is repeated from the Laocoön plate. Dr. Thornton mentions Dr. Johnson. Blake notes—

The beauty of the Bible is that the most ignorant and simple minds understand it best. Was Johnson hired to pretend to religious terrors while he was an infidel, or how was it?

Nicholas Breakspear, the only Englishman who was ever made Pope (who was choked by a fly in the fifth year of his pontificate), composed a version of the Lord's Prayer in rhyme, that English children might learn it. He took a symbolic view that would have pleased Blake, even of the daily bread, praying—

> That holy bread that lasteth ay
> Thou send it ous this ilke day.

With regard to the crucifixion and our duty of considering and pondering upon that, Blake says in his marginal notes to Dr. Thornton—

The only thing for Baconian and Newtonian Philosophers to consider is this—whether Jesus did not suffer Himself to be mocked by Cæsar's soldiers willingly. To consider this to all eternity will be comment enough.

Mere jibes follow. Some are directed at Dr. Thornton's heaven (because he seems to look for it outside himself) as a "heaven seen through a lawful telescope." "The Holy Ghost and whatever cannot be taxed is unlawful and witchcraft." He puns on the word "spirit," and suggests that there *is* a kind that can be taxed, and so made "lawful."

Dr. Thornton, resenting the thoughtless and parrot-like repetition which is taught to children as saying the Lord's Prayer, observes, " Men from their childhood have been accustomed to mouth the Lord's Prayer."

Blake will not take it as it is meant.   He notes—

It is learned that mouth, not the vulgar.

Blake suggests a prose meaning of a purely free-trade, if not even socialistic description, if we must needs have one—

Give us the bread that is our due by taking away money, or a price, or a tax upon what is common to all in thy kingdom.

As for the " which art in heaven," Blake notes—

Who, that, and *which* are equally right, and Basileia (he writes it in Greek letters) is not kingdom, but kingship.

He suggests another paraphrase to Dr. Thornton's expressions, or another expression of his views—

I, Nature, Hermaphroditic Priest and King, live in the real, substantial, natural Born Men, and (assert) that spirit is the ghost of matter, and God is the ghost of Priest and King, who exist wherever God exists, not except from the effluvia.

He draws some more inferences which Dr. Thornton might not have countersigned :

··· Here is . . . (at this point are one or perhaps two words, but quite illegible), and two names which are too holy to be written.   Thus we see that the real God is the Goddess Nature, and that God creates nothing but what can be touched, and weighed, and taxed, and measured.   All else is heresy against Cæsar, Virgil's only God.   For all this we thank Dr. Thornton.

Here follows one more note, valuable as an interpretation of Blake's technical and philosophic use of the word Female (which he applies not as meaning a woman at all).   " Dim at the best," says Dr. Thornton, " are the conceptions we have of a Supreme Being who, as it were, keeps the human race in suspense, neither discovering nor hiding himself."   Blake simply notes, " A Female God," and we think of " Nobodaddy."

" The female will " (Blake says elsewhere " of which there is none in Heaven ") is to converse concerning weight and distance in the wilds of Newton and Locke " (*Jerusalem*, page 34, line 40, and elsewhere).

This pamphlet of Dr. Thornton belongs to the Linnell brothers.

For the more positive side of Blake's ideas about salvation, apart from distinctive criticism of the materialistic Christianity which he strikes at here through Dr. Thornton, we naturally turn to the poem where he tells us to look for it—*Milton*.

The reader of *Milton* will ask himself fifty times how this book relates to eternal salvation, and why the "words" of it should be "marked" as doing so.

The end of *Jerusalem* gives a hint.

The "visions of time and space" which man saw in his deadly sleep of six thousand years are, of course, "the vast form of nature," and, of course, are like "a serpent." Line 12 of page 96 compares with line 80 of page 89, and the same line where it is repeated in *Vala*, Night III, line 101.

The *self* of false forgiveness "is to be annihilated, as we see by the lines on one of the pictures in *Milton*."

Luvah is told to "go die the death of man for Vala, the sweet wanderer," in line 66 of page 29 of *Jerusalem*.

"Man cannot exist without mysterious offering of self for another" (*Jerusalem*, page 90, line 20).

Self is disapproval, censoriousness, and this means the desire to cling to a little self-conscious virtue. It is annihilated when replaced by love, and that redeems the weak, who are loved instead of being found fault with. This is the last page of *Jerusalem* and all *Milton* in a few words.

The most essential passages in *Milton*, those which explain Blake's repeated assurance to any reader that, his salvation being the subject of the poem, he ought to mark its words, are in the ninth page.

Satan stands for the attractiveness, especially the sexual attractiveness (called *precious stones* in the symbology; compare *Jerusalem*, page 59, line 1, and page 96, line 12) of Nature. His Druid sons are the same as Albion's on account of the commingling of the selfhood of Albion and Satan at Albion's darkening after he has fallen and closed his western gate — an act related often, once at the end of page 29. It causes the death of Luvah, who dies like the Saviour, who also dies *in* him and his robes of blood. A portion of this is told in *Jerusalem*, page 89, lines 65, 70. The 80th line of the same page, being the same as the 101st of the Third Night of *Vala*, sheds a little more light on the connection of the mass of symbols.

The class of Satan is called the elect, and he is created morning by morning and is the pet son of Enitharmon (Space) and dwells where God does *not* dwell, in that void, for the region of nature in art is void of symbolic imagination. The contrasted doctrines are found in the dramatic speech in *Jerusalem*, page 23, line 29. Taking the word "feminine" as meaning materialistic imagination, not the kind Blake calls "human existence itself," this passage and *Milton*, page 9, lines 7 to 26, help one another. With the remembrance that all these names stand for real human qualities, and that the myth contains the earliest psychology of Christianity of which we have any record—a kind destroyed with Gnosticism by the Roman Church, and also not forgetting that this was written by a man brought up on the latest kind, that of Swedenborg, Blake's own words will be found more lucid and explanatory than any note. Page 24 of *Jerusalem*, particularly from line 23 onwards, must be read with this, and also page 25 of *Jerusalem*, for what is newer (in literature) even than Swedenborg, though consonant with what is oldest in faith.

The word "feminine" in the prose sentences at the end of page 27 is also explanatory.

That bodily love must not be a rejoicing, but a licensed privilege, to be taken as grimly as possible, with the sole intention to produce offspring, with as little enthusiasm as may be, is what Blake was taught by his modest wife to think "morality" meant, his parents having shown him that it must include a complete absence of vision also. Page 36, lines 41 to 48, showed what Blake had to teach Catherine Bouchier of the larger purity.

Lines 25 and 27 of page 41 of *Jerusalem* are a further revelation; also page 42, lines 37 to 45. What is told in lines 35, 36 of page 43 naturally follows. Mystically, lines on Ulro, 21, 22 of page 44, and on Jerusalem, lines 38, 40, help.

All page 49 is particularly explanatory, lines 28 and 29, 46, 66, and 75 in especial. Line 11 of the next page recalls the first part of line 30 of page 44.

Knowing what we know of Blake's idea of "sin" (page 30, line 44), line 25 of page 50 turns out to be the very last thing we should have expected, from what people still tell about him, for it is a defence of public modesty.

On the other hand, in higher life modesty is a sin, however sweet and lovely as an indulgence (page 53, line 11). We are here in the region of symbolism again.

2 B

Of the difference between forgiveness and atonement, page 61 of *Jerusalem*, lines 15, 25, are the most emphatic, and must be read with lines 20 to 27 of page 96.

Lines 18 to 20 of page 62 of *Jerusalem* help the difficulty of the 9th page of *Milton* also.

What may be called the ultimate of Blake's theology on the Christian side is to be found in lines 21 and 22 of page 75 of *Jerusalem*, which are excessively dangerous reading to a hasty eye. The prose line 15 of page 27 is perhaps the closest to what is usually called "salvation," however. While on creation, line 34 of page 83 is the most emphatic and clear, with lines 6 to 8 of page 85, and line 42 of 86, and line 52 of page 88.

Let line 34 of page 90 be put up visibly as a warning and, for those to whom it is of use, line 34 of page 91, and the Miltonic trouble about atonement and the Satanic paradox will be evident enough, perhaps, as parts of that Real Blake whom we are seeking to make live once more, without further intrusion of the interpreter.

CHAPTER XXXII

MARGINAL NOTES [1] TO THE 'DISCOURSES' OF SIR JOSHUA REYNOLDS, 1798

(*On title-page.*) "This Man was Hired to Depress Art." This is the opinion of Will. Blake. My proofs of this opinion are given in the following notes.

(*At foot of page.*) Advice to the popes who succeeded to the age of Rafail (*sic*)—

> Degrade first the Arts, if you'd Mankind Degrade,
> Hire Idiots to Paint with cold light and not shade.
> Give High Price for the worst, leave the best in disgrace,
> And with Labours of Ignorance fill every place.

(*On fly-leaf.*) Having spent the vigour of my youth and genius under the oppression of Sir Joshua and his gang of cunning hired knaves, without employment, and, as much as could possibly be, without bread, the reader must expect to read in all my remarks on these books nothing but indignation and resentment. While Sir Joshua was rolling in riches, Barry was poor and unemployed except by his own energy. Mortimer was called a madman, and only portrait painting applauded and rewarded by the rich and great. Reynolds and Gainsborough blotted and blurr'd one against the other and divided all the English world between them. Fuseli, indignant, almost hid himself. I am hid.

(*On table of contents.*) The arts and sciences are the destruction of tyrannies or bad government. Why should a good government endeavour to depress what is its chief and only support.

To : "Much copying discountenanced."

Blake : To learn the language of art, copy for ever is my rule.

(*At foot of first page of table of contents.*)

Blake : The foundation of empire is art and science. Remove them, or degrade them, and the empire is no more. Empire follows art, not *vice versa* as Englishmen suppose.

---

[1] The date of these is either 1820, when Blake was sixty-three, as he says in a verse written to Discourse I, or in 1810, when most of the epigrams on the same subject were written in the MS. book, when he was fifty-three. The epigrams in the MS. book suggest that the notes were written in 1810, but since Blake himself dates them 1820, we must suppose they were written in the mood of his notes to Dr. Thornton's Lord's Prayer, and in the same year—unless the epigram alone was added in 1820 by an afterthought as already suggested, or, what is really far more probable, "aged sixty-three" in its last line is a mere slip of the pen, and Blake meant "aged fifty-three," which was the fact.

(At foot of table.)

On peut dire que le Pape Lion Xme en encourageant les Etudes donna les armes contre lui-même. J'ai oui dire à un Seigneur Anglais qu'il avait vu une lettre du Seigneur Polus, ou de la Pole, depuis Cardinal, à ce Pape : dans laquelle on le fêlicitant sur ce qu'il etendait le progrès de Science en Europe, il l'avertissait *qu'il etait dangereux de rendre les hommes trop savants.* Voltaire, *Mœurs (et l'Esprit) des Nations.* (?) Tom. 4.

O Englishmen, why are you still of this foolish Cardinal's opinion ?

(On fly-leaf—opposite Dedication to the King, and over it.) Who will Dare to Say that Polite Art is Encouraged or Either Wished, or Tolerated in a Nation where the Society for the Encouragement of Art Suffered Barry to give them his labour for nothing. A Society Composed of the Flower of the English Nobility and Gentry——Suffering an Artist to Starve while he Supported Really what They under Pretence of Encouraging were Endeavouring to Depress.—Barry told me that while he did that Work he Lived on Bread and Apples. O Society for the Encouragement of Art, O King and Nobility of England, Where have you hid Fuseli's Milton ? Is Satan troubled at his exposure.

The Bible says that Cultivated Life existed First. Uncultivated Life came afterwards from Satan's Hirelings. Necessaries, Accommodation, and Ornaments are the whole of Life. Satan took away Ornament first, next he took away Accommodations, and then he became Lord and Master of Necessaries.

(This is written as note to the statement in the dedication that " the regular progress of cultivated life is from necessaries to accommodations, from accommodations to ornaments.")

" To give advice to those who are contending for Royal liberality has been for some years the duty of my station in the Academy "—says Reynolds.

To this, Blake : Liberality ! We want no liberality. We want a Fair Price and proportionate value, and a General Demand for Art.

(At foot of page.) Let not the Nation where Less than Nobility is the Reward Pretend that Art is encouraged by that Nation. Act is First in Intellectuality, and ought to be First in Nations.

(At head of account of Reynolds's life.) Invention depends altogether upon Execution or Organisation ; as that is right or wrong, so is the Invention perfect or imperfect. Whoever is set to undermine the Execution of Art is set to destroy Art. Michael Angelo's Art depends on Michael Angelo's Execution Altogether.

To : " Raffaelle appeared to him superior to the most illustrious names."

Blake : Why, then, did he not follow Rafael's Track ?

To : " The better taste of Reynolds put an end to Hudson's reign."

Blake : Hudson drew correctly.

To a long account of how first impressions of Raffaelle at the Vatican disappointed Reynolds and other students and visitors.

Blake : Men who have been Educated with the Works of Venetian Artists under their Eyes cannot see Rafael, unless they are born with determinate Organs.

I am happy that I cannot say that Rafael Ever was from my Earliest Childhood hidden from Me. I saw, and I knew immediately the difference between Rafael and Rubens.

> Some look to see the sweet Outlines,
> And beauteous Forms that Love does wear :
> Some look to find out Patches, Paint,
> Bracelets and Stays and Powdered Hair.

To : " I found that those persons only, who, from natural imbecility, appeared to be incapable of ever relishing those divine performances, made pretensions to instantaneous raptures on first beholding them."

Blake : Here are Mocks on those who saw Rafael.

To : "Not relishing them" (the works of Raffaelle) "as I was conscious I ought to have done . . . I felt my ignorance and stood abashed."

Blake : A liar. He never was Abashed in his Life, and never felt his Ignorance.

To : "I viewed them again and again. I even affected to feel their merit and admire them more than I really did. In a short time a new taste and new conceptions began to dawn upon me, and I was convinced that I had originally formed a false opinion of the perfection of art, and that this great painter was entitled to the high rank which he holds in the estimation of the world."

Blake : All this concession is to prove that Genius is Acquired as follows on the next page.

(On next page.) " I am now clearly of opinion that a relish for the higher excellencies of art is an acquired taste. . . . We are often ashamed of our apparent dullness ; as if it were to be expected that our minds, like tinder, should instantly catch fire from the divine spark of Raffaelle's Genius."

Blake : A Mock.

To : "The excellence of his style is not on the surface, but lies deep, and at the first view is seen but mistily."

Blake : A mock.

To : " It is the florid style which strikes at once, and captivates the eye for a time."

Blake : A lie.

The Florid Style such as the Venetian or Flemish never struck Me at Once nor At All. The style that Strikes the Eye is the True Style, But a Fool's Eye Not to be a Criterion.

To : "I consider *general copying* as a *delusive style of industry.*"

Blake (after underlining the words) : Here he Condemns Generalising, which he almost always Approves and Recommends.

To : "How incapable of producing anything of their own those are who have spent most of their time in making finished copies. . . ."

Blake : Finished. What does he Mean ? Niggling Without the Correct and Definite Outline. If he means that Copying Correctly is a hindrance, he is a Liar, for that is the only School to the Language of Art.

To : " It is the thoughts expressed in the works of Michael Angelo, Correggio, Raffaelle, Parmegiano, and perhaps some of the old Gothick masters, and not the invention of Pietro di Cortona, Carlo Maratti, Luca Giordano, and others whom I might mention, that we seek after with avidity."

Blake : Here is an Acknowledgement of all that I could wish. But if it is True—Why are we to be told that Masters who could Think had not the Judgment to Perform the Inferior parts of Art, as Reynolds artfully calls them. But that we are to learn to Think from Great

Masters, and to Learn to Perform from Underlings? Learn to Design from Rafael, and to execute from Rubens?

(*More is added, but cut off by the binder.*)

To a description of "Mr. Mudge, the clergyman," often seen at Sir Joshua's house, as a "learned and venerable old man," very conversant in the Platonick Philosophy, and very fond of that method of Philosophising.

Blake: Hang villainy.

To an account of two different reports, one saying that Dr. Johnson and the other that Burke had written Reynolds's *Discourses*.

Blake: The Contradictions in Reynolds's *Discourses* are Strong Presumption that they are the work of several Hands. But this is no proof that Reynolds did not write them. The Man, either Painter or Philosopher, who Learns or Acquires all he knows from Others, Must be full of Contradictions.

To a note on Mr. Moser, Keeper of the Royal Academy, of whom it is said that he "might in every sense be called the Father of the present race of Artists."

Blake: I was once looking over the Prints from Rafael and Michael Angelo in the Library of the Royal Academy. Moser came to me and said, "You should not study these old Hard, Stiff, and Unfinished Works of Art. Stay a little, and I will show you what you should Study." He then went and took down Le Brun's and Rubens' Galleries. How did I secretly rage. I also spoke my mind.

(*A line follows, cut off by the binder, so as to be illegible.*)

I said to Moser, These things that you call Finished are not even Begun; how can they then be Finished? The Man who does not know the Beginning never can know the End of Art.

To the statement of Sir Joshua that he "consoled himself by remarking that these ready inventors are extremely apt to acquiesce *in imperfection.*"

Blake (*after underlining* "*imperfection*"): Villainy—a Lie.

To: "How difficult it is for the artist who possesses this faculty (invention) to guard against carelessness and commonplace invention is well known, and in a kindred art Metastasio is an eminent instance, who always complained of the great difficulty he found in attaining correctness in consequence of having been in his youth an *Improvisatore.*"

Blake: I do not believe this anecdote.

To: "There is nothing in our art which enforces such continued exertion and circumspection as attention to the general effect of the whole. It requires much study and much practice; it requires the painter's entire mind: whereas the *parts* may be finishing by nice touches, while his mind is engaged on other matters: he may even hear a play or a novel read without much disturbance."

Blake: A Lie. Working up of Effect is more an operation of Indolence than the making out of the Parts as far as Greatest is more than Least. I speak here of Rembrandt's and Rubens's and Reynolds's Effects. Real effect is Making out of Parts, and it is Nothing Else but That.

To an editor's note on the lost secrets of colour-mixing known to the old Masters.

Blake: Oil colours will not do. Why are we told that Reynolds was a great colourist and yet inferior to the Venetians?

To an editor's note on a list of prices obtained by Reynolds, stating that being "without a rival he continues to add thousands to thousands."

Blake : How much did Barry get ?

To : "Many of the pictures of Rubens being sold in 1783, in consequence of certain religious houses being suppressed by the Emperor, he (Reynolds) again in that year visited Antwerp and Brussels, and devoted several days to contemplating the productions of that great painter."

Blake : If Reynolds had really admired Mich. Angelo he never would have followed Rubens.

To : "His (Reynolds's) deafness was originally occasioned by a cold he caught in the Vatican, by painting for a long time near a stove, by which the damp vapours of that edifice were attracted, and affected his head. When in company with only one person he heard very well without the aid of a trumpet."

Blake : A Sly Dog. So can everybody ; but bring Two People, and the Hearing is Stopped.

To a note from "Retaliation," a poem by Dr. Goldsmith, in which he has drawn the characters of several of his friends in the form of epitaphs to be placed on their tombs—with the quotation—

> Here Reynolds is laid, and to tell you my mind,
> He has not left a wiser or better behind.
> His pencil was striking, resistless, and grand ;
> His manners were gentle, complying, and bland ;
> Still born to improve us in every part,
> His pencil our faces, his manners our heart.
> To coxcombs averse, yet most civilly steering,
> When they judged without skill he was still hard of hearing ;
> When they talked of their Raffaelles, Correggios, and stuff,
> He shifted his trumpet and only took snuff.

Blake : Such Men as Goldsmith ought not to have been Acquainted with such Men as Reynolds.

To an editor's note saying of Reynolds : "It is clear from his manners and his writings that in the character of his eloquence he would have resembled the perspicuous and elegant Lælius, rather than the severe and vehement Galba."

Blake : He certainly would have been more like a fool than a wise man.

To : "He was a great generaliser . . . generalising, and classification is the great glory of the human mind."

Blake : To generalise is to be an Idiot. To Particularise is the Alone Distinction of Merit.—General Knowledges are those Knowledges that Idiots possess.

To : "Such was his love of his art and such his ardour to excel that he often declared he had, during the greater part of his life, laboured as hard with his pencil as any mechanick working at his trade for bread."

Blake : The Man who does not Labour more than the Hireling must be a poor Devil.

To a quotation from Pope, appropriate to " the ferocious and enslaved Republick of France," ended in these words :

> They led their wild desires to woods and caves
> And thought that all but savages were slaves.

Blake :

> When France got Free, Europe, 'twixt fools and knaves,
> Were savage first to France, and after—slaves.

To a note on the prosperity of England, stating that the national trade having doubled between 1784 and 1796, amounted then to THIRTY MILLIONS, and that the price of land, war notwithstanding, was nearly as high as in times of profound peace, and that these FACTS ought to be sounded from one end of England to the other, and furnish a complete answer to all the SEDITIOUS DECLAMATIONS that have been or shall be made on this subject.

Blake : This whole Book was written to some Political Purposes.

To the account of Reynolds's death in 1792.

Blake :

> When Sir Joshua Reynolds died
> All Nature was degraded ;
> The King dropped a Tear into the Queen's Ear ;
> And all his Pictures Faded.

To the account of his funeral, where the pall was borne up by three Dukes, two Marquises, and five other noblemen.

Blake : A Mock.

To : "Sir Joshua Reynolds was, on very many accounts, one of the most memorable men of his time."

Blake : Is not this a Manifest Lie ?

To : "In taste, in grace, in happy invention, in the richness and harmony of colouring, he was equal to the great masters of the renowned ages."

Blake : Barry Painted a Picture for Burke, equal to Rafael or Mich. Ang. or any of the Italians.   Burke used to show this Picture to his friends and say, "I gave Twenty Guineas for the horrible Daub, and if any man would give . . ."

(*The rest cut off by the binder.*)

Such was Burke's patronage of Art and Science.

(*So end the notes to Reynolds's Memoir.   Then, on the fly-leaf of the dedication of the Discourses to the Members of the Royal Academy, and on the blank spaces of that dedication :*)

Blake : I consider Reynolds's *Discourses* to the Royal Academy as the Simulations of the Hypocrite who smiles particularly when he means to Betray.   His Praise of Rafael is like the Hysteric Smile of Revenge.   His Softness and Candour the hidden trap, and the poisoned feast.   He praises Michel Angelo for qualities which Michel Angelo abhorred : and He blames Rafael for the only qualities which Rafael Valued.   Whether Reynolds knew what he was doing is nothing to me : the Mischief is the same whether a man does it Ignorantly or Knowingly.   I always considered true Art and true Artists to be particularly Insulted and Degraded by the Reputation of these *Discourses*, as much as they were Degraded by the Reputation of Reynolds's Paintings, and that such Artists as Reynolds are at all times hired by the Satans for the Depression of Art.   A Pretence of Art : To destroy Art.

The Neglect of such as Milton in a Country pretending to the Encouragement of Art is Sufficient Apology for my Vigorous Indignation, if indeed the Neglect of My own Powers had not been.   Ought not the Employers of Fools to be Execrated in future Ages. They Will and Shall. Foolish Men, your own real Greatness depends on your Encouragement of the Arts, and your Fall will depend on their Neglect and Depression. What you Fear is your true Interest. Leo. X was advised not to encourage the Arts. He was too wise to take this Advice.

DISCOURSE I

The Rich Men of England form themselves into a Society to Sell and Not to Buy Pictures. The Artist who does not throw his Contempt on such Trading Exhibitions, does not know either his own Interest or his Duty.

> When Nations grow Old the Arts grow Cold,
> And Commerce settles on every Tree ;
> And the Poor and the Old can live upon Gold,
> For all are Born Poor, Aged Sixty-Three.

To the commencement of the first Discourse.

Blake : Reynolds's opinion was that Genius May be Taught, and that all Pretence to Inspiration is a Lie and a Deceit, to say the least of it. For if it is a Deceit the whole Bible is Madness. This opinion originates in the Greeks calling the Muses Daughters of Memory.

The Enquiry in England is not whether a Man has Talents and Genius ! But whether he is Passive and Poetic and a Virtuous Ass, and obedient to Noblemen's Opinions in Art and Science. If he is, he is a Good Man : if Not, he must be Starved.

To : " After so much has been done by His Majesty, etc."

Blake : 3 Farthings.

To : " Raffaele, it is true, had not the advantage of studying in an Academy, but all Rome, and the works of Michael Angelo in particular, were to him an Academy. On the sight of the Capella Sistina, he immediately from a dry Gothick, and even insipid manner, which attends to the minute accidental discriminations of particular and individual objects, assumed that grand style of painting which improves partial representation by the general and invariable ideas of nature."

Blake : Minute Discrimination is not Accidental. All Sublimity is founded on Minute Discrimination.

I do not believe that Rafael taught Mich. Angelo, or that Mich. Ang. taught Rafael, any more than I believe that the Rose teaches the Lily how to grow, or the Apple tree teaches the Pear tree how to bear Fruit. I do not believe the tales of Anecdote when they militate against Individual Character.

To : " I would chiefly recommend that an implicit obedience to the *Rules of Art*, as established by the practice of the GREAT MASTERS, should be exacted from the *young* Students. That those Models, which have passed through the approbation of ages, should be considered by them as perfect and infallible guides ; as subjects for their imitation, not their criticism."

Blake : Imitation is criticism.

(On a page on the importance of directing the studies of youth at first to what is substantially necessary for their artistic knowledge, lest they should pick up brilliant and superficial tricks early on, and not have the courage to go back afterwards, and learn essentials.)

To: "A facility in composing . . . a masterly handling . . . are captivating qualities to young minds."

Blake: I consider the following sentence is Supremely Insolent, for the following Reasons :—Why this Sentence should begin by the words, A Facility in composing, I cannot tell, unless it was to cast a stigma upon Real Facility in composition by assimilating it with a Pretence to and Imitation of Facility in Execution. Or are we to understand him to mean that Facility in composing is a Frivolous pursuit? A Facility in composing is the Greatest Power of Art, and Belongs to None but the Greatest Artists, the Most Minutely Discriminating and Determinate.

(*To the next pages which are about the "useless industry" that makes executants of mere boys with mechanical facility, about its danger as a source of corruption and error as shown in Foreign Academies, about frivolousness of the ambition of a student who wants to show dashing effect, not to attain exactness—and about a warning against the impetuosity of youth seeking short paths to excellence, and needing to be told that labour is the price of fame, and that however great their genius, there is no easy method for them to become painters.*)

Blake: Mechanical Excellence is the only Vehicle of Genius.
This is all False and Self-Contradictory.
Execution is the Chariot of Genius.
This is all Self-Contradictory; Truth and Falsehood Jumbled Together.

To: "When we read the lives of the most eminent Painters, every page informs us that no part of their time was spent in dissipation. . . . They pursued their studies . . ."

Blake: The *Lives of Painters* say that Rafael Died of Dissipation. Idleness is one Thing and Dissipation is Another. He who has Nothing to Dissipate Cannot Dissipate. The Weak Man may be Virtuous Enough, but will Never be an Artist.
Painters are noted for being Dissipated and Wild.

To: "When they (the old masters) conceived a subject, they first made a variety of sketches, then a finished drawing of the whole ; after that a more correct drawing of every separate part,—head, hands, feet, and pieces of drapery ; they then painted the picture, and *after all re-touched it from the life.*"

Blake (*after underlining*): This is False.

To: "A Student is not always advancing because he is employed ; he must apply his strength to that part of the art where the real difficulties lie. . . . The Students, instead of vying with each other which shall have the readiest hand, should be taught to contend who shall have the purest and most correct outline."

Blake: Excellent.

To: "I must beg to submit . . . to Visitors . . . a matter of very great consequence. . . . The students never draw exactly from the living models which they have before them . . . drawing rather what a figure ought to be than what it appears. . . . This obstacle has stopped the progress of many young men. . . . I very much doubt whether a habit of drawing correctly what we see will not give a proportionable power of drawing correctly what we imagine."

Blake: This is Admirably Said. Why does he not always allow as much.

To: "He who endeavours to copy nicely the figure before him not only acquires a habit of exactness and precision, but is continually advancing in his knowledge of the human figure."

Blake: Excellent.

(*At the close of Discourse I.*)

Blake: The Laboured Works of Journeymen employed by Correggio, Titian, Veronese, and all the Venetians, ought not to be shown to the young Artist as the Works of original conception, any more than the Engravings of Strange, Bartolozzi, or Woollett. They are Works of Manual Labour.

DISCOURSE II

(*At the head of Discourse II.*)

Blake: What is laying up materials but copying.

To : " When the Artist is once enabled to express himself . . . he must collect subjects for expression . . . amass a stock of ideas . . . learn all that has been known and done before . . . perfections which lie scattered amongst various masters . . . united in one general idea . . . to enlarge his imagination."

Blake: After having been a Fool, a Student is to amass a Stock of Ideas, and, knowing himself to be a Fool, he is to assume the Right to put other Men's Ideas into his Foolery.

To : " Though the Student will not resign himself blindly to any single authority when he may have the advantage of consulting many, he must still be afraid of trusting to his own judgment, and of deviating into any track where he cannot find the footsteps of some former master."

Blake: Instead of Following One Great Master, he is to follow a Great Many Fools.

To : " A Student unacquainted with the attempts of former adventurers is always apt to overrate his own abilities ; to mistake the most trifling excursions for discoveries of moment, and every coast new to him for a new-found country."

Blake: Contemptible mocks.

To : " The productions of such (*i.e.* uneducated) minds are seldom distinguished by an air of originality ; they are anticipated in their happiest efforts ; and if they are found to differ in anything from their predecessors, it is only in irregular sallies and trifling conceits."

Blake: Thus Reynolds Depreciates the Efforts of Inventive Genius. Trifling Conceits are better than Colouring without any meaning at all.

To : "How incapable those are of producing anything of their own, who have spent much of their time in making finished copies, is known to all who are conversant with our art."

Blake: That is most false, for no one can ever design till he has learned the language of art by making many finished copies both of Nature and art, and of whatever comes in his way from earliest childhood. The difference between a bad artist and a good one is : the bad artist seems to copy a great deal ; the good one really does copy a great deal.

To : "The great use of copying, if it be at all useful, seems to be in learning to colour ; yet even colouring will never be obtained by servilely copying the model before you."

Blake: Contemptible. Servile copying is the great merit of copying.

To: "Following these rules, and using these precautions, when you have clearly and distinctly learned in what good colouring consists, you cannot do better than have recourse to nature herself, who is always at hand, and in comparison of whose true splendour the best coloured pictures are but faint and feeble."

Blake: Nonsense. Every eye sees differently. As the eye, such the object.

To: "Instead of copying the touches of those great masters, copy only their conceptions. . . . Labour to invent on their general principles."

Blake: General Principles again! Unless you consult particulars you cannot even know or see Michael Angelo or Raphael or anything else.

To: "But as mere enthusiasm will carry you but a little way. . . ."

Blake: Mere enthusiasm is the All in All! Bacon's philosophy has ruined England. Bacon is only Epicurus over again.

To: "Few have been taught to any purpose who have not been their own teachers."

Blake: True.

To: "A facility of drawing, like that of playing upon a musical instrument, cannot be acquired but by an infinite number of acts."

Blake: True.

To: "I would particularly recommend that after your return from the Academy . . . you would endeavour to draw the figure from memory."

Blake: Good advice.

To: "But while I mention the port-crayon as the student's constant companion, he must still remember that the pencil is the instrument by which he must hope to obtain eminence."

Blake: Nonsense.

To: "The Venetian and Flemish schools, which owe much of their fame to colouring, have enriched the cabinets of the collectors of drawings with very few examples."

Blake: Because they could not draw.

To: "Correggio and Baroccio have left few, if any, drawings behind them. And in the Flemish school, Rubens and Vandyck made their drawings for the most part in colour or chiaroscuro. . . . Not but that many finished drawings are made under the names of those artists. More, however, are undoubtedly the work either of engravers or their scholars, who copied their works."

Blake: All the paintings said to be by these men are the laboured productions of journey-work. They could not draw.

To: ". . . He who would have you believe that he is waiting for the inspirations of Genius is in reality at a loss how to begin, and is at last delivered of monsters with difficulty and pain."

Blake: A stroke at Mortimer.

To: "The well-grounded painter . . . is contented that all shall be as great as himself, who have undergone the same fatigue. . . ."

Blake: The man who asserts that there is no such thing as softness in art, and that everything in art is definite and determinate, has not been told this by practice, but by Inspiration and Vision, because Vision is determinate and perfect, and he copies that without fatigue. Everything being definite and determinate, softness is produced alone by comparative strength and weakness in the making out of forms. I say these things could never be found out from nature without con—— or innate science.

DISCOURSE III

(*At the head of Discourse III.*) *Blake*: A work of genius is a work "not to be obtained by the invocation of memory, and her syren daughters, but by devout prayer to that Eternal Spirit who can enrich with all utterance and knowledge, and sends out his Seraphim with the hallowed fire of his altar to touch and purify the lips of whom he pleases."—*Milton*.

The following discourse is particularly interesting to blockheads, as it endeavours to prove that there is no such thing as inspiration, and that any man of a plain understanding can, by thieving from others, become a Michael Angelo.

To: "The genuine painter . . . instead of endeavouring to amuse mankind with the minute neatness of his imitations, must endeavour to improve them by the grandeur of his ideas."

Blake: Without minute neatness of execution the sublime cannot exist. Grandeur of ideas is founded on precision of ideas.

To: "The moderns are not less convinced than the ancients of this superior power existing in their art (the power of a fixed idea of perfect beauty)."

Blake: I wish that this was true.

To: "Such is the warmth with which both the ancients and moderns speak of this divine principle of the art; but, as I have before observed, enthusiastic admiration seldom promotes knowledge. Though a student by such praise may have his attention roused, and a desire excited of running in this great career, yet it is possible that what has been said to excite may only serve to deter him. He examines his own mind and perceives there nothing of that divine inspiration with which, he is told, so many others have been favoured. He never travelled to heaven to gather new ideas, and he finds himself possessed of no other qualifications than what mere common observation and a plain understanding can confer. Thus he becomes gloomy amidst the splendour of figurative declamation, and thinks it hopeless to pursue an object which he supposes to be out of the reach of human industry."

Blake: And such is the coldness with which Reynolds speaks! And such is his enmity. Now he begins to degrade, to deny, and to mock. Enthusiastic admiration is the first principle of knowledge and its last. The man who on examining his own mind finds nothing of inspiration ought not to dare to be an artist. He is a fool, and a cunning knave, suited to the purposes of evil demons. The man who never in his mind and thoughts travelled to heaven is no artist. It is evident that Reynolds wished none but fools to be in the arts, and in order to this, he calls all others vague enthusiasts and madmen. What has reasoning to do with the art of painting? Artists who are above a plain understanding are mocked and destroyed by this President of Fools.

To: "Most people err not so much from want of capacity to find their object, as from not knowing what object to pursue."

Blake: The man who does not know what object to pursue is an idiot.

To: "This great ideal of perfection and beauty are (*sic*) not to be sought in the heavens but on the earth . . . upon every side of us . . . only to be acquired by experience."

Blake: A lie. A lie. A lie.

To: ". . . and the whole beauty and grandeur of the art consists, in my opinion, in being able to get above all . . . details of every kind."

Blake: A folly; singular and particular detail is the foundation of the sublime.

To: "The most beautiful forms have something about them like weakness—minuteness, or imperfection."

Blake: Minuteness is their whole beauty.

To: "But not every eye can perceive these blemishes. It must be an eye long used to the contemplation and comparison of these forms."

Blake: Knowledge of ideal beauty is not to be acquired. It is born with us. Innate ideas are in every man, born with him; they are truly Himself. The man who says that we have no innate ideas must be a fool and a knave, having no conscience, or innate science.

To: ". . . From reiterated experience an artist becomes possessed of the idea of a central form."

Blake: One central form composed of all other forms being granted, it does not, therefore, follow that all other forms are deformity. All forms are perfect in the poet's mind, but they are not abstracted or compounded from nature, but are from imagination.

To: "The great Bacon treats with ridicule the idea of confining proportion to rules. Says he: '. . . The painter must do it by a kind of felicity and not by rule.'"

Blake: The great Bacon he is called—I call him the little Bacon—says that everything must be done by experiment. His first principle is unbelief, and yet he says that art must be produced without such method. This is like Mr. Locke, full of self-contradiction and knavery.

What is general nature? Is there such a thing? What is general knowledge? Is there such a thing? Strictly speaking, all knowledge is particular.

To: ". . . It may be objected, there are various central forms . . . Hercules . . . Gladiator . . . Apollo."

Blake: Here he loses sight of a central form, and gets to many central forms.

To: "There is one central form belonging to the human kind at large . . . in each class there is one . . . central form . . . common form in childhood . . . common form in age."

Blake: Every class is individual. There is no end to the follies of this man. Childhood and age are equally belonging to every class.

To: ". . . highest perfection not in Hercules . . . Gladiator . . . Apollo . . . taken from all . . . activity of Gladiator . . . delicacy of Apollo . . . strength of Hercules."

Blake: Here he comes again to his central form!

To: "There is likewise a kind of symmetry or proportion which may be said to belong to deformity."

Blake: The symmetry of deformity! Here is a pretty foolery. Can any man who thinks talk so?

To: "A figure lean, or corpulent, tall or short, though deviating from beauty, may still have a certain union of the various parts which may contribute to make them, on the whole, not unpleasing."

Blake: Leanness and fatness is not deformity. But Reynolds thought character itself extravagance and deformity. Age and youth are not classes but properties of each class. So are leanness and fatness.

To: ". . . when he has reduced the variety of nature to an abstract idea . . ."

Blake: What folly!

To: "The painter must divest himself of . . . age . . . country . . . local and temporary ornaments . . . he addresses his work to people of every country and every age . . . and says with Zeuxis, *in æternitatem pingo.*"

Blake: Generalising in everything the Man would soon be a Fool, but a Cunning Fool.

To: "Albert Dürer—as Vasari has justly remarked—would have been one of the first painters of his age . . . had he been initiated into those great principles . . . practised by his contemporaries in Italy."

Blake: What does this mean? "*Would have been one of the first painters of his age!*" Albert Dürer Is! Not *would have been*. Besides, let them look at Gothic Figures, and Gothic Buildings, and not talk of Dark Ages, or of any Age. Ages are all equal, but Genius is always above The Age.

To: "Though the painter is to overlook the accidental discriminations of nature, he is to exhibit distinctly, and with precision, the general forms of things."

Blake: Here he is for Determinate, and yet for Indeterminate. Distinct General Form Cannot Exist. Distinctness is Particular, Not General.

To: "A firm and determined outline is one of the characteristics of the great style in painting, and let me add that he who possesses the knowledge of the exact form which every part of nature ought to have, will be fond of expressing that knowledge with correctness and precision in all his works."

Blake: A Noble Sentence! Here is a Sentence which overthrows all his Book.

To: "I have endeavoured to reduce the idea of beauty to general principles . . . the only means to . . . give rest and satisfaction to an inquisitive mind."

Blake: Bacon's Philosophy makes both Statesmen and Artists Fools and Knaves.

DISCOURSE IV

(*At the head of Discourse IV.*)

The Two Following Discourses are Particularly Calculated for the Setting Ignorant and Vulgar Artists as Models of Execution in Art. Let him who will follow such advice; I will not. I know that The Man's Execution is as his Conception and not better.

To: "Gentlemen, the value and rank of every art is in proportion to the mental labour employed in it, or the mental pleasure produced by it. As this principle is observed or neglected, our profession becomes either a liberal art or a mechanical trade."

Blake: Why does he not always allow This?

To: "I have formerly observed that perfect form is produced by leaving out particularities, and retaining only general ideas."

Blake : General Ideas again !

To : " Invention in painting does not imply invention of subject, for that is commonly supplied by the poet or historian."

Blake : All but Names of Persons and Places is Invention, both in Poetry and Painting.

To : " The usual and most dangerous error is on the side of minuteness."

Blake : Here is Nonsense !

To : " All smaller things, however perfect in their way, are to be sacrificed without mercy to the greater."

Blake : Sacrifice the Parts ; what becomes of the Whole ?

To : " Even in portraits the grace, and we may add the likeness, consists more in taking the general air than in observing the exact similitude of every feature."

Blake : How Ignorant ! (*Unknown commentator*—" No ; 'tis true !")

To : " A painter of portraits shows the individual likeness. A painter of history shows the man by showing his actions."

Blake : If he does not Show the Man as well as the Actions, he is a poor Artist.

To : " He cannot make his hero talk like a great man. He must make him look like one. For which reason he ought to be well studied in those circumstances which constitute dignity of appearance in real life."

Blake : Here he allows Analysis of Circumstance.

To : " Certainly nothing can be more simple than monotony, and the distinct blue, red, and yellow colours which are seen in the draperies of the Roman and Florentine schools, though they have not that harmony which is produced by a variety of broken and transparent colours, have the effect of grandeur which was intended. Perhaps these distinct colours strike the mind the more forcibly from there not being any great union between them, as martial music which is intended to arouse the nobler passions has its effect from the sudden and strongly marked transitions from one note to another, which that style of music requires. Whilst in that which is intended to move the softer passions the notes imperceptibly melt into one another."

Blake : These are Fine and Just Notions. Why does he not always allow as much ?

To : " In the same manner as the historical painter never enters into the detail of colours, so neither does he debase his conceptions with minute attention to the discriminations of drapery."

Blake : Excellent Remarks.

To : " Carlo Muratti was of opinion that the disposition of drapery was a more difficult art than that of drawing the human figure."

Blake : I do not believe that Carlo Muratti thought so, or that anybody can think so. The Drapery is formed alone by the Shape of the Naked.

To : " Some will censure me for placing Venetians in this inferior class. . . . Though I can by no means allow them to hold any rank with the nobler schools of painting, they accomplished perfectly the thing they intended . . . elegance."

Blake : They accomplished nothing. As to Elegance, they have not a Spark.

To : " Paul Veronese, although a painter of great consideration, had—contrary to the strict rules of art—in his picture of Perseus and Andromeda represented the principal figure in the shade . . . His intention . . . effect of light and shadow . . . everything sacrificed to that . . . capricious composition suited . . . style."

Blake: This is not a Satisfactory Answer. To produce an effect of True Light and Shadow is Necessary to the Ornamental Style, which altogether depends on Distinctness of Form. The Venetian ought not to be called the Ornamental Style.

To: "The powers exerted in the mechanical parts of the art have been called *the language of painters*. . . . The language of painting must be indeed allowed these masters (the Venetians)."

Blake: The language of Painters cannot be allowed them. If Reynolds says right at p. 97. He there says that the Venetian Will Not Correspond with the great style. The Greek Gems are in the Same Style as the Greek Statues.

To: "Such as suppose that the great style may be happily blended with the ornamental—that the simple, grave, and majestic dignity of Raffaelle could unite with the glow and bustle of a Paolo or Tintoret, are totally mistaken. The principles by which each is attained are so contrary to each other that they seem in my opinion impossible to exist together, as that in the same mind the most sublime ideas and the lowest sensuality should be at the same time united."

Blake: What can be better said on this Subject? But Reynolds contradicts what he says continually. He makes little Concessions that he may take Great Advantages.

To: ". . . the Venetians show extraordinary skill . . . their colouring . . . I venture to say . . . too harmonious to produce that solidity, steadiness, and simplicity of effects which heroic subjects require, and which simple or grave colours only can give to a work."

Blake: Somebody else wrote this for Reynolds. I think Barry or Fuseli wrote it—or dictated it.

To: ". . . the principal attention of Venetians, in the opinion of Michael Angelo . . . study of colour . . . neglect of ideal beauty of form . . . general censure from the sight of a picture of Titian's."

Blake: Venetian attention is to a Contempt and Neglect of Form Itself, and to the Destruction of all Form or Outline, Purposely, and Intentionally.

As if Mich. Ang. had seen but One Picture of Titian! Mich. Ang. knew and despised all that Titian could do.

On the Venetian Painter

> He makes the Lame to walk we all agree,
> But then he Strives to blind all who can see.

If the Venetian Outline was right, his Shadows would destroy it and deform its appearance.

> A pair of stays to mend the shape
> Of Crooked, Humpy Woman;
> Put on, O Venus! Now thou art
> Quite a Venetian Roman.

To: "When I speak of Venetian painters . . . I mean . . . to the exclusion of Titian. . . . There is a sort of senatorial dignity about him."

Blake: Titian, as well as other Venetians, or far from Senatorial Dignity appear to me to give always the Characters of Vulgar Stupidity. Why should Titian and the Venetians be Named in a Discourse on Art? Such Idiots are not Artists.

> Venetian! All thy Colouring is no more
> Than Boulstered Plasters on a Crooked Whore.

To: "The Venetian is indeed the most splendid of the schools of elegance."

Blake: Vulgarity and not Elegance. The Word *Elegance* ought to be applied to Forms—not Colours.

To: ". . . elaborate harmony of colouring . . . brilliancy of tints . . . soft transition . . . merely a gratification of sight. Properly cultivated where nothing higher than elegance is intended . . . unworthy . . . when work aspires to grandeur and sublimity."

Blake: Broken Colours,—Broken Lines,—and Broken Shapes are equally Subversive of the Sublime.—Well Said Enough.

To: "Rubens,—formed on Venetians . . . took figures from people before him . . . more gross than they (the Venetians) . . . all err from the same cause. Paolo introduced gentlemen, Bassano, boors of district of Bassano . . . called them patriarchs and prophets."

Blake: How can that be called the Ornamental Style of which Gross Vulgarity forms the Principal Excellence.

To: "Some inferior dexterity, — some extraordinary mechanical power is apparently that from which they seek distinction."

Blake: The words Mechanical Power should not thus be Prostituted.

To: "An History-Painter Paints man in general: a portrait painter a particular man."

Blake: A History-Painter Paints the Hero, and not Man in general, but most minutely in Particular.

To: "Thus, if a portrait painter desires to raise and improve his subject . . . he leaves out all the minute breaks and peculiarities . . . and changes the dress from a temporary fashion to one more permanent which has annexed to it no ideas of meanness from being familiar to us—etc."

Blake: Folly! Of what consequence is it to the Arts what a Portrait Painter does.

To: "Of those who have practised the composite style,—the foremost is Correggio."

Blake: There is no such thing as a composite style.

To: ". . . The errors of genius."

Blake: Genius has no Error. It is Ignorance that is Error.

To: "On the whole it seems to me that there is but one presiding principle which regulates and gives stability to every act. The works which are built on general nature live for ever."

Blake: All Equivocation is Self-Contradiction.

DISCOURSE V

(*On fly-leaf.*) *Blake*: Gainsborough told a Gentleman of Rank and Fortune that the Worst Painters always chose the Grandest Subjects. I desired the Gentleman to Set Gainsborough about one of Rafael's Grandest Subjects, Namely, Christ delivering the Keys to St. Peter, and he would find that in Gainsborough's hands it would be a Vulgar Subject of Poor Fishermen and a Journeyman Carpenter.

The following Discourse is written with the Same End in View that Gainsborough had in making the Above assertion, Namely To Represent Vulgar Artists as Models of Executive Merit.

To: "Nothing has its proper lustre but in its proper place. That which is most worthy of esteem in its proper sphere becomes an object, not of respect, but of derision, when it is forced into a higher, to which it is not suited."

Blake: Concession to Truth for the sake of Oversetting Truth.

To: "If you mean to preserve the most perfect beauty *in its most perfect state* you cannot express the passions."

Blake: What Nonsense! Passion and Expression is Beauty Itself. The Face that is Incapable of Passion and Expression is deformity Itself. Let it be Painted and Patched and Praised and Advertised for Ever, it will only be admired by Fools.

To: ". . . Cartoon and other pictures of Raffaelle where the excellent master himself may have attempted the expression of passions above the powers of art. . . ."

Blake: If Reynolds could not see varieties of Character in Rafael Others Can.

To: "The ancients . . . when they employed their art to represent Jupiter confined his character to majesty alone."

Blake: False! The Ancients were chiefly attentive to Complicated and Minute Discrimination of Character. It is the Whole of Art. Reynolds cannot bear Expression.

To: "A stature in which you endeavour to unite stately dignity, youthful elegance, and stern valour must surely possess none of these to any eminent degree."

Blake: Why not? O Poverty!

To: "The summit of excellence seems to be an assemblage of contrary qualities, but mixed in such proportions that on one part is found to counteract the other."

Blake: A Fine Jumble!

To: ". . . transcendent, commanding, and ductile genius . . . is fitter to give example than to receive instruction."

Blake: Mocks!

To: "The principal works of modern art are in *Fresco*, a mode of painting which precludes attention to minute elegancies."

Blake: This is False. Fresco Painting is the Most Minute. Fresco painting is like Miniature Painting. A Wall is a Large Ivory.

To: "Raffaelle . . . owes his reputation to fresco. . . . His easel works stand on a lower degree of estimation . . . he never aimed at such perfection as to make him an object of irritation."

Blake: Folly and Falsehood. The Man who can say that Rafael knew not the smaller beauties of the Art ought to be Condemned, and I accordingly hold Reynolds in contempt, and his critical Pretences in particular.

To: "When he painted in oil his hand seemed so cramped and confined that he lost, etc."

Blake: Rafael did as he Pleased. He who does not Admire Raffaelle's Execution does not Ever See Raphael.

To: "I have no desire to degrade Raffaelle from the high rank which, etc."

Blake: A lie!

To: "Michael Angelo considered art as consisting of little more than sculpture. . . . He never attempted those lesser elegancies or graces in art."

Blake: According to Reynolds Michael Angelo was worse Still, and Knew Nothing at all about Art as an Object of Imitation. Can any Man be such a fool as to believe that Rafael and Michael Angelo were incapable of the mere Language of Art, and that Such Idiots as Rubens, Correggio, and Titian knew how to Execute what they could not think or Invent.

To: "Along with these he rejected all the false, though specious, ornaments which disgrace the works of even the most esteemed artists."

Blake: Here is another Contradiction. If Mich. Ang. Neglected anything that Titian or Veronese did, he Rejected it for good Reasons. Sir Joshua in other places owns that the Venetian cannot Mix with the Roman and Florentine. What does he Mean when he says that Mich. Ang. and Rafael even are not worthy of Imitation in the Lower parts of Art?

To: "Raffaelle had more taste and fancy, Michael Angelo wise genius and imagination."

Blake: What Nonsense!

To: "Michael Angelo's works have a strong, peculiar, and marked character. Raffaelle's materials were chiefly borrowed. . . . The . . . structure is his own . . . the propriety, beauty, and majesty of his characters, the judicious contrivance of his composition, the correctness of drawing . . . etc."

Blake: If all this is true, why does not Reynolds recommend The Study of Raphael, and Mich. Angelo's Execution? At page 17 he allows that the Venetian Style will Ill correspond with the great Style.

To: ". . . Such is the great style, in this search after novelty has no place. . . ."

Blake: The great style is always Novel or New in all its Operations.

To: "But there is another style, the characteristic . . . Salvator Rosa, . . . has that sort of dignity which belongs to savage nature. . . ."

Blake: Original and Characteristic are the Two Grand Merits of the Great Style. Why should the words be applied to such a Wretch as Salvator Rosa? Salvator Rosa is precisely what he Pretended to be. His Pictures are high laboured Pretensions to Expeditious Workmanship. He was the Quack Doctor of Painting. His Roughnesses and Smoothnesses are the Production of Labour and Trick. As to Imagination, he was totally without Any. Savages are Tops and Fribbles more than any other Men.

To: "Everything is of a piece, even to his (Salvator Rosa's) handling."

Blake: Handling is all that he has, and we all know that Handling is Labour and Trick. Salvator Rosa employed Journeymen.

To: "Rubens . . . a remarkable instance of the same mind in all the various parts of art. The whole is . . . of a piece. . . ."

Blake: All Rubens' Pictures are Painted by Journeymen, and so far from being all of a Piece, are the most wretched Bungles.

To : " His colouring, in which he most excelled. . . ."

Blake : To my eye Rubens's colouring is most Contemptible. The shadows are of a Filthy Brown, somewhat of the Colour of Excrement. These are filled with tints of yellow and red. His lights are all the colours of the Rainbow laid on Indiscriminately, and broken into one another. Altogether his Colouring is Contrary to the Colouring of Real Art and Science.

To : " Opposed to this, . . . Poussin . . . etc."

Blake : Opposed to Rubens's Colouring, Sir Joshua has placed Poussin. But he ought to put all men of genius who ever painted. Rubens and the Venetians are Opposite in everything to Fine Art, and they Meant to be so. They were hired for this Purpose.

To : " Poussin in the latter part of his life changed from his dry manner to one richer . . . not at all comparable to his dry manner. . . ."

Blake : True.

To : " The favourite subjects of Poussin was ancient fables, and no painter was ever better qualified to paint such subjects."

Blake : True.

To : " Poussin seems to think that the style and language in which such stories are told is (*sic*) not the worse for preserving some relish of the old way of painting. . . ."

Blake : True.

To : " If the figures which people his pictures had a modern air or countenance, . . . if the landscape had the appearance of a modern view, how ridiculous would Apollo appear instead of sin, an old man, or nymph, with an urn to represent a river or a lake ? "

Blake : These remarks on Poussin are Excellent.

To : " It is certain that the lowest style will be the most popular, as it falls within the compass of ignorance itself, and the vulgar will always be pleased with what is natural in the confined and misunderstood sense of the word."

Blake : Well said.

To : " I mention this because our Exhibitions, while they produce such admirable effects by nourishing emulation, and calling out genius, have also a mischievous tendency by seducing the painter to an ambition of pleasing indiscriminately the mixed multitude who resort to them."

Blake : Why, then, does he talk in other places of pleasing Everybody ?

DISCOURSE VI

(*On fly-leaf.*) *Blake* : When a Man talks of Acquiring invention, or of learning how to produce Original Conception, he must expect to be called a Fool by Men of Understanding. But such a Hired Knave cares not for the Few. His eye is on the Many—or, rather, on the Money.

To : " Those who have represented art as a kind of *inspiration*, a gift . . . more captivating than he who attempts to examine whether . . . art may be acquired."

Blake : Bacon's philosophy has Destroy'd true Art and Science. The Man who says that Genius is not Born but Taught, is a Knave.

O, Reader, behold the Philosopher's grave !
He was born quite a Fool, but he died quite a Knave.

To : " To derive . . . nothing from another . . . is the praise which men bestow . . . naturally lightened by a supercilious censure of the low, the barren, the grovelling, the servile imitator."

Blake : How ridiculous it would be to see the Sheep Endeavour to walk like the Dog, or the Ox striving to trot like the Horse—just as Ridiculous it is to see one Man Striving to Imitate Another. Man varies from Man more than Animal from Animal of Different Species.

To : "The truth is that the *degree* of excellence which proclaims genius is different in different times and different places."

Blake : Never ! Never !

To : "We are very sure that the beauty of form, the expression of the passions, the art of composition, even the power of giving a general air of grandeur to a work, is at present very much under the dominion of rules. These excellencies were heretofore considered merely as the effects of genius, and justly, if genius is not taken for inspiration, but as the effect of close observation and experience."

Blake : Damned fool.

To : "He who first made these observations . . . had that merit . . . as art shall advance its powers will be still more and more fixed by rules."

Blake : If art was Progressive, we should have had Mich. Angelos and Rafaels to Succeed and to Improve upon each other. But it is not so. Genius dies with its Possessor, and comes not again till Another is born with It.

To : "Even works of genius, like every other effect must have their cause."

Blake : Identities, or things, are Neither Cause nor Effect. They are Eternal.

To : "Our minds should be habituated to the contemplation of excellence . . . the substance which supplies the fullest maturity of our vigour."

Blake : Reynolds thinks that Man Learns all that he knows. I say on the Contrary, that Man Brings All that he has or Can have Into the World with him.

To : "The mind is but a barren soil. . . ."

Blake : Man is Born Like a Garden ready Planted and Sown. This World is too poor to produce one Seed. The Mind that could have produced this sentence must have been a Pitiful, a Pitiable Imbecility. I always thought that the Human Mind was the most Prolific of All Things, and Inexhaustible. I certainly thank God I am not like Reynolds.

To : "(The mind) will produce no crop or only one, unless continually fertilized with foreign matter."

Blake : Nonsense.

To : "Nothing can come of nothing."

Blake : Is the Mind Nothing ?

To : "We are certain that Michel Angelo and Raphael were equally possessed of all the knowledge in art which had been discovered in the works of their predecessors."

Blake : If so, they knew all that Titian and Correggio knew. Correggio was two years older than Michel Angelo. Correggio, born 1472; Michel Angelo, born 1474.

To : "It is not that I advise any endeavour to copy the exact peculiar colour and complexion of another man's mind. . . . The copy will be ridiculous."

Blake: Why then Imitate at all?

To: "Art in its perfection is not ostentatious. It lies hid, and works its effect itself unseen. It is the proper study and labour of an artist to uncover, and find out the latest cause of conspicuous beauty, and from them form principles of his own conduct. Such an examination is a continual exertion of the mind ; as great, perhaps, as that of the artist whose works he is studying."

Blake: This is a Very Clever Sentence. Who wrote it God knows.

To: "Peculiar marks I hold to be generally, if not always, defects."

Blake: Peculiar marks are the Only Merit.

To: "They are always so many blemishes, both in real life and in painting."

Blake: Infernal Falsehood.

To: "The great name of Michel Angelo may be used to keep in countenance a deficiency, or rather a neglect, of colouring. . . . In short, there is no defect that may not be excused, if it is a sufficient excuse that it can be imputed to considerable artists."

Blake: No Man who can see Michel Angelo can say that he wants either Colouring or Ornamental parts of Art in the highest degree, for he has everything of Both. He who Admired Rafael, must admire Rafael's Execution. He who does not admire Raphael's execution, Cannot Admire Raphael.

To: "In this (strength of parts) certainly men are not equal, and a man can bring home wares only in proportion to the capital with which he goes to market."

Blake: A confession.

To: "In order to encourage you to imitation . . . a skilful painter . . . in no danger of being infected . . . under the rudeness of Gothic essays, will find original, rational, and even sublime inventions."

Blake: This sentence is to Introduce another in Condemnation and Contempt of Albt. Dürer.

To: "The works of Albert Dürer . . . afford a rich mass of genuine materials, which, wrought up and polished to elegance, will add copiousness to what perhaps, without such aid, could only have aspired to justness and propriety."

Blake: A polished Villain, who Robs and Murders !

To: "The greatest style . . . would receive an additional grace by the elegance and precision of pencil."

Blake: What does Precision of Pencil mean ? If it does not mean Outline it means Nothing.

To: "I can easily imagine that if he (Jan Stein) had lived in Rome, and been blessed with Michel Angelo and Raphael for his masters . . . he now would have ranged with the great pillars and supporters of our art."

Blake: Jan Stein was a Boor, and neither Rafael nor Mich. Ang. could have made him any better.

To: "Men, who thus bound down by the almost invincible powers of early habit . . ."

Blake: He who can be bound down is no Genius. Genius cannot be Bound. It may be Rendered Indignant or Outrageous. "Oppression makes the wise man mad."—*Solomon*.

DISCOURSE VII

(*On fly-leaf.*) *Blake* : The purpose of the following discourse is to Prove that Taste and Genius are not of Heavenly Origin, and that all who have supposed that they Are so, Are to be considered as Weak-headed Fanatics. The obligations which Reynolds has laid on bad Artists of all classes will at all times make them his Admirers, but most especially for this discourse, in which it is proved that the stupid are born with Faculties Equal to other Men, Only they have not Cultivated them, because they have not thought it worth the trouble.

To : " We allow a poet to express his meaning, when his meaning is not well known to himself, with a certain degree of obscurity, as it is one source of the sublime."

Blake : Obscurity is Neither the Source of the Sublime nor of anything Else.

To : " But when in plain prose we talk of courting the muse in shady bowers, waiting the call and inspiration of genius, . . . we generally rest contented with mere words, or at best entertain notions not only groundless but pernicious."

Blake : The Ancients, and the wisest of the Moderns, are of the opinion that Reynolds condemns and laughs at.

To : " I am persuaded that scarce a poet is to be found who preserved a sound mind in a sound body . . . whose latter works are not all replete with the face of imagination as those which he produced in his more youthful days."

Blake ; As Replete, but not More Replete.

To : " To understand literally these metaphors or ideas expressed in poetical language seems as absurd as to conclude that because painters sometimes represent poets writing from the dictates of a little winged boy or genius, that this same genius did really inform him in a whisper what he was to write. . . ."

Blake : The Ancients did not mean to Impose when they affirmed their belief in Vision and Revelation. Plato was in earnest. Milton was in earnest. They believed that God did visit Man really and Truly, and not as Reynolds pretends. How very Anxious Reynolds is to Disprove and Contemn Spiritual Perceptions !

To : " Genius and taste . . . pretend . . . that great works are produced . . . and an exact judgment is given, without our knowing why . . . one can scarcely state these opinions without exposing their absurdity. . . ."

Blake : Who ever said this ? He states Absurdities in Company with Truths, and Calls both Absurd.

To : " The prevalent opinion . . . considers the principles of taste as . . . less solid . . . than really . . ."

Blake : The Artifice of the Epicurean Philosopher is to Call all other Opinions Unsolid and Unsubstantial than those which are derived from Earth.

To : " We often appear to differ in sentiment from each other from inaccuracy of terms."

Blake : It is not in Terms that Reynolds and I disagree. Two Contrary Opinions can never by any Language be made alike. I say Taste and Genius are Not Teachable nor Acquirable, but are both born with us. Reynolds says the Contrary.

To : " We apply the term *taste* to . . . like or dislike . . . we give the same name to our judgment on a fancy . . . and on unalterable principles. However inconvenient this may be, we are obliged to take words as we find them."

Blake : This is False. The Fault is not in Words but in Things. Lock's Opinions on words and their Fallaciousness are hurtful opinions and Fallacious also.

To : " The same taste relishes demonstration . . . resemblance of a picture . . . and harmony."

Blake : Demonstration, Similitude, and Harmony are Objects of Reasoning Invention. Identity and Melody are Objects of Intuition.

To : ". . . as true as mathematical demonstration. . . ."

Blake : God forbid that Truth should be Confined to Mathematical Demonstration. He who does not know Truth at sight is unworthy of Her Notice.

To : " In proportion as prejudices are . . . long received, . . . taste . . . approaches certainty . . ."

Blake : Here is a great deal to do to Prove that All truth is prejudice, for all that is Valuable in Knowledge is Superior to Demonstrative Science, such as is Weighed and Measured.

To : " As these prejudices become more narrow, this secondary taste becomes more fantastical. . . ."

Blake : And so he thinks he has proved that Genius and Inspiration are All a Hum.

To : " Having laid down these propositions I shall proceed with less method."

Blake : He calls the Above, proceeding with Method.

To : " We will take it for granted that reason is something invariable."

Blake : Reason—or a ratio of all we have known—is not the same it shall be when we know More. He therefore takes a Falsehood for granted to set out with.

To : " We will conclude that whatever goes under the name of taste which we can fairly bring under the dominion of reason must be considered as equally exempt from change."

Blake : Now this is supreme Fooling.

To : " The arts would lie open for ever to caprice and casualty if those who are to judge of their excellencies had no settled principles. . . ."

Blake : He may as well say that if man does not lay down settled Principles the Sun will not rise in a Morning.

To : " My notion of nature comprehends . . . the internal fabric . . . of the human mind and imagination."

Blake : Here is a plain Confession that he Thinks Mind and Imagination not to be above the Mortal and Perishing Nature. Such is the End of Epicurean or Newtonian Philosophy. It is Atheism.

To : " This (Poussin's Perseus with Medusa's head) is undoubtedly a subject of great bustle and tumult . . . the eye finds no repose anywhere . . . I remember turning from it in disgust. . . ."

Blake : Reynolds's Eye cannot bear Characteristic Colouring or Light and Shade.

To : " This . . . I hold to be improper to imitate. A picture should please at first sight."

Blake : Please whom ? Some Men Cannot see a Picture except in a Dark Corner.

To: "No one can deny that violent passions will naturally emit harsh and disagreeable tones."

Blake: Violent Passions emit the Real Good and Perfect Tones.

To: "If it be objected that Rubens judged ill . . . to make his work so very ornamental. . . ."

Blake: Here it is Called Ornamental that the Roman and Bolognian Schools may be Insinuated not to be Ornamental.

To: "No one will dispute that the Roman or Bolognian Schools would have produced a more learned and more noble work."

Blake: Learned and Noble is Ornamental.

To: "This leads us to weighing . . . the different classes of art. . . ."

Blake: A fool's Balance is no criterion, because though it goes down on the heaviest side, we ought to look what he puts into it.

To: "If a European who has cut off his beard, put false hair on his head, or tied up his own, and . . . with the help of the fat of hogs covered the whole with flour . . . issues forth and meets a Cherokee Indian, who has bestowed as much time on his toilet . . . laid on his ochre . . . whichever of these two despises the other for this attention to the fashion of his country . . . is the barbarian."

Blake: Excellent.

To: "In the midst of the highest flights of the fancy or imagination, reason ought to preside. . . ."

Blake: If this is True it is a devilish Foolish Thing to be an Artist.

DISCOURSE VIII

(*On fly-leaf.*) *Blake*: Burke's treatise on the *Sublime and Beautiful* is founded on the Opinions of Newton and Locke. On this Treatise Reynolds has grounded many of his assertions in all his *Discourses*. I read Burke's Treatise when very young. At the same time I read Locke on the *Human Understanding*, and Bacon's *Advancement of Learning*. On every one of these Books I wrote my opinion, and, on looking them over, find that my notes on Reynolds in this book are exactly similar. I felt the same Contempt and Abhorrence then that I do now. They mock Inspiration and Vision. Inspiration and Vision was then, and now is, and I hope will always remain, my Element, my Eternal Dwelling-place. How can I then hear it condemned without returning Scorn for Scorn ?

To: "Principles of art . . . in their excess become defects."

Blake: Principles according to Sir Joshua become Defects.

To: "Artists should learn their profession from endeavouring to form an idea of proportion from the different excellencies which lie dispersed in the various schools of painting."

Blake: In another discourse he says that we cannot mix the Florentine and Venetian.

To: An instance occurs to me of two painters—Rembrandt and Poussin. . . . Rembrandt's manner was absolute unity. . . . Poussin has no principal light at all."

Blake: Rembrandt was a Generaliser ; Poussin a Particulariser.

To: "The works of Poussin are as much distinguished for simplicity as those of Rembrandt for combination."

Blake: Poussin knew better than to make all his pictures have the same light and shade. Any fool may concentrate a light in the Middle.

To: "We may compare . . . the portraits of Titian, where dignity, seeming to be natural and inherent, . . . has the appearance of an inalienable adjunct. . . ."

Blake: Dignity an Adjunct.

To: "When a young artist . . . is told . . . certain animating words of Spirit, Dignity, Energy, Grace, greatness of Style and brilliancy of Tints . . . he becomes suddenly vain of his newly acquired knowledge."

Blake: Mocks.

To: "Art in its infancy, like the first work of a student, was dry, hard, and simple. But this kind of barbarous simplicity would be better named Penury, as it proceeds from mere want; from want of knowledge, want of resources, want of abilities to be otherwise. Their simplicity was the offspring, not of choice, but of necessity."

Blake: Mocks. A lie.

To: "In the second stage they are sensible of this poverty . . . ran into a contrary extreme. But . . . we cannot recommend them to return to that simplicity . . . but to deal out their abundance with a more sparing hand. . . ."

Blake: Abundance of Stupidity.

To: ". . . it is not enough that a work be learned; it must be pleasing."

Blake: If you Endeavour to Please the Worst, you will never Please the Best. To Please all is Impossible.

To: "Again, in the artificial management of figures, it is directed that they shall contrast each other according to the rules generally given. . . . But when students are more advanced, they will find that the greatest beauties of character and expression are produced without contrast. St. Paul preaching at Athens, far from any affected academical contrasts of limbs, stands equally on both legs, and both hands are in the same attitude; add contrast, and the whole energy and unaffected grace of the figure is destroyed. Elymas the Sorcerer stretches both hands forward in the same direction, which gives perfectly the expression intended."

Blake: Well said.

To: "It may not be improper to give instances where the rule itself, though generally received, is false. . . . It is given as a rule by Fresnoy: That *the principal figure of a subject must appear in the midst of a picture, under the principal light, to distinguish it from the rest.*"

Blake: What a Devil of a Rule.

To: ". . . what those proportions are cannot be so well learned by precept as by observation on pictures, and in this knowledge bad pictures will serve as well as good."

Blake: Bad pictures are always Sir Joshua's friends.

To: "It ought, in my opinion, to be indispensably observed that the masses of light in a picture be always of a warm mellow colour—yellow, red, or yellowish white; and that the blue, the grey, or the green colours be kept almost entirely out of these masses, and used only to support and set off these warm colours, and for this purpose a small proportion of cold colours will be sufficient."

Blake: Colouring formed on these Principles is destructive of All Art, because it takes away the possibility of Variety, and only promotes Harmony, or Blending of Colours one with another.

To: "The conduct of Titian in the picture of Bacchus and Ariadne has been much celebrated, and justly, for the harmony of colouring."

Blake: Such Harmony of Colouring is Destructive of Art. One Species of General Hue over all is the Cursed Thing called Harmony. It is like the Smile of a Fool.

To: "The illuminated parts of objects are in nature of a warmer tint than those that are in the shade."

Blake: Shade is always cold, and never, as in Rubens and the colourists, hot, and Yellowy Brown.

To: ". . . fulness of manner found in perfection in the best works of Correggio and, we may add, of Rembrandt. This effect is produced by melting and losing shadows in a ground still darker than those shadows. . . ."

Blake: All this is destructive of Art.

To: "A picture I have of Rubens; it is a representation of moonlight. . . . The Moon in this picture does not preserve so great a superiority in regard to the object which it illumines as it does in nature. This is likewise an intended deviation, and for the same reason. If Rubens had preserved the same scale of gradation of light between the moon and the objects which is found in nature, the picture must have consisted of one small spot of light only, and at a little distance from the picture nothing but this spot would have been seen."

Blake · These are Excellent remarks on Proportionate Colour.

To: "Before and above all things it is necessary that the work should be seen, not only without difficulty, but with pleasure and satisfaction."

Blake: If the Picture ought to be Seen with Ease, surely the nobler parts of the Picture, such as the Heads, ought to be Principal. But this is never the case except in the Roman and Florentine Schools, not, I (?) trust the German in the Florentine school.

To: ". . . Sketches give the pleasure of imagination . . . the imagination supplies more than the painter probably could produce."

Blake: What Falsehood !

To: ". . . Everything shall be carefully and distinctly expressed as if the painter knew with correctness and precision the exact form and character of whatever is introduced into the picture. This is what, with us, is called Science and Learning, which must not be sacrificed and given up for an uncertain and doubtful beauty which, not naturally belonging to our art, will probably be sought for without success."

Blake: Excellent, and contrary to his usual opinion.

To: "Mr. Falconet has observed in a note . . . that the circumstance of covering the face of Agamemnon was probably not in consequence of fine imagination of the painter . . . he thinks meanly of this trick of concealing. . . ."

Blake: I am of Falconet's opinion.

So end the notes on Reynolds. Comparing them with the "Public Address," the likelihood that they really belong, with it, to 1810 seems so strong that an apology is due to the reader for not printing them nearer to it in this biography, in defiance of Blake's "aged sixty-three."

CHAPTER XXXIII

VISIONS AND DANTE

THOUGH August 1820 was the year of most of Varley's "visionary heads," Blake continued to do more and more of these. His theory of a permanent mental substance into which he could dip his own mind and find—by the resulting visions—a means of remembering people who had "died from the earth" before he was born is now, of course, easily recognised as one that hardly differs from what is being scientifically proved to be as near to an account of the truth as any other which tries to describe etheric movements and changes in terms of more subtle and more unusual experiences than those that come to us every day through our five senses. These terms have hitherto belonged, in this, as in all sciences not yet scientific, to magicians and occultists. There is one thing of which we need continually to remind ourselves. Myth is the natural language of occultism in the mouth of primitive nature. It lays us open to new and fascinating mistakes, such as are made by children who try to understand poetry. When locomotives were first introduced into Turkey, a delightful science of demonology suited to their explanation grew up. It was a mistake, of course, but the terms of it hardly differ from those in which the most experienced American engine-drivers speak of their machines as if they were persons, attributing to them not only personal names but personal qualities. That there is even a scientific justification for this is seen in that wittiest book of last century, Samuel Butler's *Erewhon*, and recently we have had an expert in metal work telling us that he is so impressed with the *life* of iron that when he sees a big bar he takes off his hat to it. Poor Blake has been derided for having been reported to have done this to a vision of St. Paul while he was walking with a corporeal friend in the streets of London. The anecdote is of doubtful authenticity. A mistake is easily made in telling such tales.

When a man is right about visions we call him a tele-pathist, a prophet, or a magician; when wrong, he passes for a madman. The day will come when we shall be sane enough ourselves to remember that in these difficult subjects he may be wrong without being mad, for he is *more likely* to be wrong than right, and that in reasoning normally about his abnormal experiences he is practically certain to talk *as though* he had lost his reason.

Crabb Robinson's notes about Blake's later visions tell us so many interesting things, and with so evident a sincere avoidance of exaggeration, that he must be quoted at some length. There are two forms of his reminiscences, not in the same words. He altered and condensed the second from the first. The presence of some specially significant words in the condensed account, absent from Gilchrist's quotations from the original journals, suggests that these were doctored by the biographer.

In speaking of the 1820 period of visions Gilchrist notes that Varley's "critical friends" discovered traces of his "receipt for a face" in them, and hints by this expression that they were all sham and made up to impose on Varley. Crabb Robinson, with similar ignorance of the working of the artistic mind, whether or not it is aided by the visionary mind, thinks he has found an inconsistency in Blake, which he notes. Here is the whole paragraph. It contains more than one obvious error of judgment:

There was nothing *wild* about his looks. Though very ready to be drawn out to the assertion of his favourite ideas, yet there was *no warmth, as though he wanted to make proselytes*. (The italics are ours; Crabb Robinson had not peeped into Blake's notebook and read—

> He's a blockhead who wants a proof
> Of what he can't perceive;
> And he's a fool who tries to make
> Such a blockhead believe.)

Indeed one of the peculiar features of his scheme, so far as it was consistent, was indifference, and a very extraordinary degree of tolerance and satisfaction with what had taken place—a sort of pious and humble optimism, not the scornful optimism of *Candide*. He warmly praised some compositions of Mr. Aders; and having brought for Aders an engraving of his *Canterbury Pilgrims*, he remarked that one of the figures in it resembled a figure in one of the works then in Aders' room, and that he had been accused of having stolen from it. But he added that he had drawn the figure in question twenty years before he had seen the original picture. "However, there is no wonder in the resemblance, as in my youth I was always studying that class of paintings." I have forgotten what the figure was. But his taste was in close conformity with the old German school. This is somewhat at variance with what he said, both this day and afterwards—implying that he copied his visions.

It is, as we all know now, not at variance at all, only in supplement. His art did not always copy " vision," it often "composed" like that of other people, and even when it copied " vision " it often copied visions that were altered or " infected " by other mental activities.

Blake certainly had the Socratic theory about art, that it is a proof when genius cannot analyse it of the existence of the gods. He said, " Art is inspiration. When Michelangelo or Raphael in their day, or Mr. Flaxman does one of his fine things he does them in the spirit." Blake gave Flaxman's name in this connection long after the quarrel with Flaxman about the " Screwmuch " conspiracy, and therefore after Flaxman, who had been accused of joining those who wished to keep down Blake's prices, refused all further intercourse. It is a pure piece of artistic magnanimity on Blake's part. He told Crabb Robinson that he had " seen Shakespeare," who was like his portraits, especially the " old engraving " ; that he had seen Milton often, once " as a very old man " with a long flowing beard, and that Milton had asked him to correct in a poem or picture an error of his in *Paradise Lost.* " But I declined; I said I had my own duties to perform." The error that Milton wished corrected was that sexual intercourse grew out of the Fall—of course a most anti-Blakean view of the Fall, which did not very substantially prove the " devils' account " of it in the *Marriage of Heaven and Hell,* a marriage absolutely different from the erroneous reconciliation of contraries which leads to that hateful thing an aggregate, or *bloated general form,* that was in his mind connected with the evil idea " Morality," *Jerusalem,* page 91, line 27. Milton did not grow to be a very old man. He only lived sixty-six years on earth, and never wore a beard. We are in a " spiritual " sphere in this conversation. Voltaire came to Blake much and talked what might have been French, Blake said, but was English to his ear. Milton was perhaps a shaven spirit, but appearing to Blake was bearded *to his eye.* This again shows the impersonal surface, yet personal depth of these visions. Voltaire, in this wordless language, said to Blake, when speaking of his enemies, that they had blasphemed the Holy Ghost *in* him, which should not be forgiven, though it *would be* forgiven him that he had blasphemed the Son of Man.

He did not say that this *had* been forgiven him. Crabb Robinson does not seem to notice that the doctrine of Purgatory is implied here—a doctrine naturally absent from so practical a church as ours, practical in its dealings with a free and married clergy as well as with its laity. Voltaire was, said Blake, commissioned by God to expose the Scriptures *when read in their literal sense.*

The most important opinion on religion given by Blake, and the one that would have arrayed the narrower clergy against him more than all his belief in the "Saviour" would have attracted them, was that reading the Scriptures in the literal or "natural" sense "takes all sublimity from the Bible." This is his answer to those who consider explaining the Biblical myths to be nothing else than "explaining away."

Crabb Robinson's note on Swedenborg and Dante is:

Incidentally Swedenborg was mentioned. (Blake) declared him to be a Divine teacher; he had done, and would do, much good, yet he did wrong in endeavouring to explain to the reason what it could not comprehend.

Did Swedenborg do so? Cannot the reason comprehend that a mask is a mask? Of course it, in Blake's use of the word, cannot be said to understand the *face* that Swedenborg claimed to have found *under* the Old Testament mask. Swedenborg himself says that we cannot comprehend it till we have "soaked ourselves" for long in our celestial mental faculties, and that it is "irksome" to the everyday parts of our minds—the "Natural Man."

He seemed (Crabb Robinson goes on, speaking of Blake) to consider, but that was not clear, the visions of Swedenborg and Dante as the same kind. Dante was the greater poet! (When was Swedenborg anything but the essence of prose?) Yet this did not appear to affect the estimation of Dante's genius (why should it?) or his opinion of the truth of Dante's visions. Indeed when he even declared Dante to be an atheist it was accompanied by the highest admiration, "though," said he, "Dante saw devils where I saw none."

Crabb Robinson then puts down in his journal some "insulated remarks" of Blake:

Jacob Boehmen was placed among the divinely inspired men. He praised also the designs to Law's translation of Boehmen: "Michelangelo could not have surpassed them." "Bacon, Locke, and Newton are the three great teachers of Atheism, or Satan's doctrine." "Irving is a highly gifted man; he is a *sent* man, but they who are sent sometimes go further than they ought." (It will be remembered how Blake in his notes to Lavater admits his own feeling of temptation to do this in order to produce more effect.) "I saw nothing but good in Calvin's house. In Luther's there were harlots." He declared his opinion that the earth is flat and not round, and just as I had objected the circumnavigation, dinner was announced.

It is a loss that this did not go further. Of course, around the size of the earth *is* an eternal plane *to a spectator* walking on it. Blake was speaking purely about its result on the emotions of man through his eye, by means of which " we become what we behold," and the vision of the earth in each of us is that of a plain that *leaves off* at the horizon. It is even a cup, concave like a " Mundane Shell."

By way of an example of the difference between the natural and spiritual sun (a very strong point with Swedenborg), Blake says to Crabb Robinson :

You never saw the spiritual sun ? I have. I saw him on Primrose Hill. He said : " Do you take me for the Greek Apollo ? No. *That* " (pointing to the sky) " is the Greek Apollo. He is Satan."

Readers of *Jerusalem* and *Milton* are grateful to Crabb Robinson for that. Satan: Apollo: Greek materialism, reason : nature : death. Blake also said : " I know what is true by internal conviction—a doctrine is stated ; my heart tells me it must be true."

Of course we all get our convictions, most of them at second or third stages, from some original conviction, in precisely the same way. Of course, also, Blake had at his hand his Bible, in which he might have read (Jeremiah xvii. 9): " The heart is deceitful above all things and desperately wicked." He does not seem, however, to have reflected that from this arises the plain duty of every religious man to be a doubter, nor does he reproach his own impatience for constantly rebelling against this hardest of all religious duties.

Crabb Robinson gives a number of further notes about Dante, which form a useful help to understanding the few pencillings by Blake found among the designs to the *Divine Comedy* made for the Linnell brothers.

Blake declared him (Dante) a mere politician and atheist, busied about this world's affairs, as Milton was, till in his old age he turned back to the God he had abandoned in childhood. I in vain endeavoured to obtain from him a qualification so as not to include him (Dante) in the ordinary reproach. Yet he afterwards spoke of Dante as being then with God.

Blake's designs to Dante are made in thinly-washed water-colours in a large thick sketch-book which was probably bound for the purpose. It is a heavy folio several inches thick. Its pages measure fourteen by eighteen inches, but look more and more gigantic as one turns them over, on account of the largeness of style in the designs and the trance-producing influence that passes from them to the mind of any one who lends himself to their power. Only a few were engraved by Blake. To aid himself in comprehending the scheme of the poem, he sketched a diagram of Dante's "circles," No. 1 being at the bottom. They are placed above the other with a note: "This is upside down, but right when viewed from purgatory after they had passed the centre." This recalls the descent of the angels in the *Marriage of Heaven and Hell* until they get so low that they hold on by the roots of trees and hang over a nether void, and the bending down of Milton into Albion's "bosom of death," until "what was under soon seemed above." "In equivocal worlds," Blake notes to Dante, "all is equivocal." He has also drawn what looks like a target. The bull's-eye is labelled "Purgatory," and the rings have these names:—the innermost ring, "Terrestrial Paradise: it is a limbo"; then "Moon, Mercury, Venus, Sun, Mars, Jupiter, Starry Heavens"; and for the exterior ring of all, "Vacuum." He also notes: "It seems as if Dante supposes that God was something superior to the Father of Jesus, or, if he gives rain to the evil and the good, and the sun to the just and the unjust, he can never have builded Dante's Hell, nor the Hell of the Bible, as our parsons explain it. It must have been originally framed by the dark Spirit itself, and so I understand it."

He begins again:

Whatever task is for vengeance for sin, and whatever is against forgiveness of sin, is not of the Father but of Satan, the accuser and father of hells.

He is now speaking of the Father *after* Jesus has become God. Blake had then ceased to consider the First Person of the Trinity (either as Jehovah or as Elohim) as separate from the Second, though he at one time did so very often, with the result that he has left this note in his MS. book:

Thinking as I do that the Creator of this world is a very cruel being, and being a worshipper of Christ, I cannot help saying to the Son, O how unlike the Father! First, God Almighty comes with a thump on the head, and then Jesus Christ comes with a balm to heal it.

This recalls a still earlier note made in the same book in the same quaint and grotesque style, like that of some Gothic ornaments. It was made after he had written the dedication to Stothard (who had a long nose) of the "everlasting gospel," that begins—

> The vision of Christ that thou dost see
> Is my vision's greatest enemy.
> Thine has a long hooked nose like thine,
> Mine has a snub nose like mine.

I always thought that Christ was a snubby, or I should not have worshipped him, if I had thought he had been one of those long spindle-nosed rascals.

Returning to the book of Dante drawings, once Blake makes a cartoon where Homer is seen crowned with laurels and armed with a sword in the centre ("the classics devastated Europe with wars"), and a series of circles surround him. The first is labelled "Swedenborg"; the rest are illegible. A note tells us—

Everything in Dante's *Paradise* shows that for tyrannical purposes he has made this world the foundation of all, and the goddess Nature, —Memory,—not the Holy Ghost . . . in her empires. . . . As poor Cha-Bell said, "Nature, thou art my goddess." Round Purgatory is Paradise, and round Paradise is vacuum, or limbo. Homer is the centre of all—I mean the poetry of the heathen—stolen and perverted from the Bible, not by chance, but by design, by the kings of Persia, their generals, the Greek heroes, and lastly the Romans. Swedenborg does the same in saying that the world is the ultimate of heaven. This is the most damnable falsehood of Satan and the Antichrist.

This is one of the "old falsehoods" of which Swedenborg is accused in the *Marriage of Heaven and Hell*, where, unfortunately, they are not specified.

This is all that we have of Blake's ideas about Dante. He learned Italian in order to read him in the original after studying Cary, whose translation he spoke of approvingly. It was as easy to win Blake's praise as to incur his vituperation. Any faithful service done to a visionary or even to an outlining artist—any receiving a prophet as a prophet— would be rewarded by his blessing. As for the contrary, we must be either sheep (of the true fold) or goats—outcast in the wilderness, or, as he calls it, "the indefinite," an expression whose amusing inappropriateness when it is applied to Newton he did not see.

Of the many designs made in the third book for John Linnell, only seven were engraved. The subjects are (1) Paolo and Francesca, (2) Devils tormenting Ciampolo, (3) Devils tormenting each other, (4) Brunelleschi and the serpent, (5) Donati and the serpent, (6) The falsifiers, (7) The traitors.

It is easy, and melancholy, to see what cause for application to his own experience Blake had in his mind while engraving these designs. None is carried very far. The style of Marc Antonio is almost distressingly evident in the shading. The figures contain Blake's usual merits and defects, and it is exceedingly difficult to find in the figure of Dante himself any attempt to bring before us the "long-nosed rascal" that it is supposed to represent.

Death interrupted the engraving of the series.

CHAPTER XXXIV

'JOB' AND LINNELL

PERHAPS the chief work, however, of Blake's last years—for the exact date of the hundred designs to Gray in the Duke of Hamilton's collection is not known to the present writer —and surely the chief artistic work of his life, is the series of twenty-one engravings to the *Book of Job*, for which two sets of drawings were made. These engravings are well known from the reproductions that have been published from time to time since they were first printed from very good " photo-intaglios " in the second volume of Gilchrist's *Life*. Their presence here will always make that book sought after till a comfortable edition of them replaces it.

They were produced in Fountain Court, and " published as the Act directs" on March 8, 1825. It will be noticed that in the first picture of Job and his family the date is 1828. Of course, in numbering so many it is not surprising that the figure 8 from " 8th of March " was repeated once by error at the close of the date of the year, which is given as 1828, for all the dates were added together on the outer margins of the twenty-one plates. This trifling error is probably responsible for the belief of the earlier biographers that Blake died in 1828, and makes the year of his death unforgettable by the sadness of the mistake, for as he died the year before, in 1827, this plate can by no possibility be accepted as engraved in the year to which Blake assigns it.

The work was all done after Blake left South Molton Street and went to Fountain Court, Strand (again a house-hold move for economy's sake), where he had rooms on the first floor, whose back windows looked between two high houses on to the river. Great reduction and destruction of the contents of the sixteen packages that made up his luggage when he went to Felpham must have now been necessary.

He had less room than ever. When Crabb Robinson called on him there was not even a sound spare chair, so that the visitor sat on his bed. Gilchrist says (on page 321 of the Biography) that No. 3 Fountain Court, Strand, was "a house kept by a brother-in-law named Baines," who was, as Tatham records, the husband of Mrs. Blake's sister, who is only mentioned once, and then in this connection. The removal from South Molton Street, and the consequent break in daily poring over one class of work, had its usual effect of putting a new edge on Blake's artistic nerves—which his misguided belief in industry was continually deteriorating. To this is due the vigour and freshness of the *Job* designs, which contain nothing to suggest that when they were published the artist was an old man, worn and ready to sink under an illness that would never have attacked him had he sat less constantly at his work-table. That he ate only just enough to support life for years, and that he was often at his press turning its handle, explains why he was alive at all and had not died of sedentary habits. For two years, it is said that he never left the house. His only relaxation was reading the Bible, which he consulted in several languages. That it was a relaxation, and not a pious and stupefying duty, is his debt to Swedenborg.

At Fountain Court he was able to forget all the old Hayley trouble and Cromek struggle. From now—in fact, from a little before the removal—he had never a moment's real anxiety about being able to find enough to eat while doing his own best work. John Linnell has to be thanked for this. Butts, Blake's other best patron, full of his drawings, and losing the eyesight that enabled him to see them, after buying the first set of *Job* drawings, is no longer heard of. He had been a true believer and a persistent supporter in a very quiet and inexpensive way. But he had never been a real mental companion. In John Linnell Blake had at last found, if not a reader who could follow his symbols, at least some one who would give him help and employment and sympathy that was not patronage. The days are over now of the "injurious doubts" with which Hayley had, in his kindest moments, done his artistic nerve much irreparable harm, and obliged him to labour like "Milton" striving with "Urizen." There is a direct reference in many passages that spring from this experience. Freedom from employers, unsympathetic, however well-meaning and affectionate, accounts for the value of the *Job* as a work of art, and is in itself an indictment against Hayley, whose memory will never be able to answer it.

Little fragments of encouragement from different sources came now to Blake, as it were, spontaneously, like the sun and rain.

Wainewright, who used to write in the *London Magazine* under the name of "Janus Weathercock," replaces the unknown enemy on the *Examiner*, who vanishes from the stage. Gilchrist tells us that Wainewright wrote under other pseudonyms also. He concealed cleverness under an air of flippancy. He recognised the value and seriousness of the figure in art, whether drawn by the great German outliner Moritz Retzsch, or our own Stothard (the Walter Crane of his day), or Etty (its Sir Edward Poynter). He also took up Blake, tried to puff his *Jerusalem* smilingly, a hopeless task, and bought a copy of his *Songs of Innocence and Experience*. He painted also, and Blake said, pointing to a picture of his in the Academy of 1823 or 1824 (as Samuel Palmer recalls), that it was "very fine." Samuel Palmer remembers that Blake wore that day his plain black suit and *rather* broad-brimmed, but not Quakerish, hat. He used to wear knee-breeches—then already becoming old-fashioned—out-of-doors, and the more modern trousers at home. He must have despised this garment, and looked upon it as a sort of pinafore for the legs, for he used to lay his engraved plates on his lap till the knees of his trousers were shiny.

It is to be hoped that Wainewright has been admitted to heaven as an appreciator of Blake, at least to the corner of it to which holiness does *not* give access, for he ended by using strychnine to poison a beautiful girl who was his sister-in-law, in order to obtain £18,000 from the life-insurance offices. After committing this and some lesser acts of infamy, he died wretchedly as a convict (also perhaps of his own strychnine), and his memory forms a curious comment on the Latin tag about study of art tending to soften the manner of life and forbid its ferocity, which is one of the few really humorous passages in our school Latin grammar.

Among the little bits of good fortune that came to Blake at Fountain Court was a donation of £25 from the funds of the Royal Academy in recognition of the merit of the designs to Blair's *Grave*. It is to be hoped that the critic of the *Examiner* heard of that gift. If Cromek had ever known of it he would have attributed it to his own "herculean labours" for a man who was "predetermined not to be served." Gilchrist records that Collins and Abraham Cooper recommended the grant, and Baily and Richard Bone were the movers and seconders of the vote granting it.

But in 1823, before the permanence of Linnell's help was assured, Blake began the year with very short commons. It was now that he borrowed the *Job* designs that he had sold to Butts, and showed them about in the hope of employment, with the result that Linnell gave him the order for their engraving, and for a "duplicate" set of drawings. They are not identically the same; and the first set (which it would be a mistake to call the originals) were sold eventually by Lord Houghton, into whose possession they had come.

In the arrangement about the *Job* engravings, Blake for the first time received a proper agreement about his work, drawn up and signed. For the designs and copyright he is to have £100, payable in instalments, and out of the profits after the engravings are sold he is to receive another £100. If there were no profits, then of course nothing beyond the first £100 was due to him; in fact, it is not clear that anything was due unless the profits exceeded £100. There were practically none, and Linnell gave Blake £50 "out of" their absence.

There was an element of grandeur in the air of cold and business-like dignity with which Linnell surrounded all he did for Blake, and on the Blakean principle that "grandeur of ideas is founded on precision of ideas," the exact sums that passed shall now be set down and recorded.

In the little sketch of a memoir, elaborated only on the few points where a correction of or addition to previous records was needed, that was tacked on to the Quaritch edition,—where it was intended to serve as a supplement to Gilchrist and a source of information to some future biographer,—the present writer said : "In 1825, the date when the first complete proof of the *Job* was made, payments began to pass for a series of coloured drawings done for Mr. Linnell (the Dante series). . . . They were paid for by instalments, about £52 being given in all, so far as record remains."

Fortunately, the misunderstanding of some information and figures supplied by the Linnell family, which caused this mistaken statement, is corrected in a long and valuable letter from the eldest surviving son, who writes :—

January 7, 1893.

DEAR MR. ELLIS—I have as yet had time only to glance at a very few parts of your new book (the Quaritch edition), and I instinctively

FROM THE "BOOK OF JOB."

"When the Morning Stars sang together and all the Sons of God shouted for joy."

turned to those subjects as to which I have knowledge, and that have relation to J. Linnell, viz. those chapters describing the execution for J. L. of the *Job* engravings, and the Dante drawings, and plates, etc. I at once noticed a few inaccuracies and certain statements that are not in agreement with the real facts. Now, I am the only one of my family who has taken the pains and the time to examine my father's papers, and his diary, memoranda, etc., and thus I have obtained from these both certain and definite information as to some particulars in the transaction between him and Mr. Blake not known to everybody. The above documents are the ultimate authority for determining the facts in these matters. . . .

Here follows a gentle reprimand to the present writer from Mr. Linnell for not having applied to him for information, and for not having submitted the MS. of the memoir to him. The more assiduous conduct of another biographer, writing the life of another subject, is held up at some length to show what should have been done :

. . . Certain statements would then have been made correct which are now misleading. See p. 131 (vol. i.), we read : " While the engraving of the *Job* series was in hand, etc." I believe it would be more correct to say : " On the completion of the engravings of the *Job*, J. L. commissioned W. B., in return for the different payments he made to W. B. (since the final payment on account of the *Job*, October 30, 1825), to illustrate Dante's poem by drawings in the book J. L. gave him, W. B. doing as much or as little as he chose."

From this we see that the date upon the proofs of the plates themselves, which says that they are " published as the Act directs, March 8, 1825," was only the date on which Blake himself first thought that he might consider the plates complete, and that proofs, retouches, and afterwards prints, were taken from them at leisure, and that the real " publication" took place the following year. The proofs were published at £10 : 10s. the set, and the prints at £5 : 5s. the set, bound in cardboard covers of terra - cotta colour, with white labels pasted in the middle upon which the price is written in pencil.

We know that the *Job* plates which were begun in March 1823 were completed in November 1825. In Blake's letter to J. L., November 10, 1825, he speaks of the final touches to the *Job* plates, and says: " I hope a few days more will bring us to a conclusion."
The plates must have been in the printer's hands in the latter part of 1825 and the beginning of 1826, for the book was published in March 1826. Now the *Job* was virtually finished and paid for before the work of Dante, and the payment of various sums on account of it commenced. Blake, in letter February 1, 1826, asks for a copy of the *Job* to show to Mr. Chantrey, showing that copies were being issued at that date. . . .

A few lines condemning another biographer follow, and the letter is resumed :

Now from the contemporaneous accounts and receipts of the payments made by J. L. to W. B., it is certain and proved :—Firstly, the final payment for the *Job* plates was made October 1825. (The payments were from March to December 1823, during the year 1824, and from January to October 1825, for the *Job* plates.) [A word of general praise for another biographer follows.] This is given wrongly in your book, p. 135. *All the proofs* that have been taken of the plates were taken at this first date [Which ? The proofs themselves, with the accidental exception mentioned, bear date March 8, 1825], before the publication, and after the proofs a certain number of *prints* were taken, which were also sold in March 1826. Of course no more " proofs " can follow after the " prints." Secondly, that the payments to W. B. of various sums on account of the Dante designs, both the drawings and the plates, for these were carried on together, commenced at the latter part of the year 1825, and continued till August 1827 (the last payment to W. B. was on August 2, 1827). Further, these payments added together amount to £103 : 5 : 6 (the total actually paid by J. L. to W. B. himself). This sum is cut down in p. 137 of your book to £52 !

The " your book " here referred to is the memoir to the Quaritch edition. In justification, the present writer can but conjecture that the figure, which he did not invent, but received from one of the Linnell brothers, must have been taken from a note made by J. Linnell at some date or other when he had really paid only £52, and that notes of further payments were made later, which not being shown to the present writer when he was taking down the figures, he was left to infer, mistakenly, that this was the latest record, and represented the total payment.

After W. B.'s death, J. L. paid to Mrs. B., from September 1827 to September 1828, about £46 (including burial of Mr. B., £10 : 15s., the rent of Fountain Court, etc.). Of the above sum, J. L. reckoned about £20 would be allowed to Mrs. B. for taking care of the house in Circuit Place, and the remainder he considered as additional payment for the Dante work, drawings and plates. I kno' in a letter March 1831, by J. L. to Fred Tatham, in reply to his question how much would have to be repaid to J. L. if the Dante were sold at an enhanced price for the benefit of Mrs. B., etc., he quotes these payments and says : Taking the £103 he paid to Mr. B. from (?) December 1825, and the £47 paid to Mrs. B., with £20 deducted for the housekeeping at Circuit Place, it leaves £130 to be repaid to himself if the drawings were resold, in which case the seven plates would be given up to Mrs. Blake. (That is all about the payments. The letter continues :) Further, I notice in page 168 an extraordinary statement—" How the MS. of *Vala* escaped and found safe keeping is not known by his own family " ! ! *This is utterly untrue.*

Unfortunately, the present writer had, when compiling

this part of the memoir, only questioned other of the Linnell brothers, whose memories, then as now, were less accurate and complete than that of the elder, who alone had retained and studied their late father's papers.

I have perfectly known as far back as I can remember how it escaped ; there never was the slightest doubt about the matter. Since the death of Mr. Blake and onwards, my father *often told me as well as others* that Mr. Blake gave him the MS. The exact date of the gift he said nothing about, as of no consequence. Certainly I never heard anything about his " death-bed." This is a pure invention of some one.

The other Linnell brother who was the present writer's informant did not use the phrase " death-bed," but said that the MS. had been given to his father by Blake when he was ill, and during the latter or last days of his life. Blake's final illness was of an intermittent character, and he was drawing for J. Linnell, *sometimes in bed*, on and off, up to a short time before he actually died. There is every probability that the gift was really made on " his death-bed," though long before the day of his death. The sentence to which Mr. Linnell takes such energetic exception in his letter is as follows : " How the MS. of *Vala* escaped " [that is, escaped destruction from Tatham's hands when other MSS. were ruthlessly burned], " and found safe keeping with Mr. John Linnell is not known by his own family. It is believed to have been given by Blake himself on his death-bed as a recognition that he owed more to his last patron than the short hours that were left to him would let him accomplish." " Death-bed " is not offered as a quotation of any one's exact words. Mr. Linnell's letter here does not deny the substantial accuracy of the recollections of his brother as followed in the memoir, though he appears to believe himself to be doing so. But he suggests a reason for Blake's not allowing Tatham to get at the MS., which may perhaps be the real answer to the question *how* it escaped.

Blake gave it to J. L., no doubt because he knew that he would be the one most likely to appreciate and preserve it, as at first it contained some rather extraordinary illustrations.

" *At first* " refers to the fact that later on it did not contain all of these " extraordinary illustrations," because J. Linnell used the india-rubber to one in particular, to make it less audaciously defiant of the proprieties,—the drawings were in pencil only. Their subjects include the distinguishing

characteristic of the ancient god " Priapus," an object fitted
for sacred art before the degrading spirit of a later civilisation had vulgarised it, but not fitted for secular art, other
than medical, at any period of the world's history. In one
design to *Vala*, the Priapic attribute is represented as
nearly the height of a signpost: three figures are bowing
down to it. They presumably represent Bacon, Newton, and
Locke worshipping Nature. The association of the symbol
with this rendering is found in its character of being that
which most causes man, apart from argument, to believe
in external nature (the great delusion), and the design
represents the fact that all rationalistic and experimental
philosophy depends upon for support, and therefore worships
as its god, the great source of temptation to a belief in
external nature, for without external nature they are nothing.
On this also depends Morality, which is necessary, if they be
right, but is nothing and ceases to exist if there be no such
thing as temptation, which it therefore worships as its creator; of all this, however, as part of Blake's mind, and of the
meaning, in any respect, of Blake's prophetic books, neither
the late John Linnell nor any of his descendants ever had
the glimmering of an idea. The present Mr. John Linnell
continues :

Who could have misled you to make such a statement I cannot conceive, and that after Mr. Story had simply told the truth (page 170).
What will the public think of this ?

The public will understand, of course, that the present
writer had not at that date read or even heard of Mr. Story's
little book.

I have no room for more now. Excuse bad writing through haste.—
Yours faithfully,   J. LINNELL.

The letter is beautifully written in a minute handwriting,
and, notwithstanding its great length, covers only the usual
four pages of a sheet of notepaper.

The " payments," of which it gives so hard, full, and careful
an account, passed often by post, and the letters acknow-
ledging them are always pleasant, though they contain
hardly anything of those outpourings of the " spirit " that
are to be found in what Blake used to write, even to Hayley,
at times. That of November 18, 1825, referred to in Mr.
Linnell's letter, is as follows :

DEAR SIR—[Until the year before his death Blake addressed Linnell as " Dear Sir "]—I have done, I believe, nearly all we agreed on. And if you should put on your considering cap, as you did last time we met, I have no doubt that the plates would be all the better for it. [This is evidence that retouchings *in consultation* had been going on since the date on the plates of March 8, 1825.] I cannot get well, and am now in bed, but seem as if I should get better to-morrow. Rest does me good. Pray take care of your health this wet weather; and though I write, do not venture out on such days as to-day has been. I hope a few more days will bring us to a conclusion.

J. Linnell himself was a good engraver, and had engraved plates in collaboration with Blake. With regard to the house " in Circuit Place," referred to in the letter of J. Linnell's eldest son, can it have been in Cirencester Place ?

Blake wrote one letter to Mrs. Linnell at Collins's Farm, North End, Hampstead, describing a scene in which he, who had once undergone a trial, actually describes an imprisonment, though for a short term :

DEAR MADAM—I have had the pleasure to see Mr. Linnell set off safe in a very comfortable coach. And I may say I accompanied him part of the way on his journey in the coach. For we both got in, together with another passenger, and entered into conversation when at length we found that we were all three proceeding on our journey. But as I had not paid, and did not wish to pay for, or take so long a ride, we with some difficulty made the coachman understand that one of his passengers was unwilling to go, when he obligingly permitted me to get out, to my great joy.

This is the second time that Blake has set his persuasive tongue to change the intentions of a man accustomed to govern horses, and has succeeded. He must have remembered Astley and Poland Street.

It was at the house of Mr. Aders, a buyer of pictures, to whom Linnell had introduced Blake, that, in 1825, Blake met Mr. Crabb Robinson, who afterwards called on him several times, and wrote of him at some length in his journals (quoted by Gilchrist) and in his reminiscences, condensing his journals, and yet—unless Gilchrist makes misleading omissions—adding a sentence or two. These reminiscences are complete in the memoir to the Quaritch edition. His personal description of Blake at this time is :

He had a broad pale face, a large full eye, and a benignant expression, at the same time a look of languor, except when excited, and then he had an air of inspiration, but not such as, without previous acquaintance with him or attending to what he said, would suggest the notion that he was insane.

Mr. Robinson's opinion was that Blake, nevertheless, *was* insane, a victim of monomania (on the subject of art, evidently); and Gilchrist says that Mr. Robinson was the only one who thought so of all whom he had met that knew Blake.

The reason is obvious. Of Blake's friends Mr. Robinson had most general education, without having enough imagination to judge Blake. Yet he thought that he could judge and understand any sane person, and that if Blake were really sane, he *must* be able to understand him. Yet he knew nothing of symbolism, and nothing of Swedenborg. The other people consulted by Gilchrist were simpler folk, and admitted that it did not at all follow that Blake, who seemed sane, was mad merely because they could not always understand what he was saying. When their knowledge of books fails to be enough to prepare their judgments, well-educated men are dangerous.

Of Mrs. Blake's appearance Crabb Robinson says :

Notwithstanding her dress, which was poor and dirty, she had a good expression in her countenance, and, with a dark eye, remains of beauty from her youth.

She always spoke of, and to, her husband as " Mr. Blake."

CHAPTER XXXV

BLAKE AND WORDSWORTH'S IMAGINATION

IN the conversations remembered by Crabb Robinson, there are notes of a good deal besides what has already been referred to. Most of this is about Wordsworth, who had not then been put away on an upper shelf because room was wanted for Tennyson, Swinburne, and Browning; nor were men's ears rendered impatient of his wearying manner by the fascination of Keats and the tragic sweetness of Shelley, nor was the book-case filling up as now with the gradually increasing editions of Blake himself.

Crabb Robinson did not suspect, when he wrote his journals, that when his interview had ceased to be of value as explaining Blake or illuminating Wordsworth, it would still be worth reading to smile over. Least of all did he foresee that the smile would be at himself:

On the 24th December I called a second time on him. On this occasion it was that I read to him Wordsworth's Ode on the supposed pre-existent state [he means pre-natal, of course], *Intimations of Immortality*. The subject of Wordsworth's religious character was discussed when we met on 18th February and 12th May (this is all 1826). I will here bring together Blake's declarations regarding Wordsworth. I had been in the habit, when reading this marvellous Ode to friends, of omitting one or two passages, especially that—

> But there's a tree of many a one,
> A single field which I have looked upon,
> Both of them speak of something that has gone :
> The pansy at my feet
> Doth the same tale repeat :
> Whither is fled the visionary gleam ?
> Where is it now, the glory and the dream ?

lest I should be rendered ridiculous, being unable to explain precisely what I advised. Not that I acknowledged this to be a fair test. But with Blake I could fear nothing of the kind. And it was this very stanza which threw him almost into an hysterical rapture. His delight in Wordsworth's poetry was intense. Nor did it seem less notwithstand-

415

ing the reproaches he continually cast on his worship of Nature, which in the mind of Blake constituted Atheism. The combination of the warmest praise, with imputations which, from another, would assume the most serious character, and the liberty he took to interpret as he pleased, rendered it as difficult to be offended as to reason with him. The eloquent descriptions of nature in Wordsworth's poems were conclusive proofs of Atheism. "For whoever believes in Nature," said Mr. B., "disbelieves in God, for Nature is the work of the Devil." On my obtaining from him the declaration that the Bible was the Word of God, I referred him to Genesis: "In the beginning God created the heavens and the earth." But I gained nothing by this, for I was triumphantly told that this God was not Jehovah, but the Elohim ; and the doctrine of the Gnostics was repeated with sufficient consistency to silence one so unlearned as myself. The Preface to *The Excursion*, especially the verses quoted from Book I of *The Recluse*, so troubled him as to bring on a fit of illness. Those lines he singled out :

> Jehovah, with His thunder and the choir
> Of shouting angels, and the empyreal throne,
> I pass them unalarmed.

"Does Mr. W. think he can surpass Jehovah ? " There was a copy of the whole passage in the copy of Wordsworth's poems returned to my chambers after his death. There was this note at the end. "Solomon, when he married Pharaoh's daughter and became a convert to the heathen mythology, talked exactly in this way of Jehovah, as a very inferior object of man's contemplations. He also passed him 'unalarmed,' and was permitted. Jehovah dropped a tear, and followed him by his Spirit into the abstract void. It is called the Divine Mercy. Sarah dwells in it, but mercy does not dwell in him." Some of the poems he maintained were from the Holy Ghost and some from the Devil. I lent him the 8vo edition (1815), in two volumes, of Wordsworth's poems, which he had in his possession at the time of his death. They were returned to me then. I did not recognise the pencil notes he had made in them to be his for some time, and was on the point of rubbing them out when I made the discovery, and they were preserved.

To Crabb Robinson the word Mercy did not recall, as it does to us, other passages of Blake, such as—

> We were placed here by the Universal Brotherhood and Mercy,
> With powers fitted to circumscribe this dark satanic death,
> *Milton*, page 22, lines 50, 51,

because he had looked on this " dark satanic death " as life, and had never dreamed of asking himself what *powers* he had over it, or how these were to " circumscribe it." He did not know that outline is one symbol and indefiniteness another, and that one is of life and the other of death. Nor had he read another and more obvious passage in *Milton* that connects this world of the visions of Time and Space with Mercy :

Time is the Mercy of Eternity. Without Time's swiftness,
Which is the swiftest of all things, all were eternal torment,
Page 23, lines 73 and 74,

any more than he knew of the imitation of Nature's images drawn from remembrance, which is Generation, symbolically the "sixfold Miltonic female"—

Void outside of Existence, which when entered into
Becomes a womb,   Page 43, last line,

that it is the literal reading of nature and Scripture that is dipped now in blood and now in sleep, and is the origin of war and lassitude, the alternate evils of this evil world, the spectre and emanation of its senses, the severity and the lethargy—its division and delusion day and night!

Gilchrist gives a word or two from those notes that Crabb Robinson so nearly rubbed out of his Wordsworth. (How the present writer would thank the owner of the volumes if he would tell him, through the publishers, what the rest are!)

In the preface to that edition we are told that the powers requisite for the production of poetry are first those of observation and description.

Blake, passing over the obvious fact that the author only required to substitute the word *prose* for *poetry* and there would be no quarrel with his remark, gives this note: "One power alone makes a poet—Imagination, the Divine Vision," which shows us how sublimely unconscious he was of his own gift of melodious language, and how little the divine vision did, except indirectly, for this equally necessary half of a complete poetry.

On Wordsworth's line, "Bound each to each by natural piety," he makes a note, but of course he cavils at this usual and popular way of using the word *natural*, as though Wordsworth could be expected to use it in his deeply Swedenborgian manner. "There is no such thing as natural piety, because the natural man is at enmity with God."

This recalls his remark when seeing in the Gallery our full-size copy of Leonardo da Vinci's *Last Supper* that is now slowly growing leathery in possession of the Royal Academy, but is nevertheless even now more visible than the original. He looked at the faces of the apostles and said, "Each of them seems to have subdued the natural man." Has any better remark been made about that picture? Those who are disappointed with the face of the central figure should buy the photograph of Leonardo's original sketch for it, now in the Milan Museum—the most truly religious face ever drawn. It might be by a Gnostic.

On the fly-leaf, under the heading *Poems referring to the Period of Childhood*, Blake writes—

I see in Wordsworth the natural man rising up against the spiritual man continually, and then he is no poet but a heathen philosopher, at enmity with all poetry or inspiration.

At the end of the poem *To H. C. Six Years Old*, he exclaims—

This is all in the highest degree imaginative and equal to any poet, but not superior. I cannot think that real poets have any competition. None are greatest in the kingdom of heaven. It is so in poetry.

Against the heading *On the Influence of Natural Objects* he writes—

Natural objects always did, and now do, weaken, deaden, and obliterate imagination in me. Wordsworth must know that what he writes valuable is not to be found in nature.

Blake seems at times to forget that there are two moods, each called Nature, and that if Scripture has its misleading natural reading, Nature has its invaluable spiritual reading, and that though an excess of contemplation of it may stupefy our minds and render them unfit for this, so will an insufficiency. Starvation will as surely make a man feeble as plethora, and the mind is as the body. His own mind is insufficiently nourished on the material side. Yet he knew the Smaragdine table of Hermes, with its " As above ; so below," for he alludes to it in *Jerusalem*.

Blake, in these Wordsworth notes, then calls on us to read Michael Angelo's sonnet, vol. ii, p. 129, which as given by Wordsworth is worth repeating :

No mortal object did these eyes behold
When first they met the placid light of thine ;
And my soul felt her destiny divine,
And hope of endless peace in me grew bold,
Heaven-born, the soul a heavenward course must hold.
Beyond the visible world she strives to seek
(For what delights the sense is false and weak)
Ideal form, the universal mould.
The wise man, I affirm, can find no rest
In that which perishes, nor will he lend
His heart to aught which doth on Time depend.
'Tis sense, unbridled will, and not true love
That kills the soul. Love betters what is best
Even here below, but more in heaven above.

As an expression of spiritual experience this is in fact pure *Blake* in every line, and justifies Blake's instinctive delight in Michael Angelo, the man as well as the artist, from his first years. Michael Angelo was (like Socrates) "a sort of brother."

Of Wordsworth's prefaces Blake writes—

I do not know who wrote these prefaces. They are very mischievous, and direct contrary to Wordsworth's own practice.

And again, p. 341—

This is not the defence of his own style in opposition to what is called poetic diction, but a sort of historic vindication of the unpopular poets.

And at the end of the *Supplementary Essay*—

It appears to me as if this last paragraph beginning with "It is the result of the whole that in the opinion of the writer the judgment of the people is not to be respected," was writ by another hand and mind from the rest of these prefaces. Imagination is the divine vision, not of the world, nor of man, nor *from* man as he is a natural man. Imagination has nothing to do with memory.

Gilchrist gives no more of these. His printing is followed here. Blake probably used many capital letters that he has omitted.

Among the lost books of Blake besides the *French Revolution, Oothoon, Titian,* the *Book of Moonlight,* and *Barry,* a poem, is one that he was doing at this time that, of course, fell a victim soon after to Tatham's Irvingite *odium theologicum.*

Crabb Robinson records after the record quoted in an earlier chapter:

I inquired about his own writings. "I have written," he answered, "more than Rousseau or Voltaire. Six or seven epic poems as long as Homer's, and twenty tragedies as long as *Macbeth.*"

He showed me his version of *Genesis,* for so it may be called as understood by a Christian Visionary. He read a wild passage in a sort of Biblical style. "I shall print no more," he said. "When I am commanded by the spirits then I write, and the moment I have written I see the words fly about the room in all directions. It is then published. The spirits can read, and my MS. is of no further use. I have been tempted to burn my MSS., but my wife won't let me."

He incidentally denied causation, everything being the work of God or Devil. "Every man has a devil in himself, and the conflict between this Self and God perpetually going on."

On another day he said, "Men are born with an Angel or Devil."

Blake has gone beyond that wish of the Lavater period to have a man's "leading propensity" called his angel. The Blake of the time *before* he "subdued the Spectrous Fiend" (after the visit to the Truchsessian Gallery) was not the same Blake as the one we are hearing now.

"This" (the angel and the devil) "he himself interpreted as soul and body. He spoke of the Old Testament as if it were the evil element. 'Christ took much after his mother' (the Law)." (These two words, found in the Crabb Robinson reminiscences, do not appear in Gilchrist's extracts from his journals. But we already know Gilchrist's method of unconfessed omissions. He did not add this time "his mother.") "He digressed into a condemnation of those who sit in judgment on others. 'I have never known a very bad man who had not something good about him.'"

This was on the same day when Crabb Robinson told Blake of the death of Flaxman, curious to see how he would take it. "He said—with a smile—'I thought I should have gone first.'"

In one of the last letters written by Blake he speaks, almost in the same words, but with an addition that lights up all his work for us :

Flaxman is gone, and we must soon follow, every one to his own eternal home, leaving the delusions of the goddess Nature and her laws, to get into freedom from all the laws of the Numbers, into the Mind, in which every one is King and Priest in his own house. God grant it on earth as it is in heaven.

We know what "law" was "Christ's mother" now. The last sentence reveals Blake's own meaning when he prayed the Lord's Prayer, and we are cured of that horrible illness we went through in reading his laborious paraphrase of Dr. Thornton's meaning.

In the margin of a copy of Cennini's book on fresco painting that Linnell lent to Blake we read—

The Pope supposes Nature and the Virgin Mary to be the same allegorical personages, but the Protestant considers Nature as incapable of bearing a child.

Has the Pope enough habit of mystic thought to go even so far as to make this mistake ? Did any "Protestant" (between the fifth and the eighteenth centuries) know enough to set him right ?

To avoid danger of confusion from the apparent inconsistencies between Blake's different utterances, it is necessary to remember that most of the interpretation and explanation that we can collect from his works and his reported speeches has reached us from the two opposite periods of his active life. The first period is represented by the *Marriage of Heaven and Hell*, with the "Devil" triumphantly quoted, and "Hell" as a place where are to be had the "enjoyments of genius." It begins to change at once from the time when he divided the nature of man under four powers, and the states of these powers under Wrath and Pity, neither of which was good when dominant. The struggle in his mind came to its climax after the visit to the Truchsessian Gallery, when he finally seems to have made up his mind against anything but a complete yielding of the whole mental nature to a passive acceptance of inspiration, protected by a watchfulness against all impulses that arise from self-interest or from reason.

Quakers and Quietists had long ago aimed at the same perception of the value of mental calm. So had Swedenborg and Boehme. Blake describes "self-annihilation" as "inward complacency of soul," and it is evidently the same experience known in the Benediction of the Church of England as "the peace of God that passeth all understanding." Its mystic value is limited in the second part of that benediction, where peace is invoked to keep us in knowledge.

The difference between Blake and other inspirationists was that he did not seek Nirvana—which is, in this world, quietism — merely as a means of a knowledge of God, but as necessary to the one form of mental activity that he considered as Godlike: imaginative art, the life of the poetic genius, that comes to us by what Swedenborg calls influx during the absence of our personal will.

Inevitably this led him to a firm rejection of the doctrine of the Atonement as it is usually explained. Those who think carefully are already inclined to perceive that, like the Mosaic law, it was given to us "for the hardness of our hearts," and that it will soon be time for us all to pass it by. Blake, who was enthusiastically tender-hearted, would not endure it. "It kills Mercy *in* the victim" was his view. As for the justice of God being satisfied by it, and therefore it being necessary, he simply would not hear of this. God's "justice," in our human sense of the word, is too plainly a figment. "To be an error and to be cast out is part of God's plan." "Some are born to endless night; it is right it should be so." He accepted the Calvinistic view of predestination. Like the author of the Book of Job, he considered that among the infinite attributes of the Almighty was an infinite and ultimate immunity from all criticism by us, or all explanation by us, in which our ideas of Justice have any share whatsoever. They only exist to give us material for forming an idea of the meaning of the words Mercy and Forgiveness that are God's active self. Such was Blake's repeated view, to be found differently worded over and over again. One principle of thought his mind appeared to lack entirely, however dominant it may be in ours. We consider that no statement can both express truth and contradict truth. He does not.

When he says, "There is a place beneath the bottom of the graves, which is earth's central joint, where contraries are equally true," he gives what he intends to be the philosophic basis of inconsistency, difficult to express consistently, of course, but meaning, in Blake, something like this—"The peace between inconsistencies in ultimate thought is the sign that we have reached a mental place where contradiction is of no further use to us, for it exists only for progression, and does not serve where this cannot be. The contradiction of the sexes, its symbol, is equally without contest in the part of the organism where what even will do equally for both is preserved and propagated. Friendship, Sympathy, Humanity, Imagination, Heaven, and God are free from argument and from sex."

Into this peacefully luminous state of life Blake now passed at Fountain Court, Strand, and from it he no longer went out to "jostle in the street." He had really "found the word golden," as he notes in his MS. book when it first came to him as a sign of the change on May 2, 1810, and he put it into *Jerusalem* at once with the little quatrain—

> I give you the end of a golden string,
>   Only wind it into a ball ;
> It will lead you in at heaven's gate,
>   Built in Jerusalem's wall.

He had been writing it for some years now, at first with struggle, but now with peace. He was very near the gate.

The little peep of the river from Blake's back window was so treated by him when he showed it that every one felt a child-like fairy-tale fascination in it. "That divine window!" says one friend. As for the little room, " There was no misery in Blake's rooms for men who love art, a good table" (well done, Mrs. Blake!), "and warmth. I never look upon him as an unfortunate man of genius. He knew every great man of his day, and had enough." Palmer says: "Himself, his wife, and his rooms were clean and orderly; everything was in its place. His delightful working corner had its implements ready, tempting to the hand."

If we wish to know what Blake's hands were like we must look at those in the *Job* engravings, full and flexible, with finger tips not too stiff with the finger, and wrists that would bend back at a right angle in times of surprise or horror. For description from life we have only Mrs. Blake's one sentence about those hands in which she tells that she "never saw them idle."

"The millionaire's upholsterer," breaks out Palmer again, "can furnish no enrichments like those of Blake's enchanted rooms."

They were approached by a fine Queen Anne staircase with thick balustrade. The front window looked into Fountain Court. Neither had the noise or distraction of the Strand below it. This front room was the drawing-room. The one behind was bedroom, dining-room, studio, and kitchen.

Here he was living when he made to a little child that memorable speech, "My child, may God make this world to you as beautiful as it has been to me"; and this of Sir Thomas Lawrence and others of the great men of his day: "They pity me, but 'tis they are the just objects of pity. I possess my visions and peace. They have bartered their birthright for a mess of potage." It must be remembered that the "potage," in the form of a post in the Royal Family as drawing-master, had been offered to Blake in his day. He had chosen the visions, and at last he had attained to peace.

The esteem in which John Linnell held Blake, and his complete freedom from all feelings of a patron in regard to him, is shown in his proposal to christen his second son William. Blake himself expostulated. "The name of the child ought to be Thomas, after Mr. Linnell's father," he wrote; "it will be brutal, not to say worse, in my opinion and on my part. Pray consider it, if it is not too late. It troubles me very much as a crime in which I shall be a principal."

The child was, after discussion, christened James. He is still living, and has made the only coloured copies of any of Blake's designs that are good enough to be mistaken for originals. Besides his own original work, he has produced one of the best small copies of Leonardo's *Last Supper* in existence. The present writer owes much to his hospitality and sympathy while making some supplementary study of the MS. of *Vala* in his house this year (1904). The first copy of it prepared for the Quaritch edition in 1891-92 was found to contain inaccuracies and lost lines, and this having been pointed out by Mr. Fleay, the MS. was revised for the edition now issued by Chatto and Windus. The first copy of it and the sorting of the pages were done in collaboration with Mr. Yeats at the house of William, the youngest of the Linnell brothers, who has produced work of which specimens will be in our National Gallery one day. Blake's name is in the family, therefore Mr. William Linnell remembers being put on Blake's knee at two years old, but smilingly disclaims having any further knowledge of him.

Blake himself carried the quiet sorrow of the childless man throughout his life, and Samuel Palmer says : " I yet recall (his lips quivering with feeling) when, on one occasion, dwelling on the exquisite beauty of the parable of the Prodigal, he began to repeat a part of it, but at the words, ' when he was yet a great way off his father saw him,' could go no further. His voice faltered and he was in tears."

John Linnell and Cumberland and Palmer were, with Varley and Calvert, Blake's best friends in his latter years. He was quite without enemies. " Cosway, Fraser, and Baldwin of Egypt's lake " are no more heard of.

In the Screwmuch lines he alludes to " poor Schiavonetti " who " died of the Cromek." Cromek himself soon followed. Hayley, his would-be kind "adversary," had remarried. Fuseli should be counted amongst the friends, perhaps. He lived, it is true, till 1825, but latterly in retirement, and almost in mental torpor, though, as he said, "now and then a wave of imagination rises and breaks at my feet." Of the value of Tatham as a companion to Blake we can only con-jecture, knowing that his sympathy, if Blake supposed him to have any, was illusory, and hoping that it formed a pleasant illusion. John Linnell was, in religion, also conscious that he did not agree with Blake. To have clear and serious, if unobtrusive, ideas on religion runs in the Linnell family. Yet he stood up for him while he disagreed.

"Often," he wrote, "Blake said things in order to puzzle and provoke those who teased him in order to bring out his strongest peculiarities. With the froward he showed himself froward, but with the gentle he was as amiable as a child. His eccentricities have been enlarged upon beyond the truth. He was so far from being so absurd in his opinions or so nearly mad as has been represented that he always defended Christian truth against the attacks of infidels and its abuse by the superstitious. . . . It must be confessed that he uttered occasionally sentiments sadly at variance with sound doctrine."

Crabb Robinson has recorded some of these "sentiments," and they are really, when examined, as much at variance with Blake's own sound heart as with Linnell's "sound doctrine," but he was an Antinomian in theory, and tried to be one consistently.

He did not succeed exactly, for his blood getting the better of his theology, he announced that God (since Jesus had become God) was always forgiving sins, and that there were no sins.

CHAPTER XXXVI

SAMUEL PALMER

SAMUEL PALMER recalls of Blake in his old age that

He was energy itself, and shed around him a kindling influence, an atmosphere of life, full of the ideal. To walk with him in the country was to perceive the soul of beauty through the forms of matter, and the high, gloomy buildings between which, from his study window, a glimpse was caught of the Thames and the Surrey shore opposite assumed a kind of grandeur from the man dwelling near them. Those may laugh at this who did not know such an one as Blake, but of him it is the simple truth. He was a man without a mask, his aim single, his path straightforward, his wants few, so he was free, noble, and happy. His voice and manner were quiet, yet all awake with intellect. Above the tricks of littleness or the least taint of affectation, with a natural dignity which few would have dared to affront, he was gentle and affectionate, loving to be with little children and to talk about them. "That is heaven," he said to a friend, leading him to a window and pointing to a group of them at play. . . . I can never forget the evening when Mr. Linnell took me to Blake's house, nor the quiet hours passed with him in the examination of antique guns, choice pictures, and Italian prints of the sixteenth century. Those who may have read some strange passages in his catalogue, written in irritation and probably in haste, will be surprised to hear that in conversation he was anything but sectarian or exclusive, finding sources of delight along the whole range of art, while as a critic he was judicious and discriminating.

Samuel Palmer is writing of the time *after* the subduing of the "Spectrous Fiend," that Blake too hopefully had believed had been quite accomplished by his visit to the Truchsessian Gallery, was really a fact.

He thought—with Fuseli and Flaxman (or perhaps he assented when reminded that Fuseli and Flaxman thought)—the Elgin Theseus, however full of antique savour, could not as ideal form, rank with the very finest relics of antiquity. He fervently loved the early Christian art, and dwelt with peculiar affection on the memory of Fra Angelico, often speaking of him as an inspired inventor and as a saint, but when he approached Michel Angelo, the *Last Supper* of Da

Vinci or the *Torso Belvidere*, and some of the inventions preserved in the Antique Gems, all his powers were concentrated in admiration. . . .

He was fond of the works of St. Theresa, and often quoted them with other writers on the interior life. Among his eccentricities will, no doubt, be remembered his preference for ecclesiastical government. He used to ask how it was that we heard so much of priestcraft, and so little of soldier-craft and lawyer-craft.

It is to be regretted that he did not open a stall on the threshold of the Vatican for the sale of an Italian translation, dedicated to the Pope, of his *Marriage of Heaven and Hell* and *First Book of Urizen*.

The Bible, he said, was the book of Liberty, and Christianity the regeneration of nations.

In politics a Platonist, he put no trust in Demagogues. His ideal home was with Fra Angelico; a little later he might have been a reformer, but after the fashion of Savonarola.

(Samuel Palmer here reveals a dream-like state of illusion based on infantile misconception worthy of Blake himself, whose books would never have reached Fra Angelico's home, and would have been burned in the market-place by Savonarola.)

Samuel Palmer's account goes on:

He loved to speak of the years spent by Michel Angelo, without earthly reward and solely for the love of God, in building St. Peter's (he evidently never read Michel Angelo's letter saying that but for the necessity of keeping his father supplied with money he would give up art). . . . I asked him how he would like to paint on glass for the great west window (of Westminster Abbey) his *Sons of God shouting for Joy*, from the designs to *Job*. He said, after a pause, "I could do it," kindling at the thought.

(Ought it not to be done? We have his pictures, we have processes of enlargement, we have the technique of translation into glass. Where is the Blake Society? Where is the necessary Dean? Where are the subscriptions?)

He made a copy of a picture of Giulio Romano's; it hung in his room near Dürer's *Melencolia*.

There are living a few artists, then boys, who may remember the smile of welcome with which he used to rise to receive them.

After mentioning Wordsworth's pleasure in his *Songs of Innocence*, and Flaxman's general admiration of his poems, Palmer goes on in this priceless letter:

To the multitude they (his poems) were unintelligible. In many parts full of pastoral sweetness, and often flashing with noble thoughts *or terrible imagery, we must regret that he should sometimes have suffered fancy to trespass within sacred precincts.*

The italics are ours. They point out the real tragedy of Blake's life—its isolation. Samuel Palmer is quite unconscious that he understood just as little of Blake's poems as the multitude to whom they were unintelligible, and John Linnell, with his vague remark about "sound doctrine," certainly understood no more. Had there been *one* man who knew what Blake *meant*, he could have read the Prodigal Son without a tear. *He was alone.*

But Samuel Palmer was not at all foolish or shallow. His next words are full of good sense of a kind.

Thrown partly among the authors who resorted to Johnson the bookseller, he rebuked the profanity of Paine, and was no disciple of Priestley, but, too undisciplined, and cast upon times that yielded him neither guidance nor sympathy, he wanted that balance of faculties that might have assisted him in matters extraneous to his profession. He saw everything through art, and in matters beyond its range exalted it from a witness into a judge.

Yet Samuel Palmer must have often heard from Blake that ultimate maxim carved on the Laocoön plate—

The whole business of man is : the Arts, and all things in common.

In considering this view, if we are to find any religion at all in it, we must in fairness to Blake remember that almost every one who interprets the Bible does so by building all his ideas on something that he thinks God *must* have meant. We have the Latin Church in Europe now that says, " Since God cannot have meant to mock man by leaving an incomprehensible Scripture that could not be understood when read privately, therefore He *must* have left an interpreter, and *we* are that interpreter." It is true that outsiders view the interpretation with hair on end, whether they are considering its fitfulness, its insufficiency, or its policy.

Swedenborg, in the same " God-*must*" spirit, said, " Since the Bible is the Word of God, it *must* be about the Lord, and the degrading and ridiculous story of Abraham, for example, *must* be a sacred symbol from which to learn the Divine life," —and he learns it.

The Scots " Minister " says, " Since the group of southern ecclesiastics that pretends to the interpretation of Scripture was a scandal to Europe for centuries, God *must* have meant *me* to understand it without such help,—and I do."

Blake, in the same spirit, said, "Since all is Mind, and Brotherhood is the Divine purpose in man, the only form of Mind free from covet, aloof from argument, and resting on vision supplied straight from God Himself, *must* be the true religion, and that is Art."

Samuel Palmer, after recording, as others have done, Blake's boyish pleasure in upsetting the dignity of people who tortured him with matter-of-fact unappreciativeness, concludes:

Such was Blake as I remember him. He was one of the few to be met with in our passage through life who are not in some way "double-minded" and inconsistent with themselves, one of the very few who cannot be depressed by neglect, and to whose name rank and station could add no lustre. Moving apart in a sphere above the attraction of worldly honours, he did not accept greatness, but conferred it. He ennobled poverty, and by his conversation and the influence of his genius made two small rooms in Fountain Court more attractive than the threshold of princes.

With this peroration Palmer is silent, though on general grounds we must regret that he did not tell us why he thought the threshold of princes was attractive.

On June 13, 1826, Crabb Robinson records:

I saw him again. He was as wild as ever, says my journal, but he was led to-day to make assertions more palpably mischievous, if capable of influencing other minds, and immoral, supposing them to express the will of a responsible agent, than anything he had said before.

This is probable from a man who did not wear a mask, and who thought morality *wrong*, notwithstanding that he thought nothing wrong, yet who did not quite think that morality was nothing. (It was the *state* in which we are willing to sacrifice our brother to our censoriousness.)

If we wish an absolutely complete view of Blake's system on its moral and religious side, as well as its practical or social side, we need add only a few words to his formula. After, *The whole business of man is the Arts and all things in common*, the addition might take some such words as these, *The whole virtue of man is productiveness and sympathy. The whole hope of man is imagination and union.* But we must understand that the phrases are to be used in their best sense. *Productiveness* is to imply conscientious worship of beauty, *sympathy* is to imply disinterestedness and pity; *imagination* is to include vision and inspiration, and union must be taken to develop into an eternal merging of all men in One Man, the only Immortal.

CHAPTER XXXVII

LAST FRIENDS AND LAST HOURS

BUT Blake's whole business in life was now nearly over. The constant strain of his nervous system *from drawing out of his own head, and from feeling emotions of love, hatred, admiration, and even desire for the visions* that his head presented to him, just as we feel in sleep personal feelings about the beings of our dreams, was now to have its revenge upon him.

He even thought that these things were no tax on him, no source of "dissipation," but just the contrary, being mercifully given in the dull world, where, as he says,

> The Angel who presided at my birth
> Said, Little creature formed for joy and mirth,
> Go, love without the help of anything on earth,

and that they were divinely sent to repose his burning thirst and freezing hunger (*Milton*, p. 3, line 4). Doctors tell us that a man has two great nervous centres, that of the brain and spine, and that of, or at least near, the stomach. One or the other must now break down. Both had been overstrained for years. Old age had come with its reckoning. If Blake had not been the sanest of men, the nerves more closely connected with the brain (the cerebro-spinal system, as they are called) would have been wrecked, and he would have become a dangerous madman. As it was, the apparatus that enables digestion to keep the blood alive was the portion of his physique whose coherence began to be lost. Deathly chill, and symptoms resembling the sort of cholera that is said to be produced by *fear* in otherwise healthy subjects, began to come at intervals to this fearless man. Warmth and rest would drive the attack away. The keen air of Hampstead, where he lived for a while in his last years, or a

mental excitement such as he felt over Wordsworth's bom-
bastic verse about "passing Jehovah and his choir unalarmed"
would bring it on again.   Between the attacks Blake would
cast off depression and be full of hope and work as ever.
Mr. Linnell invited him to Hampstead, and was full of
kindness and sympathy.   These alternations of hope and
despair went on for a year and a half.   Blake's letters always
show consideration for his friends, and he even gently rebukes
Linnell for his solicitude when writing to congratulate him
on the birth of "another fine boy" (now William, Blake's
namesake, if not technically his godson); he says—

> I go on just as if perfectly well, except during those paroxysms
> which I now believe will nevermore return.   Pray let your own health
> and convenience put all solicitude concerning me at rest.   You have a
> family; I have none.   There is no comparison between our necessary
> avocations.

This is in July 1826.   The year following he died.

At Collins's farm, Hampstead, where he visited the Linnells,
Gilchrist found Mrs. Collins still remembering Blake as "that
most delightful gentleman."   He could hardly be better
described, and when Westminster Abbey finds room for
his bust its title is already found.

Blake was not troubled with spiritual fears of any punishment beyond the grave.   On the contrary, one sentence of
his on this subject is left that might well be added as a
motto to the title for his bust that we owe to Mrs. Collins:
" Perhaps, and I verily believe it, every death is an improvement in the state of the departed."   So the dark cloud of
Calvinistic predestination had a silver lining to it.   That
God would not take vengeance for sin, he had always believed,
and through the little side-gate of " Perhaps" his mind was
coming to understand that even folly might not exclude us
from heaven for ever.

Meantime he began designing nice, well-lettered chapter-
headings for that Bible "as understood by a Christian mystic"
of which he read a few chapters (quite in vain) to poor Mr.
Crabb Robinson.   Their titles almost make up for their loss
to readers of his existing works :—

> Chap. I. The creation of the Natural Man.
> Chap. II. The Natural Man divided into male and female, and of
> the Tree of Life, and the tree of the knowledge of good and evil.
> Chap. III. Of sexual nature, and its fall into generation and death.
> Chap. IV. How generation and death took possession of the Natural
> Man. Of the Forgiveness of Sins written on the murderer's forehead.

Here ends what the Linnells possess. Blake probably did not live to do any more.

A fragment in the MS. book seems to have belonged to this. It is all crossed out with one long pencil stroke, as if to note that it had been copied out elsewhere—perhaps among the MSS. that Tatham thoughtfully destroyed after Blake's death, lest they should do harm.

The Combat of Good and Evil is eating of the Tree of Knowledge. The combat of Truth and Error is eating of the Tree of Life. These universal and particular. Each are (*sic*) personified. There is not an error but has a man for its agent; that is, it is a man. There is not a truth but it has also a man. Good and evil are qualities in every man, whether a good or evil man. These are enemies, and destroy one another by every means in their power, whether of deceit or open violence. The Deist and the Christian are but the results of these opposing Natures. Many are Deists who, under certain circumstances, would have been Christians in outward appearance. Voltaire was one of this number. He was as intolerant as an inquisitor. (Samuel Palmer seems not to have seen this sentence when writing about Blake's views of ecclesiastical government.) Manners make the man, not habits. It is the same in art. "By their fruits ye shall know them." The knave who is converted to Deism and the knave who is converted to Christianity is still a knave. But he himself will not know it, though everybody else does. Christ comes, as He did at first, to deliver those who are bound under the knave, not to deliver the knave. He comes to deliver Man the Accused, not Satan the Accuser. We do not find anywhere that Satan is accused of Sin. He is accused of unbelief, and thereby of drawing man into sin that he may accuse him. Such is the last judgment—a deliverance from Satan's accusation. Satan thinks that sin is displeasing to God. He ought to know that nothing is displeasing to God but unbelief, and eating of the tree of knowledge of good and evil.

As we read this appalling statement we remember Blake's use of the word *is*, and his statement to Crabb Robinson, "Jesus is the only God;—and so am I,—and so are you," and that the portion of the only God that *was*. Blake himself was exceedingly conscientious in his own dealings and scrupulously considerate, and ready to boil up into furious rage at the least sight of cruelty or knavery, or even any lack of thoughtfulness or of sympathy.

So ends that amazing cry of the heart—Blake's life. Gilchrist has sought and recorded every little detail of the kindness of his latest friends, and the modesty, courage, and probity with which Blake worked for his living even while dying, his last commission receiving extra care because so much as three guineas and a half had been paid for it "within a few days" of the end.

One letter, whose last sentences have been already quoted

in reference to the death of Flaxman, must be given here complete, as only two later ones are known as written by Blake before his death.   They are short, and Gilchrist has already published them.   This one is not in his *Life*, though he gives a facsimile of the " little card " done for Cumberland by Blake, and referred to here.   This letter appears by the reference to *Job* to be an answer to one from Cumberland referred to in Blake's letter to Linnell dated March 15—a month earlier—printed by Gilchrist, in which he tells how Cumberland has bought a copy of *Job*, and is trying to get other people to do the same.

DEAR CUMBERLAND—I have been very near the gates of death, and have returned, very weak and an Old Man, feeble and tottering, but not in the Spirit and Life, not in the Real Man, the Imagination, which Liveth for Ever.   In that I am stronger and stronger as this Foolish Body decays.   I thank you for the Pains you have taken with poor *Job*. I know too well that the great majority of Englishmen are fond of the indefinite, which they measure by Newton's doctrine of the fluxions of an atom,--a Thing that does not Exist.   These are Politicians, and think that Republican Art is inimical to their Atom.   For a Line or Lineament is not formed by Chance ; a line is a line in its minutest subdivisions.   Straight or Crooked, It is Itself, and not Intermeasurable with, or by, any Thing Else.   Such is *Job*.   But since the French Revolution Englishmen are all Intermeasurable, One by Another, certainly a happy state of Agreement, to which I for One do not Agree.   God keep me from the . . . (word illegible) of Yes and No too, the Yeay Nay Creeping Jesus, from supposing Up and Down to be the same thing as all Experimentalists must suppose.

You are desirous, I know, to dispose of some of my works and to make them (?) Pleasing.   I am obliged to you and to all who do so.   But having none remaining of all that I had Printed I cannot Print more, Except at a great loss.   For at the time I printed those things I had a whole house to range in.   Now I am shut up in a Corner, therefore I am forced to ask a price for them that I scarce expect to get from a stranger.   I am now printing a set of the *Songs of Innocence and Experience* for a Friend at 10 guineas, which I cannot do under six months consistent with my other work, so that I have little hope of doing any more of such things.   The Last Work is a poem entitled "Jerusalem the Emanation of the Giant Albion," but find that to print it will cost my time to the value of Twenty Guineas.   One I have finished.   It contains 100 plates, but it is not likely that I shall get a Customer for it.

As you wish me to send you a list with the prices of these things, they are as follows :—

America	£6	6	0
Europe	6	6	0
Visions, etc.	5	5	0
Thel	3	3	0
Songs of Inn. and Exp.	10	10	0
Urizen	6	6	0

2 F

The little card I will do as soon as Possible, but when you Consider that ·I have been reduced to a Skeleton, from which I am slowly recovering, you will, I hope, have patience with me.

Flaxman is gone, and we must All soon follow, every one to his Own Eternal House, Leaving the Delusive Goddess Nature to her Laws, to get into Freedom from all Law of the Numbers, into the Mind, in which every one is King and Priest in his own House. God send it so on Earth as it is in Heaven.—I am, dear sir, yours affectionately,   WILLIAM BLAKE.

12 April 1827, No. 3 Fountain Court, Strand.

The letter is addressed—

> George Cumberland, Esq.,
> Culver Street,
> Bristol.

In the next letter, a very short one, written to Linnell and dated April 25, 1827, after giving thanks for ten pounds received that day and for an introduction promised to Mr. Ottley, who was likely to buy books or pictures, and assuring Linnell that he is going on better every day "both in health and in work," Blake says :

I go on without daring to count on futurity, which I cannot do without doubt and fear that ruin activity, and are the greatest hurt to an artist such as I am. As to *Ugolino*, etc., I never supposed I should sell them. My wife is answerable for their having existed in any finished state. I am too much attached to Dante to think much of anything else. I have proved the six plates and reduced the fighting devils ready for copper. I count myself sufficiently paid if I live as I now do ; and only fear that I may be unlucky to my friends, and especially that I may be so by you.

This allusion to his wife recalls how closely she had come to live with him. She even once (at least) brought him a spiritual message. It was in South Molton Street. On the 87th page of the MS. book is this note :

Sunday, August 1807. My wife was told by a spirit——

Here the copy of the entry made by the present writer stops. He cannot now remember whether the record continued. Probably it broke off there.

The original book has gone back to America. These few words, however, are enough to show that the wife *had* a message, and that the husband cared to record that she had one—things notable as far as they go, and showing that Mrs. Blake was more than Blake's housekeeper, and more than his "beloved." Even beyond domestic matters there was give and take :

For many years (Smith writes of Blake) he was in the habit of lighting the fire and putting on the kettle for breakfast before his Kate awoke. Having never been a mother, to this devoted wife Blake was at once husband, lover, and child. She would get up in the night, when he was under his very fierce inspirations, which were as if they would tear him asunder while he was yielding himself to the Muse, or whatever else it could be called, sketching and writing, and so terrible did this task seem to be that she had to sit motionless and silent *only to stay him mentally*, without moving hand or foot, this for hours, night after night.

The italics are ours. Tatham relates in almost the same words the value of her silent presence. Blake wanted to be stayed nervously rather than mentally. He has recorded the scene in *Jerusalem* in few words, with no allusion to the mental staying, which would, if it existed, have come into the poem :

Trembling I sit, day and night, my friends are astonished at me,
Yet they forgive my wanderings. I rest not from my great task
To open the Eternal Worlds, to open the immortal Eyes
Of Man upwards, into the World of Thought, into Eternity,
Ever expanding in the Bosom of God,—the Human Imagination.

Gilchrist says, however, of Catherine Blake that "she too learned to have visions, to see processions of figures wending along the river in broad daylight, and would start when they disappeared in the water."

Both Butts and Linnell possessed drawings by Mrs. Blake, her own compositions, that if looked at carelessly would be considered to be Blake's own.

Now, in his last illness, he turned to her and said, " I have no grief but in leaving you, Catherine. We have lived happy, we have lived long, we have been ever together, but we shall be divided soon. Why should I fear death ? Nor do I fear it. I have endeavoured to live as Christ commanded, and have sought to worship God truly in my own home, when I was not seen of men."

But the truth began to press upon him.

" Kate," he said, " I am a changing man. I always arose and wrote down my thought, whether it rained, snowed, or shone, and you sat beside me. This can be so no longer."

Garth Wilkinson kept these few words for us. Gilchrist has collected all else that there is to tell of the end : how when he was lying waiting for death, with no one but his wife beside him, he said, " Stay ; keep as you are. You have ever been an angel to me ; I will draw you." Tatham described the drawing as "a phrenzied sketch of some power—highly interesting, but not like."

She consulted him about where he would be buried. He chose Bunhill Fields. Perhaps it would be better to lie there, where his father, mother, aunt, and brother lay, but so far as his own feelings were concerned, she might bury him where she pleased. He chose for funeral service that of the Church of England.

As the mid-day passed on August 12, 1827, an uprising of joyous emotion seized him. He began to sing aloud new songs to new melodies, as he did in early days when the *Songs of Innocence* began and were sung to Mrs. Mathews at Rathbone Place. His voice was powerful. In his ecstasy he "made the rafters ring." He said of these songs, "My beloved, they are not mine! no, they are *not* mine!" Then, in happier mood than when he had spoken of their being divided, he told her that they would not be parted, and that he would always be there to take care of her. It appears that he did so. His convictions supported her mind and enabled her to live quietly and not feel too lonely, since he was always really near, and she died at peace. Even in a physical sense he took care of her. His books and drawings gave her the food she ate while waiting to cease to require to eat food.

Then silence fell. The colour of his face changed, and, so quietly that the watchers did not know the exact hour, he ceased to breathe.

"I have been at the death of a saint," said a neighbour who had come to help his wife in that last hour.

POSTSCRIPT

CUMBERLAND notes on the blank page of the letter dated 12th April 1827, here given in full, "He died August 12, 1827, in the back room on the first floor of No. 3 Fountain Court in the Strand, and was buried in Bunhill Fields Burying-ground on 17th of August in 25 feet from the north wall, No. 80."

Gilchrist says, "That particular part of the burying-ground was not added till 1836; in 1827 it was occupied by houses, then part of Bunhill Row. On reference to the register now kept at Somerset House I find the grave to be numbered 77 east and west, 32 north and south. As it was an unpurchased 'common grave' (only a nineteen-shilling fee was paid), it was doubtless (to adopt the official euphemism for the basest sacrilege) used again, after the lapse of some fifteen years, as must have been the graves of those dear to him."

When antiquaries of the future desire to identify the remains for a monument, the skull measurements, when verified by the cast of the head now in possession of Sir William Richmond (see Frontispiece to this volume), will give means for a complete and authoritative identification.

Mrs. Blake, when a widow, received a gift of £100 from the Princess Sophia, which she returned "with all due thanks, not liking to take or keep what, as it seemed to her, she could dispense with, while many to whom no chance nor choice was given might have been kept alive by the gift."

She lived chiefly by the sale of Blake's remaining books and works. Mr. Cary, the Dante translator, bought an *Oberon and Titania*, and Lord Egremont a group of Spenserian characters from the *Faerie Queene*.

Tatham says that Mrs. Blake coloured more of Blake's designs than was generally believed. He was useful to her in helping to find purchasers. When she died she bequeathed all that remained to him, and he continued to sell them. He told Mr. W. M. Rossetti in 1862 that he had sold Blake's "works" for thirty years, and at about the same period said, when visiting Dr. Garnett, that he had "destroyed some of Blake's manuscripts and kept others by him, which he had sold from time to time."

He looked on Mrs. Blake with veneration, and relates touchingly how "she suffered the remains of her dear husband to leave the house" on the day of the interment, ". . . set out herself the refreshments of the funeral, and parted with him with a smile."

"For some time" after this she lived with and kept house for Tatham,—who was young enough to be her grandson,—and then returned to the same lodgings where Blake had lived with her and where he had died; where constant sorrow caused her to suffer such pain when she took food that at last, after a specially bad attack lasting a day and a night, she died; grief, and grief only, having slowly killed her in four years. Tatham, Mr. Bird the painter, Mr. Denham the sculptor, Mr. and Mrs. Richmond, and another friend unnamed were at her funeral.

But though she died of no illness but bereavement, she did not lament or repine. Neither the thoughts of her last years, nor of the whole of her married life since her husband finished her education, can be understood unless we constantly remember how much in advance of his century he was in his intellectual perception of those actions of mind that differ from "corporeal understanding" as much as sight from hearing, and of the fact that they have their own region and atmosphere, as different from that of ordinary reason as ether from the atmospheric air that we breathe, and that conveys sound but not light.

We must not rashly consider that this occult mental power, which Blake called "Imagination," was like our ordinary imagination, though it had a kinship. It exceeds it sometimes as the fancied fourth dimension of space exceeds the usual three, has its own *here* and *there,* its own *before* and *after,* a Time where Successivity does not rule, and a Space where Place has other laws. So he called it Eternity, and by it the Real Blake is yet with us, his posterity, as he was with Catherine his widow.

INDEX

THE END